How can I ever thank you for your constant support in those "early" years — & throughout the next thirty! Much love,

Julian Schlossberg

Letters From the Prophets

Letters From the Prophets

A Theatre Teacher's Memoir

Julian S. Schlusberg

Authors Choice Press
San Jose New York Lincoln Shanghai

Letters From the Prophets
A Theatre Teacher's Memoir

All Rights Reserved © 2001 by Julian S. Schlusberg

No part of this book may be reproduced or transmitted in any form or by any means, graphic, electronic, or mechanical, including photocopying, recording, taping, or by any information storage or retrieval system, without the permission in writing from the publisher.

Authors Choice Press
an imprint of iUniverse.com, Inc.

For information address:
iUniverse.com, Inc.
5220 S 16th, Ste. 200
Lincoln, NE 68512
www.iuniverse.com

ISBN: 0-595-18230-5

Printed in the United States of America

Antigone

For Cousin Jeff
"Every exit is an entrance somewhere else."
Tom Stoppard

Contents

Foreword xi
Prologue xv
Acknowledgements xxi
Letters from the prophets 1
Chapter One
    The Early Years 3
Chapter Two
    The Plays 59
Chapter Three
    Endings and Beginnings 227
Chapter Four
    The Shakespeare Plays 245
Chapter Five
    A Fitting Conclusion 295
Chapter Six
    The Special People 319
Chapter Seven
    Other Stages 331
Chapter Eight
    Deaths and Inheritance 355
Chapter Nine
    Foote Summers 385
Chapter Ten
    Awards 403
About the Author 427

Foreword

The author of the book that you are about to read claims that he learned a great lesson from the Hotsons (Professor Leslie Hotson, the great Shakespearean scholar, and his wife, Mary)—*the importance of listening*. The book belies that fact. Julian Schlusberg seems to have learned to listen from infancy, and he learned to remember *all* that he heard.

Listening is not an easy habit to cultivate. Young people have an uncanny resistance to it. Young people who grow into adults seem to avoid the habit. If one reads a play by Anton Chekhov or John Millington Synge, one might be shocked to hear the play's population intent upon hearing only themselves talk. To listen and to hear another takes compassion, humility, curiosity, and joy in nurturing the habit and pleasure of listening. And for a teacher, listening is the first *necessary* talent to exercise. Without the ability to listen, a teacher is doomed to cheat the student.

But listening means you hear not only the voice, not only the heartbeat, but also the silence of the student. The most common, private, and hidden condition that all students bring with them is the desire to be discovered by a teacher. That experience can *only* happen if the student is fortunate enough to be placed in a classroom with a teacher who hears with his or her ears, eyes, heart, and soul. The students in Hamden, Connecticut, were blessed with the good fortune to have in their community such a teacher. It is that teacher's experience as a director in the theater, as a teacher in the classroom, as a humanizing force in contact with young people that this book is all about.

In another of his books, *Lessons for the Stage*, Julian Schlusberg announces in his opening sentence, "Teaching acting is one of the greatest joys in the world." Although Schlusberg surmises, "I'm sure most drama teachers share that sentiment," I would ask him for additional evidence. I do not wish to berate drama teachers, but I have seldom witnessed the degree of joy in his statement from my contact with acting teachers over the past fifty years. Perhaps I do them a disservice. If so, I apologize. But I don't do disservice to Schlusberg. His statement is a genuine fact of his life illuminated by thirty round, firm, and fully-packed years of working with young people in acting classes, directing them in well over a hundred productions, and supervising them in an exceptional, unique theater program which he organized and energized.

During my years as a university instructor, professor, and administrator, I urged members of the faculty in both the Humanities and Sciences to consider adding an acting course to their curriculum in the training and educating of their students. My justification for this request was that acting teaches listening. One cannot act with credibility (the ultimate objective) unless one learns to listen to the person to whom the actor is expected to respond. This obligation puts the actor in the position of considering another human being, requires the actor to honor the humanity of another. That action is the first principle of humanizing a young person, the act of considering the humanity of another individual. For many, drama itself is the conflict of one's self interest with that of another's. In fact, our lives may be that daily diet, our self-interest in conflict with the interest of another. To be aware of that *other* is the actor's duty.

An actor has an additional humanizing factor in her or his development. As Schlusberg demonstrates, an actor transforms herself or himself into another person, a stranger, in an act known as empathy. Empathy is an action by which one puts one's self in the service of another's self, not from sympathy only, but from an awareness of being in that person's shoes. That transformation is accomplished by the actor's gift and the actor's developed craft. When Schlusberg describes Tom Edwards' convincing Othello in their production, *Othello*, he does not say that Edwards *was* Othello. He cannot be Othello because he cannot give up being Tom Edwards. But he must convince me he is Othello, for if he were *really* that character he would kill Desdemona on the stage. Theater people like to tell the story of Laurette Taylor who, while playing Amanda Wingfield in the opening of *The Glass Menagerie* in Chicago, was greeted backstage by a young, aspiring actress from Northwestern University. The student said to her, "Miss Taylor, when you do Amanda Wingfield, are you really Amanda Wingfield?" Taylor's response was, "No, dear, I am an actress." What can be more schizophrenic than acting. To be successful in putting one's self in another's shoes takes tolerance, patience, imagination, and craft. The actor is being both himself or herself *and another's* self. What training for living a *human* life!

This book details a young instructor's introduction to teaching and then follows him through thirty years of diligent devotion to and training of his charges. The book is startlingly informative and relentlessly inspiring. It is also about to move the reader to tears and considerable heartbreak. It is a rare accomplishment. Anyone reading it will learn from it, will be educated by it, will be delighted by it, will be saddened by it. Schlusberg's educational accomplishments are extraordinary, as are those of his students. But the book is its own accomplishment. The reader will find herself/himself in the company of a document that will astonish not only the teachers of this nation, but also the citizens, the parents, and the children who populate it.

I have known Julian Schlusberg for thirty years and have had frequent contact with him. But I never expected to have the extreme joy and awareness of reading his vocational journey. From my point of view, no one teaching youth of any age, nor those raising children of their own should be without it.

Howard Stein

Professor Emeritus
Columbia University

Prologue

A student in one of my acting classes, Ravenna Michalsen, once suggested that I write my memoirs. At the time I laughed, feeling rather embarrassed and responding that only "famous" people write memoirs—politicians, celebrities-certainly not high school teachers. But I must admit that I've thought about Ravenna's suggestion many times over the subsequent years, thinking that there is much to share, many stories to tell. However, unlike memoirs meant to entertain or perhaps share dark secrets, mine are meant to help teachers. Perhaps on one of these pages there may be some bit of information, an insight that will help in some way—solve a problem, inspire a lesson, select a play for production. My good friend, Howard Stein, Professor Emeritus from Columbia University, once said that the great Yale acting teacher, Robert Lewis, required students to come to every class because one could never tell what might be said that could change the rest of a person's life. Likewise, maybe one of these chapters or some random thought or reminiscence will open a new horizon for an unsuspecting teacher or student of the theater.

In the summer of 1999, just after my retirement, I had dinner with Ann Altman, the mother of one of my former students and a very dear friend. Even after her daughter, Leah's, graduation, Ann and I kept in close contact. This extremely busy person seemed to flit in and out of my life at the most opportune, and often, "needy", moments, always offering a suggestion, always radiating a warmth and appreciation for life, and always modeling the behavior of one who has too much to do in too little time. While we sat at dinner that night, I must admit I wasn't sure what life held in store for me. It seemed as if my entire adulthood had been consumed with teaching and directing plays. My work day never ended at the conclusion of the school day, but rather went on until nine o'clock in the evening. It also included Saturdays from morning until late afternoon, and often school vacations provided the needed continuous number of hours to complete major technical or acting projects. I guarded the students' time, however, making sure that they were with me only when necessary, and even then, that they had time for their homework and families. I felt such a strong commitment to my students and to the Theater program. I suppose the relationship to both bordered on the parental. More so than the time commitment was the emotional one, feeling a need to be available for troubled students, or sharing happy times, attending their concerts, being invited to their homes. As I reflect back upon those days, there was such a gradual blending of my personal and professional lives that I really couldn't tell where one began and the other ended; and perhaps they didn't. Maybe it was just one life, totally consumed with the art of the theater and the people who made it work in Hamden, Connecticut.

Ann Altman remarked that most people who retire are ecstatic and noticeably free of stress, but this was not the case with the man sitting opposite her. Rather, she noticed my angst, and the inability of my smile to mask my shaking hands. And being an observant and tell-it-like-it-is kind of person, Ann made me aware of it as well. She knew I had written a book and several articles for educational magazines, and she knew also how passionate I felt about writing, all of which led her to suggest that I put my feelings into words and perhaps free myself of the demon inside. I might also add that Ann is an editor herself and is therefore well versed in the power of words.

Soon after my dinner with Ann, Ned Ostojic, another parent of yet another wonderful theater student, Claudia, spoke to me at a get-together. He said that until his daughter's involvement, he didn't attend the theater on any regular basis, and therefore this world was a new one for him. He was "hooked" on plays after seeing the first one that Claudia was involved with, and as he began to observe more and more, he was bewildered with the vast array of talent in Hamden High School. Ned asked me if this would be the case for any given school in any given section of the country.

How could so many talented students happen to be in one school at one time? I wasn't sure how to answer Ned. I've been asked this question a number of times, and I could never answer it before either. I began to explain that what Ned was observing was only one part of a long chain of events and of a theater tradition that had been flourishing for thirty years, growing stronger all the time. How does one go about explaining how a program spawns professional actors and technicians and directors and designers; playwrights and filmmakers and magicians and even comedians? How does one account for a program imparting skills that make people better at whatever they choose to do? That makes teachers and doctors and social workers and even parents *better*? And most importantly, how does one find the words to explain how a program makes its students better human beings; people concerned with their world and trying hard to make it a better place to live? It certainly isn't possible in a momentary conversation, and I don't even know if it can be done within the covers of a book. But it is too important not to try, and so Ned provided one more reason to sit down and write the story that I have lived for so many years.

As a matter of fact, it seemed like I was bombarded with reasons to write, or maybe I was just looking for them. The story of Hamden Theater involves hundreds and hundreds, perhaps thousands of students, and yet it is so very personal for me as well.

Now life stretches before me, and I am in a transition period, the length of which I am not sure. I am humbled by wonderful employment opportunities, but I feel the work at hand, this chronicle of a three-decade-long student success story—not to mention teacher-student love affair—is too important to ignore. It needs the respect of time and unencumbered responsibility. I have set out to do what Ann suggested and to try to answer Ned's seemingly unanswerable questions. These two influences, and Ravenna's suggestion so long ago, seem to have joined forces, and now that I have started the process, it almost controls me, compelling me to remember, to close my eyes and envision the past like some sense memory acting exercise. And the more clearly people and events come into focus, the more I remember about the students, their unbridled enthusiasm, the plays, the teaching, and the successes and awards they earned to put Hamden in the national spotlight of educational theater, the more I realize that this is a story that must be told for so many reasons. One of those reasons comes to me in the shadowy form of a theater teacher/director who wonders whether the loneliness and anxiety of an uphill battle is worth the effort and time it takes to create a solid theater program in a school system that doesn't understand the *importance* of such a venture, or even what the theater is in the first place. Another one, a very important one for me, is to record what has happened in this town; what forces combined in a miraculous way and under circumstances that existed at one point in time to create a Camelot-like experience that lasted thirty years.

Just recently I received a letter from Joann DePalma, a student in my very first class in 1969. She is now an elementary school teacher and I happen to know that she has won accolades for her work, including Teacher of the Year. Joanne, or "Joby" as I knew her, heard about my retirement and wanted to share some feelings with me. Her words were simple and came from her heart, but the feelings they produced within me were profound. She told of how the Theater, way back in the late sixties, helped her to find her "voice;" that she didn't have much self-confidence in those days, despite the wonderful and supportive family she had. Her "voice" continued to grow and mature, and she realized that her gift was the ability to teach others, and this ability had made a major difference in her life. Knowing Joann, I would add that it has made a major difference in the lives of her students as well.

It is not often that a person receives such heart-warming confirmation of his or her work, yet Joann's letter is probably very much like those received by many teachers who have helped students find their purpose through the power of educational theater. I have also had conversations with students during and after their secondary school experience, and these have provided great comfort for my entire career, often being the source of the energy and inspiration I needed to get through any given day. So much is expressed in their unpretentious and honest words—appreciation, anecdotes expressing their amazement at realizing a goal or overcoming a problem, awareness of self-growth, telling how their Theater training has helped them understand a situation better, relating how they have come to feel better about themselves, and a host of other subjects as well. Often I receive these letters years after a student has graduated, when he has come to finally understand something we spoke about in class or perhaps in a friendly conversation a great while before. My late acting teacher, Constance Welch, once jokingly reprimanded a student who was talking in her class rather than paying attention, "Even if you *were* listening to me," she began, "you wouldn't *understand* this for another ten years!" In so many cases, this is an accurate observation. Sometimes people need to "grow into" a concept or a theory; they need time to witness it, assimilate it, and subsequently understand its relevance.

The letters I have received are warm and heartfelt, and I am touched by students' recognition of their own growth. Perhaps there is nothing that could fulfill a teacher more than this. Their lives have been changed for the better; their self-concept has been bolstered. They have a better sense of who they are, and that is one of the most important things about life.

Wisdom and knowledge are related, but not the same. My father, for example, went to school until the eighth grade and never had an opportunity to gain a great deal of knowledge in a formal classroom situation. Yet I feel he was one of the wisest people I ever knew. In his seemingly simple manner and with relatively few words he could be erudite and impart worlds of information. I remember he used to tell me that I could learn more from listening than from talking a great deal, and I think that was one of his greatest lessons. My father knew so much about life and tried to guide his children so that we could gain this wisdom as well.

In the famous Sistine Chapel ceiling fresco there is a space between the fingers of God and Adam. In that seemingly invisible and minimal amount of space a world begins, filled with the electricity and the explosion of possibility. It represents the space between our eyes and what we see; between our ears and fingers and tongues and all that we experience through our senses. It is the connection we feel when we look within ourselves and see the universe. If we could only find a way of representing this space—this all-too-brief moment in time when so much happens—on the stage as well as help our students become aware of and feel the magic of that space, then we will have done a great deal more than direct a play or teach a class.

Judging from the letters I have received through the years, I feel very fortunate that many of my students have indeed visited that special place. And I'm so happy that it has been the theater that has inspired them. I keep thinking of the future when *they* become the teachers and the leaders of their time. I have witnessed their inspiration not only as part of a theatrical company, but in their use of the Theater to improve their lives, to realize their responsibilities to society, to uphold the basic tenets of a civilized world. They not only heed the words of the great playwrights, but, in fact, *practice* those lessons.

The "letters" have not only arrived in the written and spoken forms, but have been manifested in their acting, designing, and technical work; in their directing, choreographing, dramaturgy and playwriting. I have been truly moved by them in classes, in their provocative and mature discussions, in the respect they have for each other and the various viewpoints they propose. I see and feel their intensity and passion in every phase of our work. Yes, they are indeed the prophets, and I can't help but feel great optimism and confidence in our world because they are out there spreading their word and their influence.

How interesting it is to "re-live" one's life, even if it is only in the mind, and how fortunate I am to have that opportunity. Suddenly the events and people that all too often drift into a cloudy past are re-emerging. Faces...I see many, many faces and my mind echoes with the sounds of voices like sweet, distant music. Who knows... maybe this venture will also show me the path to the future as well.

Acknowledgements

A theater program cannot attain a level of excellence without the help of many people. Certainly I have seen a veritable parade of designers, choreographers, artisans, and workshop leaders who have, over the course of thirty years, taught, enriched, and affected the lives of the students in Hamden High School's theater program. Each has given humbly, yet his or her expertise has been hungrily devoured by these most wonderful and enthusiastic students. The cumulative effect has been staggering and has enabled us to achieve a level of proficiency that many would deem impossible on a high school stage. Perhaps, then, my gratitude is more of a tribute to the combined efforts of teachers and students working together, ignoring what many would consider the limits of what can be achieved by young people. Their work speaks for itself. And so I thank the professionals, many of whom are Hamden Theater graduates, who gave their time, talent, and caring to a to a most special group of students.

A special thank you to Thomas J. McVety, whose graphics enhance this book in spectacular fashion. A graduate of Hamden Theater himself, Tom always makes the time to "give back" to the department that nurtured him and so many others.

Howard Stein wrote the Foreword to this book, and I am particularly grateful to him. The Professor Emeritus from Columbia University has been a source of great inspiration for me. Through his teaching over so many years, Howard has helped shape the American Theater, and while his students are some of our most distinguished theatrical figures, he gives of himself generously to anyone who desires to learn. His knowledge is rare, but his wisdom is even moreso. I am very lucky to have had Howard touch my life.

I would also like to thank Michael Lee and Virginia Corbiere, the technical "wizards" at the Foote School in New Haven, Connecticut, who helped me immeasurably as I prepared this manuscript for publication. The staff at Rollins Printers in Hamden, Connecticut, also have provided much assistance.

This book will illustrate my good fortune in crossing paths with many illustrious people who humble me with their kindness, and from whom I have learned so much. They also have affected my work in Hamden: from Professor Leslie Hotson, a foremost Shakespeare scholar, to the late and terribly missed Jason Robards who became a good friend; from Margaret Tyzack, the famous and talented English actress to Armand Zimmermann, the late and legendary theater teacher from Connecticut who impacted an entire State with his love for educational theater and his insistence on its importance in our schools' curricula. And finally, Constance Welch, my own acting teacher who was, herself, pivotal in the growth of the Theater in this country and even abroad. All of these people and so many, many more startle me with the vast storehouses of their knowledge about the Theater, and with their facility to communicate to students and audiences with passionate vision.

And finally I thank my family for epitomizing what that word means. The rhythm of my family, like that of an intimate dance where two people hold onto each other to share the warm sensation of caring hands, has been one of love and support for as long as I can remember. And now the dance includes new children, seeming to appear faster than ever-Kyle Jeffrey, Joseph Richard, Joseph Anthony, Erica Hope, Andreya Skye, Andrew Michael , Kathryn Sidney, Samuel Lane, and Rachel Lane, Daniel Jay, Jonathan Michael, Zachary Stuart, Olivia, Keith, and Richard. How fortunate they are to be guided through this life by their bright, sensitive, observant parents, whose own births were not so long ago, at least in my eyes.

The Theater takes us places that everyday life cannot. I offer a special thank you to my students throughout the years who shared that journey with me.

I just thought I'd drop you a note to say hello. I've been thinking about you a lot lately. It's hard to put into words exactly why. I'm in this sort of "re-inspiration" place. I find myself remembering and re-exploring the reverence I have for the theater; I have been caught up in something else at this school, I think. I've been studying the nature of this business as a business and forgetting about what is really important. And so my mind has been traveling to you all the time lately. I keep remembering what it was like when theater was important on so many levels and money was not the most important one. It was spiritual and political and human and other-worldly and full of great passions. I sit in a dead, empty acting class that concerns itself primarily with discovering how I am marketable and I hear your voice saying, "People come to the theater because they have need of us," and "The road to truth is paved with humility." It is when I think of you that I can identify most clearly for myself why I am doing this, what is really important. I continue to learn from you as I look back on things you've said and learn them again in ways I didn't understand them before. I miss you... It's been a long time since I've sat alone in an empty theater. I'm going to do that tomorrow.

Kate

Letters from the Prophets

A Thousand Clowns, 1969

Chapter One

The Early Years

Portrait of author, 1969

"The greatest teacher I ever had once had another great teacher. This teacher's spirit so filled my greatest teacher that everywhere he went he could not help but follow in his own teacher's footsteps. My greatest teacher filled his students with the same knowledge, pride, and confidence that his teacher had instilled in him many years before. He did it because he could not help it; because he had to; because my teacher knows the circle is endless."

Noah

"I don't think I have ever learned as much in all my life about love, warmth, and caring as I did while working in the Theater."

Jennifer

I began my teaching career at Michael Whalen Junior High School in Hamden, Connecticut in September of 1969, although I student-taught there the previous year. At the time I was fresh out of college and bursting with desire to teach the subject that had provided such a feeling of exultation, and for which I had a love that would be difficult to describe in words. In those days my feet barely touched the ground! Everything was exciting and new and celebratory, and the Theater, like some kind of mysterious, invisible guiding force, propelled me swiftly and passionately through both my professional and even personal life. And as I think about things now, that feeling hasn't changed much over the years, albeit the initial excitement is now combined with a comfort, and, to some degree, confidence borne of experience, patience, flexibility, and the solace that seems to naturally emerge as we grow older. Today I like to think of having matured from not only those appreciated successes of my life, but from the risk-taking that youth embraces, the experimentation that tantalizes the aspiring "artist," and even the failures that embarrass us and which we quickly try to sweep under the carpet. In the late sixties, however, my mind was still filled with visions of the "TV Studio" at Southern Connecticut State College (now University) in New Haven, and my senses were bombarded with its smells and shadows and looming dramatic adventures. This space, this living, thriving, pulsating heartbeat, was where I had taken all of my acting courses and where I had performed countless times; it was the place where I would find my closest friends and, in fact, anyone of any educational or professional importance-and in those days what else mattered? It was a place that enveloped me with its thick, comforting arms and whispered to me that I could do more than I ever expected of myself. And now I was trying to recreate the thrill of what had transpired in that black box of a room in a new place; one that was to become my "home" in the neighboring town of Hamden. I could never have known at that time that Hamden would welcome and nurture educational theater over the next thirty years, and that the program would even capture national attention one day. Southern provided a supportive and secure environment in which to learn about Theater; where I seemed to be joyously inundated with experiences on a daily basis-from performing in productions to preparing scenes and monologues for acting classes, learning physical and vocal warm-up exercises, writing research papers on Shakespeare and Ibsen and Chekhov and Strindberg, even watching a memorable video on Julian Beck and Judith Malina's Living Theater while discussing Jerzy Grotwoski's work and subsequently engaging in heated debates over the contour of the entire Theater scene. Each day brought with it new ideas, new perspectives, and the unexpected.

And then there was the cast of characters, many of whom I think I idolized. I was younger in many ways, and, as a relative newcomer, I remember sitting spellbound during their performances-the beautiful Mary Ellen Crown whose resonant voice, long flowing hair, and expressive eyes made her absolutely captivating to watch; and the talented George Blahodatny who could not only act, but miraculously direct as well; And Connie Wozny and Bob Brueller and John Talbot and Ed White and Joann

Greenman. I felt no envy at all; I was just mesmerized by them. The day would come when I would act with them, and just trying to live up to their standards kept me working and rehearsing at a fevered pitch.

I worked hard to be accepted into the existing world of Theater at Southern, although my beginnings were anything but sophisticated. I remember being asked by an upperclass directing student to perform in a scene from O'Neill's *Desire Under the Elms* . I was to play Eben Cabot in the play's sensuous parlor scene where my father's sultry new wife attempts to seduce me. Looking back on that experience makes me laugh, for seduction was a new word in my vocabulary. I was still fresh off the New York streets playing stickball and stoopball with my friends and running from the police whenever my left-handed brother, Joey, hit a softball through the windows of the neighboring apartment house, and yet here I was, not two inches from the smoldering lips of this passionate, emoting older woman, looking over her shoulder at the exit door and wishing I could run through it immediately-all the way back to New York.

I also worked for student director Bob McDermott who kindly miscast me as the handsome Jonathan Harker in Bram Stoker and Hamilton Dean's *Dracula* , a "cutting edge" production for those days, albeit rather quirky as well. I never drove a stake through Dracula's heart in the McDermott production, but somehow a giant crucifix was projected onto his chest from a nearby lighting instrument and he seemed to melt, much like the wicked witch in *The Wizard of Oz*. But, then again, it was the Sixties, and we were all caught up in the tremendous revolution of the time, making us question the status quo and opt for new interpretations and expression. This play was done "in the round" as many plays were done in the TV Studio. This meant that the audience sat on all four sides of the acting space, pulling them into the action through their proximity to it. That play provided the long-awaited opportunity to work with Mary Ellen Crown who played "Lucy," the beautiful engenue-turned-vampire. In one scene she and I were seated on her bed, deep in the throws of passion, and as we embraced, I remember glancing into the audience and directly into the eyes and grinning face of my father sitting in the first row, not eight feet away from me. He was a simple man who didn't have any experience with Theater, but he was swelling with pride that night, feeling that his son must have truly made it in the theater world to be able to play a love scene with this beautiful woman, even though, as I look back upon it now, I wasn't very good. That was a humorous moment, and even a bit embarrassing, but it was one my father would talk about for a long time to come.

I was much happier with my next acting project, playing Estragon in a student-directed production of Samuel Beckett's *Waiting for Godot*. Here again the play selection, with its heavy existentialist theme, mirrored the times. George Blahodatny was the director and I was swept up in the admiration everyone in the department seemed to have for him. He had won the previous year's Best Actor award, and I was honored that he cast me in this prestigious role. I just hoped I could live up to his expectations. I played opposite Ken Woolley as Vladimir. Ken and I hit it off immediately, which is fortunate since those two roles must work so closely. Whenever we saw each other, even years later, there was a bond, a feeling of kinship that had its roots in that special production.

George, Ken, and I worked relentlessly on this play. I wasn't familiar with it before, but found myself making discoveries about the text and about myself that were fascinating and enlightening. There was a freedom to try almost anything in rehearsals, and if George seemed to like it, Ken and I were encouraged to experiment even more. Vladimir and Estragon, or Didi and Gogo as they are also referred to, were very much like clowns, yet under the surface there was a desperation and longing, a loneliness and sadness that were extremely poignant. I was able to relate to both sides of the character easily, and for perhaps the first time in my life, I felt that I was able to channel some of my long-hidden and repressed subtext into my acting. It was really quite liberating, making *Godot* one of the best experiences of my life.

I remember acting in the play and not only feeling totally at ease, but almost as if Estragon were some real-life extension of Julian Schlusberg; or maybe it was the other way around. I remember so much from the actual performances, and that was a long time ago. I remember the shafts of amber light and the deep blues of evening. And I remember the point in the play where Vladimir needs to leave the stage for a moment, and I felt so terribly lonely. And I *really* did! There were undoubtedly some very strong connections going on between the character, the play, and me.

Godot was largely responsible for me winning the Best Actor Award that year, an unheard of accomplishment since I was only a sophomore. But I never thought of myself as working for any kind of recognition during this play or any other. I was simply enjoying myself unlike I had ever done before.

Interestingly I've seen *Godot* a few times since then, and only once did it truly work for me. I felt that the other productions stressed the comedy too much, or the pathos. Or maybe we never really like other people's productions of plays we toiled over with so much energy and love. But *Waiting for Godot* remains a very special play for me.

Although my acting classes were very traditional in nature, the productions, depending on the director, were sometimes more avant garde. This included faculty-directed plays as well as student-directed pieces. I remember playing "Tranio" in a faculty-directed production of The Taming of the Shrew , wearing "mod" clothes-gold corduroy bellbottoms and a burgundy and gold polka dot shirt, and acting in the wedding scene to the musical strands of "Winchester Cathedral" in the background. This play was actually a great deal of fun to be a part of, as all of the plays were in those days at Southern. There was always an unrestrained spirit and enthusiasm that surrounded them so that we all participated in one way or another, in just about anything that was presented.

All of these diverse, yet fervent experiences and unique personalities seemed somehow to fit into my beating, throbbing heart, and my blood carried my passion for the Theater to every part of my body. If there is any truth to the phrase, "living and breathing Theater," this young, naive, awe-struck, seemingly misplaced, lower-middle class Jewish kid from New York was the living example.

Southern was also where I met my close friend, Ann Gabriel, who would play a major part in my professional and personal life for many, many years. So often over the next thirty years I would rely on Ann's "theater eye" to tell me if my productions were on target. Not long ago Ann and I revisited the TV Studio and its adjacent hallway, the center of our lives where so many of us lived in the constant buzz of theater activity. During our visit the space was hauntingly quiet. The Theater Department had long since moved to the Performing Arts Center on campus, our theater friends had gone on with their lives, and most of our professors had died—but our brief time there rekindled memories; and in that quiet we could hear and feel the spirit of a glorious past.

It was the Sixties, and society at large was turbulent, dynamic, and invigorating. New Haven was a particular hotbed of activism, as might be expected since it was the home of Yale University as well as several other colleges. It was a college town with many young people giving it a vibrancy and liberalism, and even a radicalism that might have appeared frightening to some. But there was also the feeling that New Haven was a solid place, well-steeped in its past and reflecting a culture and intellectual capacity that would remain constant and reaffirming and strong enough to cope with any temporary change in the social geography. These were the days of Watergate and the Viet Nam War and the "love generation." And New Haven seemed, in a way, to epitomize what was going on nationally.

In 1970, Black Panther Bobby Seale stood trial in New Haven and fifteen thousand people gathered on the New Haven Green to support him. He and other members of the Black Panthers were on trial for murder and conspiracy, and while everyone listened to speeches, other Black Panthers did their best to prevent riots by attempting to convince the crowd to remain calm and non-violent. Looming nearby were 2,500 National Guardsmen ready to do battle if necessary. It was a potentially explosive situation, with each side menacingly awaiting the first sign of intimidation from the other. That was a frightening time, especially since this national news story was taking place in our own back yard. I remember listening to radio reports of tanks rolling down Whalley Avenue to quell night time looters in the downtown area of the city. Those tanks were parked in the lots of our very own college.

It was also during this turbulent time period that there were political and social protests of all kinds, much of this, as it had been for centuries, reflected in the Theater. Guerrilla Theater made its appearance and the manifesto of the Living Theater, a group which dates back to the 50's and early 60's-"to increase conscious awareness, to stress the sacredness of life, to break down the walls"-seemed to find its way into a new emerging Theater of ideas and experimentation. One of our theater professors at Southern was very excited about Jerzy Growtowski's recent arrival in New York with his Actor's Research Project, another new and different influence on Theater of those days. I also remember the hoopla surrounding the arrest of actors in a Yale production who had taken off their clothes and run into the adjoining streets.

These were the times...and there I was, seemingly like a fish out of water; a pretty innocent kid from Mt. Vernon, New York, independent for the first time in my life and living in this fast-paced city alive with activity. And how I loved it! It seemed that all of my excitement for the times and the place could be mirrored in the zeal with which I pursued my theater studies. And I think I was in the right place at the right time to be able to study with remarkable teachers:

Dr. Kendall was the chair and founder of Southern's Theater Department. A tall, impressive looking man with distinguished white hair, his appearance belied his genuinely soft-spoken nature. His friendly smile and and benign personality made him totally approachable, and I needed that quality in a teacher. Interestingly, I never acted in one of Dr. Kendall's plays, but I took several classes with him. He was the father figure of the department. I remember taking a playwrighting class with him and creating perhaps the worst play ever written. Yet, with his characteristic soft smile, he complimented me on its few positive features, and then recommended that I turn it into a script for the screen since the stage effects I called for were impossible to create. I also remember his surprise retirement dinner and the crowded banquet hall. A totally shocked Dr. Kendall humbly addressed his former students with his typical sense of style and class, diminishing his own accomplishments over those years and praising those of his students. It was at times a bit difficult to believe that this soft-spoken man had a rather intriguing past in the military, meeting Maria, the woman who was to become his wife, in Italy where she was a member of the underground movement against the Nazis. He labored hard to begin the formal Theater program at Southern, or New Haven State Teachers' College as it was then known. He founded the Crescent Players, the college's theater organization, in 1954, although there was some theater activity on campus prior to then. From then on he worked tirelessly, nurturing its growth by attracting high quality teachers and exposing students to all kinds of plays. I remember his insistence on selecting play scripts of note, feeling that the script must be deserving of the countless hours that would be spent bringing it to life.

I have always felt close to my alma mater, and not long ago I attended a play there. I was dismayed that many students in the Theater program did not know who Dr. Kendall was, other than the Drama Lab in Lyman Center was named after him. Of course, they didn't know about the other acting teachers either, A. Richard Coakley or Constance Welch, both of whom have since died. I'm not sure why such a situation bothers me. I just feel that, as Linda Loman said, "Attention must be paid;" that we should always respect the memory of those who initiated what we enjoy today. It is always important to know what has gone before. In this way we can understand the present more clearly. Certainly Dr. Kendall, Miss Welch,and Mr. Coakley were pioneers of sorts, and spent much of their lives infusing us with an ardor and a discipline that enrich us today.

The same is true of a gentleman named Armand Zimmermann who was a great high school theater teacher in Connecticut. He also was a pioneer and devoted so much time and energy into organizing the Connecticut Drama Association, the State's official secondary school theater group and an organization very dear to my heart, having been a member of it for over twenty-five years. Armand died some years ago after a most distinguished career. He sued a local school system which tried to force him into an unwanted retirement due to his age, and made quite a splash in doing so, capturing national attention. He forced school systems to face the issue of mandatory retirement. He was a dynamic man who, when forced to leave high school teaching, went on to teach in a private elementary school. I remember him showing me drawings that his students made, displaying them as proudly as he was of any award-winning play he directed; intently describing each child and why his or her drawing was a unique accomplishment. He was an amazing man and I was lucky to know him. He "took me under his wing," so to speak, at the beginning of my career, and I learned a great deal from him. I convinced the Connecticut Drama Association, although I must admit I didn't have to push too hard, to institute a scholarship in his name for students planning to teach theater or be involved in it professionally. Somehow hearing the name, "The Armand Zimmerman Scholarship" makes me feel that he is still with us.

The outstanding characteristic of A. Richard Coakley had to be his infectious laugh. He had an outlandish sense of humor and was at his best, in my opinion, when he directed comedy. I played Arnolphe for him in Moliere's *The School for Wives* and think that his one goal during that rehearsal period was to get me to break character! I know he appreciated my serious approach to the work, but I think he also placed a high value on levity in the workplace. His goal was achieved when I misjudged the distance to a bench to which I was blindly backing up, and I landed on the floor. Everyone broke character, including me. Once that happened, it seemed as if Mr. Coakley could return to the business of directing the play. My human foible seemed to be important to him; or maybe he just understood that I needed to "lighten up" a bit. Arnolphe was a challenging role to say the least, and one that required so much work. I remember learning lines at two in the morning, *every* morning. But it was all worth it, for this was one of the most rewarding acting roles I ever had. I was always thankful to Mr. Coakley for trusting me with it.

In 1971, after I graduated from Southern, Mr. Coakley asked me to return to play Scrooge in his production of *A Christmas Carol* which was to be presented at the new Lyman Center for Performing Arts on the college campus. At first I turned down his offer as I was a new teacher and working constantly with lesson plans, starting to build my own theater program, and the other multitudinous tasks associated with those first years at a new job. But I soon realized how much I wanted to play the part, and I phoned Mr. Coakley to accept the role. It really was a wonderful experience. Mr. Coakley had adapted the play himself and had incorporated many of the unknown, or lesser known, carols into the production. Thom Peterson designed a magnificent set, and I remember feeling, during the performances, that this environment felt so real. My current fascination with Dickensien times and characters probably started with this production.

One day during the rehearsal process, Mr. Coakley came into the dressing room to discuss my character. He felt that I was making Scrooge too sympathetic. I look back on this conversation with a bit of amusement because I can certainly understand how that would happen. Being the "serious" actor at the time, I remembered the lesson we learned about finding something good in evil characters and vice versa, thereby giving the role a well-rounded, more complete characterization. Of course, Mr. Coakley wasn't exactly interested in the Stanislavsky-type approach I was taking and wanted instead the good, old-fashioned Scrooge that everyone happily hated. We discussed areas of the character rather seriously, but I don't think he felt he was making any progress. Finally, he pulled two aspirins from his pocket. He instructed me to look at my face in the mirror while chewing the aspirins. I did as he asked me to, although I thought it was a rather odd request, and suddenly witnessed my face contorting from the acrid taste I was experiencing. I remember he said to me, "Do you see that face? Now THAT is Scrooge!"

And thus, with this seemingly-simple device, I had found the character very quickly. Of course, there was much more to it than merely the taste of the aspirin; it created some kind of physiological change within me as well, and an accompanying mental picture of the man. It was as if that bitter taste filtered into the entire life history of the character. I remember the aspirin episode clearly and fondly. I wonder how long Mr. Coakley was going to give me to justify my work before he pulled out those tablets. And so I experienced an early lesson in troubleshooting and being prepared; a lesson and a trait I would come to value as a teacher and a director.

A Christmas Carol played before full houses of sixteen hundred people for two weeks. It was immensely enjoyable for so many reasons. I was very excited to be acting again, I was pleased with the character I had developed, and the company was, once again, like a family. I reconfirmed by intention of creating this same feeling of support in my fledgling group at Michael Whalen, and can now look back on my thirty years with the understanding that this may have been one of the greatest causes of the success that Hamden's Theater program experienced over the years. There has always been that trust and support among the students throughout those years, making Hamden Theater a place of comfort and acceptance.

Mr. Coakley died a few years after this production. He had been quite ill even during my college years. Rumor had it that he died during a run-through of his play near the end of the rehearsal period, but I think the truth is that he died at home. His death was a great loss to Southern's Theater program, and certainly to all of the students who learned so much from him and loved him dearly. His infectious laughter still echoes in my mind.

Anthony Mark Watts was an Englishman who impressed me greatly with his vast storehouse of knowledge. I took several theater literature courses with him, often struggling to pull a "B", but I learned a great deal. I also acted in several of his plays and remember the fast pace of his rehearsals and how he would frequently become animated, moving briskly on the stage and throughout the theater. He would also throw new ideas at us repeatedly, but not the kinds of ideas with which one could immediately improvise or experiment; rather, we had to think about what he wanted, what his metaphors meant, and how we could embody them in our performance. Just prior to opening night of Anne Jellicoe's *The Knack* he called us together and told us to radically change our characters-which threw us into a great turmoil! What was wrong with what we were doing? If we were bad, why didn't this come up before? How could we save the play, the performance, and our own self-dignity? A kind of uncomfortable heat enveloped us as we huddled together without our director trying to determine what we could do to save the play. We finally realized that nothing was wrong with us technically. The execution of our blocking was fine as was every vocal inflection we used. However, we had become stale in our performances; our reactions didn't seem fresh and as if they were happening for the first time. I was never one to enter the controversy over which is more difficult to direct or act in, comedy or drama, but I can easily see how the loss of spontaneity in a comedy could have devastating results. Mr. Watts' comments were upsetting, to say the least, and they definitely made us rethink and re-invent.

I admired Mr. Watts for his intelligence, often totally immersed in his lectures about Ibsen, Chekhov, and Strindberg. He became an important figure in my professional development, serving as my thesis advisor (again putting me through an exhaustive research period, but one from which I benefited), and also someone I could talk to through the years. I thought I had completed my thesis comparing and contrasting five plays dealing with the life of Joan of Arc many times, but Mr. Watts always seemed to find more material that he suggested I research. Finally, when the project was finished, he needed to read the entire paper and accept or reject it before a rapidly approaching deadline. He phoned me from Boston one day to tell me that he was traveling to New York, and that the train would stop in New Haven at a certain time. I was to meet him on the train platform and give him the thesis draft. I remember doing just that, never questioning the practicality of the idea, and soon I was to watch the departing train with an empty feeling in the pit of my stomach as it carried away my only copy of a project on which I had worked for several years. I stood there in a quandary, in an absolute whirlwind, listening to the diminishing sound of the train and thinking about the long hours of writing and the arduous research. Was this truly the most prudent way of handling the impending deadline? But I was becoming more familiar, although not necessarily more comfortable, with Mr. Watts spontaneous suggestions, and I did, after all, have faith in him.

Robin Hall taught Children's Theater. Mrs. Hall was a bit older, or maybe she just seemed to be. She was a beautiful woman, elegant and statuesque. I only took one course with her, but when I think of all of the Children's Theater work I've done over the years, I realize that she made a major impact on me. During those years when I was building the foundation of what I felt was important about Theater, Mrs. Hall figures prominently. She also garnered a great deal of respect from people in the field. She was truly a lady in every aspect of the word.

Sigurd Jensen was hired as the technical director in 1967-68 during my second year of involvement with the Crescent Players. Sig was an energetic man who I didn't know very well because I never availed myself of the opportunity of working on the technical aspects of productions. I wanted to learn as much as I could about acting, never realizing that I would one day be teaching theater and needed some technical knowledge. Actually, Sig did several workshops at Whalen in 1969 and 70, teaching the students basic construction techniques. Sig and I would become good friends in later years.

When I first began my theater studies at Southern, I enjoyed the closeness of the theater students. They were a fairly close-knit group, although there were two distinct factions as I remember them. There were the upperclassmen, a group of very independent New Haven-based apartment dwellers and their respective circle of friends who had nothing to do with theater or Southern for that matter. There were also the younger, more college-oriented students, most of whom lived on campus.

I remember the older group as being very streetwise. Their concerns were more worldly, some of them were already married and parents, and many of them lived in the only areas of the city where they could afford the rent, those being rather dangerous sections at best. I recall going to their parties which were often attended by rather unsavory characters, many of whom I suspect walked in uninvited. The fact that these older students accepted me wholeheartedly into their circle, or perhaps it would be more accurate to say on the periphery of their circle-by my own choice-made me feel very good, for what could I ever offer them by way of friendship or anything else. I was so naive in those days that I didn't even recognize the constant smell of marijuana wafting through the air. Yet they seemed to genuinely enjoy my company, never pressuring me to participate in their smoking or drinking, a fact that impressed me.

I was able to comfortably straddle both groups of students, finding great and lasting friendships and taking away life lessons in my associations. One friend, Linda Lawrence, was a local girl who lived at home with her family. As all of us always confided in each other, friends started to notice Linda distancing herself from us and acting a bit different. She was dressing older for some reason, but what I noticed the most was a glow I had not seen before. We finally discovered that Linda was dating Sig Jensen, which was quite a shock in those days. The idea of a student and a teacher dating seriously had many people gossiping, but to this very day I can see the joy in Linda's eyes as we stood in the hallways outside the TV Studio. I knew this was right for her, and I was very happy for them. They eventually married and had two children, the older one of whom, Jon, was friendly with my own daughter, Jennifer, when they were very young.

Another member of the faculty was a young designer named Thom Peterson. I always thought of Thom as bringing some real technical "class" to our department. His set and costume designs were sophisticated and advanced and unlike any I had seen before. We were always excited to hear his new ideas for the productions. As with Sig, I didn't have much contact with Thom due to my immersion in the acting area of the program, but as the years passed, well after I graduated, I became more friendly with him. I think a major turning point in our relationship was when I was asked to direct William Inge's *Picnic* in 1984. Thom and I worked closely on the look and feel of the production, and I think it took until then for Thom to realize that I truly respected his work, and also that I greatly valued the technical end of production.

And then there was Constance Welch. I could devote a chapter to her alone, for she had such an enormous influence on my life, and subsequently on the lives of the Hamden students through the years. I first met her in an acting class of eight students. It was my sophomore year at school, and somehow I mustered up the courage to take an acting class. It had long been a dream of mine. I'd done work in elementary school, and believe it or not, I remember those wonderful plays so vividly, specifically a sixth grade production of *I'll Eat My Hat* directed by our English teacher, Rhoda Engel, and in which I played a teacher who, upon losing a bet, had to eat a hat made of cream-filled vanilla lady fingers! It's funny how those memories of times long ago remain so vivid. The school system in my hometown of Mt. Vernon provided me with wonderful learning experiences and superb teachers. Actually, I was privileged to have fine teachers who encouraged me throughout my entire educational career. Mrs. Colton in high school and Adelaide Amore at Southern were particularly supportive of my writing and encouraged me to do as much of it as possible. In high school I was too shy to audition for the drama club's plays, but I did play roles in English class projects. I played Hamlet in a scene from that play for Miss Cahalan's English class, and she told me I had promise. I don't know how this came about, or even how I was given this role, but I smile now as I remember her words, as they were the first words of reassurance I received in this field. I also remember the trepidation that certain members of the drama club felt when word spread around that I did a good job. I noticed several of them starting to chum around with me, perhaps trying to discover whether I would start to audition and give them any competition! But that wasn't the case at all. I still was basically too shy to engage in the major productions in any way. But I do remember going to them, often alone, for every performance of every play. I sat by myself in the school's balcony and wanted so much to be a part of the play. I was particularly struck by our school's vibrant and colorful production of the musical, *Brigadoon* , never knowing at that time that I would direct it three times in my career.

Miss Welch's acting class of eight was inspiring. I walked into the TV Studio with great fear that first day, even thinking about dropping the course before I took the initial class. The Studio was painted black and was a large square room. This was different than any classroom I had ever encountered. But there was something very comfortable about it right from the start. I examined the other students, mostly attempting to determine if they were nice people, or if they would laugh the first time I embarrassed myself in front of them. There was a curiously older woman sitting in one of the folding chairs as well. I remember her wearing a neat suit, her hands folded in her lap, and a pleasant half-smile on her face as if she were far away in her thoughts. I wondered why this woman would take an acting class, but one of the exciting things about college life was the mixture of students of all ages and backgrounds in any given course.

At the start of the class, the woman who had been sitting alone so calmly even before I entered the room, stood up and moved before us. She introduced herself as Constance Welch, and in that moment my life began to change. Miss Welch was simply the most dynamic, engaging, interesting person I had ever met. She was a brilliant teacher who, over the course of the years to come, allowed me to learn so much about myself and brought out feelings I never knew I had.

The first few classes were strange and new to me. Once Miss Welch handed out a slip of paper to each of us on which was written an inanimate object. Our task was to incorporate a major attribute of that object into a human being. Mine was a jack-in-the-box, and, of course, I misinterpreted the assignment and jumped around the room impersonating the object and not a human at all! I was terribly embarrassed and could easily understand why the class laughed hysterically. After a while, I joined them. When my friend, Ann Gabriel, acted out her object, she moved stiffly around the room in a very odd, upright manner. We suppressed our giggles as well as we could, and I certainly was in no position to laugh at the work of anyone else! A long while passed and no one could guess what object was written on Ann's piece of paper. She eventually told us that it was a piece of spaghetti. When we questioned Ann about her interpretation, she said she was unsure whether the spaghetti was cooked or not, so she decided that it had just come out of the box, and the reason that she walked so stiffly was because she was proud of her Italian heritage! Needless to say, we couldn't suppress our giggles anymore, and we suddenly convulsed in laughter once again. When I think about it now, these assignments taught us a lot I'm sure, and I used them throughout my teaching career. But I'm also sure that Miss Welch used them to relax us, and to bring us together as a tight-knit group.

Our class bonded quickly, and we soon felt a need to "investigate" the background of the woman with whom we were falling in love. We learned that she had taught at Yale for thirty-eight years, and with a new regime taking over at the Drama School under the leadership of Robert Brustein, she was lured to Southern by Dr. Kendall. Since then I've read Brustein's book in which he denies the accusation that he forced Miss Welch out of Yale. He had been criticized harshly by her students in this regard for many years. I've also read Elia Kazan's account of studying with Miss Welch during his Yale years. We soon discovered that Miss Welch was considered the finest acting teacher in the country at one time, and had a list of students who were now leaders in the American Theater. She studied with Maria Ouspenskaya, one of Stanislavsky's first acting pupils at the Moscow Art Theater. Ouspenskaya came to the United States to teach the new techniques Stanislavsky had been experimenting with in Russia.

One day during class, Miss Welch was called out for a phone call. This was highly unusual for she would never miss a moment of instructional time. She received an urgent phone call from New York and was asked which of two actresses she would recommend to play the lead in a new Broadway comedy called *Forty Carats*. Julie Harris won the part. Ms. Harris had been a student of Miss Welch's at one time. We were all so impressed by the phone call, and realized then that this humble woman with whom we were blessed to be studying was also incredibly powerful as well. We also learned that she was often hired to privately coach actors in professional plays and movies, Susan Strasberg being one of them, as well as Raymond Massey in the famous movie, *Abe Lincoln in Illinois*.

Miss Welch used to compare creating a character to peeling an onion; there is always another layer of life that lies under the surface. And so it was with Miss Welch herself. Her life and background unfolded over time, and we realized what an honor and opportunity it was to be taught by her.

I took every course possible with Miss Welch, and acted in all of her plays. She instilled a great love of Theater in me. More importantly, she made me feel special. She gave me the confidence I so sorely lacked up until then. As Miss Welch did not drive a car, I often provided her transportation home after rehearsals. The rides to downtown New Haven were filled with the most wonderful conversation. She would often treat me to a light late-night dinner, and on one occasion took me to the prestigious Yale Faculty Club. I felt a bit uncomfortable, concerned more with using the correct fork than the conversation. There are many things to say about Miss Welch. In short, she was inspiring, and if I studied with her for a hundred years I could not have learned all she had to teach. She had a way of chipping away our acting problems one at a time, so that we were never overwhelmed with the myriad of problems we had, and she made us feel good at the same time. Roderick Bladel, the head theater librarian at the New York Public Library at Lincoln Center and also a student of Miss Welch's, dedicated his book, *Walter Kerr's Analysis and Criticism* to her. His words are poetic and true, and capture the feelings of so many of her students:

"I didn't understand Miss Welch; yet she understood me perfectly. She had a gift for understanding, and sometimes it was an almost instantaneous thing. There must be hundreds and hundreds of people who, because Miss Welch lived, can say, 'At least once in my life somebody understood me and took me seriously.' Like Linda Loman, she believed that 'attention must be paid.' I saw her engaged in conversation with John Cochrane when he was no more than six years old, and she listened as attentively to that child as if she were listening to Aristotle. Which she may be doing these days. She was full of surprises like that."

When friends get together and talk half-humorously, half-seriously about aging and all that comes with that process, we always return to the fact that we didn't meet Miss Welch until she was sixty-eight years old. And then we think about the enormous effect she had on our lives. There is certainly a lesson to be learned there.

When Miss Welch died in June of 1976 we felt lost. Her wake was a very sad event, and a handful of us felt as if we were temporarily disconnected from the rest of the world. It was a strange, frightening, and lonely feeling to think of the Theater without Constance Welch; indeed, to think of the world without Constance Welch. I was terribly reluctant to walk up to her body in the open casket, and could only do so with the help of friends. Looking at her expressionless face only reinforced my discomfort, and when I finally found what little comfort I could standing alone in the rear of the room I realized that this was not my acting teacher; this was merely the body that beautiful soul inhabited. Miss Welch's burial was in a New Haven cemetery, attended by her admiring students and her only relatives, two nieces from the midwest. It was simple and quiet, the way she would have liked it. Prior to her death, when my close friend, Bruce Connelly, was at her bedside and obviously distraught at the inevitable conclusion of her life, Miss Welch looked into his eyes and told him, with that characteristic care and humility in her voice, not to worry; that death was merely like exiting quietly behind a curtain in the wings-as simple as that. Constance Welch taught me many things while she was alive, and I think she taught me as many, if not more, after she died.

After her death, Miss Welch's nieces weren't sure what to do with her belongings. Many of them eventually were donated to the Lincoln Center Theater Library, but there were several boxes of correspondences and notes that the Library couldn't house for lack of space. Somehow I ended up with them. I have often gone through those boxes, the fragile, flaking pages unveiling a rich and textured history of a young woman's growth into a major figure of the theater. There are notes from her early days when she studied law, and there are lectures she delivered, old programs of plays she directed, newspaper articles, research papers she wrote concerning the

Contance Welch (photo by Samuel Kravitt)

with Jason Robards

as Scrooge in A Christmas Carol (1971)

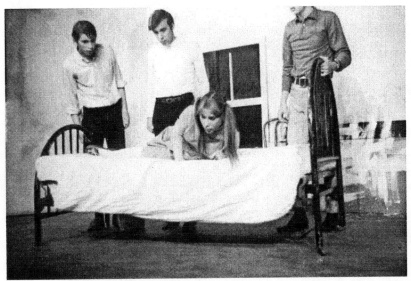

Julian Schlusberg with James Marko and Claudia Iverson in Ann Jellico's The Knack (1966)

with John Swanson in Moliere's School For Wives **(1968)**

with Janice Morin in Anna Sophie Hedvig by Kjeld Abell (1969)

relationship between the voice and emotion, and letters that reflect a colorful professional life. I have the letter wherein the famous George Pierce Baker, head and founder of the Drama School, invited her to come from the midwest and teach at Yale. Interestingly, none of the letters seem to convey a "personal" life. Perhaps this was more guarded in those days, although there are veiled references of her turning down a suitor in letters sent to her by a friend. It is almost difficult to think of Miss Welch having time for anyone or anything else beside Theater and her students. She was very attentive to us, and I like to think she lives on through us to those we teach and those who are important to us. One of Miss Welch's Yale students, Marcia Kravitt, was very devoted to her and cared for her during her last years. Marcia's husband, Sam, is a professional photographer and took a most striking portrait of a young Constance Welch in

1948. Marcia and Sam gave me a copy of the photo which I treasure and which now hangs in my theater office.

Miss Welch had a close friend named Mollie Gassner, to whom she introduced me. Mollie was the wife of the late famous theater historian and critic, John Gassner. It was said that he loved his wife so much that he had a portrait of her hung on his living room wall, positioned in such a way that he would immediately see it in the reflection of his bathroom mirror as he shaved each morning. I never met John Gassner, but I feel like I knew him through the numerous conversations I had with Mollie. She was a kind and gracious woman with a sparkling wit. I remember a long drive we shared to Providence, Rhode Island, where Mollie was giving a playwriting award in her late husband's name. We talked so much that the ride seemed to be only a few minutes long. I also remember that we stopped at an elegant restaurant in Sturbridge, Massachusetts for dinner, and she wouldn't allow me to pay for any part of it. Mollie was like that. She and Miss Welch were similar in many ways, and both of them treated me very well.

The first time I met Mollie Gassner was a rather embarrassing situation. An upperclass acting student was directing and acting in a two person play by Luigi Pirandello called *The Man With the Flower in His Mouth* . When his partner in the project dropped out unexpectedly with approximately a week left prior to the workshop performance, the upperclassman asked me, a sophomore and novice at the time, to play the role. Needless to say, I was greatly impressed and honored at the request and gladly accepted. I knew there was very little rehearsal time before the performance, but I was so flattered by the offer. I began to learn my lines immediately. I look back on those days, when I knew absolutely nothing about theater, and little about anything else as well, and I wonder at my audacity at jumping into projects so suddenly. The director/actor made elaborate plans for our few rehearsals, which even included us cutting classes one day, something I would have never done and certainly never shared with my parents. He assured me that we could easily overcome the time problem. But he never appeared for our first rehearsal. Nor did he show up for the second or third. The day before the performance I was numb from fear, but he told me we would rehearse all day, and the following day as well right up to curtain time. As might be expected by this time, he never appeared, and we went into the performance without a single rehearsal! His final instructions to me were to merely sit at the small cafe table which was our entire set and he would do all of the blocking around me. I will never forget the feeling of dread and panic I experienced. I can still feel the heat of the amber stage light as well as the streams of perspiration running down my face. I froze. I never said a single word and the upperclassman improvised the entire one-act play.

I knew I had to face Miss Welch after the performance. She was sitting in the first row of seats, accompanied by Mollie Gassner and a few other influential theater friends from the Yale Drama School. I apologized to them simply and with few words, for there really was no excuse to be so unprepared. Miss Welch gave me one of her famous one-line responses: "Julian, don't ever let this happen again." I hung my head in the most extreme embarrassment I can remember. A few days later Miss Welch told me that she brought these colleagues from Yale because she wanted them to see "this new boy with great potential." Again, I was humiliated. I wanted to run as far away as possible. I saw the end of my brief theater career before my eyes. I even thought I hated Theater. But Miss Welch remarkably brought me back; gave me challenging scenes to perform in class and excellent roles in her plays. She taught me to overcome obstacles and helped me regain my faith in myself, and all of this with few words but great trust.

I tell this story, as disconcerting as it may be, to all of my theater students. While I wish I could bury it, it was, in its own way, one of the most profound learning experiences I've ever had. I learned the value of preparation and focus, of discipline and organization. More importantly, I learned that I had the potential to surmount a problem and come out of it with a higher self-esteem.

During my senior year I applied to direct one of the annual student-directed plays. Usually these were one-act plays or at least shorter than a full-length play. I, however, fell in love with Herb Gardner's three-act play, *A Thousand Clowns*. I had seen the movie starring Jason Robards and liked it a great deal. I met Mr. Robards some years later at a drama festival at Choate Rosemary Hall School in Wallingford. As I was President of the host organization at the time, the Connecticut Drama Association, we were introduced by a colleague who then abruptly ran off to take care of some business, and before I realized it I was alone with this famous actor. After what seemed like a hour-long awkward silence, I blurted out, "I loved you in *A Thousand Clowns!*" which, of course, could have been the dumbest thing in the world to say since he made the movie about twenty years before! He, however, must have understood the situation. He laughed and quickly allayed any nervousness I had, and we proceeded to have a wonderful and comfortable evening together. Mr. Robards and I were to meet on several occasions in the future.

The faculty granted me permission to direct *Clowns* and the auditions were heavily attended. One actor impressed me for the role of Arnold Burns. I remember his large physical build, his deep, slightly raspy voice, and sincere eyes. But most of all I felt his acting was totally honest, even vulnerable. And so I cast this man in his first-ever acting role. It was Dan Lauria, now a well-known television and movie actor, although Dan does a great deal of stage work as well. Dan and I became close friends, and I'm glad to say that friendship is still as strong today. He told me years later that Miss Welch had spotted him on the football field as he was a football player at the time. Of course, I never figured out why Miss Welch was on that field! She strongly suggested that he audition for *A Thousand Clowns*; that the director was "someone he needed to work with."

I felt good when I learned this as it represented a final "forgiveness" for the Pirandello experience two years before. I guess I had harbored the guilt of that dreadful experience all this time, but the fact that Miss Welch thought I could help actors through my directing was a great encouragement to me.

Of course there was a great deal of activity between the Pirandello debacle of my sophomore year and the wonderful experience of *A Thousand Clowns*. In February of my junior year I was asked to direct a piece for another of those afternoon workshops. It was a two-character, one-act play by Ed Baerlein called, *Push Button 13 and Watch the Machine Go Boom!*. All that I knew about the playwright was that he was a college student from somewhere in the United States, and at the time I didn't think it was at all strange that we would be producing his play. Dr. Kendall was always searching for new and interesting material, and I knew he had many connections to other colleges and universities. The play was a futuristic piece, the theme of which was very much like George Orwell's *1984* or Aldous Huxley's *Brave New World*. Most of the personnel that worked on the play were seniors, and I was initially surprised and quite flattered that the faculty asked me to direct. My two actors were John Talbot and Connie Wozny, both of whom were very well respected in the department. John had received a major acting award the previous year, and I was taken by his graciousness in being named Best Supporting Actor while I, a year younger and a relative newcomer, had won the Best Actor Award. But John never had a problem with this. In fact, he looked after me that sophomore year as I tried to learn the ins and outs of this daunting Theater machine. He referred to me as his "little brother," and I remember feeling a great loss when he graduated and moved away.

I always felt that Connie was somewhat overlooked as far as her talent was concerned. I had seen her do some magnificent work (you'll remember I was quite the silent observer), yet the major roles in department productions seemed to elude her. If anything, she made quite an impression with her performance in this workshop, and people took a fresh look at her. She always said she was grateful to me for casting her, but I never doubted that she and John were responsible for the positive impact of this play.

Push Button 13 was received well, and the review of the play praised every aspect of it., also stating, "The workshop...was a tribute to Mr. Schlusberg's direction." I was amused at the use of the title, "Mr." for I thought of myself as an inexperienced post-adolescent at best in those days. But the reference seemed to signal a strange new attitude towards me. I started to feel that people were paying more attention to me and listening to what I had to say. The faculty seemed appreciative and approving of my work on the play which they showed, quite interestingly but also quite characteristically, through their subtle smiles and a difficult-to-describe, longer-than usual look in their eyes. It almost seemed as if they were trying to "size me up," and I remember feeling both flattered and unnerved by their attention. Soon after, Miss Welch laughingly began an acting class by saying that she had just come from a Theater faculty meeting where a debate took place over who "discovered" me. I remember feeling that familiar sudden warm flush of embarrassment force me to look down instantly. My heart pounded and I could feel the stares of my classmates. Truthfully, I also felt humbled to think that the faculty was at all pleased with my work.

Not long ago I saw an advertisement for a play by Ed Baerlein in *American Theater Magazine*. I was instantly overcome with a flood of memories of that play written so long ago, and I felt some kind of personal satisfaction that I was entrusted with his work when he was just starting his journey. I experienced a momentary feeling of kinship although we never met, for, unknown to him, we at Southern played some small part in his "history."

Southern provided me with the opportunity to play some wonderful roles. While many of them were from the classical theater, one I felt particularly challenging was in a little known play called *Anna Sophie Hedvig* by the Danish playwright, Kjeld Abell. Miss Welch directed it in my senior year. It seemed quite a departure from the theater fare at Southern over the years, and we wondered why Miss Welch had chosen it. As it turned out, the play was significant in its theme; that people must take action when they see injustices in the world. Abell was an outspoken man whose work was highly symbolic. He wrote *Anna Sophie Hedvig* in 1939 as a warning about the rise of the Nazi movement. In 1944 a fellow playwright, Kaj Munk, was murdered by the Nazis, and the next evening Abell interrupted a play at the Danish Royal Theatre to ask the audience to pay homage to the memory of Munk. Abell had already spent time in a Nazi concentration camp and therefore had to go underground where he joined the resistance movement.

The play was a stark drama, and even the atmosphere during rehearsals seemed to be very serious, even foreboding. The impending sense of danger that the Nazis represented to the playwright seemed to work its way into the TV Studio, and we all shared a feeling that we were working on not only a very important play, but one of those that had established Miss Welch's reputation as a foremost acting teacher and director in the country. And she was brilliant as she directed us! She moved around the theater, in and out of the action; she interrupted us to make us aware of forces and events; she suggested subtextual changes. This was Miss Welch at her best-dynamic, forceful, intense, driven, yet never dictatorial or tunnel-visioned. She still guided, coaxed, and cajoled in the most patient and flexible manner. When I worked for her in such a situation, my blood rushed through my body like never before, and I knew this experience would change me for the rest of my life.

It was difficult to separate the rehearsals and the play from our personal lives. The anxiety and tension felt by the characters often attempted to invade. But I think this happened because the whole experience meant so much to us. I played the son of the house, John, who was newly married to a woman named Leila. The role was different for me and I wondered if I could pull it off believably. He was brazen and hot-tempered; perhaps a bit spoiled as well.

The cast was a large one, some twenty-three of us, and it was wonderful to witness everyone exploring parts of their being that they had never allowed to surface before. One person who always comes to mind when I think of this play was the woman who played my mother, "The Lady of the House." She was an English woman named Violet Thompson-Allen who was now pursuing a college degree in her late 50's or perhaps early 60's. Violet was charming and warm and kind. I remember her self-effacing nature and her great sense of humor, often at her own expense. One night during rehearsal I noticed her seated offstage and watching me intently. If I weren't so fond of her I might have thought it intimidating. After my scene she told me how fascinated she was with my use of my hands. She said that my fingers seemed to cut the air, visually expressing my emotions precisely and honestly. I recall being very flattered by her observation. No one had ever said anything like that to me before and I was honored that she would even take the time to watch me.

It wasn't difficult to imagine myself her son as Violet assumed a maternal relationship to many of us, albeit never imposing or disciplinary. She felt like one of us and rarely, if ever, excused herself from an activity due to age. She invited some of us to her home in Hamden once. Situated by a lake, I recall its furnishings as being so elegant and sophisticated. Violet certainly was a woman of class, yet, in her own way, very down-to-earth and simple. She also collected clocks and they adorned all the walls and furniture. I loved Violet, and was distressed at her death several years later. Her delightful, playful, and enchanting personality was soothing and comforting. She played a significant role for me in those days.

The play had a very successful run. More importantly, however, I think I connected with its theme in a very personal way. I always valued the *idea* of speaking out for what I believed in, but I never thought I could find the courage to actually do it. Likewise, I had an idea of what John was all about, but had doubts that I could create this character in a truthful way. Miss Welch helped me overcome my tentative feeling about the latter, and while that was slowly evolving, I was simultaneously and even unknowingly discovering a courage within me as well. That theme is a principal I hold dearly today, and I have advocated it to my students throughout the years. Yes, that play that I had never heard of before and have never seen or even heard of since "spoke" to all of us and changed our lives as well.

Late in the school year 1969 I, along with seven others, were inducted into the National Collegiate Players, a theatrical honorary fraternity and a member of the Association of College Honor Societies. This was one of the greatest honors at Southern, and was particularly meaningful to Dr. Kendall. What mystified me was that the ceremony, and even the membership to an extent, was shrouded in a kind of secrecy. We were never told what to expect or anything that we had to do to prepare for the ceremony. The eight of us-Douglas Bennett, Karen Burgess, Leonard Caplan, Ann Gabriel, Cara Lehman, Joyce Seretny, and Donna Whitham, and I-were brought into a room almost entirely lit by candles except for some stage light which shone on a long center table. Around the perimeter of the room were seated unrecognizable figures, largely in shadow. These were other members of the fraternity, many of whom had graduated several years before and whose names I would recognize later on. After Dr. Kendall and some others spoke, we inductees were given small books containing passages from the great plays and from which we had to read with no previous preparation. I remember Dr. Kendall asked me to read the famous "To Be or Not to Be" speech from *Hamlet*. My heart raced, partly because the entire ceremony made me nervous, but also because he was entrusting me with the one soliloquy he regarded in an almost reverent way. As I read, I remember being very aware of the fact that I felt absolutely nothing at all. It was an merely a collection of words to me, and I felt guilty that I was not illuminating or even highlighting any of Shakespeare's poetry or philosophy while I read. I just wanted to get through it. The eight of us were all relieved after the ceremony, and even felt proud that we were now members of this prestigious group. But I remember questioning the secrecy of the induction. We were given very nice membership pins, but what I really wanted was a copy of that little book. But just as the ceremony was cloaked in secrecy, the books disappeared quickly and I never saw one again.

Almost immediately after the induction I saw an advertisement for a performance by the famous mime, Jean-Louis Barrault. He would be bringing his show, *Words and Music From the Court of the Sun-King, Louis XIV* to Yale on May 12. I knew this was a rare opportunity and I decided that I had to see this master. I managed to get a single ticket. It was a magnificent performance, and as I watched spellbound from the balcony in the darkened theater, I knew I was witnessing a genius. Every move of his body, large or subtle, was so expressive and communicated so much. I was hypnotized by Barrault and remember feeling like I was the only one in the theater. And as my mind seemed to be a sponge in those days, I realized how communicative the body can be, and was once again reminded of the importance of the physical in creating a character. I felt that this performance was one of those important events in my life, and what I learned from it would greatly affect my future work.

The end of my senior year brought the usual excitement and trepidation that any soon-to-be-graduate feels. I anticipated being out of school and beginning a new phase of life, yet I knew I would miss the home that the Theater Department provided. At the honors convocation I was presented with my third consecutive award as Best Actor of the Year and felt both speechless and deeply touched that the department respected my work so much.

Many years later, in 1994, Southern's Alumni Association presented with me an Alumni Citation Award for "outstanding contribution to the performing arts." As I listened to the speeches at this beautiful and formal affair, my mind wandered back to those days when we studied and worked so hard, realizing how crucial and influential they were for my teaching career and my own personal development. I envisioned the TV Studio and the many rehearsals; I saw visions of my good friends and acting partners Ken Woolley, John Swanson, Janet Sheiffle, Bruce Connelly, Patty Bariuso, Dan Lauria, Jim Marko, Lois Look, Nancy Katz, Larry Olszewski, Joyce Seretny, Marshall Hitch, Jimmy Lucason, Charles Mackey, Vicky LaFortune, Lenny Caplan, Carol Paglia, and so many more. And my friends, the technical artists who worked so diligently on the crews, contributing to the overall success of the plays: Jamie Gallagher, Mike Duffy, Tom Swetts, Lois Sarasin, Paula Altieri, Karen Burgess, Sarah Stein, Bonnie Strickland, Sue Andriso, Barbara Skopic, Patty Stone, Bill Roberts, Kathy Begina, Dina Shein, Michael Blinn, Cindy Latella, Donna Whitham, and a host of others. All of these faces, like ghosts, swirled before my eyes; I pictured us in performance, in rehearsals, and deep in discussion; I saw faces laughing and arms and hands gesturing and felt the tight embrace of shared joy. And I thought of Shakespeare's line, "I count myself in nothing else so happy as in a soul remembering my good friends." As I came back to the present and looked at the many faces before and around me and the candle-lit elegance of this marvelous evening, I became suddenly lonely, wondering where those college friends were, and I realized how much I missed them.

The three acting awards did much to provide some greatly-needed confidence back in 1969, and I thought the world was at my finger tips. I eagerly planned to go to New York and join the ranks of struggling actors, understanding that I might not "make it," but also knowing that it didn't matter so very much. At that moment in time I felt good and I felt courageous. When I seriously considered my options at that crossroads, however, I realized that several friends of mine already in New York seemed to be struggling a bit more than I personally wanted to. So I decided to save some money before I joined them, and at least be able to put some food on the table while I looked for employment in the Big Apple. Things were not to unfold in quite the manner I had planned , however.

It was with this background that I began my teaching career. I took the job with the thought that I would only teach for a year, saving what money I could before I ventured into the City. I student-taught at Michael Whalen under the tutelage of Joseph Cristiano, an English teacher of the highest standards. He was the head of the department, an innovator, and he helped me enormously. He still does, as we have maintained a friendship all these years. Joe was responsible for the introduction of many teaching techniques which are still current and valuable, but now they have more "trendy" names. I quickly learned that the method of communication was all-important in teaching, and that the subject matter itself is flexible enough to fit into just about any technique or format. With the content I had learned at Southern and with Joe's skill guiding me to communicate that content, I felt I was on the right path. Quite simply, Joe was an excellent teacher, mentor, and leader, and I can attribute my being taught by him once again to Fate putting me in the right place at the right time.

I had a wonderful time when I was student-teaching. Joe's classes were large, but enthusiastic. Actually, these very students would become involved in the first theater productions at the school, and while I didn't know it at the time, they would become important to me for many, many years to come.

I must admit I was nervous during those first days of student-teaching, and I give those classes a great deal of credit for being so tolerant. I also gave them quite a "show" through my own anxiety and clumsiness. On one of my first days in front of the class, I tripped over the trash can and fell behind the teacher's desk. The fall wasn't nearly as embarrassing as having to stand up and face the group of shocked, as well as very amused students. I remember trying to use my acting skills to create a little comedy routine as a way of "saving face." Another time I was leaning over the desk making some point or other during a heated class discussion. I shut the top desk drawer not realizing that my tie was hanging down and had gotten caught in it. Of course the class was hysterical when I attempted to straighten up and was jerked down due to the restriction of the tie. No comedy routine would help me in this instance. And yet on another occasion, a student from the Home Economics class entered my room in the middle of the teaching period and proudly presented me with a large piece of cake that she had just made. I left it on a corner of the desk, resumed teaching, and planned to eat it later on. Naturally, I became involved in the class activity, and later in the period leaned over and, forgetting that the cake was in front of me, forcefully put my hand into it. I guess my classes were filled with surprises like that. Who knows, maybe my awkwardness made them feel comfortable with me on some level. They certainly were relaxed and open to the subject matter. Our shared excitement for Shakespeare vaulted the students into exciting independent projects, and class discussions were often exhilarating as we examined classic novels. I remember performing Shakespearean soliloquies for the students, and they would then perform them for me. Often Joe would ask administrators to observe classes, for the students were becoming increasingly creative, and their critical thinking and discussion skills were developing rapidly. Time went by quickly and the daily classes were filled with a feeling of joy and discovery.

As I think back on it, I realize that Joe had an ulterior motive for inviting high ranking Hamden school officials to the class. I believe he was trying to pave the way for my being hired. He was like that; extremely helpful and wonderfully kind in a quiet and reserved way. When a job did, in fact, open at the school for the 1969-70 school year, Joe phoned me, asking me if I was interested. I gladly accepted it. I was able to teach English and Drama, which really excited me. And it was wonderful to teach next to Joe. I learned so much, and he, in turn, encouraged the growth of the theater program in those early days. He and his wife, Fran, not only attended the plays, but supported me in a time when theater was thought of as nothing more than a frill. It helped to have someone of Joe's stature and influence support the struggling young program, giving it credence and a sense of importance.

During the first week of school I asked a school administrator if I could teach acting on the stage in the auditorium rather than in a classroom. He smiled in a condescending way and said to me, "Son, in this school, drama is on the bottom of the barrel." I took that to mean "no." I smiled politely, thanked him for his time, and made a silent vow to make him "eat those words." Many years later at that administrator's retirement dinner, long after the theater program had won accolades nationwide, I gently and good-naturedly reminded him of those words. He surprisingly not only denied having spoken them, but, in fact, felt largely responsible for the birth and growth of the the program! Sometimes I'm amazed at people's recollections of events. In this case, however, I knew that his admiration for the program was sincere, and it felt good to hear him boast of his role in its development. I could tell that he was proud of our students' accomplishments and, after all, his recognition of their success was very important. I wonder about the many school administrators who feel the same way as he did initially, and what it would take to change their minds; to see the enormous educational value in such a program. But for now, I could only thank him once again, this time, however, with much warmth and good feeling.

Prior to my student-teaching tenure at Michael Whalen, a group of students had approached English teacher, Barbara Mastroianni, asking her to direct the first play at the school. I knew Barbara from my days with the Crescent Players at Southern. She was a few years older than I, and I remember how involved she was with the group. She and I remained good friends and professional colleagues until her death from cancer some years later. Barbara had a verve, a vivacity for life. She fought that cancer as best she could, and even when she was near the end of her life she had the idea to remarry her former husband. And so she had the nurses dress her, and she decked herself with long flowing ribbons of every color and description, and she was married on the outdoor patio of the hospital. The picture of her simple ceremony, of her laughing face, of her defiance of death, and yes, even of the ribbons comes to mind whenever I think of her. Now there was a lady of courage and elegance.

Barbara was about to begin the play, but when I arrived, she asked me if I would like to direct it. I gladly consented, and together with my friend and fellow student teacher, Ann Gabriel, we set out to direct the first full-length play in the Hamden Public Schools in a long while, and the first ever at Michael Whalen-quite appropriately *Our Town* by Thornton Wilder. There had been some kind of Theater in Hamden since 1935, although there was no formal structure or program. It consisted mostly of drama club productions, with various teachers sharing the responsibilities through the years. Interestingly the woman who founded the then-new Hamden High School producing group, "The Theatre Guild," was my speech teacher at Southern, Ethel Miniter Wiggins. I remember that Mrs. Wiggins was the first instructor I met at Southern, walking into her classroom as a nervous freshman on that very first day of my college career. Her face was stern and her hair formed into a tight gray bun on the top of her head. She promptly informed the women in the class that, although slacks were permitted on campus beginning that year, there were to be no slacks in her classroom! An auspicious beginning, indeed, as she continued to teach the class with an austere, no-nonsense approach. She also told me that my speeches sounded like sermons, which made sense to me at the time since the most influential public speaker in my life thus far was the rabbi in our synagogue. I listened to him nearly every Saturday morning for my entire adolescence. Mrs. Wiggins softened as the course progressed, and I actually started to like her somewhat. But it did seem ironic to me that she would have initiated the program in Hamden. It was one of many "connections" I would recognize over the years to come.

Ann allowed me to do most of the directing of *Our Town* while she supervised every other phase of the production. To this day, she is an assistant to the director in West Haven (Connecticut) High School. I know Ann would be a wonderful director in her own right; she has "lived" with the theater for over thirty years, and has an eye for detail, but she prefers the "assistant" role.

Thornton Wilder was a resident of Hamden for many years, living in an impressive home high atop a hill not far from Whalen. Often I would feel inspired during rehearsals, knowing that his home was literally only blocks away from the school. After his death, his sister, Isabel, continued to reside there. Hamden has always been proud of Wilder. In April of 1997 the United States Postal Service issued a stamp in his honor and held the ceremony at Hamden's Miller Memorial Library. I was asked to provide a brief performance and asked one of my directing students, Michael

Mattie, to work on this project. Michael was about to graduate that spring. I had a great deal of faith in his ability and wanted to honor his four years of diligent work. He selected a one-act play by Wilder called, "The Penny That Beauty Spent," and the performance was excellent. I recall being impressed by Michael's calm in the presence of so many dignitaries on local, State, and national levels. I can only attribute this to having confidence in his work. I like to think that I am also confident, but I readily admit to fighting off attacks of the nerves on numerous occasions.

Our Town was a grand success. There's nothing quite like a group of young people who feel good about their accomplishments and themselves. I remember the auditorium reverberating with the sound of laughter and excitement as the students basked in the praise of their parents. Miss Welch came to see the play and commented, "There's genius up on that stage." Once again I wasn't sure what she meant. As in college days, we never questioned her or asked her to explain herself, but often would get together and try to find meaning in her sparse verbal response to our work.

Emily's death scene was particularly moving in that production. The students, in all of their innocence, truly felt the outward pain of the scene, yet also understood the complex subtext of Wilder's message as well. Their black umbrellas and the deep blue cyclorama background created an impression which I still remember, and one professional theater person in the audience spoke for many years of that moment as being so totally honest that all anyone could do was weep at its simple beauty. I often wonder if that moment was created by sheer luck. How could such young, inexperienced people move an adult audience so! But I found this to be true throughout my career as I have observed the work of students of all ages in many, many schools. Their relative innocence and lack of adult "baggage" allows them to get to the heart of a scene rapidly and honestly, and their youth and enthusiasm as well as their trust in their directors allows them to be vulnerable and risk-taking. It may sound bizarre, but I often think young people can and do perform as honestly as most professionally trained actors.

I also remember imploring a college friend, Bruce Connelly, to play the part of Simon Stimson, the Grovers Corners' resident drinker, because the boy playing the role became ill at the last minute. Bruce performed it very well and with very little rehearsal as I remember. Those early days required a lot of "mending and patching," last minute problem-solving, and getting help from anyone willing to come to our rescue. Fortunately, many of my friends from Southern lived close by and were kind enough to help whenever they were needed. I think they were excited for these students just starting their theatrical journey, and I also think they felt like they were, in some way, a part of the whole experience; that they felt an "ownership" in this experiment. I remember my college friend, Mike Duffy, spending a great deal of time at Whalen, teaching the students about technical theater. There were others as well, and I felt good that my students were having the opportunity to learn from them.

The *Our Town* cast was large and spirited for this initial theater project at the school. We rehearsed after school for several hours each day until the performance dates arrived. When I look back at that first play I think about how simplistic it was in comparison to the sophisticated and complex productions that would characterize the program in years to come. Yet this was the foundation for all that followed, and those young students worked so hard. I often think of them as the pioneers who started it all, and I feel so good that many of them still keep in touch some thirty-plus years later. They became the core of the theater program for the next several years, and when they went on to Hamden High School, they expressed a strong desire to continue their training with me. We decided to meet on Saturday mornings, calling ourselves, "The Studio Players." It was wonderful to work with students who had such drive and love for what they were doing. Interestingly, the younger junior high school students would take advantage of the opportunity to work with the older students, and a true feeling of collaboration and cooperation emerged. These, then, were the people who began the Theater as we know it today in Hamden.

Whalen benefited from being termed a "community school," a title I didn't quite understand at the time except that it enabled many of the school's extracurricular activities to be funded, and while there wasn't enough money to provide frills for those activities, it at least secured the existence of many after-school groups. Ours was one of them. Albert Baldino was the coordinator of the Community School Program and became a good friend. It's difficult to describe Al in terms of the "modern" administrator of today. While he certainly had the required organizational skills, I always recognized a kind of paternal quality in him. He loved all of those children in the many activities the program made possible. He went out of his way to help them, giving them rides to events, throwing pizza parties, showing his concern and his affection at all times. Al was a sensitive man and, looking back on those years, brought a great deal of happiness into the lives of many young neighborhood children. Al's generosity was symbolic of the school system in those days. Others shared this family-style approach, working well after the school day ended for little or no pay, but just because they cared; people like Al's brother, John, Joe Cristiano, Joe Cirasuolo, John Carusone (who later became mayor), Gary Burgard, John Edmonds, Carmen ("Skip") Vegliante. Hamden was fortunate indeed to have these people.

The community school title also enabled me to run a summer theater program, and that first summer I chose to direct George Bernard Shaw's *Pygmalion* . Robert Silverman played Henry Higgins and Marie Loggie played Eliza Doolittle. Rob now teaches music in New York City, and I received a warm and welcome letter from Marie last spring when my retirement was announced. Rob wrote a poem for me dated January 27, 1969 entitled, "To Be Alive." I was very touched by this expression of his affection and admiration, and I've held onto that poem all these years. And then he wrote another which he had published some twenty years later. These "bookend" poems mean a great deal to me for they reflect an author who is sensitive to and appreciative of his world.

I remember once, during those very early years, receiving a panic-stricken phone call from Rob in the middle of the night. He had a major fight with his parents and was calling me from a public phone booth. It was winter and he was without a jacket. The urgency in his voice alarmed me, and I drove to meet him immediately, bringing with me a warm coat. We went to an all-night diner where I bought him some hot soup, forced him to call his parents and let them know that he was safe, and then tried to calm him down. Rob had several issues he was dealing with during his high school years, making him no different than any other high school student. I think a lot of this was due to his maturity and "free-thinking" nature. He also had a love for music that made him want to devote himself to his trumpet rather than go to college immediately upon graduation. His parents, on the other hand, wanted him to begin his college education immediately, and this caused friction between them. While I find that it is not uncommon today for high school graduates to wait a year before entering college, it was not so acceptable in those days-especially for academically gifted students. Finally Rob's parents relented, and Rob spent his post-high school years developing his talent for music. He eventually did take the college path, and combined his love of music and education to become a teacher. He even teaches classes in drama.

Rob's story is not unique. I can't begin to describe the frustration teenagers feel during these years, and how many metaphoric warm coats and bowls of soup have to be doled out. I try not to take sides, but I must say that the youth and relative inexperience of students does not make them the problem all of the time. I've encountered some bewildering parenting practices over the years; parents who believe that discipline can only be achieved through punishment; parents who threaten to pull their child from a play a week before it is to open, not understanding that such an action only humiliates the child while causing a multitude of problems for the other students and the director.

The Studio Players continued to meet while I ran the Whalen Players simultaneously. In 1969 the older group decided that it wanted to do a full-length production in addition to their Saturday acting classes, so we chose to work on Tennessee Williams' *The Glass Menagerie*. This was to be the first high school play I ever directed. Williams had been a favorite of mine for as long as I could remember. I was really affected by him, O'Neill, Miller, Hellman, O'Detts, Inge-those realistic playwrights who managed through their genius to portray the poetry of the human condition. *The Glass Menagerie* seemed like a fitting first play for the Studio because it offered not only the power and sentimentality of the story, but the lyricism of the text as well. Interestingly, the group also wanted a small-cast play for its first production. Deborah Zelitch played Amanda Wingfield. It was Debbie who first approached Barbara Mastroianni about starting a theater group, and I would often tell her that she was responsible for the whole program. Debbie was bright, had a wonderful sense of humor, and worked hard for the players. Roy Mazzacane played Jim, the Gentleman Caller. Roy's mother, Mary, studied opera at Yale, and I also discovered years later that she studied with Constance Welch while there. I still talk to Roy today as he is a leading voice teacher in the area, as well as a fine singer. I've had the honor of directing him in several operas in recent years, and it felt good to work with him again.

In subsequent years the Studio Players went on to present Arthur Miller's *The Crucible,* Marcel Maurett's *Anastasia* translated by Guy Bolton, Maxwell Anderson's *Elizabeth the Queen* , and William Gibson's *The Miracle Worker.* When *The Miracle Worker* won accolades at the State Drama Festival as "Outstanding High School Production in Connecticut" in 1974, public awareness of the seriousness and professionalism of our students greatly increased. The program seem to win its "legitimacy." I must say that the public was kind as well. While it seemed demanding so far as quality was concerned, a trait I like to think our work instilled in the audiences, Hamden provided a very supportive environment for the growth of educational theater. Even before 1974 the school system and the town were quick to recognize and applaud the efforts of its students. Letters were written to the local newspapers, plays began to be reviewed, and there was a general feeling of happiness surrounding this new, growing, expanding, and successful program.

There were many students who, collectively through their talents, played a crucial role in the emergence of the Studio Players as an exemplary and award-winning troupe. In addition to Rob and Marie and Debbie and Roy, there were Kirsten Summers, James Gold, Margaret Adair who later became a resident stage manager at Yale, Promise, Connie, and Syd Ahlstrom, James Abrams, Rachel Green, Colleen Ledig, Donna Urquhart, Ron Munson, Ann DeMatteo, John Howard, Ann Muttilainen, Gail Grate, Sean Morgan, Chester Overlock, Olga Podryhula, Rachel Bernstein, Charles Aprea, Lisa Sette, Adam Bernstein, Lisa and Lauren Miller, Debbie Lewisohn, Greg Wiltshire, Melissa Widmer, Tom and Susan Baratz, Heidi Ahlstrom, Lissy Trachtenberg, Terri Daddio, Joan Sullivan, Debbie Winch, Karen Listro..... the list goes on and on.

It's also difficult to separate the names of those who contributed to the Studio Players from those who worked so industriously as Whalen Players. The line of demarcation where one ends and the other begins is blurred by the idea of a "company" of people working together and not divided into age brackets. While high school students might have helped with certain aspects of the junior high school productions, they never appeared in them. However, the reverse was not true, and helped to provide some advanced training for the younger students.

Michael Whalen was a great place to begin my career as a teacher and director. The staff was enthusiastic and shared a common goal of providing the best possible education. The administration welcomed the enthusiasm of the students for this new program and did its best to accommodate the large number of them desiring to take drama classes during the day. By the school year 1973, there were nine daily drama classes with an enrollment of nearly 200 students. There were two separate theater courses, an introductory course and a more advanced one that studied Shakespeare and the classics and performed touring children's plays for the elementary schools.

However, what provided a rich fabric for this school was its diversity. It was located in a neighborhood surrounded by Yale professors, a large African-American community, and an Italian neighborhood where a high percentage of the children spoke only their native language. The school was the beneficiary of this mixture of cultures, each with its own interests and attitudes, concerns and problems. What each had in common, however, was the best interest of its children, and they worked hard to make that school function smoothly. The Theater program was contributed to by all, and it was a lesson in understanding to watch everyone collaborate on a production. I was an advocate of what some would call "color-blind" and "multi-ethnic" casting, and often had students of all denominations acting as a family or as love interests on the stage. This, I felt, not only opened up doors of possibility and encouraged all students to participate, but actually demonstrated, in a tangible way and with a product to show for it, an ability of all kinds of people to get along with each other. This has always been an important principle to me. I'm reminded of audiences springing to their feet as a young African American actress named Gail Grate literally stopped the show twice during each performance of *Brigadoon* with her amazing talent; and of David Bowles, another African-American actor whose comedy genius and timing made him a school and community hero; and I'm thinking of the numerous students of Jewish, Italian, Hispanic, Asian, Polish, and other backgrounds acting and building sets and painting together-but most notably, laughing together and hugging each other and supporting each other.

In a way, I was in a very good position in those days because each community had a vested interest in my work. While many people didn't know much about live theater, they knew where their children were, at school and happy. Parents brought lunches on weekends for the entire group, and often remained to watch their children building a set, or painting-and the parents often became involved as well, working alongside their own children and those of their neighbors. On production evenings, the community filled the auditorium wearing their best clothing, putting their best foot forward out of respect for their children's endeavors.

But our community, like any other, was not immune to the tenor of unrest that was rifling through the country in the early seventies. Whalen had a very tense school year in 1972-73 and we experienced a "riot" in our cafeteria, much like the ones other schools were trying to quell. That school year saw the exit of many veteran teachers upon whom the tension took a terrible toll. Yet, within months, that very cafeteria was the scene of the cast and crew of our production of *Fiddler on the Roof* spontaneously rising and singing during the lunch hours, engaging the entire student body and staff in song and camaraderie. Some people attributed that minor miracle to the power of the Theater; I attribute it to the power of people who recognize the absolute need to understand each other and the importance of getting along. There simply is no other way for the community and society to progress.

The Whalen musicals were extremely popular in those days, and rarely was there an empty seat in the auditorium that held some five hundred spectators. Our four performances were usually sold out. We did those wonderful school musicals like *Bye Bye Birdie, Guys and Dolls, Oliver!, Brigadoon, Fiddler on the Roof, My Fair Lady, Carousel, Funny Girl, Carnival, Camelot, The King and I, The Sound of Music, Bells Are Ringing,* and *Wonderul Town.* They became more complex as the years passed, and the talent became more pronounced as the program developed. Today the array of musicals is wider, and the style is noticeably different from those written in the 1950's and 60's. I look at the musicals I currently direct for the Foote School Summer Theater in New Haven such as *Sunday in the Park With George, Joseph and the Amazing Technicolor Dreamcoat, Pippin,* and I recognize the change in the American musical theater. I suppose schools will always opt for the oldies, and I understand their value, but I sometimes worry that theater educators and directors get stuck in those all-too frequently done musicals and neglect the fresh, contemporary material out there. New material reflects the world in which these young people are growing, and they need exposure to it as they form their values. Sadly, some directors even select three or four musicals and present them in rotation over the years, never venturing into anything new at all. They often save and pull the same sets out of storage, merely reproducing the play as it appeared previously. I feel that students are terribly cheated in such instances. They deserve more respect than that.

Whalen, from the very fact that it was a hub of serious drama as well with the residence of the Studio Players, also did numerous non-musicals. I tried to choose plays that offered a variety of experiences, ranging from subject matter to production style. I was also very concerned about exposing the students to quality material written by fine playwrights. Many people argue that students should never play adults on stage. I disagree. Many people argue that students should only be exposed to the most simplistic kinds of plays until they are old enough to appreciate more sophisticated material. I disagree again. I believe in challenging students to open their minds and hearts to plays that are enlightening, that force them to think, and that may even be a bit controversial.

Probably the most important aspect of our work as teachers and directors is using common sense, tact, and sensitivity in selection, rehearsal procedure, and presentation. Of course, in our case, the resident high school actors performed the more sophisticated plays, while the junior high school students assisted and sometimes appeared, playing smaller roles. I carefully selected the material for the latter as well, and these plays also provided considerable challenges. Over the years at Whalen, the Players presented Noel Coward's *Blithe Spirit,* Garson Kanin's *Born Yesterday* , Edna Ferber and George Kaufman's *Stage Door* , John Patrick's *The Curious Savage* , Peter Shaffer's *Black Comedy* , the Frederick Knott thrillers *Wait Until Dark* and *Dial 'M' for Murder* , Herb Gardner's *A Thousand Clowns,* Neil Simon's *The Good Doctor,The Odd Couple* , and *The Star-Spangled Girl* , Leonard Gershe's *Butterflies Are Free* and many others. The rehearsal periods of these plays overlapped those of the Studio

Players, and there were also children's plays that toured the Hamden elementary schools as we attempted to arouse the interest of the very young as well. In short, there was a great deal of theater activity going on. I realize that the reader may wonder what type of quality could be expected from junior high school students. Let me assure you that the quality was high. There was no condescension in our theater. Our work was serious.

Whalen was gaining more and more attention and even fame throughout the local community and the State. In 1978 I was requested by Professor Robin W. Winks, the Master of Berkeley College at Yale, to meet with James R. Mason, a Walter Hines Page Scholar from England who was touring the United States. Mason was studying the placement of drama in the secondary school curriculum and spent that year observing schools and their programs throughout the country. I remember the cordial Mr. Mason and how impressed he was with the range and seriousness of theater activity at Whalen. Not long after he left New Haven, I received a thank you note from Professor Winks in which he said how happy Mr. Mason was to start his tour with our group and that it set a high standard for other schools to live up to.

That same year, the late Arthur Pepine, a producer at the Yale School of Drama, wrote me a letter telling me that he had heard of the excellent work going on at Whalen, and he wanted to encourage the students by inviting them to attend Thursday night Drama School performances. We were quite happily surprised by the generosity of Mr. Pepine's offer, and attending those productions provided us with a standard of excellence as we prepared our own work. Arthur Pepine was a fascinating man. He studied acting at Yale until an unfortunate diving accident physically handicapped him for the rest of his life. Yet he never lost his passion for the theater and went on to become a prestigious member of the theater community in New Haven.

There are many endearing memories of theater at Whalen. In addition to the excitement of the performances themselves, there were so many "moments"-those seemingly little occurrences that tend to get swallowed up in the overall excitement of a production, but are memorable because they are significantly human, both touching and funny. There was the letter of gratitude I received from a student who was so excited before the opening night curtain that he wrote it with an eyebrow pencil, and also an anonymous hand-written letter, the last sentence of which says, "I will not sign this so that you can think of this as coming from all the people who have ever been in one of your plays." I remember the irony of a burgeoning theater program which didn't have the money to replace hammer heads when they fell off during crew sessions. There was also a note I found on my desk from an elated student stating quite simply, "There is so much love floating around here!" and then there was a note from a student dated May 24, 1975 which said, "Maybe in ten or twenty years you'll go through your memory chest and you'll pull this letter out and remember me..." and feeling like I had opened a time capsule, I did just that on October 21, 1999, recalling her with great fondness. I remember placating a student who begged me to allow his pet goose to appear in *Carnival*, and the subsequent humor of trying to "direct" it, obviously with no success as it eventually stole the scene by crossing downstage, and squawking at the audience. I also recall being "stabbed" by a student while teaching him to fence for *Camelot*. Then there was the touching, brief note I received from a girl working on *A Thousand Clowns* in which she said, "I want to thank you for the experience of being part of a group, something I don't usually get a chance to do because of my shyness. I rehearsed saying this and it sounded silly, so I decided to write it instead." I was struck by this girl's honesty and maturity. There was also the time we received a hand-written letter from the playwright, Neil Simon. We were opening *The Odd Couple* at the time, and he was in New Haven where his new play, *The Gingerbread Lady*, was opening at the Shubert Theater. He heard about Whalen through the tightly-knit theater community and sent us a flattering note wishing us luck. This meant a lot to the students who went out on the stage that night knowing they had the support of the famous playwright himself.

I also remember directing *The King and I* when the actors playing Anna and the king were working so hard on the mechanics of the dance steps that they were missing the exultation of that famous moment in musical theater; when both characters temporarily lose themselves in the ecstasy of swirling around the stage to the accompaniment of Rogers and Hammerstein's exhilarating music. I remember literally pulling the musical director, Lauren Loro, out of the pit and, as the orchestra played "Shall We Dance", Lauren and I danced with abandon around the large stage. Elizabeth Harlow, the vocal director, still talks of that moment and what it represented: a kind of freedom that permeated our work, where all facades were let down and all one hundred of us could openly laugh and have fun. That was Liz's first play with me, and we still enjoy working together so many years later. Of course, Liz also remembers the not-so-good experience when I felt the actors did not prepare themselves for rehearsal, so I apologized on their behalf to the orchestra and musical staff and dismissed them. The actors, however, had a night of rigorous work ahead. But I feel that this too is important: just as there should be a certain lightheartedness about rehearsals, there must be first and foremost discipline and diligence. These are only a few of the literally hundreds of reminiscences that are indelibly etched into my mind.

I remember the growing challenges as well; the numerous things I had to learn about directing through experience. In *Camelot* , Lancelot, played by Lawrence Iannotti, was much taller than Guenevere, portrayed by Christine O'Day. I knew this would be a concern from the moment I cast the play, but they were both outstanding at the auditions, and I knew they would be superb in these roles. I also didn't believe that height or any other physical attribute should prevent a person from having the opportunity to learn and experience. And so I learned to minimize height differences through "creative" blocking, such as the taller person sitting, while the shorter stands. I also used darker colors, which minimize the silhouette, on Larry and lighter colors on Christine. We experimented together and overcame the problem.

There were also outstanding performances; performances that seemed to contradict the young age of these students. I'm not certain how to account for them other than give credit to the learning environment, the presence of serious older students whose passion for their work was contagious, and perhaps the feeling that we were all involved in something powerful and thrilling. There was Edith Meeks as the blind Susy Hendrix in *Wait Until Dark* which caused one audience member, a person with no Hamden connections, to write, "I don't know which to praise more: her skill in making the stage business her own then-and-there activity, or her ability to deliver lines as though they had never been memorized, or her ability to be 'blind,' which she pulled off without a hitch"; Heidi Ahlstrom's magical performance as Madame Arcati in Noel Coward's *Blithe Spirit* ; Neal Augenstein's moving Tevye in *Fiddler* and Michelle Klotzer's comical Yente in that same production; Alison McWeeney's impressive Eliza Doolittle; Doug Mann's outrageous Leo Herman, or "Chuckles the Chipmunk" in *A Thousand Clowns;* Adam Bernstein as both the maniacal Mr. Roat in *Wait Until Dark* and Henry Higgins in *My Fair Lady* ; Ann Macaione's wonderfully wacky and yet poignant Fanny in *Funny Girl* ; Carla Franzoni and Bill Gunn in *Born Yesterday* ; Eloise Goddard and Sarah Haller in *Wonderful Town* ; Maureen Creegan and Jay Friedler as Carrie and Mr. Snow in *Carousel.*

Carousel was an enchanting piece. The characters of Julie Jordan and Billy Bigelow were played by Patty Pesticci and Paul Teitelman. When I first announced my plans to direct this play, many people thought I had chosen a vehicle well out of the range of students on a junior high school level. But I had faith that this particular group of students could readily handle this challenge. The singing was extremely demanding, and for that reason I cast it several months in advance. Patty and Paul, two exceptionally devoted students, studied diligently. Both of them were fine actors and had beautiful voices. Of particular difficulty was Billy's "Soliloquy" which Paul worked on endlessly. The product of Patty and Paul's efforts was simply incredible. They gave the most moving and inspiring performances. Ed Meyer designed the set, Lauren Loro conducted an extremely talented orchestra, Joanne Koob choreographed, and Deborah Finkelstein coordinated the costumes.

Patty told me after the play that if she would one day have a daughter, she would name her Julie. And many years later Patty did, in fact, do just that. Her married name is Jarvis, and so the world now has a Julie Jarvis...which is pretty close to Julie Jordan. This is yet one more anecdote in the Hamden Theater family, for I truly believe our strong family bond extends over thirty years. Recently I saw Patty's mother, and she informed me that Patty's son, a precocious young boy, is an avid participant in his school's drama activities. I'm sure his mother watches him with great pride, perhaps recalling the days of her own heavy involvement. If he could only have seen his mother in *Carousel*!

Students stand out in my memory as I recall those days; students who contributed to the foundation of our unique program as it exists today. All of these students, no matter how different they may have been in ethnic or religious background, socioeconomic levels, or any other category worked industriously and with great spirit; seriously and with sensitivity; with a warmth that filled the theater as they shared their time and their efforts. I remember the wonderful Michelle Klotzer, Alison McWeeney, Ellen Meeks, the three sisters Jeanne, Christine, and Mia O'Day, Jeff and Judy Lettes, Jamie DeLong, Keith Erikson, the four Hirshfield brothers-David, Andrew, James, and Russell, Larry Fitzgerald, Carla Franzoni, Bill Gunn, Laurie and Steven Pitts, Lisa Haynam, Bill and Justin Garvey, Robert Cedro, Greg Wiltshire, Debbie Wells, Richard Funaro, Mark Caplan, Paul Teitelman, Rita Cerisi, Tanya and Noelle Larson, Carolyn Riordan, Nancy Snyder, Ralph and Tom Burr, Maureen Creegan, Charles Aprea, Steve Villano, Geoffrey Kanner, Sharon Sullivan, Susan, Mary, and Marsh Richards, Janet Paier, Jay Friedler, Stuart Seltzer, Tom Tozzo and his sister, Nancy, Paul Gross, Alex and Elizabeth Kenney, John Maria (who I recently went to see in an off-Broadway production in New York), Dan Burns, Jeff Bogens, Stuart Farber, JoAnn Coppola, Beth Hardy, Patty and

Debbie Winch, Ann Levatino, Debbie Munson, Lisa Mikolinski, David Stern, Miriam Schmir, Bill and Bob Liebeskind, Marissa Puopolo, Nan Hyde, Maureen and John Donohue, Shari Rothstein, Paul Hunt, Lisa Lowney, Eloise Goddard, Jessica Thomson, David Dippolino, Jared Haller, Andrew and Daniel Whitman, Diane and Ted Stevens, Laura Saller, Susan and Glenn Noffsinger, Sonja Hendrix, Ken Christianson, Kim Hajus, Reggie Lindsay, Lisa Sette, Lynn and Barbara Festa, Mitzie Cole, Ginny and Jeff Aten, Chris Westberg, Seth Messinger, Hope Singsen, Laura Hortas, Laurie and Brian Meltzer, Kirsten, Lisbeth, and Gordon Shepherd, Diane Willis, Helena Whalen, Anne Augenstein, Stuart Seltzer, Ed Romanoff, Diane Tomkinson, Stuart Farber, Jesse Dale Riley, Paula Runlett, Louis, Phil, and Sally Weinberg, and so many, many more. As I write these names and think of others, I am filled with both happiness at recollecting these special people, and also with melancholy, for I truly miss them very much.

Hundreds and hundreds of Whalen students found happiness in the theater. Their youthful energy, their work ethic, and their human qualities of trust and responsibility can never be minimized, for these were the very students who provided the groundwork for what was to become one of the strongest educational theater programs in the country; that would win recognition from the State, the Region, and the Country; that would be saluted by the Rockefeller Foundation, and private businesses and industry; that would be designated as the "model" theater program and would be visited by educators from this country and abroad; that would produce professional actors, designers, technicians, playwrights, tv scriptwriters, and directors of stage and screen; that would be the subject of a national and internationally distributed documentary on educational theater. To think that all of this began in the hearts and the dreams of junior high school students in the late 60's is overwhelming. But it proves once again that there are no limits to what human beings can achieve if they have the passion and the commitment. I count myself very lucky to have been a part of it.

Chapter Two

The Plays

Antigone, 1966

"Going back to Hamden put me in touch with the reason why I thought about acting as something important to me. It has given me the highest expectations, and by highest I do not mean to imply loftiness. I expect discipline and I expect community among actors and director and crew."

Martin

"I would never have guessed anything from high school would mean so much to me. Our theater tradition is part of who I am, much to my wonder and joy. I didn't realize it until this summer. I was warming up before a play and suddenly I knew that Hamden Theater was with me. I carry it in my heart. When I close my eyes, I can see it all perfectly. I can hear that excited silence, smell the dust on the curtains, feel the lights on my face. You take it with you. I didn't know that. I didn't know that could happen. I love it."

Jesi

Theater is a very personal thing for me. I feel that people come to the theater-both educational and professional-because they have a need for it; that it answers a longing in the soul. While it may be looked upon as entertainment for many, there is no doubt that we can measure our society by it; that it reflects our mores, strengthens our convictions, and exposes our shortcomings. Over the past thirty five years it has also provided a spiritual journey for me as I begin to understand the connections between the great playwrights and philosophers of today and the oracles and prophets of the past. Therefore Theater is of utmost importance, and teaching it implies a serious responsibility. And while it can be taught as an art form unto itself, it would be difficult for me to separate it from what it can do for people educationally; what it can do to enhance a person's self-esteem; how it can raise our consciousness about society and how to improve it. In my opinion the theater is a tremendous vehicle for vividly illustrating such issues as assuming responsibility to civilization, combating racism and bigotry, introducing students to other time periods and other cultures, and also acquainting them with more limited worlds, such as that of the handicapped or the terminally ill. I also believe that *performing* the classics can bring these plays alive as no in-class reading and dissection of the text can. Watching a person act out a story gives it a sense of relevance and immediacy; it allows us to feel that we are being let in on a big secret.

For these reasons, play selection is extremely important. Plays that are notable and significant speak to an audience in an eloquent and poetic manner. They are often sophisticated and advanced, and the approach to them must mirror their mature subject matter. I believe that directors, teachers, and students must be bold enough to tackle productions that present extraordinary challenges and that provoke thought and excitement and even controversy. They must work with integrity, choosing material by authors who provide, through their language and imagery, subject matter, themes and characters, a unique and positive literary experience that comes to life on stage. Obviously, a well-rounded program includes plays of all types, but whatever the choice, I've always encouraged my colleagues across the State to select "worthy" material. I recall one of my college professors, Dr. Robert Kendall, claiming that a play script must be deserving of the time devoted to bringing it to life.

Over the years I have directed productions of *The Great White Hope, The Elephant Man, Dancing at Lughnasa, The Shadow Box, Desire Under the Elms, Becket, Summer and Smoke, The Lion in Winter,* and *The Little Foxes*—to name a few. Also classical plays have included *Cyrano de Bergerac, A Midsummer Night's Dream, Othello, Richard III, As You Like It,* and *Much Ado About Nothing.* It has been uplifting for me to witness the numerous positive short and long term effects these plays have had on the students: they have been challenged intellectually and artistically; they have been engaged in dialogue that has added dimension to their lives;

and they have been empowered to see the unlimited possibilities that lay ahead. I believe that these plays, as difficult and mature as they may be, offer great "life" lessons for the students, in addition to exposing them to truly fine literature and all that that entails. Naturally, these plays must be approached in a sensitive way, ensuring comfort for all of the participants. This is difficult territory, but the benefits far outweigh the difficulty, and I've seen, read, and heard of too many positive results to ever relinquish my belief in these pieces of work. They have a good effect on young people; they address issues that young people can and should handle; they make them think and form viewpoints, all of which helps a person gain a strong self-concept.

The plays that have been presented by Hamden Theater students have been astonishing pieces of work. From the very outset, in those early days of the late sixties and early seventies, the students could be characterized by a seriousness of purpose. While doing plays was always fun, there was the pervading feeling that we were making a statement, sharing something very important with our audiences, and also, in our own way, contributing to this thing called, "art." As thirty years passed, the work took on a sophistication that grew out of a richness of tradition and a high respect for those who previously had devoted themselves to this practice . There was always the feeling that we were in the process of growing, and each new generation of students felt compelled to continue that growth. Even when Hamden was setting records with award-winning productions and even when it was in the national spotlight, there was never a complacency. Rather, students worked *harder* to maintain the reputation created by their older "brothers and sisters." In general, while students were proud to be a part of Hamden Theater, a wonderful sense of humility prevailed throughout those years, a trait I feel is of utmost importance in the arts. How can we learn unless we realize how much more there always is to do?

The program benefited greatly from guest artists throughout the years, and jumped to new technical levels of expertise with the addition of Orten

Pengue, Jr. as technical director in 1982. There seemed to be nothing that Ort couldn't build or fix, and soon students clamored to learn carpentry skills from him-often using formulas they learned in math class. His positive attitude and his feeling that anything was possible encouraged the students to strive harder as they built two story sets, revolving sets, utilities with running water and electricity, and even an entire functioning beauty salon.

Frank Alberino, a former student in the program, became the third member of the artistic team in 1997, although he was my designer at the Foote Summer Theater Program for several years before. Frank's degree in set and costume design from The State University of New York at Purchase entitles him to work professionally, but this kind and talented man desires to "give back" to the students some of what he's learned and therefore show his gratitude to Hamden Theater. Together, Ort and Frank are nothing less than incredible and have accomplished things on stage that are unheard of in high school theater, and probably most college and university theaters as well. In Hamden, unlike many other schools, it is prestigious to be a member of the technical crew, and what the students learn from Frank and Ort is immeasurably valuable for the rest of their lives.

I am often asked which of the plays I've directed is my favorite. I could never begin to answer this question, for each is special and reflects the backgrounds and personalities of a specific group of students of which I was extremely fond. I suppose this is similar to asking a parent which of his children he likes best, and obviously there is no answer to that question either. The discussion of the plays that follows will hopefully do some justice to each one, perhaps illustrating why I consider it unique. The process of directing a play, however, from doing the research-which often begins months before auditions-to the final performance is so complex and so full of details that it would be impossible to recall all of the events which surround each play. I have tried to share some important information about the plays and the people who were responsible for bringing them to life. Each group was extremely devoted to the work, and they brought great pleasure to their audiences.

Hopefully those audiences were enlightened and left the theater a bit wiser than they were upon entering it. That's one of the many joys of the Theater-its ability to inspire in often the most subtle of ways, making us all better people for having had the opportunity of both sharing it as a group and experiencing it in a very personal way as well. Here, then, are the plays. Perhaps a director or two will be inspired to explore one of the following texts and thereby offer his or her students that wonderful opportunity to gain the insight that the Theater can provide.

The Miracle Worker was part of a theater season that was very exciting, but I know I must have been very young and energetic to create it. In addition to the high school production of *The Miracle Worker*, 1974 saw Whalen productions of the Frederick Knott thriller, *Wait Until Dark* , Leonard Gershe's comedy, *Butterflies Are Free* , the musical, *Fiddler on the Roof* , and a touring children's theater production of *Cinderella* . Those were exciting days, and the theater at Michael Whalen Junior High School was a hub of great activity. High School and Junior High School School students worked together in both the performing and technical areas, proving what educators have been saying for a long time: that students teaching students can be one of the most effective forms of education. The place was buzzing with activity, especially on Saturday mornings when we would have acting classes attended by all of them.

William Gibson's *The Miracle Worker* has become, over the years, standard "high school fare," and by that I mean that it is very popular, almost always placing in the list of the top ten most frequently produced plays on high school stages nationwide. I always found this somewhat deceptive in that it might give the impression of being easy to do. This is not the case at all. The play is a very difficult piece dealing with complex character relationships. In addition, the actor playing Helen Keller must appear both blind and deaf, and the actor playing Annie Sullivan must give the impression that she *was* blind and has recently regained her sight. There is also that tumultuous dinner table scene which places the two women in an intense, physically combative situation. And under all of this action there must be a story that is so very sensitive and filled with love. Annie Sullivan wrote, in 1891

> "At another time she asked, 'What is a soul?' 'No one knows,' I replied, 'but we know it is not the body, and it is that part of us which thinks and loves and hopes...and is invisible...'
> 'But if I write what my soul thinks,' she said, 'then it will be visible, and the words will be its body.'"

How does one go about to capture the beauty expressed in these lines, yet I feel that such emotion, such sensitivity and insight *must* be the spine of this play.

I decided to direct *The Miracle Worker* in a three-quarter round style. The Whalen stage was a large and deep one, and was conducive to such staging. I felt that it was important for the audience to be close to the action and hopefully be drawn into it. I'm sure I was influenced also by my own acting days at Southern Connecticut State University where we always performed in the TV Studio. When I recently went back to visit , I realized that it was smaller than I remembered, but still the feeling of all that had taken place in that space-all of the glorious plays, the smell of the make-up and costumes, the color of the lights, and working with really devoted people-came back to me in a sudden rush of emotion. This is what I was trying to recreate at Whalen. I remembered how audiences in the TV Studio enjoyed the close proximity to the actors, and I remember that the audiences at Whalen did also. I would do many more such intimate productions over the course of my career in Hamden. When I began directing on the Hamden High School stage in 1975 I was happy and relieved to find it large enough and easily adaptable for such staging. Many years later when Hamden was considering a new high school, or renovations to the current one, I was asked what I thought would be needed for theater of the 21st Century. I suggested a Black Box as well as a proscenium theater, for the flexibility provided would enhance students' education tremendously. I'm happy to say that both were built in the new theater complex at the renovated Hamden High School.

Colleen Ledig played Annie Sullivan and Donna Urquhart played Helen Keller in that wonderful 1974 production, and they were superb. The cast was combined of both high school and junior high school students working as a true ensemble. The production was the first Hamden winner of the Connecticut Drama Association's "Outstanding High School Production in Connecticut" Award at the statewide drama festival that year, and all of Hamden was thrilled about the accomplishment. This award, the highest given at the Festival, was not a surprise to most of the Festival attendees, although it was to me. I remember the announcement of our placement nearly knocked me off my chair. The directors and executive officers of the CDA kindly told me later that they immediately recognized the quality of the production as being outstanding. It did, however, cause quite a stir among the old guard of Drama Association members as they wondered who these upstarts were.

There was great excitement in school on the Monday morning following the Festival. Great tribute was paid to the company during the morning announcements, and even those who hadn't considered Theater a major activity in the school were now offering their congratulations and looking at the program with closer scrutiny. This prestigious award had established Hamden as a leader and drew a great deal of attention to the town, the school system, and the theater program. I was also pleased because those were days where we had very little in the way of facilities or financial support. We depended on what Tennessee Williams would call, "the kindness of strangers." And there was great kindness indeed as many people volunteered to help us, loan us props, and donate costumes. I felt that the success of the program in those early days was a tribute to the efforts of the students because it clearly illustrated that *people* make a program and not necessarily facilities or even money.

So much time has passed since those days, and I meet so many directors and theater teachers today who seem to be in that same precarious place. They tell me of the lack of support, of the dire financial situation, and of poor facilities. How can I begin to encourage them to pursue their goals, and to be *good* at it! Those who have the power to change the conditions will do so eventually, but they have to be convinced that the program is one of consistently high quality. I can only smile calmly and try to be supportive. It doesn't take much to break a theater teacher's spirit, especially where there is little or no belief in the value of educational theater in a local school system or community. The individual has to be driven by his or her own inner conviction and passion.

When Hamden was announced the winner at the drama festival, I remember the elation and pandemonium that broke out in the theater. Our students were crying in disbelief, although, when I look back at the weekend, there were many indicators that we would do well. The festival adjudicators were unanimous with their praise, our own Hamden audiences who had seen the production prior to the festival were very moved by it, and the newspaper-which actually reviewed school theater in those days-called it an "outstanding production." But I suppose we never thought this victory would come our way, especially since the eighteen other schools seemed so much more established than we did.

Donna and Colleen both were awarded "Outstanding Actress" awards. And then the adjudicators did something they had never done before. They created a special award for Colleen in honor of her outstanding performance as Annie Sullivan. Within in the next week, another adjudicator sent Donna a gilt-bordered first edition copy of Helen Keller's autobiography because she was so moved by Donna's performance.

The Miracle Worker certainly put us "on the map", so to speak. The only negative side of this is that with such attention comes a scrutinizing public eye. Would we be watched now so that everything we did needed to be as successful as this play? Would we lose our freedom and enjoyment of experimenting with the art form, even falling flat on our faces in a failed attempt at trying something new. We seemed to be at a crossroads.

There are so many wonderful memories connected with this production, but one that stands out in my mind was watching the moment when Helen finally "understands" and tries to say "water" as it pours into her hands from the outdoor pump. Annie is frantically spelling the word into Helen's palm and pumping the water simultaneously. When Helen makes the connection between the word and the object, a moment that will open the door on the rest of her life, she says, "Wa-wa." She says it over and over, slowly at first, and then building in momentum until the two women wildly embrace each other. During one of the performance nights, I watched an elderly gentleman witness this moment. He was sitting in the front row, leaning on his cane, and when Donna struggled to say "wa-wa", a tear rolled down the old man's cheek. I will always remember that moment. It told me all I needed to know for the rest of my career. What a tribute to those actors who moved that gentleman so; who enabled him to visit that invisible, special place in his heart that unifies all of us.

Robin Burkholz and James Abrams played Mrs. and Mr. Keller respectively. I've seen Jim a few times over the years and at a recent reunion we seemed to slip back in time so easily and happily to the days of *The Miracle Worker*. Jim is now a political leader in the State, who, I am glad, but not surprised to say, represents his district with honesty and integrity, the same traits that characterized him during his high school years. Other members of the cast included Beth Hardy, Ann DeMatteo (now a successful newspaper reporter and journalist), Ron Munson, Geoffrey Kanner, and Gail Grate. The blind children who were so innocently moving and convincing in their stage appearances were Maureen Creegan, Sean and Brendan Ledig, Terry Puleo, Michele Plant, Diane Willis, and Diane Tomkinson. Bill Garvey was our lighting designer. Bill played a large technical role in these early days of Hamden Theater, and now is a talented technician in the professional theater, having worked on just about every big-name production. Chuck Aprea also worked on the play as did Anna

Sadiwskyj, Sue Baratz, Steve Villano, Ann Pearlin, Mark Batti, and Heidi Ahlstrom (yet another successful journalist).

It is truly fulfilling to be able to look back upon this time and realize that so many of these students still keep in touch. Hamden Theater meant a lot to them. It might be considered a bit of the "soul" that Helen Keller questioned, for by devoting themselves so earnestly to this important work at such an early age, they made the soul visible, "and the words became the body."

1975 saw two major high school productions. In November I directed *A Midsummer Night's Dream* , a noteworthy venture in that it was our first experience with Shakespeare. Students wanted to perform a Shakespeare for several years, but I didn't feel we were quite ready for it. Now, however, with the training provided by the Studio and the crest of pride and accomplishment felt with the success of *The Miracle Worker*, I felt we were ready to tackle the project. I don't think I realized then how important *Midsummer* would be, and as I look back on it so many years later, I am overcome by the fondest memories of that play.-and also its importance as the first play of my career taking place on the Hamden High School stage, thus beginning my intimate and strong feelings for a place that would soon become "home." Joseph Cirasuolo, the Director of Learning Services in Hamden at the time and a great fan of the theater program, convinced me to direct at Hamden High School and he, Joseph Juliano Jr., the theater teacher/director at Hamden's other junior high school, and I worked on creating a program that would include classes and productions there. It was a time of great excitement and a crucial moment in the development and expansion of the Hamden Theater. More details about *Midsummer* can be found in the Shakespeare chapter of this book.

In March of 1975 the Studio presented James Goldman's *The Lion in Winter*. By this time the Studio's popularity was at an all-time high, especially after having won the Outstanding Production Award at the Connecticut Drama Association Festival the previous year. However, what most impressed me was the students' driving passion for the Theater and their strong desire to learn as much as possible. Amidst all the public accolades was this intense group of students who seemed oblivious to the praise surrounding them. They were totally focused on the work. Carroll P. Cole, whose son, John, was in *Lion* wrote to me afterward, stating, "When I see what kids are capable of doing it almost drives me wild to see how little they usually settle for." I'm glad to say that in all of my years of teaching, my students never "settled" for anything less than they were capable of. In fact, they always wanted *more*. Perhaps much of this is based on the accomplishments of their predecessors which always seemed to loom before them. It's so satisfying to feel that our productions have enjoyed a long afterlife, for they are talked about constantly. Throughout my career students often asked me about previous plays; about the actors and style of production, about the plots and the technical components. Current students have always felt a great respect for those who have gone before them. They always ask me if their productions are "as good" as the previous ones, but never better. I think that says a great deal for them and the modesty that drives them to work hard.

The Lion in Winter needed two strong actors to play Henry II and Eleanor of Aquitaine, his wife. Fortunately I still had Colleen Ledig whose stage presence had matured to an even greater level, an observation that surprised me for I didn't think she could get much stronger than she was as Annie Sullivan. Her delivery of Goldman's lines, many of which are simultaneously humorous and bitter, sensitive and sarcastic, was superb. The review in the newspaper said, "Colleen Ledig is Eleanor of Aquitaine; forceful, intelligent, regal. The part could have been written for her to play; more than that, Eleanor herself could have existed simply so Miss Ledig could one day portray her-and this sweeping statement, you understand, comes from one who considers Eleanor one of the most fascinating and admirable people in history. We have noticed that fidelity of character in other parts Miss Ledig has played and were not surprised to see it now; this is an actress!" This review was prophetic in that Colleen is a now professional actress and a successful one at that.

Charles Shanley played Henry. He was a "new" actor. My choice of Charles for this major and important role was a surprising one to many, but I was impressed with his intelligence, his smooth, resonant voice, and his mature physical appearance. There was also something about Charlie's eyes; they seemed to have a clarity and yet a mystery to them.

The idea of mystery surrounding a character has always intrigued me. Many years ago I attended a family wedding, the reception for which was outdoors. I remember the weather as being nearly perfect, although the previous day's rain made the ground a bit soggy. At one point, a cousin I hadn't seen in years came from the house and stood on the porch which was a good deal higher than the yard. He scanned the crowd below him, he stood alone and a bit imposing. My aunt happened to be standing next to me at the time, when she took my arm and said, "Look at Ricky. He looks like he knows something that we don't." And that one simple statement spoken so matter-of-factly suddenly struck me like a lightning bolt, for this, I realized, was a major component of fine acting. I think this is why I was so taken by Charlie's audition; while he delivered the lines so well, there was a sense of the unknown lurking almost eerily behind those eyes, and I knew at once that this would work so well for the role of Henry.

In a similar manner, another memory that dates back to my childhood is of my father's friend known simply as "Skeetz." I was very young at the time, so I don't remember too much about him other than the fact that he would suddenly appear, seemingly out of nowhere. He was a bachelor, or at least it seemed that way because he was always alone. Slight of build with numerous streaks of gray in his hair, he had a face that was at once friendly, yet interestingly worn-looking. His intense eyes and deep facial lines implied a history I wanted to know about, but which always remained a mystery to me.

Charlie did an excellent job playing opposite such a talented Eleanor. The other members of the ensemble were strong also and included Donna Urquhart of *The Miracle Worker* as the French princess and Henry's young lover, Alais; Ron Munson, who had done extensive work at Michael

Whalen for several years and contributed so much to the success of *The Miracle Worker*, as Richard, the oldest of Eleanor and Henry's three sons; Chester Overlock, another core member of the Whalen group as Geoffrey, the middle son; John Cole as John, the youngest son; and Bill Garvey as Philip, the King of France. As I noted previously, Bill was to become a Broadway technician with an extensive list of credits. However, he wanted to try his hand at acting, and performed Philip very effectively.

We performed *Lion* in the three-quarter round style characteristic of the Studio plays before it. This time, however, Ed Meyer designed the lighting, as he did for the earlier 1975 production of *Midsummer*. Ed owned and operated Stage Lighting Rental Service in New Haven, and was a graduate of the Yale Drama School and Carnegie Mellon University. Ed would play a pivotal role in these early days of Hamden Theater. He taught our students a great deal, and I think he relished working on the plays because it allowed him to to have a great deal of contact with them.

I feel that the Hamden students have been an impressive group throughout the years. So frequently I have heard the highest praise for them from visiting choreographers, designers, community members, even substitute teachers. They have, for thirty years, radiated a kindness and a warmth, and their desire to learn makes our visiting artists feel special and appreciated. I also think that Ed learned a lot himself as we were all experimenting and growing alongside each other. It was an exciting time from that point of view; the burgeoning talents of so many young people, the electricity in the air at rehearsals and classes, the various styles and kinds of productions-from dramas and comedies to musicals and children's plays. All of these things combined to make Hamden a special place.

Ed and his wife, Katherine, lovingly known as "Tink," had lived through the most horrific tragedy some years before. They lost both of their teenage children in a house fire. Ed and Tink were the kindest of people, genuinely caring and loving, and I have always questioned why such a horrifying event would happen to them. Life presents unanswerable questions so often, and we fragile humans learn resiliency the hard way. After this, Ed and Tink abandoned their goals of becoming physicists and returned to their original love-theater. They moved from Long Island, New York, back to New Haven where they began their lighting company, and, in a way, Hamden students became their surrogate children. Ed and Tink spent a great deal of time working on and teaching them. Years later Tink would lose her battle with emphysema. I remember her near the end of her life, carrying around her breathing apparatus, but still attending the plays and occasionally spending time in rehearsals. Tink provided a lesson in courage. Despite the terrible misfortunes that befell her, she managed to go on, mustering her courage and finding her own peace and happiness.

A few years later Ed married Beryl Normand, a lovely woman with a strong moral, political, and civic character. She felt a responsibility to society and was active in many community services. Beryl and her daughters, Samantha and Meg certainly soothed and brought joy back into Ed's life. They are heroes to me, for they have given so much of themselves to Ed, demonstrating the goodness in the human soul.

These were still the days of small budgets and a reliance on support from anyone who would offer it. I am amused when I think back to Colleen Ledig making a costume from some old draperies that my wife, Lynn, took down from our living room windows. I still recall Colleen sitting on a chair and sewing that costume herself, and I can also see the big empty window in my apartment, realizing that I had better do something to replace the drapes.

Despite the modesty of our resources, *The Lion in Winter* was a great success. The newspaper drama critic wrote, "What constantly amazes this critic is the depth of mature understanding and compassion these performers consistently bring to their roles. There is no one in this cast older than seventeen, and yet they look, act, and are the people they so ably portray. They not only understand, but make an audience feel the complex emotions of people whose lives are completely outside their own experience. These performers are without parallel." I agree with this last statement, but I would replace "performers" with "human beings."

The Prime of Miss Jean Brodie was our major production in 1976 and took place on the Whalen stage. Even today it remains a special play for many people in the Hamden community. I'm not sure why this production stands out. Certainly there have been many plays over the years that were truly outstanding; many that won numerous awards at drama festivals and that have been lauded by theater scholars, critics, adjudicators, professional theater people, and even the Governor of the State. But *Brodie* remains, even twenty-five years later, a favorite. Several of the cast and crew members went on to careers in professional theater, but I don't think that played a role in *Brodie*'s popularity. Perhaps it has something to do with the fact that our department was so much smaller in those days, and the success of any production was a tribute to the many people in the community who who helped out. Even the custodian, the late Sal DeFalco, helped by having tickets printed for us on a regular basis. This simple contribution made Sal feel like he was part of the program, and that was very important to him.

When I first met Sal he wasn't used to students being in school after regular hours when he performed most of his cleaning tasks, and he used to get upset over the theater students' use of the lavatories-especially after he had just cleaned them. After a while it became very humorous to see our students try to refrain from using the bathroom because the custodian wanted to keep them clean. But as Sal became more familiar with the students and their long hours of rehearsal, when he started to see how important theater was to them and that they were actually good at it, his attitude changed radically, and he did all he could to help. He even taught carpentry skills to some of the beginning students. And he would always steal a peek at rehearsals. I remember several visits to his home during Christmas time where he and his wife, Marie, would shower candy canes on my infant daughter, Jennifer.

But it seems like everyone wanted to help out in those days. Joseph Cirasuolo, mentioned above, used to come down to the theater after school and watch rehearsals. He grew to adore the students, and upon my recent retirement, wrote me a beautiful letter recalling those days. He said, "This administrator found in the times I spent with you and your students affirmation in my chosen career, acceptance that went beyond the role that I played in the school organization, and renewed faith in the basic goodness of people. My time as an administrator at Whalen would have been much more difficult if I could not have dropped in on rehearsals and if I could not have sat there in the audience filled with all sorts of positive emotions when those kids enhanced and engaged all of us who were there." I also remember riding in Al Baldino's car as we went to pick up props at a student's house. Al, a busy man in his job as Community School Coordinator, would always find time to shuttle us around whenever we needed to beg or borrow from someone. During one of these rides, Al told me that he knew the theater program would grow very large one day, and while that would be a wonderful dream-come-true, I would one day long for these simple days when everyone was close-knit and there was a true sense of community. I remember that conversation so clearly, and I promised myself then that I would always promote a sense of "family" in our department; that I would let everyone know that there are no "stars" among us, and that, in fact, we were all after the same thing-learning, and enjoying ourselves while we did so.

I believe that the sense of family has grown stronger as the years have gone by, and that our students, during all of those years, cared for and about each other very much. They taught each other and helped each other out in bad times. We were always there when there were problems to be solved, and believe me, there were many of them. I'm reminded of the line from Lorraine Hansberry's play, *A Raisin in the Sun* : "When do you think is the time to love somebody the most: when they done good and made things easy for everybody?...It's when he's at his lowest and can't believe in hisself 'cause the world done whipped him so." If anything has made Hamden Theater strong over the years it has been a genuine feeling of family, of friendship, and of love.

These were the days also when many teachers volunteered their help. Diane Elliott would sell tickets, and Risa Nitkin would paint scenery. Risa's father even helped out by having our show posters printed. A woman in the community, Bev Latham, volunteered to make Jean Brodie's costumes, and Bev didn't even have children in the Hamden school system. She just recognized the industriousness of these students and wanted to be involved. Frank Carter, an English teacher, would often help out, as did Martha Zinn and Betsy Olsen, art teachers, and Deborah Finkelstein helped with several plays, her jobs ranging from business manager to choreographer. Teacher Peter Boppert took publicity photographs of the plays, and Susan Boppert was the orchestra director for several musicals. Even spouses of teachers, John Madden and Dottie Russo, were there. All gave freely of themselves because they were caught up in the excitement surrounding Theater, and they wanted to be involved.

This, then, was the background, the environment in which *The Prime of Miss Jean Brodie* was undertaken. I liked the script a great deal and knew that I would need very strong actors. But the presence of high school and junior high school students studying together at Whalen provided a large selection. Gail Grate, now a high school junior, was an ideal Brodie. Gail had achieved a great deal of success in her theater work thus far, having shown a remarkable ability to play both dramatic and comedic roles. She actually stopped our production of *Brigadoon* twice as Meg Brockie-and this as an eighth grader. The audience went wild over her, and everyone predicted a Broadway career for this young junior high school student. How pleased they all must have been to find that Gail has indeed played Broadway many times as well as regional theater all over the country and television and film. I was in the audience for the Broadway opening of Robert Schenkkan's Pulitzer Prize-winning drama, *The Kentucky Cycle*, beaming and weeping with pride watching Gail perform. I have also seen her as Eliza Doolittle and in Suzi-Lori Parks' *The America Play* at the Yale

Repertory Theater and in plays at the Long Wharf Theater. Much of her work is at the Arena Theater in Washington where she played the title role in Shaw's *Saint Joan* and at the Joseph Papp Theater in New York.

Gail's Brodie was marvelous. Although she was only seventeen at the time, her maturity in that role belied her age. Her stately physicality and her rich, resonant voice combined to create an exquisite character. To everyone in that audience, Gail *was* Jean Brodie. She played every nuance of the role to perfection. I remember a young and wide-eyed David Rosenberg Korish (who went on to study with Eugenio Barba and is now an artistic director of a theater in South America), a junior high school student at the time who would go on to play major roles in his Hamden Theater career, coming to *Brodie* every night just to watch Gail. David and Gail met on a New York City street quite by accident some years later as she was exiting an awards ceremony, and they had a wonderful reunion. I love to hear of Hamden students reunited in their adulthood, once again enjoying the bonds that were initially made so many years before.

The cast was comprised of wonderfully talented people. Donna Urquhart, who had made such a splash at the Connecticut Drama Festival with her Helen Keller in *The Miracle Worker*, played Sandy, a school girl who becomes Brodie's "assassin." Donna was one of the best instinctual actors I've ever had. She had an ability to know just how much emotion was needed, and her final confrontation scene with Brodie was absolutely electric. Donna created many fine roles in her theater career, and I think of her as a pillar of the department. Her excellent work in play after play set a standard for actors of future generations.

Helena Whalen played Miss MacKay, Brodie's nemesis and the headmistress of the Marcia Blaine School when Brodie teaches. Helena, as well as Diane Willis as the beautiful Jenny, Sarah Cash as Monica, and Honor Winks as Mary MacGregor created a solid cast of characters playing Brodie's students. Each of them had much experience and used it well. Malcolm Smith played Teddy Lloyd, Brodie's suitor. Malcolm fit the role perfectly with his good looks and velvety voice. He went on to become a talented writer in California. Theron Albis played the bumbling Gordon Lowther with a charm and amiability that made him an audience favorite. Terry is now a playwright in New York. Several years ago I was sitting in a restaurant booth in New Haven, and I heard a familiar voice nearby. As the wooden divisions between the booths were high, I couldn't visually identify the speaker, but I knew that voice. I peeked over to see Terry busily working on the script of what was to become his first New York production. Not long after I saw a full page ad on the back cover of a theater magazine advertising Terry's play, *An American Passenger*. Currently he is also a featured writer for Stage and Screen, a popular performing arts book club. Terry is a talented man, and I'm certainly proud of him-as I am of all of these students.

Tanya Larsen played Sister Helena. I remember her large, expressive eyes so vividly. Tanya had a way of underplaying the role, and by doing so, making it even more dramatic. She was calm and dignified and focused. Doug Affinito played Mr. Perry, the reporter, Debbie Lewisohn added great humor to the play as Miss Campbell, the gym teacher, and Ralph Burr played McCready, the gardener.

The two age groups made casting the older and younger schoolgirls an easy task, with the older ones played by Joyce Barbiero, Linda Cherokyle, Amy Heimerdinger, Donna Palleria, Meg Russett, Kimberly Smith, and Diana Weaver; the younger ones were played by Karen Casper, Maureen Creegan, Joanne Furtak, Nan Hyde, Margaret LeGrand, Ann Macaione, Lisa Mikolinski, Laura Nelson, Lisa Russo, Judy Ursini, and Miriam Schmir. Steve Villano and Cathy Collett were my assistants for the play and helped tremendously with this major production.

It is interesting and a little known fact that various members of the Hamden school administration were initially perturbed by my selection of *Brodie*. I even postponed the play for a year as I tried to dissuade them of their fears that the play was anti-Catholic. It is true that Jean makes some statements critical of the Church, yet she is the very character who is defeated at the end of the play for her views and convictions. I must admit that I thought twice about fighting to do the play, but I had great faith in it and in the students who would bring it to life. I also knew that those who objected to the play had probably never read it as is usually the case with censored material in schools. My method was to postpone directing it for a year while I slowly and methodically presented my point of view. I did not want to be overly aggressive and draw attention as many people do in this kind of situation. I never was a hell-raiser when it came to these things anyway, but always believed in a slower, more rational and objective approach where there is discussion and various viewpoints are respected. I was relieved that my tactics worked, and I feel that the skeptics were happy with the production when they saw it. *Brodie*'s success at the drama festival and the plaudits that it won from the public and the newspapers also helped to convince them of the play's merits. This was the only time in my career that I met with any kind of censorship concerns. So many directors and teachers have fought major battles in this arena through the years, but I have always been grateful to the Hamden School System and the community at large for their unwavering support of our play choices.

Brodie did exceptionally well at the Drama Festival that year. The play won the Outstanding Production in Connecticut, and Gail won the Outstanding Actress Award. Donna was appointed to the All-Connecticut Cast and Honorable Mention Awards were won by Malcom, Terry, and Helena. To this day, many of the veteran members of the Connecticut Drama Association will talk about *Brodie* and the effect it had on them. It certainly was a special production, but, to me, more special than the production were those hard working students. They brought great honor to our school and to our town, and they helped to firmly establish Hamden as a leader in educational theater.

Brodie stirred up a great deal of interest in our Theater program from students outside of the department. The next production, Edmond Rostand's classic ***Cyrano de Bergerac*** had an enormous turnout for auditions. I cast some forty-three people-the largest cast to date. It amazes me, when I look back upon this year, that *Look Homeward, Angel*, the spring production of that same year, also had a large cast, and most of these actors were not even in *Cyrano* . Obviously, then, the popularity of the program was growing quickly.

The classical theater has always drawn me to it. I am fascinated with the timeless themes it presents and its glorious use of language. I was fortunate to have a large group of students who, contrary to those would be skeptical of adolescent tastes, also shared my love for the classics. Josh Stein played Cyrano, and we spent long, long hours together privately as we worked on the character's long speeches, some phrases of which, in Brian Hooker's translation, still make my skin tingle. Cyrano speaks the following lines as he courts Roxanne from the shadows beneath her balcony:

> In my most sweet unreasonable dreams,
> I have not hoped for this! Now let me die,
> Having lived. It is my voice, mine, my own,
> That makes you tremble there in the green gloom
> Above me-for you do tremble, as a blossom
> Among the leaves-You tremble, and I can feel,
> All the way down along these jasmine branches,
> Whether you will or no, the passion of you
> Trembling...

Josh had a facility with the words. I frequently watched him from a very close proximity during rehearsals, and I was so often swept away by his love for the language. Every sound of every word was crystal clear and bathed in a rich subtext.

Josh's father, Howard Stein, was one of those rare people a person is blessed to meet in life. When I first met Howard he was the Associate Dean of the Yale Drama School. Since then he moved to the University of Texas at Austin and then to the Oscar Hammerstein II Center for Theater Studies at Columbia University. We have maintained a close friendship all these years, and I am proud to call him my mentor. Howard primarily focused on playwriting, although he knows nearly every major figure in the professional and university theater world. His humility belies the fact that he is one of the most prestigious figures in the American Theater. I was honored that he wrote the afterword for my book, *Lessons for the Stage, An Approach to Acting* (The Shoe String Press, North Haven, Connecticut, 1994). Whenever I spoke to Howard I was overwhelmed with his knowledge and wisdom. I wanted to write everything down that he ever said to me. Howard brought a friend, Jerry Crawford, to a final rehearsal of *Cyrano*. I remember Jerry, from our one meeting, as an enthusiastic and energetic man. I'd like to think he was enthusiastic about the rehearsal he had just witnessed. Some days later he sent me a gift, a copy of his book, *Acting in Person and In Style* (Wm. C. Brown Co., Publishers, Dubuque Iowa, 1976), and I've used it constantly over the years. It's a wonderful book-perhaps one of the most valuable to me in my thirty years of teaching.

Howard was a colleague of my late acting teacher, Constance Welch. They met at Yale where Miss Welch taught for thirty-eight years. I felt good when I would occasionally see them together because they were the two most important people in the theater world to me. Miss Welch had died on June 20, 1976-just prior to *Cyrano*, and I dedicated the production to her. One of her Yale students, Marcia Kravitt, was to become a very dear friend of mine. Marcia saw the play and read my dedication, after which she wrote me a lovely note saying that Miss Welch would live on in the hearts of the Hamden students. It was a thought that brought me pleasure and peace. I started an award in her name that year to honor graduating seniors who in any way served as instructors to other students. In those days high school students served as teaching assistants in the junior high school drama classes, and they were often the recipients of the award. The practice has continued all these years, except that in the last years of my career, the assistants worked in my Special Education Drama Classes.

I remember a great deal of happiness in those *Cyrano* rehearsals. I must admit that particular group of students had a collective sense of humor that was bold, to say the least. And yet they were disciplined, perhaps from their experience of working on many other plays, and realized the enormous task that lay ahead.

Michele Durocher was an ideal Roxanne, the object of Cyrano's intense passion, and Malcolm Smith used his swaggering, handsome looks as well as a boyish innocence and gullibility as Roxanne's suitor, Christian de Neuvillete. I think Malcolm may have set the Hamden record for the most death scenes in his high school career, most of which he would purposely overact during rehearsals, causing convulsions of laughter among the cast and crew members, and often bringing rehearsals to a complete halt.

When I began work on the play, I realized the need for an impressive first entrance for Cyrano. The script calls for his voice to be heard offstage, and then he suddenly appears, "arising in the centre of the floor, erect upon a chair." I knew I had to think of something equally as sensational. Our theater had a balcony in it and I wondered about having Cyrano slide down a rope that would bring him from the balcony to the stage. When I discussed this with a colleague who taught physics, he informed me that the angle and distance of the approach would create enough speed to plunge poor Cyrano through the back wall of the stage, so I decided to try something different. I ended up having him toss a rope over the balcony, climb down the rope, and enter through the aisle of the theater. This action had a wonderful effect, and was, I suppose, somewhat safer than my original idea.

Bill Burns acted as the fencing master for the play. Bill was a local filmmaker at the time who had earned great praise with his documentary on the high school's ice hockey team under the outstanding coaching of Lou Astorino. Bill was sincerely interested in young people and volunteered his services often during the ensuing years. During one rehearsal, Josh slashed through the air with his sword, extinguishing the flame of a candle. We all gasped in awe at this deed, and the naive director said to Bill and Josh, "Keep it! I love it!" whereupon Bill broke out in hysterical laughter. He later explained that what Josh had accidentally done probably couldn't happen again in a hundred years. We would have to show Cyrano's prowess with a sword in another way. We accomplished that by slicing a candle in half, having Josh whip his sword just above the candle, and then lifting the top half, giving the impression that his sword was so fast that it went right through the thick candle without disturbing it. That effect worked impressively.

I was also lucky to have the first of several excellent student teachers. Valerie Mickish was a Yale student, and an enormous help. She took it upon herself to build Cyrano's famous nose, which was quite a relief for me. But Val did a great deal more than that. She was not only an effective and talented student teacher, but also wonderfully supportive of the students and the production. I often wonder where she is today. She wrote me a thank you note in which she expressed her hope to one day have a theater program like Hamden's. I'm sure she does. She was one of those people who would never compromise, but always sought the best.

When I look at the cast list I am impressed by the talent. Numerous people in smaller roles had held major roles previously, and their sense of professionalism provided a model for the newer members of the ensemble. The cast benefited from the talents of such department stalwarts as Adam Bernstein and Neal Augenstein who played Felix and Oscar respectively in the Whalen production of *The Odd Couple*. Adam also played a variety of roles ranging form the maniacal Harry Roat, Jr. in *Wait Until Dark* to Henry Higgins in *My Fair Lady*. Today Adam is a major film director. Neal played Tevye in *Fiddler on the Roof* at Whalen. There were also such experienced actors as Susan Noffsinger, David Stern, Maureen Creegan, David Hirshfield, Peggy Carnine (who now runs a local theater company in New Haven), Jeff Vanderlip, Nancy Snyder, Mark Caplan, Matt Kaufman, Bob Sader, Carolyn Riordan, Bill Liebeskind, Carlotta Violette, Kate Warfel, Alison McWeeney, Sue MacArthur, Meg Russett, Marsie Karis, Doris Carlson, Louis Weinberg, Scott Shultz, Tom Trower, Robert Hendrix, Heidi Ahlstrom, Lisa Mikolinski, David Ambrose, and Steve Rosenbloom. Also Marcus Stern, Tom Stevens, David Rosenberg, Honor Winks, Debbie

Lewisohn, Margaret Emley, Andrew Hirshfield, Theron Albis, Paul Teitelman, Diane Willis, Edith Meeks, and Steve Simon, all of whom would soon play major roles in upcoming productions if they hadn't already. Four talented musicians from the Music Department appeared in the play: Tricia Macaboy, Jahna Calandrelli, Karen Storz, and Judy Monson.

Tim Veno was a crew member who was invaluable to the department. I had watched Tim grow over the years. He was an extremely talented young man, dedicated to the department, and seemingly able to do just about anything. Through it all he was always polite and respectful. Today Tim has worked his way up through the police force in New Haven. Other crew members included Jonea Gurwitt, Karen Hauser, Kathy Shanley, Amy Heimerdinger, David Ambrose, Sheila Dennis, Pam Milford, John Hanlon, Marci Popkins, Chris Long, Art Tannenbaum, Fred Beimler, Jean McEnerney, Brian Sheehan, Tom Veno, Sandy Norvell, Gail Grate, Patty Pesticci, Debbie Smith, Karen Bormanis, and Glenn Noffsinger.

Glenn, or G.R. as he was always known, grew up in Hamden Theater. He was one of the very young boys in *Fiddler on the Roof*, and remained involved throughout all of this junior high school and high school careers, becoming one of the most proficient technicians we ever had. Although his love was always in the technical area, he was acting in the Whalen production of *Dial 'M' for Murder* when he played a key role in one of Hamden Theater's most memorable stories. In this junior high school production, G.R. played a murderer hired by a man to kill the latter's wife. The plan goes awry, however, and, while trying to defend herself, she manages to stab and kill him with a pair of scissors. One night the scissors was missing, having been mistakenly removed from the set during a scene change by a prop crew member. The wife, played by Miriam Schmir, improvised by pushing the murderer away and running around the set, trying to elude him. I'm sure Miriam was also trying to think of a solution to this problem. G.R. played along and chased her, although I'm not quite sure he knew what the problem was. He knew Miriam for the talented and disciplined actor that she was, and I'm positive that he figured she would not spontaneously change her blocking unless something was desperately wrong. He pursued her with great intensity, jumping over the couch and tossing chairs out of the way. Finally, Miriam picked up the closest object, which happened to be a phone, hit G.R. in the stomach with it, and he "died." Everyone was stunned, not the least of whom was me, although for a different reason. I overheard audience members discussing the death scene as they left the theater that night, and one said, "Oh, that's why they call it *Dial 'M' for Murder*. She kills him with the phone!" I guess the audience believed the business, although I doubt whether you can kill a person by hitting him in the stomach with a phone. But audiences, including myself, have been known to believe anything that happens on stage as long as it is done convincingly. I look back on that episode and congratulate Miriam for her fast thinking and G.R. for adapting so quickly. I also admit that it was one of the most frightening times I've encountered in my directing experience.

Joanne Piscitello was the Assistant to the Director for *Cyrano*, Doug Johnson, a department graduate, came back to design the lighting assisted by Laura Velardi, and Alan Tiernan served as the Master Carpenter. Alan died some years later in a mountain climbing accident. I think of Alan often, as I do of the other Theater students who have died over the years. It is difficult for me to reconcile their loss in light of the exuberance and energy they had, and the laughter that so freely flowed from them. To "wax poetic", I often think of them as the stars in the dark night sky- always there, always bright, always shining down on the rest of us. I miss them a lot.

Also during the 1976-77 season I directed **Look Homeward, Angel** based on Thomas Wolfe's novel and adapted for the stage by Ketti Frings. It was a very different piece of theater than *Cyrano*, and I was glad to be able to offer the students the opportunity to work on two such contrasting plays. Frings won both the Pulitzer Prize and the New York Critics' Award for the play in 1958. The play, as the novel, is basically autobiographical, with the character of Eugene Gant representing the fictional version of

Wolfe himself. The play explores his complex feelings, his intense loneliness and need for love, his interaction with his often-brawling parents, and his attraction to a beautiful woman some six years his senior.

When I first read the play I felt an immediate attraction to it. It touched something inside me as I identified with many of Eugene's feelings. One of the exercises I assign in my acting classes is called a "score," and requires the student to compose a logical and sequential series of actions which illustrate part of a story. One of many play choices I provide is *Angel*, and I ask them to deal with Eugene Gant coming onto his porch late one summer evening and listening to the soft moan of a distant train. This moment is so similar to many of my own childhood memories, although I was much younger than Eugene Gant at the time. I remember so many summer nights when I would lay in bed under the open window, inhaling the scent of lilac and listening to the songs of a thousand crickets. I would lie awake for hours, watching the shadows of the trees on the flagstone patio below my window, and listening to that train whistle off in the distance. How I fantasized about the destinations it would take me and the adventures to which it would lead me.

The story of the play was a serious one, with few moments of comic relief. I knew the potential for the play to become rhythmically slow because of the pervasive dramatic elements, and knew that I would have to find and direct many different rhythms to keep the play flowing and exciting. I decided to use a three-quarter-round style for the play, also a marked difference from *Cyrano* which was played in a proscenium style.

I had, once again, a wonderful and strong cast and crew. My assistants were Lisa Miller and Noelle Larson, both of whom were mature and disciplined. They were also well organized, and maybe the fact that I had known them for many years enabled them to predict many of the things I might say or need. Lisa and her younger sister, Lauren, and also Noelle and her older sister, Tanya, were two sets of siblings that were amazing young people. The four of them had in common a sense of calm and patience, an enthusiasm and kindness that made me think of them as colleagues rather than students. They were largely responsible for the success of any play in which they were involved.

Gail Grate played Eugene's mother, Eliza Gant. Gail was riding on a crest of popularity since her work in *Jean Brodie*, and I think she may have felt the pressure to create an equally compelling character. This is yet one more instance where the goals of educational theater and the pressures of a watchful if not critical public seem to clash. While theater teachers and directors are trying to guide a student through a continuing development and self-exploration, the audience demands a characterization even better than the last one. But Gail had faced this for many years as she had quite a following in Hamden since her days in junior high school.

Opposite her was Julio Caro as W.O. Gant, Eliza's husband. Julio was new to theater, this being his first play. He was a physically impressive young man, one who easily could easily pass for an older character. Complementing his physicality were his dark hair and dark eyes that contributed to an imposing stage presence. Gant was a heavy drinker, and Julio and I worked many, many hours on playing the required drunkenness. We worked to avoid the cliche manifestation, one which all-too-often evokes audience laughter due to the broad overplaying and unrealistic mannerisms. I remember how important it was to Julio that he appear appear believable.

David Rosenberg played Eugene and was able to draw upon his own sensitivity in creating the character. David had truly developed his acting talents since his early days at Whalen, and it seemed as if this part were written for him. David told me how impressed he was with Gail in *Brodie*; in fact, he almost idolized her, and now that he would be acting with her excited him tremendously. Their scenes together were truly superb, and the play provided a foundation for a friendship that grew very strong over the years. David eventually changed his surname back to its original European "Korish", went on to earn his MFA in directing from Carnegie Mellon University and has directed in theaters around the world. He studied with Eugenio Barba, and is currently the artistic director of a theater company in Costa Rica named Teatro Abya Yala where he works with his wife, Roxana Avila.

Malcolm Smith played Eugene's brother, Ben, who dies in the play. If you remember, he died earlier that year in *Cyrano* as well. Malcolm had a strong sense of humor. I will never forget the April Fool's Day rehearsal when the entire cast camped up Malcolm's death scene. To my chagrin at the time, one actor was more outrageous than the next as they donned costumes and played the death scene like it was a poor overblown melodrama. The straw that broke the camel's back was when Malcolm appeared in a skirt! I think I canceled the rehearsal when I realized that there was no way we could make any progress that day. In those days I would *never* have canceled a rehearsal, and looking back on it, I probably over-reacted to their innocent fun. It actually was hilarious, but it interfered with my goal that day, and that's all I seem to have cared about. I'm glad to say I've grown and lightened up a bit since those days also! I never knew for sure, but I always suspected Malcolm of being the culprit behind those *Angel* shenanigans. But no matter what I thought of it at the time, those actors were creative and original.

Another interesting story about Malcolm occurred when he moved to New York City many years later. One day he was sunbathing on the roof of the apartment building where he lived. He struck up a conversation with another young man, and soon they discovered that they were from Connecticut, from Hamden, had both attended Hamden High School, and had both been intensively involved in Theater. The other man was Larry Iannotti who had been in many plays including *Becket* and *The Great White Hope*. Although he had never seen Malcolm act, Larry immediately recognized the name, and the two felt an immediate bond and spent many hours talking. These are kinds of experiences that have always excited me, probably because it means that Hamden Theater was very important in students' lives, and that it remains in their hearts even after high school.

Edith Meeks played Helen Gant Barton. As with all of her work, Edith was outstanding. She always had a fine instinct for finding the soul of her characters, and that was evident even in her junior high school performances. A close friend who is a professional actor remembers seeing Edith as the maid in *Blithe Spirit* and recalled how she stole the attention of the audience through her meticulous work. He was impressed that Edith treated this small part as seriously as if it were the most crucial role in the play. While she was hysterical in the part, she was, most of all, honest and focused. Her work in *Angel* was marked with this same honesty, and she gave a very moving performance. Edith went on to teach acting at the H.B. Studio in New York.

The newspaper review of the play was extremely positive. It stated, "The players are worthy of the play. They have achieved the highest goal of acting-to seem not to be acting at all. There is no sense of being at a play: rather the audience, sitting on its own front porch across the street form the Dixieland Boarding House, is intimately involved in what seems actual events; privileged spectators to the private agonies and triumphs of what seem real people." The reviewer also stated, " (The play) is a highly moving, never maudlin or over-talkative drama with a reality of emotion and a truthfulness of character portrayal no audience will ever forget."

I was very pleased with *Angel*. I remember that we almost weren't able to get the royalties to perform it, however. While we were into the rehearsal period, it was announced that a new musical based on the play would be opening in New York soon, and the rights were taken off the market. I wondered how this was possible, since we had already been granted them. How could royalties be revoked? I asked my good friend, Howard Stein, who had many ties with the professional theater world, to investigate this for me. Howard, as I might have suspected, knew the producers, and we were given permission to perform. As it turned out, the musical adaptation did not succeed in New York and did not have many performances. I might be a novice in certain areas, but I didn't know how a musical version of this play could work anyway. At the time I was so heavily into the novel and the play's text, and it had a certain quality that I found immediately provocative and sensitive, but one which I didn't think would be appealing to large crowds of entertainment-seeking tourists.

Angel was successful for many reasons, not the least of which was the strides the students made in performing a play of a totally different style and ethos from the department's earlier production that season, *Cyrano de Bergerac* . It seemed like this group of students could accomplish just about anything that came its way.

I directed Arthur Miller's *The Crucible* twice in my career, having a great affinity for this play. I also taught it every year in my Literature of the Theater class, and never did that play lose any of its power for me. The play epitomizes courage to me, not only in the text, but also the very act of writing it. I think of the play as a bold accomplishment for Miller, especially when Congressional power in the 1950's could have exacted considerable damage on him. The play is obviously a criticism of McCarthyism, paralleling the Salem witch hunts of 1692 to the communist scare of 1952. Yet the play's timeless quality is testified to by theaters and production companies who view it as a vehicle denouncing bigotry, single-mindedness, violation of due process of law, and defying those forces attempting to suppress individualism and freedom of thought, speech, and action. I recently read that *The Crucible* is performed nearly every day of the year in some area of the world, and that it can suit the interpretation of any company.

My own interpretation of the play was man's search for self-value. I always marvel that even in the darkest of times we human beings can call upon some hidden reserve, a courage we never knew existed, and survive. John Proctor, the protagonist of this play, is faced with death, yet he finds a "shred of goodness" in himself, a reaffirmation of the soul which gives meaning to his life.

The barrenness of winter often makes me think of *The Crucible* . I look into the woods, smell the crispness in the air, see some birds fly from tree to tree, and feel an icy loneliness. I think to myself that this is what Salem must have been like in 1692. For some reason I feel an excitement about this quiet time given entirely to nature's starkness; it seems as if it is the perfect time for something to happen, some adventure or mystery to unfold. So my connection to the play is more than a social, moral, or political one; it is an emotional and dramatic one as well, and I feel that this kind of affinity to a play immediately stimulates creativity.

My research taught me that Salem Village was not the place to live in 1692, and this wasn't entirely because of the witchcraft accusations. Such accusations were not as unusual as we think. Europe saw executions numbering in the hundreds to every one in Salem during this time. The Village was torn by factionalism, by economics, and by social and even geographic turmoil. Certainly, then, the complex web of human passion had been growing for more than a generation prior to the climactic witchcraft trials.

Into this society Miller places John Proctor, the common man, whose chief concern is his family. But to make him vulnerable, the playwright has Proctor commit adultery with Abigail Williams. The latter's love for him, combined with her fear of losing him, causes her to accuse Proctor's wife, Elizabeth of witchcraft. He subsequently exposes Abigail's intentions as he attempts to save his wife. However, in attempting to do so, Proctor is also accused of witchcraft and imprisoned.

While this is a synopsis of the action, *The Crucible* traces the spiritual growth of Proctor and Elizabeth. Elizabeth, a straight-laced, honest Puritan woman, is obsessed with her husband's infidelity. He, in turn, is obsessed with trying to attain her forgiveness. He says, "Learn charity, woman. I have gone tiptoe in this house all seven month since she (Abigail, who used to work for the Proctors) is gone. I have not moved from there to there without I think to please you, and still an everlasting funeral marches round your heart."

From this point in the play onward, Elizabeth undergoes a personal development in human courage. We witness this in her telling the "brave lie" in the court, claiming that John did not commit adultery. This pivotal point of the play is probably the first lie of her life, and she does it to save her husband's reputation. She values her husband's good name over the truth, not realizing the tragic effects of the lie. In Act IV her spiritual growth continues as she confesses her own inadequacies: "I have sins of my own to count. It needs a cold wife to prompt lechery." Her ultimate sacrifice, of course, is her decision not to plead with John to save his life. When he decides that he must sacrifice himself for the sake of his name, she realizes that she cannot take his newly discovered soul from him. She speaks the final words of the play, saying, "He have his goodness now. God forbid I take it from him."

Proctor attempts to find his own dignity in the play. At first he defies the witchcraft proceedings and refuses to conform. Later when he is jailed he is asked to sign a confession that he is the "devil's man." He does this, but refuses to hand it to Deputy Governor Danforth, the refusal representing one more step in Proctor's quest. He has signed it because he feels his infidelity has already robbed him of what honesty he had, and it would be more dishonest to die a martyr like the good Rebecca Nurse. However, when he is told that he will hang if he does not relinquish the signed confession, he tears the paper and proclaims his reason:

> Because it is my name! Because I cannot have another
> in my life! Because I lie and sign myself to lies! Because
> I am not worth the dust on the feet of them that hang!
> How may I live without my name?

Proctor's concern for his name, or his dignity, is more profound than the "reputation" aspect of a name found earlier in the play. In the act of tearing his confession Proctor finally realizes his goal: "For now I do see some shred of goodness in John Proctor. Not enough to weave a banner with, but white enough to keep it from such dogs."

I realize I have written a great deal on these pages about this play, but if there is any piece of dramatic literature that I feel most closely akin to, it is this one. I continue to be tremendously moved when I read or hear the lines from it. I continually find instances of similar situations in newspapers and magazines and in the everyday lives of each of us. Acts of courage, large and small, are often lonely and easily intimidated-especially in the face of overwhelming opposition. But believing in one's self is much too important to deny the responsibility we owe to our society, to our world, and to ourselves. The message of the play is so vibrant, so important, and I believe so strongly in it that our work on the play became a kind of mission.

In 1978, I decided to use an arena style for the production, with the audience sitting on all four sides of the actors. I wanted an intimacy between the actors and the audience so that the latter could become a part of the play. We performed it on the stage at Whalen, a rather large space which afforded enough seating, and also a place in which most of us felt extremely comfortable. I knew the nearness of the audience would mean that each and every actor in this large cast had to be focused and committed. I was thrilled, then, to receive a letter from the Associate Dean of the Yale Drama School who had seen the production, stating, "The single most impressive feature of the production was the group playing. I didn't see one poor performance, one performance that called attention to itself because of its weakness."

Joshua Stein played Proctor, Joanne Piscitello played Elizabeth, Michele Durocher played Abigail, and Marcus Stern played Deputy Governor Danforth. Marc went on to become a nationally-known, professional director and professor at Harvard.

An interesting story concerning Mark occurred about two years ago. There was a rather large article about him and containing his picture published in American Theater Magazine. I clipped the article out and posted it on the bulletin board backstage at school, as this was someone and something we Hamden Theater people could all be proud of. I then received a visit from Leah Altman, a graduate of ours who was attending Harvard. She asked me why I had a photo and article about Professor Stern on the bulletin board. When I told her that Marc was from Hamden, Leah was stunned. She sat in his class at Harvard totally unaware that both of them were products of the same high school theater program. What's more, Leah confided in me that Marc was very serious and seemed unapproachable at times. I laughed and told her that Marc was always receptive and fun to work with and that she needed to introduce herself to him as his "younger sister" from Hamden. When she requested an appointment with him and told him that she too came from Hamden, she said that his eyes widened with surprise and the recognition of sudden kinship. He stood up, came to her, and embraced her. Since then, Marc has acted as her advisor on a production of *Angels in America* that she directed at Harvard. When I went to see the play, I was standing in the crowded lobby, and I suddenly felt pressure on my shoulder. Someone's head was there! And it was Marc, the dignified Professor and famous director. We looked into each other's eyes and rediscovered each other after so many years. What a wonderful night that was-to enjoy the unique talents of Leah's directing and to reconnect with Marc. Naturally, my major source of fulfillment was seeing the two of them working together.

Josh was an incredible Proctor. There are some Hamden performances that stand out in my mind and heart, and his was certainly one of them. When he spoke Miller's magic words, it brought thrills to the audience, as did his Cyrano the previous year. I always felt close to Josh. He was not only a fine actor, but a good friend. That may sound strange as far as a teacher-student relationship is concerned, but I feel it is an accurate description. We had many long talks over the years. There was a special bond between us.

Joanne also was radiant. One judge at the Drama Festival noted her "quiet dignity." She was the perfect Elizabeth Proctor. I had a photo of her in the role and gave it to her mother for a gift, and now, some, twenty-two years later, it is still hanging on the wall of her mother's apartment. Joanne was, even at an early age, a person of calm and common sense. I admired her for this and hoped that my own daughter would one day have the qualities that made Joanne such an exceptional person.

Josh and Marc both were awarded Outstanding Actor awards at the Drama Festival that year, and Joanne was appointed to the All-Connecticut Cast. Michele Durocher's Abigail won her an Honorable

Mention in Acting award. She was excellent as the evil character, creating a person who was manipulative and conniving. The subtlety of her sly and victorious smiles were a trademark of this role.

The entire ensemble was strong in this play. Ralph Burr, usually a quiet young man, played the paranoid Reverend Parris with the required fanaticism and ardor; David Rosenberg played Reverend John Hale, and Kyle Elise Holmes played the Barbados slave, Tituba. Carolyn Riordan, Donna Palleria, and Maureen Creegan played the young girls afflicted with witchcraft with a believable hysteria. Their "crying out" scene was frenzied and forceful and really affected the audience. Honor Leigh Winks was excellent as the beleaguered Mary Warren, a pivotal role in the play, and Debora Lewisohn and Larry Zeisner played the Putnams effectively as well. Adam Bernstein who had been such a central member of theater during his Whalen days played the eccentric Giles Cory. Rebecca Nurse is another important role and a truly fine actress is needed in this part. I was lucky to have the talented Edith Meeks play Rebecca, adding it to an already impressive list of well-defined characterizations. The cast was rounded out with the strong performances of Steven Simon (who wrote a biographical play which I enjoyed very much after he graduated from Syracuse University. I remember seeing it performed in a very small off-off Broadway house.), Tom Stevens, Ellen Krinick, and Martin Carl. Marty Carl now runs a successful theater company in New Haven. Heidi Ahlstrom, a wonderful and well-known reporter these days, and Noelle Larson served as my assistants for the play, and added their much-needed organizational skills.

The Crucible won considerable acclaim in our town. It was the third play from Hamden to win the Outstanding High School Play Award at the annual Connecticut Drama Association Festival. A judge called it, "the finest high school play I have ever seen." It then represented Connecticut at the New England Drama Festival in Providence, Rhode Island. The New England Theatre Conference bestowed its prestigious Moss Hart Memorial Award on it as the outstanding play in New England-high school, college, university, community, professional-extolling human dignity. Our students were tremendously proud of this achievement.

There were many things about this production that moved me. Besides the professionalism demonstrated by the entire company, there was a feeling of friendship that made our time together so wonderful and comforting. The company also presented me with the most heartfelt gift on the closing night of the play. They had been meeting at the home of one of the cast members each evening after rehearsal to work on a quilt, and each actor and crew member designed and made individual patches that were sewn into it. It was a touching gift and one that meant a lot to me. I still have it, and have shown it to numerous students since then. I have used it as a unique learning tool when I teach the play, but, more importantly, it is a quilt that will always remind me of those very special human beings.

I enjoy the plays of Eugene O'Neill immensely. They seem to have some kind of mystical hold on me and have had that effect since my college days. I'm attracted to the passion in them, the rawness in the work that is both honest and bold. I am also entranced by the way his poetic use of language makes the highly dramatic and sometimes abhorrent elements of plot that much more dynamic. In my earlier days I identified with much of what he wrote. There is a haunting loneliness in much of his work as well as a longing quality, and certainly the experimental nature of his plays is to be esteemed.

There was something rakish about O'Neill in his youth; the unsavory characters with whom he often associated, his drinking binges, and his voyages on those old frigates to South America found their way into much of his writing. On a personal level, I must admit a certain attraction to that part of his life, although I can't identify with it. Perhaps it is the adventure he sought and found and the yearning I have always had to seek my own. I also admire his ability to change the course of his life, from that of a man in the lowest pits of despair to one who became one of the greatest playwrights in the world. The fact that he revolutionized the American Theater brings him great distinction, and his effect on it will forever be felt.

I had the good fortune of meeting Jason Robards several years ago at a drama festival held at Choate Rosemary Hall School in Wallingford, Connecticut. Robards' career was launched when he played Hickey in O'Neill's *The Iceman Cometh*. His daughter was a student at Choate when we met, and he graciously consented to give the welcoming address to theater students from throughout New England. As I was serving at President of the Connecticut Drama Association, I had the opportunity of not only meeting him, but spending the entire evening together talking about the Theater and even being interviewed on a radio show that night. He and I struck up a genuine friendship and we met several times during the following years. I remember the look on my daughter, Jennifer's, face when he surprised her on her sixteenth birthday, greeting her warmly in his dressing room after a performance of *Ah, Wilderness!* at the Yale Repertory Theater. And we also met for coffee after a workshop performance of a new play at the Long Wharf Theatre in which he was appearing. The playwright was hospitalized and dying, and revisions to the script could not be made. I remember we discussed acting choices for various areas of the text. But even on this occasion, as on every other, O'Neill crept up into the conversation like some ghost who made his presence felt at every turn. Robards is a devoted O'Neill actor, and he told me of a large contingent of such actors who would gladly perform in O'Neill plays anywhere and any time just because of the rarity and the richness of the material. Robards' close friend, the late Colleen Dewhurst, said that one does not "wade into" an O'Neill play, but must plunge into it headfirst and trust the material to keep the actor afloat. Given the nature of the plays, I find this metaphor most accurate.

My long-time and close friend, Ann Gabriel, smiles impishly when I go into one of my vehement conversations about O'Neill , for, although she respects the playwright and my feelings for his work, she does not share them. She laughingly says that a person either loves O'Neill or hates him. I can see her point of view. I wouldn't categorize O'Neill's plays as entertaining for the masses, but they are masterpieces that compel us to think about the human condition.

I felt it was important to expose students to O'Neill, and selected one of my favorite plays, *Desire Under the Elms*, for production in 1979. I began my research at the Yale Drama School Library. I love that old building. It also brings me closer to my late acting teacher, Constance Welch, who taught there, having been hired by the famous George Pierce Baker and brought to New Haven from the Midwest. The Yale Drama School is steeped in tradition; you can almost feel it when entering the building on York Street with its gothic architecture, narrow winding stairways, and rooms upon rooms of books. There is a palpable energy here, and you can't help but feel that this is a place that nurtured the growth of the American Theater. O'Neill attended Yale for a while as he studied with Baker, and when I first entered the library I came face to face with a bust of the great playwright. I recall that the intense eyes seemed to animate that bust.

I discovered that O'Neill's manuscripts were left by his widow, Carlotta Monterey O'Neill, to Yale, and I headed off to the Beineke Rare Book Library where they were stored. Yale was on vacation, and I was one of very few patrons in the library. I asked the librarian if I might be able to see the manuscript of *Desire*, and she went off to locate it. When I was alone I wondered what I might encounter. The librarian never said the manuscript was locked away and unavailable, nor did she say it could only be viewed in the presence of a library employee due to its value. As a matter of fact, she said nothing at all. She gave me a polite smile, a nod of her head, and with that she disappeared. I was caught up in some kind of nervous excitement and anticipation that actually made me shake.

Soon the librarian appeared with a large manuscript in her hand. She explained that she couldn't find *Desire*, but that she would let me see *Mourning Becomes Electra*. I wasn't disappointed at all, for seeing and handling any original O'Neill manuscript would have been equally as thrilling. After that visit I wondered about the whereabouts of *Desire*. I thought all of the playwright's work was there. That missing manuscript still piques my curiosity. There were very few people around, and the librarian trusted me to peruse *Mourning* on my own. I couldn't believe I had the original manuscript in my hand. I handled each page so carefully, spending hours examining O'Neill's tiny notes in the margins, the stains on the pages, and almost feeling that I was in the presence of the playwright himself. I think I "absorbed" Eugene O'Neill that day; that he became some visceral part of me. My feelings deepened, my instincts in directing the play felt more secure and certain than ever, and I felt an overpowering commitment to honor the man through the best possible production of his work.

Desire Under the Elms is influenced by the Greek plays, *Medea* and *Hippolytus*, the former play dealing with a mother murdering her young sons for revenge, while the latter concerning itself with a woman falling in love with her stepson. O'Neill, greatly influenced by the theater of the ancient Greeks, felt that these themes could be translated to the American stage undiluted. He used them, however, as a springboard from which he expounded his own philosophies. This play explodes with violence, passion, greed, revenge, pride, and the most horrible of crimes-infanticide, incest, attempted patricide, and adultery. I think back to Ann Gabriel's smile when she said that O'Neill wasn't for everybody. Briefly, the story is that of Ephraim Cabot, a seventy-five year old farmer who has lived a hard life and relishes the values it has taught him. He brings home his third wife, Abbie Putnam, who is much younger than he, and having lived a hard life of her own, she is obviously only interested in owning the Cabot farm herself. She meets Eben, Ephraim's young and handsome son, and after an initial confrontation, they fall in love and have a child. Ephraim thinks the child is his, and when he tells Eben things that would make the latter doubt Abbie's love, Eben retaliates by saying that he hates her and wishes that their son were never born. She, desperate to show her love, kills the baby. She is arrested for the deed, but Eben, in a final demonstration of his love for Abbie, admits to his part in the baby's death, and the two of them go off to face their punishment together. Of course the play has many other twists of the plot that intrigue and totally captivate the spectator. Even reading this play with my Literature of the Theater class every year produced amazing emotional responses. It is a play with events unfolding almost uncontrollably and each more dramatic than the one before.

The cast for *Desire* was very strong, particularly the the actors who played Ephraim, Abbie, and Eben. Paul Teitelman, Margaret Emley, and David Rosenberg faced the challenges presented by this material with enthusiasm. I often think about the intensity of the scenes and marvel at their ability to plunge into it. I was careful to exercise the cast physically and vocally, as I do for every production, for a long period of time before each rehearsal. I wanted the actors to approach the work refreshed and relaxed. They grew into the roles magnificently, producing some of the best acting I have ever witnessed. The play was very physical, and we worked hard to make the stage violence totally believable, yet always safe. All three actors had a good deal of experience and knew the procedure of rehearsal well, and this helped as we slowly molded the play into its final form. David's Eben was intense, and I remember his eyes often reminded me of that bust of O'Neill. There was a passion in them that David used so well to create this character. He had previously played Eugene in *Look Homeward, Angel*, Reverend Hale in *The Crucible*, and other difficult roles that helped him create a foundation for Eben. And while he could be angry and violent, David had the capacity to play tenderness as well. His scene in the parlor with Abbie was soft and gentle, and the way he looked down into the baby's cradle at the end of Act I was filled with love and a quiet awe.

Paul, currently a theater teacher in a New Hampshire high school, showed tremendous progress from his early days at Michael Whalen. His Ephraim was cold and often heartless, yet he managed to show the vulnerability under this harsh exterior. This layering of characterization separated Paul from many other actors. It would have been so easy to create a flat and linear character in this instance. People commented that they never thought they could feel sorry for Ephraim until Abbie's wild denunciation,

"He wa'n't yewr son! Think I'd have a son by yew? I'd die fust! I hate the sight o' ye an' allus did! It's yew I should've murdered if I'd had good sense! I hate ye! I love Even. I did from the fust. An' he was Eben's son-mine an' Eben's-not your'n." Paul chose to speak Ephraim's response softly and sensitively, "He's dead....I felt his heart...He'd ought t' been my son, Abbie. Ye'd ought t' loved me." His delivery was so plaintive, yet so simple that it only magnified the tragedy. And Margaret, upon hearing this uncharacteristic and sensitive reading of the line, was drawn even further into the tragic desperation of her character and the repulsiveness of her deed.

Margaret's Abbie was an inspiring performance. It seemed as if she knew just how much emotion to use as the play gradually built in intensity towards its tumultuous climax. I can see her now in the scene after she has murdered her baby. She sits in a rocking chair in the kitchen, clutching a pillow to her breast. Her entire face and body seemed to be in shock, and in the ensuing moments she lashes out at Ephraim with a mixture of uncontrolled hatred and remorse. It was a terrifying moment, as only O'Neill can write, but one that takes a consummate actress to execute, and Margaret was stunning. Without a doubt, Margaret, David, and Paul were tremendous in these roles. I spoke to them after the production was finished and asked them to comment on the feelings that Jason Robards and Colleen Dewherst shared about playing O'Neill-that he provided material unlike other playwrights, and that acting his work required nothing less than a full emotional and physical involvement. It is also indescribably liberating for an actor, that being one reason why actors will avail themselves of the opportunity of being in his plays whenever possible. The three high school actors, with relatively few major dramatic experiences in their personal lives with which to compare their recent *Desire* involvement, agreed that this play changed them in many ways, and that it was at once totally draining of their emotions and their energies, and yet exhilarating at the same time.

Other members of the cast included Thomas Stevens and Andrew Hirshfield as Cabot's other sons, Simeon and Peter respectively. Tom was an enthusiastic member of the department with a great sense of humor and very popular. I remember coaching him for his audition for Boston University and how he captivated me with his somewhat radical selection and his animated work. Andrew would go on to play the most compelling Iago in our future production of *Othello*, and I can't help but feel that much of his ability to do so took root in this production of *Desire*. Miriam Schmir played a neighboring farmer, and from this small role she would ultimately go on to play Desdemona with grace and beauty in *Othello*. Jeanne O'Day and Tom Edwards were also in the cast, both of whom would give stellar performances in *The Great White Hope* in 1981. Other ensemble members were strong actors and bolstered the strength and believability of the play through their individual performances: Michael Prezioso, Bill Stacey, Andrew Fraher, Tom Burr, David Simon, Gretchen Sherman, and Norah Martin.

Edwin Meyer designed the set for the play. Ed, you will remember, owned Stage Lighting Rental Service in New Haven and was fairly involved with Hamden Theater in its early days. Ed was a Yale Drama School graduate and did astounding work in both lighting and set design. His set was the largest ever to be built on the Hamden stage, and I would venture to say on any high school stage in the country. The peak of the Cabot farmhouse roof just barely touched the highest point of the proscenium, and four rooms occupied two raked levels below it. The kitchen and parlor were on the first floor and two bedrooms were on the second. A thrust built out from the stage served as the yard. It was a magnificent set for which student G.R. Noffsinger served as Master Carpenter. I wanted the house to look like an exposed heart with the passion, like blood, flowing freely from room to room. What was interesting about the design was the opportunity it afforded the audience to view characters who might not be in the current action, but who were in another part of the the house. In other plays these characters would be offstage.

The construction was non-stop, and we recycled every piece of lumber we could find anywhere. I remember the joy we all felt as we finally connected the roof, bringing closure to one major phase of the construction process. Christopher Long was the lighting designer who had the awesome task of making that huge set come to life with his selection of colors and intensities. But this is one of educational theater's strongest suits: the opportunity it affords young people to learn in a hands-on way. Chris understood the responsibility I gave him, and also the honor of lighting a set that took a great deal of time and energy to build.

I also remember directing the play from many areas of the set depending upon where the action was taking place. It took me a while to feel totally comfortable directing from the second floor bedrooms as the floor was raked and I had to overcome the idea that I would fall off at any minute. At one point, Paul Teitelman told me that he was hesitant to lie down on the bed on the second level, since that authentic antique bed had tiny wheels. I told him I could appreciate the concern, and we quickly remedied the situation.

The production was a great success. It overwhelmed our home audiences as well as the audience at the Drama Festival. The play won Hamden its second consecutive and fourth Outstanding Production in Connecticut Award as well as Outstanding Acting awards for David and Margaret. Paul won an All-Connecticut Cast Award, and the judges heaped praise on the production as a whole, noting its extreme difficulty, and calling it a "an excellent production filled with beautiful vocal variety." It was also termed, "fascinating, engaging, and superior."

We were invited to represent the State at the New England Drama Festival that year, but couldn't raise the $2,500 we needed to go. None of us, especially me, was terribly disappointed. The play had been draining, we had performed it well, and it had won great notoriety. However, a newspaper reporter chose to highlight the fact that three Board of Education members were fully funded to travel to a convention at the same time as the Drama Festival. It stirred a bit of controversy for a while, pitting a student learning experience against what the reporter made to sound like a pleasure trip for three adults. I quickly tried to quell the problem by writing a letter to the Board stating that I felt the article was unfair and inappropriate. They were satisfied and happy that I addressed the issue immediately.

Many years later David Rosenberg and I had lunch downtown New Haven. We talked about the *Desire* experience and how much it had meant to him. We also talked about the then recent murder of two children by a mother whose new boyfriend did not want to be a father. We were amazed at the strong parallel between O'Neill's fictional situation and the real life situation of that time. We also discussed O.J. Simpson's alleged murder of his wife, and noted the similarities between that situation and *Othello*. We marveled once again at the Theater's reflection of life, even in these seemingly unrealistic and highly dramatic situations.

There was no doubt that *Desire Under the Elms* continued the Hamden Theater tradition of selecting quality plays and performing them well. It also bought more and more attention to our program which was now gaining attention far outside the State of Connecticut.

In May of that same year, we presented *Forty Carats*, a delightful comedy by Jay Allen. It provided some welcome comic relief from the angst-ridden *Desire* and also balanced the season nicely. Interestingly, it was this play for which Constance Welch was asked her opinion about casting many years before. It was also this play that I saw with my wife, Lynn, on our honeymoon in 1969. I really enjoyed the play, and the fact that Julie Harris, one of my favorite actors, played the lead only increased that enjoyment. I remember our production with great fondness. There was an ambiance of fun and lightheartedness that surrounded it. The play's fast-paced plot and engaging characters, plus a cast that matched the eccentricity of those characters with their own unrestrained zaniness, filled our rehearsals with a great deal of laughter and creative energy.

The plot involves a forty-year old woman, Ann Stanley, who falls in love with a much younger man, Peter Latham, and the complications this situation causes. Miriam Schmir played Ann and Ken Festa played Peter. The characters include Ann's mother, Maude, who acts like a teenager,

Ann's daughter, Trina, who is embarrassed by the entire situation, and Ann's ex-husband, Billy, who always seems to appear unexpectedly.

This was a good role for Miriam who I had worked with several times since her junior high school years. She was a very bright young woman and was perfect for a role where the character's heart is in constant battle with her sense of reason. Ken had a sexy charm and boyishness which brought Peter alive. The two of them worked extremely well together.

Andrea Ahrens played Maud, and she was hysterical. Andrea had a unique, resonant, and throaty voice that I found very appealing, and she used it well for the characterization. Her natural sense of timing and comedy was a highlight of the production, and the audience loved her. Ann Macaione, who had played Fanny Brice so well in the Whalen production of *Funny Girl*, was the idea Trina. Ann also had a natural instinct for comedy, yet her acting was also marked by an honesty and freshness that was very endearing.

Tom Stevens played Billy Boylan, Ann's ex-husband, as only Tom could. He could be fast-talking, sarcastic, persuasive, and yet under all of this, Tom's own sensitivity gave the character truthfulness and sincerity. When he, near the end of the play, convinces Ann to follow her dream, it was a touching moment. The play couldn't have worked if Tom had not played that moment so well.

Brian Drutman played the wealthy Texas suitor, Eddy Edwards, complete with a wide-brimmed cowboy hat, a white fringed jacket, and a thick Texan dialect. Lisa Blaich, Tom Edwards, Bill Stacey, Julianne Kasten, and Deborah Donovan completed the cast and created an excellent ensemble. They were so much fun to work with. There was a youthful vigor about them that was totally refreshing. They were relaxed, flexible, willing to experiment, yet well-disciplined and totally devoted.

I was once again fortunate to have two excellent assistants, Kim Hajus and Sarah Long. I had worked with both of them before, a situation which really helps in directing a play. I found that I could trust them to make decisions and to take the initiative to organize many areas of the production. Kim went on to marry another Hamden Theater student, Paul Ryder. Sarah had performed in children's plays and had also been my teaching assistant at Whalen. She created a wonderful rapport with the younger students. Many years later I saw Sarah in two professional productions, one at the Yale Repertory Theater and one at the Long Wharf Theater, and in both of them I was struck by her superb acting. It was wonderful to talk to her after those performances and reminisce about high school days. She is an excellent actor and an exceptional human being.

I've always been attracted to plays taking place in New York City. I'm not sure why this is. Perhaps it has something to do with growing up so close to the city and feeling its distinctive rhythm; the lure of the hustle-bustle, the bright lights, the crowds rapidly moving in all directions, the street venders, the museums, the restaurants, and theaters. There was always the possibility of the unexpected happening in New York. I visited the city frequently as I grew up, either with my mother or my aunt or my cousin, and I never tired of it. It was, and still is, a thrilling experience for me. This was another attractive element about *Forty Carats* . It's setting in Manhattan seemed to allow for that unexpected to occur, and the play's seemingly unbelievable premise could readily happen. It also sent a message to the students; that anything is possible; that dreams can come true, but often it takes courage and a strong sense of independence to make them a reality.

1980—81 season was a bold and extremely successful season. Like the previous years, I directed two very different kinds of plays, continuing to expose students to a broad spectrum of plays and various styles of producing them. November saw the production of George Bernard Shaw's *The Devil's Disciple* , and in February I directed Howard Sackler's *The Great White Hope*. Once again there was a large talent pool at Hamden High School, and both of these plays offered large casts and much technical opportunity. The plays were not the only things providing experience and education, however. The training program that was begun years before was truly paying off, as students had a vast array of courses from which to choose. At one time there were twelve theater courses at Hamden High School. Later we trimmed that number down to ten as we constantly worked on the content and structure of the program. Independent Study courses and Interdisciplinary courses would further enhance the educational theater opportunities, and the productions reflected the amazing classroom accomplishments of our students by becoming more complex and sophisticated.

The Devil's Disciple was such fun. I had seen the play performed at the American Shakespeare Festival Theater in Stratford, Connecticut some years before and was quite taken by the plot as well as a period of American history that had always intrigued me-the American Revolution. As a child, my father would often take my younger brother and me to the ferry crossing in Yonkers, New York. We would travel to New Jersey where we would tour the headquarters of the British General, Corwallis. My father took us somewhere every Saturday in those days, to places like the Bronx Zoo, the Botanical Gardens, City Island, Orchard Beach, Rye Beach, carnivals, and boat rides on Long Island Sound. Most of our destinations were repeat visits, and most of them were free or cost very little. As we looked back upon those days recently, my brother, Joe, praised our parents, saying that they never let us know how poor we were. Our family had very little money, yet we children always felt no worse off than anyone else in the neighborhood. Our parents filled our weekends with visits to so many places, and we never realized that the cost of gas for the car was probably the most expensive item of the day.

It's interesting that I still, so many years later, have "sense memory" sensations about the Corwallis home. I remember the low ceilings, the musty smell of the interior, and the many personal belongings on display throughout the house. My father would tell us stories about the Revolutionary War and the heroism of the American colonists as we strolled along the water waiting for the ferry to take us to back to Yonkers.

Perhaps it was my fascination with the Revolutionary War that spurred me to select Shaw's play, or perhaps it was partly a longing for those childhood days and the security of holding my dad's strong hands; remembering the white shirt with the rolled cuffs he would wear whenever we traveled, and hearing the love in his voice as he told us story after story. Whatever the stimuli might have been, however, I attacked the play with great zeal, as did the large number of students who brought it to life.

The story of the play takes place in 1777 New England and involves Dick Dudgeon, a Puritan, who has lived all of his life in a narrow-minded Puritan society. This causes him to believe that those who follow God's teachings are, in fact, uncharitable and cause misery for each other. He wants happiness in his life, and concludes that the only way to achieve it is to consider himself a disciple of the Devil. Soon he is arrested by the British, being mistaken for the local Puritan minister, Reverend Anthony Anderson. Rather than refute the charge and put Anderson's life in danger, he continues to pose as the minister, which Anderson's wife mistakes as a sign of love for her. At the end of the play, Dudgeon is saved from hanging at the gallows by Anderson who has become a revolutionary leader.

My research on the play found some critics accusing it of being melodramatic, but I never felt that way about it at all. In fact, I found Shaw's use of language, ironic twists of plot, and colorful characterizations to be quite fresh and contemporary. Ken Festa played Dick Dudgeon, having progressed tremendously from the already fine acting he displayed in the previous season's *Forty Carats*. Ken could play a swaggering, "devilish" character well, and he also had a disarming, captivating personality on the stage. Larry Iannotti played Anthony Anderson, and with his resonant voice and good looks, appeared very much the part of the mature reverend with a defiant hidden self. Both Ken and Larry would appear in *The Great White Hope* later in the year and win major acting awards for their work. It was easy to see their obvious talent in this play as well. Anderson's wife, Judith, was played by Lisa Prezioso, who managed to evoke Judith's physical beauty as well as her childlike innocence so well.

During one of the performances, the long zipper in the back of Lisa's dress broke while she was onstage, and she calmly adjusted her blocking so that her back was never to the audience. Offstage the problem was taken care of quickly, and I'm sure Lisa was nervous about the situation, but the audience and I never knew what had happened. I often wonder about the things I'm not aware of during the performance of any play I direct. Once the production opens, I sit in the house each night, and there is an understanding that any problems must be solved by the company. Problem-solving is an important component of educational theater, although I'll admit it has raised my blood pressure on many an occasion. I also seem to have an ability to forget most problems once they're solved. So often students and members of the theater staff will recall some incident that occurred a while ago regarding one of those numerous problems indigenous to live performance, but I simply cannot remember most of them at all. Maybe it's a protective device my mind created long ago so that I would continue in this profession for a while. At any rate, Lisa's experience and ability to think quickly saved the day. But she was always like that in life. Her bubbly personality and frequent laugh belied the serious, astute, and composed person she was underneath.

Karl Fusaris played Christopher Dudgeon, a slow-witted youth who provided a great deal of humor. At one point he had to come nose-to-nose with Christopher Erikson, the actor playing British Major Swindon, and Chris had a difficult time staying in character. Karl was not only funny, but totally convincing. He added greatly to the rich fabric of characterizations Shaw offers in this play. Karl went on to study at Columbia where he befriended my good friend and mentor, Howard Stein, Dean of the Hammerstein Center for Theater Studies.

The cast was filled with wonderful actors, many of whom would play major roles in our upcoming production of *The Great White Hope*. Tom Edwards played British General Burgoyne in *Disciple* and would go one to be one of Hamden's, the State's, and New England's most celebrated actors this year for his portrayal of Jack Jefferson in *Hope*. And the young Martin Harries who played the British Sergeant would have several great performances ahead of him such as Thomas Becket and Richard III. Other distinct real-life personalities created unique characters in *Disciple*. This may have been the perfect time to do this play, for it is not common to find the vast array of talent provided by people like Jeanne Schreiber, Jennifer Peterson, Larry Fitzgerald, Sarah Sherman, Bill Gunn, David Simon, Carla Franzoni, David Pickman, Justin Garvey, James Hirshfield, Jessie Riley, James McCusker, Maura DeMaio, Debbie Konick, Meg Rausch, Jill Jason, Karen Rhodes, Julie Trachten, Amy Kaufman, Donna Norman, Sheri McDonough, and Tom Ruzsa. Many of these actors had played major roles in their junior high school years and were currently enrolled in acting classes, all of which helped them create totally believable work without regard to the size of the part.

Student Bill Stacey designed the set for *Disciple*, and solved the problem of the various locations required by using castered platforms which pivoted and maneuvered to provide different settings. I think that the very size and complexity of the set for *Desire Under the Elms* the previous year inspired Bill to be bold and creative in his design, and to understand that anything was possible. I was very impressed with Bill's work; his ability to create detailed settings despite the many changes needed, and also the way he captured the time period. There was a rough-hewn quality to some of the settings, and a more polished look to others. He also designed two enormous stone fireplaces which became a focal points of the Dudgeon and Anderson homes. As I now look back over the years, I can recall so many designs using stones of different kinds-from elaborate to simple, from field stone to cut stone- and the many crews of students who would labor for days creating them, carving them so that each stone had its distinct character.

I think that a lot of my own patriotic feelings emerged as I directed *The Devil's Disciple*. As a history student, I remember being enthralled by the bravery of the colonists as they battled the British, and now those feelings were surfacing again. Richard Dudgeon seemed to epitomize that rebellious, defiant attitude that I like to think was characteristic of our ancestors. I always enjoyed his response to Major Swindon's accusation of being a rebel when he responds, "I am an American, sir!" I also used authentic music of the American Revolution in the play. I found in the cadence of the drums and the shrill pitch of the fife the same defiance I believed to be characteristic of the spirit of our country's founders. I found it interesting that the popular tune, "British Grenediers" was used by both sides, and the lyrics reflected the respective shores of the Atlantic. One American verse was

> *Lift up your hearts, my heroes*
> *And swear with proud disdain,*
> *The wretch that would ensnare you*
> *Shall spread his net in vain.*
> *Shall Europe empty all her force*
> *We'd meet them in array*
> *And shout huzza! huzza! huzza!*
> *For brave America!*

The words alone were inspirational to me, and I like to think that the students involved with the production became somewhat more enlightened about the courage of our country's founders. Again, this was a great lesson in courage for the students as well, and hopefully many of them have found this quality in themselves as they deal with life today.

Our 1981 production of **The Great White Hope** by Howard Sackler was a brave and risky venture. It was controversial even when it appeared on Broadway in the late 60's, although it won instant fame. I believe strongly in the text of this play, and I felt that it was important to present it on the secondary school level. *The Great White Hope* deals with dignity, as we witness Jack Jefferson, played masterfully by Tom Edwards, the first black heavyweight boxing champion, try to retain his title amidst the groundswell of opposition from the white society. Epic in nature, the play begins in 1908 just after Jefferson beats Tommy Burns to win the championship and spans some three acts and nineteen scenes before it ends with Jefferson's defeat in Havana in 1915. The play's title is ironic and represents the constant hope of the white world to regain the championship.

To add to the disdain of the antagonists, and great drama to the play, Jack has a white lover, Eleanor Bachman, played by Jeanne O'Day, and the two of them are continually harassed by members of both the black and white societies. To elude them and to find some peaceful time together, Jack and Ellie find a small cabin in Wisconsin. This scene may be perceived as a difficult one since the two characters are in bed together, but Tom and Jeanne were very mature about the situation, and I felt very comfortable directing it. There have been other bedroom scenes in the history of Hamden Theater, most notably in *Camille* where the scene went on for several pages of text. The scene in *Hope* was intimate, as any bedroom scene would be, but it was one of tenderness and love, and not sex. It also contained some humor as Ellie discovers that, contrary to her former beliefs, Jack, a black man, can indeed get sunburned. The sensitivity of this scene is quickly shattered, however, when federal agents break into the cabin and arrest Jack under the Mann Act for transporting Ellie across State lines to have relations with her. It is interesting that nearly all of the the scenes in this play have some unexpected dramatic upheaval, adding to the drama and tension of the piece. I felt that *The Great White Hope* was one of the most exciting plays to work on from that viewpoint alone. Something was always about to explode.

Jack eventually escapes and thus begins his world travels, forcing himself to believe that other countries will be more hospitable, and always discovering this to be untrue. As Jack's money is dwindling rapidly, he is approached to throw the championship fight for a considerable amount, but he refuses to consider this. As time passes, however, both he and Ellie are reduced to poverty, and after a particularly agonizing confrontation where Jack tells Ellie that he doesn't love her anymore, she commits suicide. I still remember this confrontation scene as one of the most dramatic scenes I've ever worked on. Tom and Jeanne were magnificent in it, with him trying to force her out of his life because he sees how much he has dragged her down. Tom was enormous in the role; larger than life with his muscular body and booming, resonant voice. Jeanne was blond and played the role in a demure, nearly frail manner. The battle between them, then, where she begs to remain and he demands that she leave-even to the point of physically whipping her with a towel and grabbing her by the throat-was brutal and horrifying, electrifying and intense. This was a scene Hamden audiences would long remember, exemplifying one of the reasons for Hamden's strong reputation for top quality Theater that does not shy away from controversy.

As heart-wrenching as this scene was, the following one, where Ellie's dead body is carried in after she throws herself down a well, was even moreso. An image that will always be permanently imprinted in my brain is one of Tom holding Jeanne's limp body in his arms, looking upwards with such remorse and sadness, and with tears glistening in the moody stage lighting, crying out in agony, "What Ah done to ya...what you done, honey....what dey done to us..." This was one of those moments in the Theater that stops time; this is one of those moments that the Theater is all about.

This production had some thirty students in the cast, and without a doubt, they needed to be a talented group. Fortunately we had just that. Larry Iannotti was brilliant as the Federal agent as was Ken Festa as Cap'n Dan. Both of them, as well as Tom, were selected as Connecticut's Outstanding Actors at the 1981 Drama Festival. Larry and Ken possessed strong voices and created excellent physical characterizations. Jeanne won the State's Outstanding Actress Award also for her impressive work. But there were others in smaller parts whose performances were truthful and dynamic and added to the overall stunning impact of the production. These included Martin Harries as Tick, Jack's trainer; Chris Erikson as

Smitty, the sportswriter; and David Simon, as Goldie, Jack's manager. Bill Stacey, Greg Donnell, Tom Burr, Jarrett Parker, Istvan B'Racz and a host of others added depth and texture to the play with their excellent work.

I was also fortunate to have the most talented African-American actors as well: Christina Foster (who would remain with the Theater Program for several years), Yvonne Brooks as Jack's mother, Jucinda Fenn, Sherry Bostic, Lisa Davis, DeAwngellice Gore, and Sylvonia McEachern were just some of those dedicated young women, many of whom had not performed in a play before, although one would not suspect that after witnessing their excellent performances in this play.

The Great White Hope did a lot to bring our school together. It attracted a diverse audience of all ages, all of whom appreciated the importance of the theme as well as the work of the talented cast and crew. The Theater Program worked closely with the High School's Student Minority League and the Hamden Youth Services Bureau so that we could tap the resources of more people, as well as publicize the importance of this project.

The play's reception at the Drama Festival was nothing less than thrilling as people rose to their feet quickly and enthusiastically upon the final curtain. The applause was deafening and people called out their approval. One festival judge addressed the Hamden students in the oral critique following the performance saying, "You are to be praised for the courage to choose this play and for the skill to carry it off. This clearly represents some of the very finest work I've ever seen." By virtue of its receiving the Outstanding Production in Connecticut Award, *The Great White Hope* represented the State at the New England Drama Festival where it was applauded once again. Tom Edwards was given the prestigious Brother John Memorial Award for the finest actor in New England. Naturally, we were all excited for and proud of him. And he truly deserved it. Some weeks after the production we received a phone call that James Earl Jones, the actor who originated the role on Broadway and at the Arena Stage in Washington D.C., would be in New Haven, and a meeting was arranged between Tom and Mr. Jones. It was wonderful to watch them together, and perhaps the meeting served as a special bonus for Tom's hard work. I feel, however, that Tom's reward, as everyone else's, was witnessing the effect this play had on so many people.

Now that I think back on the play, I recognize the initial feelings I sometimes have of selecting a play that might be too controversial or perhaps too mature. This has happened frequently to me, making play selection frightening and lonely at times. But whenever I've had this feeling, whenever I've lost nights of sleep weighing the pros and cons, something inside me seems to take over. The importance of the project swells within me and makes me attack the project with stronger conviction than ever. I suppose it stems from my unwavering belief in the message of such plays and the gravity of that message to those wonderful people I teach. I feel that educational theater would be remiss, and I would be remiss as a teacher, if we didn't work to make this world free of bigotry and prejudice. For a time Hamden High School floated on the wings of *The Great White Hope*, and there was such good feeling-one that comes from unity and understanding. I wish it could last forever.

In November of 1981 we presented Jean Anouilh's ***Becket, or the Honor of God***. This was the second Anouilh play I directed, having done *The Thieves' Carnival* for a summer production in 1970. *Becket* is an intelligently written play, as all of Anouilh's works are, and takes place in a historical time period that I have always found fascinating. Sometimes I wonder if the historical period in which a play takes place isn't one of the most compelling reasons for me to select it. Henry II of England and Thomas Becket were good friends for a long time before the former had the idea of making the latter the Archbishop of Canterbury, thereby hoping to ease the tensions between the State and the Church. The King also felt that this would be politically advantageous to him, for he no longer would have to struggle against the powers of the Church. This simple solution to his problems was characteristic of Henry's practical thinking, although in this case it's amusing as well, considering the King's major decision of appointing his close friend to such a mighty position.

Henry was the great grandson of William the Conqueror, and during his reign there was still a large distinction between the Norman aristocracy and the Saxon peasantry. The land that William the Conqueror invaded in 1066 was little more than a wilderness with independent kingdoms randomly located throughout. He imposed his own Norman, French-speaking background in the country, thereby dividing it into social castes, with the Normans being the overlords and the vast numbers of uneducated Saxons remaining as workers. Little changed by the time that Henry II took the throne. The only real educated class was that of the Norman clergy who, as a matter of course, took on the administration of government. It could be argued, then, that while the Catholic Church produced saints and scholars, it also had its share of politically motivated men as well. Henry found himself at odds with the Church frequently, and his idea to make his good friend, Thomas, the Archbishop was, he thought, a stroke of genius. This would certainly have put the Church under Henry's power.

What Henry did not count on was Becket's sudden religious awakening; his newfound desire to honor God. In their last meeting, on the barren plain of La Ferte-Bernard in a winter blizzard, Becket says of being made Archbishop,

> "I felt for the first time that I was being entrusted with something, that's all-there in that empty cathedral, somewhere in France, that day when you ordered me to take up this burden. I was a man without honor. And suddenly I found it-one I never imagined would ever become mine-the honor of God. A frail, incomprehensible honor…"

At one point in the play, as the two men discuss the differing philosophies that pulled them apart, they have the following discourse:

Becket: Understand each other? It wasn't possible.

King: I said, "In all save the honor of the realm." It was you who taught me that slogan, after all.

Becket: I answered you, "In all save the honor of God." We were like two deaf men talking."

This, more or less, defines the conflict in Anouilh's play. Each man must answer his own calling and their coexistence seems politically impossible. Eventually Becket must be killed, for his power severely threatens and diminishes that of the King.

I felt that *Becket* was an important play to do with and for young people because it dealt with the necessity of finding honor in one's life. In a way, it seemed a natural progression from *The Great White Hope* and Jack Jefferson's quest for dignity, and even from *The Crucible* and John Proctor's search for his own self-worth. What better lessons can educational theater provide?

Lawrence Iannotti, who had proven himself a strong actor even back in his junior high school days, played Henry II. The intensity behind Larry's work, the truthfulness with which he infused the words and embodied the actions, enabled him to play Henry's many different emotions with great passion. Larry also had a rich, resonant voice and looked right for the part, with his jet black hair, tall frame, and fiery eyes. Martin Harries played Thomas Becket. Although as tall in stature, Martin had a softer look, with sandy-colored hair and eyes that could be playful at one moment and quite serious the next. Martin had undergone quite a change since his days at Michael Whalen. His wild sense of humor and boyish curiosity had matured into a more quiet and reserved nature, although there was never a doubt that those other qualities still lurked behind the sparkle in his eye. A extremely intelligent young man, it was easy to see great things ahead for him. More of Martin's genius became apparent as he went on to play Richard III.

The cast was another large one and featured other very fine actors as well. In those days the pool of actors was large and I had to continue to find plays that offered opportunities for many people. Of particular note was the wonderful Kirsten Shepherd-Barr, a young woman with her own long list of accomplishments, who played The Young Queen. When Kirsten was in junior high school, she was instrumental in the development of the Whalen Players. She was bright and enthusiastic, and her devotion to the Players went far beyond that of a member of an extracurricular activity. It was easy to tell that the Theater was important to her. Eventually, Kirsten became a university professor and the author of *Ibsen and Early Modernist Theater, 1890—1900*.

Anne Clark played The Queen Mother with regal dignity. Anne projected, even then, a sophisticated, yet warm demeanor. Her most lovely voice and perfect articulation added a quality of maturity to the character. She seemed to assume the power of this role through her understated and quiet sense of dignity and control. As Kirsten did in a university setting, Anne was to go on to teach acting in a school in New York City. This profession, I am happy to say, is shared by many Hamden High Theater graduates, among them Edith Meeks (HB Studio in New York), Paul Teitelman (high school in New Hampshire), David Rosenberg Korish (University in Costa Rica), Steven Villano (New York), Laurie Pitts (New York), and Taryn Chorney (Connecticut).

Another member of the company was Lynn Festa. This quiet, but talented young woman who did a number of plays in Hamden eventually became an occupational therapist and opened a clinic for performing artists with physical disorders. I believe Lynn is one of the true success stories of our program, for she uses the skills she learned in Theater to help others.

Strength to this ensemble was added by Larry Fitzgerald, Laurie Pitts, Brendan Ledig, Andrew Whitman, and Alexander Kenney, all of whom were like family to me since we had been together since the early days at Whalen. I remember meeting Alex for the first time. I was trying to find a costume for a student, and as I rounded a corner of our almost unwieldy collection of costumes, I literally bumped into a small, wide-eyed boy looking up at me with great curiosity. He introduced himself in a mature manner that belied and almost poked fun at his youth, and something told me that he and I would be great friends. I am happy to say that we still maintain contact although he now lives in Sweden with his wife and son, and where he is now a professional theater photographer.

There are so many others in this company who had a great effect on the quality and reputation of Hamden Theater in the days when it was still growing and expanding: Lisa Prezioso and Maura Demaio, Jill Jason and Veronica Brenckle, Gregg Donnell, Lynn Festa, Karl Fusaris, Kevin Bee, Andrea Gurwitt, Paul Gross, Laura Saller, Sean Boardman, Sarah Sherman, and David Pickman. Erika Zucker and Julie Trachten supervised props and were so proficient that I asked them to be my assistants for *Richard III* the following year.

As the drama festival approached that year, I remember feeling disconcerted by the headline of a major story in the local newspaper: "Will 'Becket' rival 'White Hope'?" Rehearsals for the festival were going very well up to this point, and I recall the sudden anxiety that came over me when I saw that bold headline and read the article. I think most Theater teachers/directors know the delicate nature of a rehearsal period. There are so many incidents that occur; so many little victories that students must win over their own respective ghosts. *Real* educational theater teaches and encourages and cajoles and nurtures, and, if lucky, inspires. I often imagine the Theater as some all-knowing, protective, and wonderfully patient parental figure who helps his students up after they have fallen down and wraps his arms around them with a strong and warm embrace when they finally succeed. Putting on the play is often the easy part.

I never compare productions. Each is too special to me because each company is unique, and now it felt like our own *White Hope* was the opposition. The department had now won four consecutive Outstanding Production Awards, capped by the huge success of *Hope* the previous year.

Obviously I was ecstatic about the successes at past Festivals, most notably the personal achievements of our students. But a few newspapers were now writing about a "Hamden dynasty", and while it was meant as a compliment, and while it sounded impressive to the tax-paying community and to the school system, I was starting to feel a pressure that the program's success was equivalent to winning the top award at the Drama Festival. I like to measure success by a student's growth.

In all fairness, I must say that the pressure never really came from within the school system. Hamden administrators, in those days and today, have always been most supportive of the program. Frank Yulo, Ed Mas, David Shaw, Jules D'Agostino, Marshall Richards, Joseph Castagnola, Alida Begina, Mary Marrandino, John Carusone, Rolfe Wenner, Carmen Vegliante, Judith Philippi, Richard Nabel, Janet Garagliano and Colleen Palmer have written letters of congratulations to students, attended rehearsals, helped with a multitude of details, and traveled to many festivals to offer their support. Dr. Begina often brought graduate classes from local universities to rehearsals where they would engage the high school students in discussions about the text, the method of putting on a play, and what the students were learning from the process. The administrators valued the arts and created an environment that encouraged their growth. They also encouraged me personally to develop, to experiment, and to take risks as our program expanded through the years. Most administrators don't get as involved in a school's Theater program as these fine people did. I count myself very lucky to have worked with and for them.

Becket did well at the Festival in the spring of 1982, earning yet another Outstanding Production Award and Outstanding Acting awards for Larry and Martin, as well as awards for Anne and Kirsten. I recall feeling more relief than joy; the pressure was off for another year. The play represented the State at the New England Festival as well and won high praise. After the hoopla of the Festivals ended, I sat by myself in the Theater for a long while reflecting on just about everything that had gone on with this play and with the others before it. These students just never stop amazing me. And just as I couldn't put my feelings into words then, I still can't today. They work so hard. They don't think of the words, "potential" and "limits" in the same breath, and with that frame of mind anything is possible. I also thought about the word, "dynasty" and what it really meant. To me it sounded like a description of a sports team. But If there *is* truth to the existence of a Hamden Theater dynasty, back in the 1980's and now, I feel that can be attributed to a long and continuous line of students who are proud to be part of a strong tradition of love and respect for the Theater and each other. They want to succeed, to contribute, and to learn; and they want to earn the respect of their predecessors, their older "brothers and sisters." They say that the wisest people can look within themselves and see an entire universe within the soul. I think my students have allowed the Theater to help them do just that. I am so proud of this theater family.

In May of 1983 we presented *The Fantasticks* , the famous and long-running musical by Tom Jones and Harvey Schmidt. It represented a departure of sorts from the powerful dramas we had been doing, and maybe a necessary one at that. This had long been one of my favorite shows, and we had never done a musical in an intimate three-quarter round style. This was a popular musical in the late 60's, and I recall seeing a fine production of it at one of the Yale colleges. It was one of those times when the ingredients were just right: a cold, wintry night, a spontaneous decision to see a play with some friends, and a really good production. It made an impression on me, and it may have been that very evening that inspired me to direct it so many years later.

My musical director was Patricia Chernow who I worked with during the summers at the Foote School Summer Theater program. Pat was the assistant musical director at the Sullivan Street Playhouse years before when the long-running New York production began, so she knew the show extremely well. We had a small orchestra, also on stage, comprised of

Pat, Rebecca Flannery, Bill Gunn who played several memorable roles at Whalen and would eventually become a music teacher in the Hamden School System, and Josh Pawelek.

The cast was small but very talented. Laurie Pitts and Brendan Ledig played the lovers, Luisa and Matt. Both had done a significant amount of work in both junior high and high school theater, Laurie having won an All-Connecticut Cast Award at the Drama Festival for her effective portrayal of Lady Anne in *Richard III*. Laurie went on to become a high school theater teacher and director. Brendan's first play was *The Miracle Worker* in which his sister, Colleen, played Annie Sullivan. Brendan was only eight years old at the time, so his association with Hamden Theater spanned a good number of years by the time he graduated from high school. Larry Fitzgerald and Karl Fusaris made wonderful fathers-Larry as Bellomy, Luisa's father, and Karl as Hucklebee, Matt's father. Larry and Karl were spirited actors and truly played major parts in the development of our program. From our earliest meeting at Whalen Junior High School, Larry was one of those students who enjoyed a challenge. There were no limits to his imagination and his accomplishments as well. *The Fantasticks* marked Larry's twenty-second Hamden Theater experience.

Martin Harries, who had been so successful as Becket and Richard III, had a great deal of fun playing Henry, the Actor, and Alexander Kenney played his partner, Mortimer, "the man who dies." Both were hysterical in this play. Alex's bio read that he "was put to the sword six times during the performances of *Becket* and was drowned for four consecutive nights during *Richard III*. Alex's first acting class assignment in eighth grade was a death scene which wasn't very good, but the teacher reluctantly remarked, 'Well...you died well.'" Perhaps that eighth grade scene was a sign of what was to come.

I always admired Alex's sense of independence as well as his courage. He did a great deal of exploring and traveling on his own as he had an unquenchable curiosity. He once took a trip to the Middle East, and during that excursion took a bus tour into the desert. The bus stopped once in a remote and unpopulated area, giving passengers an opportunity to explore. However, Alex never heard the warning to reboard and found himself stranded in the desert. I could only imagine my panic if I were in that situation, but Alex, quite characteristically, remained calm and began walking until he came upon the tent of a Bedouin. The man graciously received Alex, gave him a meal, and soon after arranged for Alex's transportation to the city. When Alex wanted to pay the man for the latter's hospitality, the man remarked that his payment would come when Alex related this story to others, for he believed he would be blessed for his good deed each time the story was told. I was so impressed with the story-impressed with the mature way in which Alex always seemed to handle every situation since his childhood, and impressed with the man's generosity. I've told the story to others often as a way of thanking that gentleman for saving Alex, and also to illustrate a genuine act of kindness.

Alex met the woman who was to become his wife in the jungles of Mexico. He was a photo journalist and she was a volunteer, helping the poverty-stricken villagers. Soon he was so affected by what he saw that he began to work with the villagers as well. Upon his return to the United States, Alex showed me a photo of an intricately constructed spinal brace that he designed and made for a deformed infant. This act epitomizes Alex Kenney perfectly; he works hard for others, never considering the time or energy he spends giving of himself in his unassuming and ingratiating manner. Alex and Ulrica were married in the village as well, and the people's gratitude and affection can easily be seen on their faces in the photographs I enjoyed viewing.

Heidi Carofano played the Mute in *The Fantasticks*. She was a wonderful dancer, and performed this role, usually played by a male, extremely gracefully. Although the role is an asexual one, I think Heidi brought an interesting feminine quality to it. And El Gallo, the handsome, swaggering narrator of the play was performed by Gregg Donnell whose past work in *The Great White Hope*, *Becket*, and *Richard III* had progressed steadily and impressively. Gregg had a great feeling for the stage, and I enjoyed directing him again at Southern Connecticut State University where I guest-directed a production of *Picnic*, with Gregg playing the central role of Hal.

Justin Garvey designed the lighting for *The Fantasticks* and Paul Gross was the Properties Master and Master Carpenter. Again, both of these students had numerous credits dating back to junior high school, and they came into this production with experience and expertise.

The rehearsals for this play were magical. First of all, the music is beautiful. Of greater importance, the work of the students was superb. Maury Rosenberg staged some of the production numbers with his characteristic zeal and humor, and I remember everyone having great fun as we worked through the rehearsal period.

The only negative experience associated with *The Fantasticks* was a letter I received from an audience member in which she objected to one of the songs in the production entitled, "It Depends on What You Pay." This song is a comical one in which El Gallo offers to kidnap or abduct a woman in any of several ways for a male suitor. The idea of abducting, however, is described with the use of the word "rape," and the audience member's letter referred to making light of a very serious situation. That person had experienced a rape in her family and was obviously still distraught over it. I understood the woman's point of view, and wrote her back apologizing for any discomfort the song may have caused her. It's interesting that not long after that experience, the professional production changed some of the lyrics in that song in an attempt to be sensitive to the situation. At that time, however, I never thought of the song as offensive, especially in its context in the production. I wondered if any other directors of this popular musical had received similar complaints, and if so, what they did about it.

At the conclusion of *The Fantasticks* the company presented me with a beautiful antique wooden box in which I found a group picture of them, a rose we used in the production, some of the confetti that the Mute threw in the air, and a letter from each of them. And as I now look at those smiling faces in the photo and read their words of thanks once again, I am deeply moved; I am transported back to a perfect time and to a perfect place. Wealth is measured in many ways. I consider myself wealthy indeed to have had these *Fantastick* people in my life.

I first began my research on **The Elephant Man** in May of 1983, planning a production of it in February of the following year. During that time I dealt mostly with the life of John (in reality, Joseph) Merrick, and I learned that Bernard Pomerance's play was, in fact, only one of several on the subject. The story fascinated me, and I enthusiastically sought more material.

The play takes place from 1884 to 1890, primarily in London, and concerns the life of John Merrick, a man terribly deformed by a disease known as neurofibromatosis. The large cauliflower-type growths that covered his body so abhorred those who looked upon him, that he was treated as a freak and generally shunned as well as ridiculed by society. Merrick's life was filled with a long succession of despairs: the death of his mother when he was a child; rejection by his father and step-mother; the steady progression of the disorder which so disfigured him that his mere presence attracted crowds ranging from the curious to the violent; his stays at the notorious English workhouses when there was no place to go and no one to turn to; his exhibition as a freak to paying crowds; the abandonment by his manager in Brussels, leaving John with no money and no means of communication; and, finally, his death at twenty-nine years of age.

Yet within that disfigured body was a soul of incomparable sensitivity; of a dignity and courage to which society can only aspire. When I think of John Merrick I do not see the beast advertised as "The Elephant Man." Rather, I see the man who, late in his brief existence, begged for a stay in the country where he could finally see what he had only read about in books. What an odd picture it must have presented-this creature limping heavily through summer fields, exulting in the many fragrances and sights.

Much that we know about Merrick was written by Dr. Frederick Treves in *The Elephant Man and Other Reminiscences*, published in 1923 by Cassell and Co. Ltd. Treves was the doctor who found and cared for

Merrick. He becomes a major character in Pomerance's play. Ashley Montagu recounted much of the story in 1973 in *The Elephant Man: A Study of Human Dignity*.

During my opening night address to the companies of Hamden plays, I often read the tender and moving scene between Merrick and Mrs. Kendal, the beautiful actress who befriends him during his stay at the London Hospital. In this scene the two discuss the Theater and Merrick tells Mrs. Kendall that were he Romeo, he and Juliet would have escaped their fate. He talks about Romeo's failure to determine if Juliet were truly dead because he never took her pulse or called for a doctor. He claims this inaction proves that Romeo does not really love Juliet, but cares only for himself. When Mrs. Kendal is moved by Merrick's sensitive interpretation of the love story, he replies, "Before I spoke with people, I did not think of all these things because there was no one to bother to think them for. Now things just come out of my mouth which are true." The scene so eloquently embodies the theme of this play-that beauty and courage come from within; that sensitivity among humans is needed in a mature and sophisticated society. Certainly, this is a great lesson for all young people.

The real Joseph/John Merrick quotes part of a poem called, "False Greatness" in *The Autobiography of Joseph Carey Merrick*:

> Were I so tall to reach the pole,
> Or grasp the ocean with my span,
> I must be measured by my soul
> The mind's the standard of a man.

For me, to think upon John Merrick is to weep in awe at his importance, his resiliency, his refusal to be beaten, and, finally, his determination to not only passively survive, but to actively revel in the breadth of life's possibilities. I think that if there were no Elephant Man the world would be, quite ironically, infinitely less beautiful.

Montagu says, "(Merrick's) story is one of the most poignant in the annals of human experience. How could a creature so afflicted and so maltreated have developed into the kind of human being he became? Merrick's life is both a triumph of the human spirit and a testimony to the power of human love."

My studies about Merrick and this play made me think about the Theater in general and about my place in it. To me, the Theater is an art form steeped in tradition, yet constantly growing. It reflects a present truth, and also illustrates the timelessness of that truth. I appreciate a certain courage, a boldness in the Theater which, through its integrity and honesty, teaches us to improve our lives. Merrick talks of "the perfect point." Whether that point is attainable or not in life may be questioned. However, I feel strongly that we must strive for it.

As we worked on *The Elephant Man*, we all felt like we were part of something very important indeed. Rehearsals attracted many crew members and I remember a good number of visitors as well who sat silently for hours and watched intently. Merrick was played by Paud Roche whose only acting experience was a non-speaking role in the previous year's production of *Richard III*. There was something very striking about Paud at the auditions, and I asked him to read again for me on the following day-just to confirm my initial impressions. As it turned out, Paud was magnificent in this role. He was a very sensitive and intelligent person, and one could easily see and feel the depth of his soul. To play the deformity, Paud twisted his body, much like photographs of Merrick. The character presented, as one would expect, an enormous physical challenge to Paud, as well as the challenge of playing Merrick's many emotions: sadness and helplessness; courage and sensitivity; his ability to love and be honest; his warmth and wit.

I think that Paud's work on this character is what brought those people to rehearsals. He was fascinating to watch, and often, between scenes, would sit by himself, rubbing his eyes, his head buried in his hands. One could see him mentally reworking something in the previous scene, or perhaps preparing for the next. I remember being so impressed with Paud's statement to a newspaper reporter that he resisted the temptation to make Merrick "seem like a saint who has endured this terrible thing all his life. There's a temptation to make him like Ghandi, or to overdo his deformities. An important part of the play is that beyond the deformities, he was a normal person. Merrick teaches a message about human dignity."

In Scene III of the play, Treves delivers a lecture accompanied by slides of Merrick's deformities. The playwright calls for the actor playing Merrick to contort himself to the respective images presented on the slides. I decided to have a scrim painted with Merrick's figure on it, and as Treves lectured, the light behind the scrim would become brighter, revealing the actor approximating the same physical position as that shown in the painting. I asked Bill Stacey to do the painting. Bill had just graduated from Hamden, having been involved in many Theater productions. He was a very talented artist who had created the poster and program cover for *the Great White Hope* . Bill painted a portrait of the boxer, Jack Jefferson, from that play, and the company signed the wooden frame. That painting still hangs in my home as a remembrance of that play. I was pleased that Bill was enthusiastic about *The Elephant Man* project. The effect of his work on the audience was mesmerizing as the painted figure of Merrick almost seemed to breathe as it slowly came to life.

I also decided to have the play signed for the hearing impaired, and for this job I hired Karen Josephson, the signer for the Interpreted Performance Series at the Long Wharf Theater in New Haven and a hearing member of the National Theatre of the Deaf in Chester, Connecticut. I was always so impressed with Karen's work at the Long Wharf, and I didn't know how she would react to being asked to sign a high school play. As it turned out, she was thrilled, and as Fate would have it, Karen was to become a key figure in Hamden Theater, not only signing many plays, but serving as our signing coach for the upcoming production of *Children of a Lesser God*. She is a wonderful and special friend who adds immeasurably to my life and to the lives of so many others.

One audience member wrote, "I was extremely pleased with your making the production available...to the deaf community. In fact, one of my friends who is deaf attended the performance that night. She found the interpreter to be excellent. In making available a meaningful production such as *The Elephant Man* to the deaf community you are furthering the concept of programming in the Arts for all individuals." And yet another person wrote, "I am a deaf person who attended the production of *The Elephant Man*. Truly it was a marvelous production; the acting of the high school students was superb...I had no difficulty understanding the characters and more important, the message of the play. The acting...was accurate of a disabled person who is *visibly* disabled. This is somewhat different than a person with a disability which is nonvisible until something "happens." In the case of deafness, it may occur when a person signs or speaks with a deaf voice, or an epileptic who has a seizure. Because visible disabilities have a great impact, people are more aware of the non-normality. Likewise, the acting and responses of the others towards John Merrick were extremely accurate."

I was very happy with the public reaction to the signed performance, and it also affected the students in a very positive way, making them even more aware of the special needs that all people have.

Brendan Ledig played Treves and Heidi Carofano played Mrs. Kendal. Both had been students of mine since their junior high school days, and both had grown and developed a great deal. I have a fond recollection of Brendan in a junior high school production of *The Star Spangled Girl*, where he played a scene in which he was sunburned from head to toe. He was so hilarious in it. We had great fun during those rehearsals in the early days, and to see him now in this sophisticated role of Treves only illustrated how well he had grown as an actor.

Heidi played her role with absolute charm, and she expertly demonstrated the marked change in her character caused by her friendship with Merrick. There is a scene in the play called "Art is Permitted but Nature Forbidden" (Pomerance assigns titles to each of the twenty-one scenes) which calls for Mrs. Kendal to disrobe for Merrick. He had never seen a naked woman, and she consents to fulfill his wishes. I decided to handle this requirement by having Mrs. Kendal standing full back to the audience. At first she opens her shawl, seemingly naked to Merrick who stands upstage of her. In actuality she was wearing a bustierre which gave the appearance of her being naked. Then she removed a clip from her hair and it cascaded down her back. I wanted the moment to be be totally silent, with no dialogue and no musical underscoring. After she completed the actions, Merrick slowly moves toward her, and leans forward to smell her hair. The backlit scene created a halo-like effect around the two actors, and the choice to smell her hair rather than peer at her body, added an unusual sensitivity to Merrick's character. The moment was played beautifully by Heidi and Paud, and during the silence I could almost hear the audience's heartbeat.

Michael Lerner played Carr Gomm, the Hospital Head Administrator. Michael also showed remarkable progress in his acting skills. He and another member of the cast, Patricia McVerry, would go on to play the lead roles in the following year's *Children of a Lesser God*.

Aaron Pawelek played a wonderful, almost Dickensien "Ross", manager of The Elephant Man; and the "Pinhead Freaks" at the fair in Brussels were played by Carine Montbertrand, Paul Knudsen, Joseph Pickman, and Jane Baird. Jane went on to appear on Broadway some years later in *Aspects of Love*. Cast members Nancy Papagoda, Heather Wainwright, and Len Van de Graaff also would play major roles in future Hamden Theater productions. As I look back I am always so pleasantly surprised at how the younger actors absorb so much knowledge from being involved in plays, using it a year or two later in difficult and complex roles. Lynn Festa, Jeff Lerner, Jim Struzinsky (Jim also served as Assistant to the Director), Michael Rothberg, and Jared Haller completed this large cast.

I recently received a letter from Jared and his wife, Andrea Marcus. Andrea worked on the crew for this production, and so many years later they renewed their friendship in California where they married. This was yet one more marriage between Hamden Theater students.

I also want to credit Paul Gross and Risa Freedman with their expert lighting design and Devra Gordon with her organizational skills as Assistant to the Director. David Morely was a Master Carpenter who worked so hard on the set as did Steven Pitts on Props and Bernadette Petrillo and David Workman on sound. One of the strongest components of education, I feel, is students learning from students. These crew heads taught younger members of the department the skills needed to carry on the work, and I feel this is one of the strongest areas of Hamden Theater as well as a reason for much of our department's success.

We did not enter the Drama Festival with *The Elephant Man*, but instead entered it in the Moss Hart Award competition sponsored by the New England Theatre Conference. One reviewer, Robert McDonald from the Theater Department at the University of Connecticut, wrote, "Let me state at the outset that this was the finest production I have seen in several years of reviewing for the Moss Hart Awards. With its inventive use of traditional theater space, fine and thoughtful ensemble acting, effective lighting, evocative music, and, above all, sensitive and clear directing, the production caught and sustained the many contrasting colors, tones, and themes in this very special and very instructive play..." He went on to say, "...Each member of the cast, crew, and design team (did) his/her very best to make the production live and breathe... Everyone seemed to care in a special way, seemed to have thought through the play's questions not only in the ensemble, but in the solitude we all encounter in life. This play needs that type of soul-searching in order to succeed and rise above the level of a 'tear-jerker.'" The play won the Regional Award for the best secondary school production in New England.

The Elephant Man was a wonderful and special experience. The students made a sizable financial contribution to the Neurofibromatosis Fund, once again illustrating their own growing sensitivity to society. I look back on this play with much warmth. The ambiance of the rehearsals, its strong theme, and most of all, its excellent production company made it a significant and memorable time.

I chose to direct Mark Medoff's powerful play, ***Children of a Lesser God*** in the fall of 1984. My decision was at first tinged with fear I must admit, for Children is a play about the deaf, requiring the director and actors to understand an experience that is completely foreign to their own. Not the least of the play's challenges is the requirement that the cast learn the language of deaf people, American Sign Language. My initial reading of the play left me emotionally exhilarated, and yet frustrated by the seeming impossibility of the play for high school production. But as the script sat on my coffee table while I was working on the previous year's production of *The Elephant Man* , it seemed to send out an energy of its own, enticing me, and soon I began to think, "Why not?"

As I look back, the decision to do *Children* seemed more difficult than the task itself. As I canvassed the students, I saw that sparkle of enthusiasm in their eyes. Next, I phoned Karen Josephson, who signed *The Elephant Man* for us the year before. Karen was familiar with the Hamden company and training program. Her first reaction was laughter, but it was a laughter filled with warmth and eagerness for the project. Almost immediately Karen was drafted as our signing coach, and *Children of a Lesser God* was underway.

Before long the New England Theatre Conference learned of the undertaking and invited us to perform at its annual convention in the fall. With the sudden reality of the accepted invitation and definite production dates looming ahead, the process began.

The month was May and *Children* was scheduled to open on the last day of October. I decided to cast immediately and have the actors playing Sarah Norman, described as "deaf from birth" and James Leeds, Sarah's teacher at the Deaf School, begin a summer of signing lessons. The next two months were filled with learning and with discovery, beginning with observing classes at the National Theatre of the Deaf. I vividly remember sitting by a beautiful waterfall with Michael Lerner (James Leeds), Patty McVerry (Sarah Norman), and Karen Josephson, learning to sign the first pages of the script, trying to make fingers work, trying out the mechanics.

We felt like we were embarking on a new and dangerously exciting journey. But it was dangerous in a positive way. The theater should have danger in it, I have often thought; a danger borne of the sheer thrill of breaking the barrier of preconceived expectations.

Preparing a play about deaf people sensitizes the participants to the world around them. It seemed ironic that we should have to travel to see performances by deaf companies when sign language was always so close to us if we had only opened our eyes. Since directing this play I have seen people communicating through sign language in our local supermarkets, in ice cream parlors and parking lots. The deaf world surrounds us. I wondered how we all could have been so unaware.

The process continued with full cast rehearsals each week, still concentrating on mechanics, still memorizing finger movements and palm orientation. I could tell the cast was growing frustrated. They wanted to block, to explore subtext, to *act* . But my plan was to move slowly for complete memorization by the beginning of school in the fall, and I wanted the sign language to be second nature by then. I told the cast that sign language was a necessary vehicle of communication, but only that. *Children* is not about a specific form of communication, but about people.

We would set a goal to learn a specific number of pages for the next rehearsal, meeting constantly with Karen, committing lines to fingers and subsequently and most importantly fingers to the heart. Soon we noticed a developing dexterity in our hands, and once or twice our hands surprised us by seeming to talk on their own.

Interspersed with strict text memorization came observations, some made firsthand and some related to us by others. We learned that one does not turn away from deaf or hearing-impaired people during conversation as one might when conversing with a hearing person; that deaf actors wear solid colors and very little, if any, jewelry to avoid distraction; that the face, the eyes, are just as important in deaf communication as in hearing.

The memorization ended on schedule, and as fall approached we were ready for our first blocking rehearsal. The production style was three-quarter round, seating approximately 140 people for each performance. This necessitated particularly careful blocking to provide as much hand and face visibility as possible. Although I had created "skeleton blocking" in advance to address this concern, we were very flexible in arriving at the final form. Often we spent three-hour rehearsals on just two or three pages, experimenting with the flow and rhythm, creating the beats which would, when finished, feed into and complement the play's overall rhythm.

The blocking rehearsals gave way to "work" rehearsals, although the distinction between these two phases lacked the characteristically sharp boundaries found in other shows. "Blending" became a key word with *Children*'s process. Nothing was rushed. Colors were carefully chosen-those of the costumes, the lighting, and the simple, multi-level set. Everything moved in its own time, and the entire rehearsal process developed a unique evolutionary rhythm.

Somewhere along this methodical process, the most beautiful thing of all happened. The play started to take on a life of its own, and we realized, more than ever, our roles as merely parts of the whole. The subtext clicked, the meaning surfaced, the communication-fingers, palms, hands, eyes, hearts-became complete. The mechanics we took such painstaking care to learn developed into something quite different, and we came to know what Sarah Norman meant when she said, "Deafness isn't the opposite of hearing. It is a silence filled with sound." The play did not come alive suddenly. Those moments of magic are wonderful when they happen, but *Children's* emergence was a gradual process. It came from constant work and nurturing by the cast. The play seemed to burst open from then on, like a time-lapse film of a flower blossoming. We knew we were part of something real and full of wonder and all-encompassing.

In educational circles there is the constant battle between the relative values of the process versus the product. The product's success, in the case of *Children* , was measurable in the play's excellent showing at both the Connecticut and New England Drama Council Festivals. The production won a total of eleven major awards, seven of these on the State level. They included the prestigious Outstanding Production Award and Outstanding Actor and Actress for Michael and Patty. The morning after we performed at the New England Drama Festival, I remember hearing students bustling around in the hotel hallway with the local Vermont newspaper in hand and they were very excited. They proudly showed me what the reviewer wrote: "When the lights came on after Hamden (Conn.) High School's rendition of *Children of a Lesser God* many eyes were wet. The audience shot to its feet in unison as if the standing ovation had been pre-rehearsed. But the joy of the moment was too spontaneous to be planned. It represented an emotional reaction to the performance... With all the (The New England Drama Festival participants') excellence, it's still fair to say that Hamden High School's *Children of a Lesser God* was the best of the best..."

After we performed at the New England Festival, we were given an oral critique by the three adjudicators. It is their responsibility to respond to the various components of the production, from the acting to the technical. It was at this critique session that I noticed one adjudicator looking at our group with a rather strange and questioning gaze. He then went on to say that he had seen Hamden productions for several years and had heard about them long before that, and while productions from other schools are of high quality, he asked, "What makes Hamden *different* ?" He was soft-spoken and genuine, trying to discover a "secret" behind the success of the productions. He asked me this question again after the critique, and I didn't have an answer for him. I've thought very seriously about this in the intervening years, and while I cannot find a definitive answer, I think it has something to do with theater students putting their soul into their work. I can best describe the Hamden students as people of character and heart whose commitment to the play and to each other is actually rather spiritual in nature. I'm not sure whether that esoteric observation answers the question or even partially answers it, but, then again, maybe it not meant to be answerable in words. There is an almost sacred intangibility that one can feel but not describe.

We were also invited to perform segments of the play at the Shubert Theater in New Haven as part of Greater New Haven's Celebration of the Arts. I was very excited for our students to be performing on the same stage as all of those wonderful shows that opened in New Haven before their long Broadway runs. And, as mentioned previously, we performed at the New England Theatre Conference Convention in Providence, Rhode Island.

There never was any debate over which was more important, the process or the product. The process simply grew into the product, and the result was a wonderful sense of gratification. Len Van de Graaff, who played a hearing-impaired student named Orin, won an all-Connecticut acting award, but his most valued prize was a comment from a festival judge who thought Len was actually deaf. Well after the production ended, Len wrote about his feelings working on the play. He said, "When we first started work on *Children* I had the feeling, and I think everyone did, that we were starting something very important, something that was in some way special to our lives. It was the feeling of a first meeting with someone you will fall in love with; an exciting feeling of 'rightness.' Looking back at the year I spent involved with the show, I now feel like part of me has been left behind; an experience that can never again be repeated. Working on *Children*, I went through all the stages of love–the tentative beginnings, the passion of full-time involvement, new-found self-awareness, increased sensitivity, and then finally the painful but necessary realization of the end..."

Sarah Haller, who played another hearing-impaired character named Lydia, received the same comment from a judge. And when a deaf member of the audience signed "Thank you" to Patty McVerry after a performance, the tears rolling down both their faces said more than all of the awards and trophies together.

The point is that *Children* worked for all of us, and much of its success was due to the fact that it was a strong example of a collaborative effort, as theater should be. An atmosphere was created in which everyone wanted and was granted input in the project. A sense of responsibility and loyalty to the production was evident from the very outset, and, with that foundation, the process grew more rewarding and exciting daily.

I remember a comment made by my friend, Howard Stein. He quoted St. Augustine as an introductory comment to a theater workshop: "From love comes understanding." I think this holds particularly true for *Children's* cast and crew. This devotion made the difference between a mechanically competent production and one that had a soul. From the director's point of view, the experience proved that a good theater program needs to take risks and requires that boldness, integrity, and even danger I spoke of before. As a teacher I saw once again the limitless potential of students who have an insatiable appetite to learn. On a more personal level, *Children* touched chords of sensitivity and humility, making all of us aware of the world around and within us. It provided a bonding of hearts and souls, of desires and energies, and made me only more aware of how fortunate I am to work with such special human beings.

In May of that year I directed Eugene O'Neill's ***Ah, Wilderness!*** This play is a major departure from the playwright's masterful tragedies and represents the autobiographical counterpart to *A Long Day's Journey Into Night*. While the latter introduces us to the brooding and painful existence of the Tyrones, *Wilderness* illustrates an innocence and humor not usually associated with O'Neill. It represents his desire for the way life could have been, O'Neill himself calling it a "comedy of recollection." The title of the play is derived from *The Rubaiyat* of Omar Khayyam, with a literary scholar theorizing that the "Ah" was substituted for the "Oh" because O'Neill felt "Ah" held a stronger sense of the nostalgic. In this play O'Neill paints his truest portrait of American life, its effect relying on the sympathetic observation of ordinary human beings experiencing, with humor and sensitivity, those growing pains so characteristic of Americana. In this regard, it falls into a category similar to our production of *The Devil's Disciple*.

The Elephant Man (1984)

Cyrano de Bergerac (1976)

The Prime of Miss Jean Brodie (1976)

Desire Under the Elms (1979)

The Crucible (1978)

Becket, or the Honor of God (1981)

The Great White Hope (1981)

Look Homeward, Angel (1977)

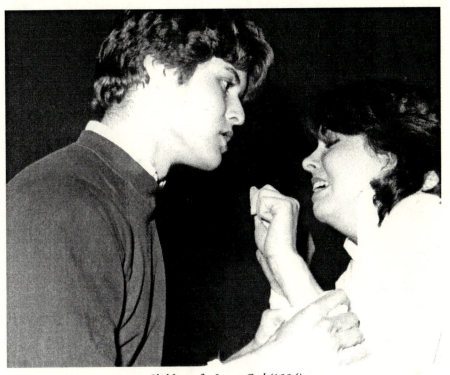
Children of a Lesser God (1984)

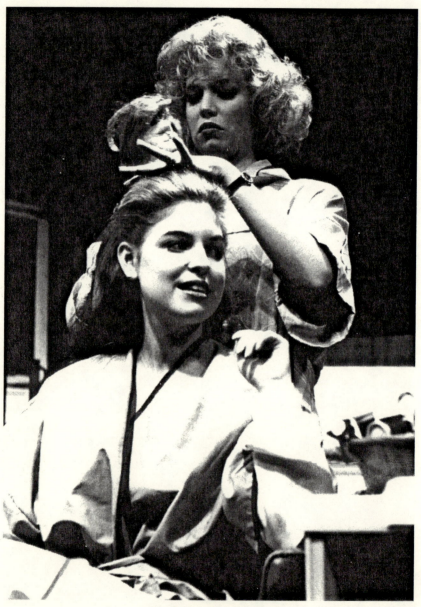

Steel Magnolias (1991)

The Shadow Box (1987)

Brighton Beach Memoirs (1988)

The Little Foxes (1990)

The Boys Next Door (1993)

Camille (1995)

Summer and Smoke (1997)

On the Verge, of the Geography Of Yearning (1998)

Dancing at Lughnasa (1994)

Central to the plot is sixteen year old Richard Miller's courtship of Muriel McComber. Muriel's tyrannical father finds Richard's love poems tucked neatly away in his daughter's wardrobe, and immediately puts a halt to the romance. Richard, however, mistakenly thinks that Muriel was the one who ended their love affair, and, feeling betrayed, sets out to heal his wounds with a trip to the scandalous Pleasant Beach House and its disreputable clientele. Of course, the play has a happy ending, with Richard and Muriel making peace, as well as the other characters solving their problems almost like a modern day sitcom. Even the characters are starkly different from those of *Long Day's Journey*, one example being the lovable Uncle Sid who some critics say is based on O'Neill's brother, Jamie. While Sid's tendency toward drink has caused Aunt Lily to reject his marriage proposals, there is no hint of the alcoholism that plagued Jamie's life. This play neatly ignores all vestiges of the pain and tragedy the O'Neills endured.

A good production company will find and evoke the time period and general feeling of the play through its selective use of externals- the costumes, props, set pieces, furniture, etc., and this production's large cast and crew immediately immersed themselves in a study of the early nineteen hundreds. Often the externals provide a path into the play's style and can also prove invaluable with character development, relationships, and an overall understanding and identification with the material. This is what happened with *Ah, Wilderness!* The time period was slowly coming alive as we delved deeper into the play. It almost seemed as if we were in a time machine, revisiting those days-as is often the case when doing a period play.

Ah Wilderness! had many special moments. I remember the nighttime beach scene between Richard and Muriel, Louise Rozett and Jeff Lerner playing it with a freshness and innocence that entranced the audience. Both of them suffused their characters with a subtle, childlike quality that was endearing and captivating. While the scene calls for a small rowboat on the sand as the only piece of scenery, we found a large and beautifully weathered piece of driftwood on the beach in Stratford and brought it up for the production. Nature's perfectly sculpted piece provided an aesthetic yet realistic feeling to the setting, and offered some good blocking possibilities as well. This scene, played in front of a deep blue cyclorama with tiny stars and with the soft sound effects of waves lapping against the shore, could not have worked better.

Another favorite was the scene in which Richard experiences the ill-famed Pleasant Beach House and one of its prostitutes, Belle, played by Eloise Goddard. Richard tries to prove his manhood by drinking, and, for the first time in his life, gets drunk. I think all directors eventually come face-to-face with the drunk scene, some of which are quite serious while others are playful and comedic. I don't think there are any "easy" drunk scenes, for all must be performed with some degree of believability. My rule of thumb for playing these or, for that matter, mental instability, is to complement the off-balanced mentality with an off-balanced physicality. I would direct actors to find their "center" (sometimes referred to as the physiovocal center, located approximately two finger-widths below the naval) and balance themselves physically, and then throw some weight to one side. This would serve as a starting point. We would then work on the speech patterns to give them a distinct sound, whether it be a slur or a drawl, and yet keep the diction totally understandable. After the mechanics are established, the actor needs to find the subtext for the scene to make it more than a physical exercise.

What helped me in directing such sequences is the realization that there is no one way to play drunk. That, in itself, offers many options. People are drunk in all different ways. I've seen people become giddy, silly, violent, and abusive. Some people laugh a lot, some shy people become outgoing, and others become morose. I remember a college friend of mine who sat perfectly still for hours and no one even realized he was drunk. When I decided to drive him home and tried to help him out of the chair, he suddenly vomited all over the floor. The wide range of visible effects of drunkenness provide great flexibility in guiding an actor to find what will work for him, all the while avoiding at all costs the cliche drunkenness too often found in poor theater productions. Jeff, I'm glad to say, found just the right manifestation for Richard's drinking experience, which, when combined with the character's inexperience in dealing with a prostitute, made the scene hilarious.

Ah, Wilderness! has a wonderful dinner table scene in it. This particular period of Hamden Theater seemed to have several of these, each with its own set of specific concerns such as blocking problems, sight line restrictions, etc. It was a funny scene, in which Essie cooks Bluefish for dinner, but calls it by another name because her husband, Nat, believes bluefish contains a "certain peculiar oil" that poisons him. Of course the entire family knows about their mother's ruse and attempts to suppress their laughter as their father obviously enjoys his meal.

One day before rehearsal I was examining the set. I was alone in the theater at the time when I saw some writing on one of the dinner napkins on the table. I thought this was rather odd, but then went on to discover more writing on the other napkins, finally realizing that the writing was actually lines from the play spoken by one particular character. The actor was insecure with the lines and had coordinated the written passages with the blocking. I was shocked and, I must admit, angry since opening night wasn't too far off. I called the actor, who I had never worked with previously, aside and conveyed my disappointment at the obvious lack of preparation. The actor was embarrassed and quickly learned the lines before the next rehearsal. In all of my years of directing, I think this was the first and only time I had encountered such a clever, albeit devious, strategy. Usually, actors just honestly admit that they didn't memorize the lines and we then decide how to best handle the situation. Looking back on the experience, I must admire the actor's planning. It's too bad s/he didn't spend as much time preparing for the rehearsal as was spent figuring out what lines needed to be written on which napkin.

Craig Walker played the bartender. He was a large and impressive looking young man, with a booming voice and good looks. Craig was a senior, and although the part wasn't extremely large, he approached it with an earnestness and sense of importance that resulted in quite an impressive job. We all can learn from such an attitude. Although Craig had never participated in theater previously, his involvement with this production excited him a great deal, and he went on to study theater in college.

Jeff's older brother, Michael, was also in the cast. Michael had achieved such success playing James Leeds in *Children of a Lesser God*, and was now playing Nat Miller, Richard's father. It was really fun to direct the Lerner brothers, especially in scenes where they appeared together. Not only were both talented, but they also shared a tremendous sense of discipline and responsibility. I think *Ah, Wilderness!* provided a transition for the Lerner family, as Michael had played several fine roles and was now about to graduate, while Jeff was beginning to emerge as a fine actor in his own right and would go on to create some excellent characterizations. Jennifer Lerner, the third and youngest child in the family, would also act in Hamden Theater. She ultimately chose to study theatrical lighting and went on to establish an excellent reputation as a lighting designer and stage technician.

Jane Baird, a lovely actress, played Essie, Nat's wife and Richard's mother. Tommy, the youngest son in the Miller Family, was played by David Brandenburg, a precocious young boy who certainly added spirit to rehearsals. Today David runs a large and successful Shakespeare company on Long Island. Len Van de Graaff portrayed Sid Davis, Essie's brother. As in the case of Michael above, Len's character benefited from his experience in previous major productions. His Jaques in *As You Like It* was excellent as was his portrayal of Orin in *Children of a Lesser God.* Len was a disciplined actor who knew what was expected of him. He was adept at creating and developing a character, yet was still learning to stretch as he found and used newly discovered aspects of himself in creating Sid.

Anne McBride played Lily, Nat's sister, with the same quiet confidence with which she created Celia in *As You Like It.* I would have to say that Anne always stood out over the years as a special person indeed. Her appreciation for fine literature, her enjoyment of the classics, and her ability to infuse her soul into her work, whether it was acting or music, made her an absolute joy. Anne embroidered two beautiful throw pillows for me, one as a remembrance of *As You Like It* and one for *Ah, Wilderness!* They are treasured possessions. Several years after she graduated, I received a beautiful letter from Anne, telling me about a speech she had to deliver before a large and possibly critical audience. She was anxious about it until she did some of our Theater exercises which soothed and relaxed her. Anne went on to state that the exercises also transported her back to her days in Hamden Theater and she reconnected with the confidence and encouragement that the program tried to provide for its theater family.

It was wonderful to note Phil DelVecchio's progress as he tackled the role of Wint Selby, a college "jock." Phil's first play was *As You Like It*, and he now seemed much more relaxed and confident. Hope Singsen, another truly fine actress and member of this cast came to visit me many years after her graduation. She and her younger sister, Molly, another Hamden Theater student, were living in California. Their Hamden ties existed no longer, but they took advantage of passing through town to seek me out. I vividly remember standing backstage and turning around to see them both approaching me. Sometimes we resign ourselves to the fact that we shall never see certain people again and force ourselves to be content with the memories of our times together. Visiting with Hope and Molly that afternoon was a special time for me, and I realized how intensely I missed them. I didn't want them to ever leave.

The cast was rounded out by Ted Fitzgerald, Joseph Pickman, Rebecca Dworkin, and Patty McVerry-all of whom contributed to the fine ensemble playing and ultimately to the success of the production. It is interesting to note that Patty played the small role of Nora, the housekeeper-this after winning New England-wide acclaim as Sarah in *Children of a Lesser God*. Some actors might have difficulty with this, but not Patty! She approached this role with the same seriousness of purpose as she did her last. I feel this not only speaks well for her, but beautifully illustrates a humility that has pervaded our program for many years. Students really understood the concept of sharing and supporting each other. In their attempts to gain a well-rounded theater experience, students played all kinds and sizes of roles, worked on technical crews, and even tried their hand at design or playwrighting or directing. I always remember a parent who saw a student mopping the stage before a rehearsal and commented that she had seen that student play the lead role in the previous department production. The parent was shocked, but then came to understand and appreciate our philosophy that everyone works together in Hamden Theater, handling all kinds of responsibilities, from acting to technical work to even cleaning up.

Ah, Wilderness! is rarely performed on the high school stage which is unfortunate. The script provides great opportunity as it challenges actors to create memorable characters and technicians to explore so many facets of production. It is also an example of the kind of dramatic literature to which students should be exposed. We had a wonderful time with it.

In 1986 I directed Peter Shaffer's magnificent play, **Amadeus**, for our fall production. The play is beautifully written, as all of Shaffer's works are, offering students the opportunity to study the most elegant use of language. It is also highly dramatic as it explores the intriguing rumor that the composer, Antonio Salieri, poisoned Wolfgang Amadeus Mozart in Vienna in the late Eighteenth Century. I remember how affected my friend, Frank O'Connor, was when he saw this play in New York with Ian McKellen and Tim Curry in the lead roles. He and I were watching the Tony Awards on television in 1981 as McKellen and the play itself captured the top awards. Frank's praise for the play was so effusive that I felt it would only be a matter of time before I seriously considered it for production. I read it soon after and found it to be a provocative play by a gifted playwright whose previous work I admired greatly. *Amadeus* would also expose my students to the kind of dramatic literature I felt was challenging and immensely gratifying.

Johann W. von Goethe said, "Mozart is the human incarnation of the divine force of creation, " but the playwright makes such a realization comprehensible to Salieri alone, who then, in his corrosive jealousy, attempts to destroy Mozart, God's musical "incarnation."

Mozart's death in December of 1791, before he was thirty-six, is shrouded in mystery and rumor. Controversy surrounds even the composer's mood while he worked on his last piece, the Requiem in D Minor, which is a major and climactic segment of the play. Some say he was obsessed with premonitions of death as he feverishly tried to finish the piece before his demise, while other scholars point to a particularly playful letter he wrote to his wife as proof that he was in anything but a somber mood at the time. The playwright opts for the former in creating this play. While Salieri's involvement in Mozart's death cannot be proven, the play strongly links the event with the former's zealous quest for fame and God's favor.

Once again I decided to present the play in a three-quarter-round style, hoping to attain an intimacy that would heighten the play's power and poetry. This production style had long ago become a popular one in Hamden. While audiences enjoyed it, it also seemed to force actors, designers, and technicians to become more detailed, as the audience's proximity made every facet of the set, every detail on the costumes, as well as every acting nuance noticeable.

Drama, to me, springs from honesty and simplicity; where no production element is obtrusive or hinders our most important responsibility-the revelation of truth and insight into the human condition. It is only then that the wonder of Theater can be realized. I was once again blessed with a company of students who approached the play in exactly this manner, for the final production was the result of hours, weeks, and months of discussion, and experimentation. I encouraged everyone to speak freely as the production was being shaped-to contribute ideas, and assume an ownership of our project. This is another wonder of Theater-a shared, collaborative effort where trust, responsibility, and sensitivity to each other are brought alive and nurtured. In this play, Man demands an answer to the question of existence and finds it in the need for recognition; to stand apart from the masses and from "mediocrity." Salieri, however, went too far-at least as far as the play is concerned-and learned that Man cannot defy God and abandon morality and virtue.

Another educational benefit of this play is the opportunity it affords students to become acquainted with Mozart's genius as so much of his music filters in and underscores numerous scenes in the play. Technical opportunities abound as well in all areas, especially costuming and set design, and a history lesson is available through the students' research of props, clothing, customs, and manners of the time. I also remember the cast and crew becoming very involved in the premise of the plot, which is understandable since mysteries have always been so popular. Overall, the theater at Hamden High School was filled with a great deal of activity as students worked on their respective areas of the production while strains of Mozart could be heard on a daily basis.

Just prior to auditions, Bill Burns, who had helped me with fight choreography for several plays such as *Cyrano de Bergerac*, *As You Like It*, and *Richard III,* approached me about working on a documentary about high school theater, answering his professional calling as a film-maker and producer. He felt that there were great lessons to be learned from watching *Amadeus* come together, especially for other theater teachers, directors, and students. I thought about it for a while. I was flattered that Bill felt we were good enough to serve as a model, yet I had real trepidations about making rehearsals, which often need to be private and sometimes can be personal, into something so public. Finally, I consented to Bill's request. After all, I knew Bill well, and I trusted him. Also, part of his production team was actually comprised of former students of mine currently in the Southern Connecticut State University Communications Department, with which Bill would be sharing this venture. I knew they would take extra care with this project since they felt protective of the Department.

I didn't realize at the time that nearly all of the rehearsals would be taped for the documentary, recording hundreds of hours from four different cameras. At first this was an awkward situation, and I learned that stopping to discuss a line or even to quiet a noisy crew member whose work was interfering with the rehearsal would not mean that Bill's cameras would stop as well. I began to feel guarded and even conspicuous, and I had to work hard to relax while the camera was constantly rolling. The situation certainly interfered with my style of directing which, at times, can be very intimate; where personal things are discussed and a trust is built between the actor and the director. I also enjoy a relaxed atmosphere during rehearsals where people can laugh and say what they please. The thought of sharing such moments with an audience was rather daunting and disconcerting, and it took some time before all of us could feel comfortable. Once I needed to quietly reprimand a student who came to rehearsal unprepared. We sat quietly in a corner as I told him that I wasn't pleased with his lack of progress, totally unaware that the conversation was being taped. These moments, Bill claimed, were important for other educational theater directors to witness as well.

Whenever I felt like I was losing patience or that the cameras were definitely impeding my progress, I would hear Bill's objective for the documentary: to heighten the quality of other schools' programs by using ours as a model. We had been doing theater for a long time, but I wondered if it were really good enough to be examined by departments throughout the country. In an interview in the newspaper Bill spoke of one of his purposes for making the film: "We show the development of the (Hamden) program and its philosophy. When you get a solid performance from Sean Penn at age 21, it's because of accelerated training. Hamden's Theater Department is a heck of a long cry from one that produces the typical high school play." And so the thought that this documentary would benefit others helped a great deal when I often reconsidered by initial agreement to collaborate on the project.

Bill's documentary, entitled, *Places Please*, was a great success. It was endorsed by the National Education Association and aired on public television many times over the next few years, being shown nationally and even internationally. I remember getting an excited phone call from a friend traveling on business through the Midwest. He was watching television in his hotel room one night and was shocked to see familiar faces and hear familiar voices. It even prompted a letter from Ernest Borgnine, the famous actor, who had grown up in Hamden. He was very excited about the program, and wished it had existed when he attended school in the town. Instead he had to find his theater training in other places.

I've always been happy for Bill's success, although I was very uncomfortable watching myself the one time that I viewed the documentary. And now, many years later, my directing style has hopefully developed, and what is seen on the tape represents part of a growing process which is very different from where I am right now. It unnerves me to think that viewers might "judge" me from the tape, but I suppose that is only human. I sometimes wish we could do the entire documentary over because I feel that Hamden Theater is on another level altogether today.

Bill interviewed many people involved with the production, including two men from Grace Recording Studio in Hamden, Fred Rossomando and Lee Walkup. In this deceivingly quiet and unassuming house in Hamden, some of the finest audio work in the country is taking place. Fred and Lee have clients that range from major Broadway shows to large corporations to individuals trying to cut a song on their own. They have always been patient and understanding as they've worked with me, technically piecing together my audio ideas and creating a sound track for countless productions over the years. I don't know what I would have done without them. Their artistry in creating and recording music and sound effects has had an enormous effect on the outcome of so many productions. More importantly, they've availed themselves and their studio to Hamden students who have been interested in this phase of production. I was always impressed with their willingness and enthusiasm to take time from their busy schedules to teach these young people.

Amadeus had a great company bringing it to life. The lighting design was created by Hamden Theater alumnus, Douglas Johnson. Doug designed many plays after he graduated, teaching the younger students about the principles of lighting while he did so. We were always fortunate that our graduates wanted to "give back" to the department; they became some of our greatest teachers.

The cast included Jeff Lerner as Salieri, Todd Billingsley as Mozart, and Mia O'Day as the latter's wife, Constanze. They were splendid. It was easy to see that they loved the material because they worked on it constantly. All three were able to find the subtext within themselves to create masterful performances. A friend of mine who possesses an advanced degree in theater training and is therefore sometimes painfully honest with me, wrote, "To see young Mozart well up with tears in the Don Giovanni scene was breathtaking, unpretentious, and real-simply real!" Todd had the ability and the vulnerability to motivate crying onstage, and often the stage lights would catch the glisten of a tear trickling down his cheek, totally capturing the audience's empathy. He used it most effectively in the following year's production of *The Shadow Box* as well.

Jeff was meticulous in his preparation for Salieri, as he was with every play he did in Hamden. He acted and looked so mature on the stage, and many people in the audience asked if he were an adult brought in to play the part. His "look", as that of every actor, is the work of our technical director who just happens to be a make-up and costume artist as well. Ort Pengue, Jr. is just an all-around genius. His research on the play, and the costumes and wigs he created, were astounding. The production was given an award for period acting at the drama festival, and I feel that much of this is due to Ort's costumes and wigs which greatly enhanced the way the students felt moving in them.

The remainder of the cast was equally as strong. Jennifer Barnhart's imposing Contessa foreshadowed the remarkable height she would attain as an actress in succeeding years, ultimately playing Regina in *The Little Foxes*. Philip DelVecchio played Joseph II with style and class. Phil is a success story, for when he first became involved in Theater, his counselor told me that Phil had some learning problems that might interfere with his progress. This young man not only disproved that possibility, but went on to play major roles, illustrating his ability to handle everything from memorization to complex character development. He also went on to do post graduate work in theater and became an accomplished director. His devotion and passion took him well beyond any preconceived expectations and supposed limitations. This has been the story of numerous individuals who have benefited from the power of educational theater.

David Schwartz's portrayal of Baron Gottfried Van Swieten was perfect as was Trisha Fast's portrayal of Katherina Cavalieri. The "Venticelli" or "purveyors of information, gossip, and rumor" were played by Audra Coassin, Ted Fitzgerald, Dan Miller, Louise Rozett, Felicia Sloin, Jon Sheehan, Christopher Stewart, and Janessa Wilson. They created an entire ambiance for this play, moving in and out of scenes deftly, often surreptitiously, and sometimes boldly. What an amazing company of actors I had, but, then again, this play requires amazing people. Several members of the cast and crew went on to study Theater in college and beyond. *Amadeus* was, without a doubt, a stronger play because of their zeal, their talent, and their kindness.

Brighton Beach Memoirs was presented in May of 1987. I may be wrong, but I think ours was the first-ever production of this Neil Simon play on a high school stage as it opened almost immediately after the royalties became available. It has been suggested that we may have staged the high school premiers of The *Great White Hope, Amadeus,* and some others as well, but there really is no way to prove this. It would, however, continue a Hamden tradition of "firsts" as Hamden High was the first school to perform Thornton Wilder's famous *Our Town*. Whether the others were premiers or not, it feels good to work on something fresh and previously unexplored by other schools. The "pioneering" aspect has had a good effect on other Connecticut schools, as it has opened doors of possibility for other theater programs statewide, and directors have used some of our play selections as encouragement to make courageous choices of their own.

The play deals with the Jerome Family in Brighton Beach, Brooklyn in 1937. Kate and her husband, Jack, have taken in Kate's sister, Blanche and her daughters, Nora and Laurie, and the already small Brighton Beach home suddenly seems much smaller. Kate and Jack have two sons, Stanley and Eugene. The play is told from Eugene's adolescent point of view-with strong autobiographical references from the playwright's life-and shows us his funny, awkward attempts to cope with his home life, his budding sexuality, and, on a more universal scale, understand the workings of the world.

This production was indeed a great deal of fun. Students had a wonderful time researching and locating time-appropriate props with which to decorate student Gary Radin's excellent set. Gary was an exceptional young man, both academically and personally. He designed the set, consisting of two levels, for a three-quarter-round production. Every bit of it was painstakingly detailed, from the moldings around the doors and windows, to the small stained glass window in the foyer, to the grass and flowers growing in the yard. I remember Gary and some crew members bringing wheelbarrows filled with earth into the theater and carefully arranging it on the lawn outside the Jerome house. Gary's intent was to create a worn look, both inside and out, yet one which was tended to daily by the inhabitants of this home. Authentic Yankee and Dodger banners hung on the walls of Eugene's bedroom, and the bedroom occupied by the girls equaled in femininity what the boys' exhibited in masculinity.

The company was tightly bonded, something which often happens in small-cast plays. But this group, portraying a family, definitely felt like a real family. The crew was very much involved with the performance as well, often watching the hilarious rehearsals and offering suggestions and opinions. Some critics have scrutinized Neil Simon's plays as being too commercial, or filled with one-liners. I, on the other hand, happen to be part of his overwhelmingly large legion of fans. Just hearing the music for the televison series, *The Odd Couple*, makes me feel instantly good.

Brighton Beach was different from his earlier works. At least I felt that way. It had in common with them an autobiographical nature, but it also had a dramatic quality and poignancy all its own. Fortunately I had a cast that could handle both comedy and drama; they could engage an audience in side-splitting laughter one moment and bring them to tears the next.

There is a strong ethos involved with *Brighton Beach* . I believe that directing this play is helped by understanding what Brooklyn was like in the 1930's, and what it was like to be Jewish in this era. Having grown up in a New York City suburb and in an orthodox Jewish family supplied me with an innate feeling for this play. As a matter of fact, this play could very well have been about my family. I, like Eugene, have an older brother named Stan who I idolized when I was growing up-and still do, as a matter of fact; I lived in a house where people literally whispered when they spoke about serious illness in the family as if mentioning it out loud would inflict the illness upon them also; I grew up in a house where, although they loved each other, my aunt and my mother were frequently at odds; I love the Yankees as does Eugene, and always wanted to be one; and, most notably like Eugene, I was sent to the store seemingly a thousand times a day. One day he is sent twice for a quarter of a pound of butter each time, and he asks why he couldn't go only once and purchase half a pound. His mother impatiently replies, "And suppose the house burned down this afternoon? Why do I need an extra quarter pound of butter?" Yes, this was the kind of logic that I also lived with in those days.

A special moment in the play occurs when Nora talks about her deceased father. She remembers how he used to invite her to go through his coat pocket where she would discover terrific things like life savers and movie stubs and nickels and paper clips. I remember the joyous sight of my own father arriving home from work each weekday, and I would run to him and hug him. And, once inside the house, he would invite me to search his pockets, and they would always include some little inexpensive, yet very special, gift for me. This play presents so many aspects with which I could identify, and directing it was like revisiting my childhood.

Andy Wildstein seemed to be born to play Eugene. His physicality, his voice, and his wide-eyed wonder as events unfolded around him helped create an excellent character. Ed Scharf, new to the Hamden stage, played

Stanley. Ed was a student in my beginning acting class, and I immediately recognized his talent. He was a senior that year and had never done any theater work before. After the play, we both regretted his lack of involvement much earlier in his high school career-he, for having missed the opportunity to work on more plays, and me for having missed the opportunity of knowing him for a longer period of time. Felicia Sloin and Trisha Fast played the sisters, Kate and Blanche respectively. Both were excellent and their scenes together were filled with sensitivity and truth. Lisbeth Shepherd's Nora was also carefully crafted. Lisbeth was such a fine actress and played a variety of roles in her career in Hamden, each so different from the others, and yet all with the utmost believability. Jeff Lerner, having just played Salieri the year before, was once again superb in the role of Jack. Jeff was, by now, a seasoned actor, having learned so much during the past years, especially in *Amadeus*. His self-confidence enabled him to continue exploring within himself for things that would make his character more truthful. And then there was Jennifer, my daughter, as Laurie, the whining, pampered younger daughter of Blanche. Jen auditioned for few plays in high school, attempting, I'm sure, to minimize any awkwardness I would feel in casting her. She was always practical and mature, even as a young girl, and always concerned about my feelings. I was just so thrilled that she was a part of Hamden Theater because there was so much the courses had to offer as well as the productions, and I knew this would help her learn about both life in general and herself in particular. Jen was in some of my classes and it was never an uncomfortable situation. But I remember working so hard as a teacher, feeling a double responsibility as father and instructor, and I wanted her and her colleagues to learn so much. And, as we always want the best for our children, I knew that Jennifer could also find meaningful friendships here, for these students were people of unique talents and special human qualities.

I remember looking forward to each day's rehearsal of *Brighton Beach*. I often felt that the anticipation of an after school or evening rehearsal made me a better teacher, for I felt buoyant in classes throughout the day. It's difficult to select a favorite scene in this play, as each one, whether comedic or dramatic, was exciting to explore. But rehearsing the dinner table scene certainly ranks as a memorable event. I often had to stress the necessity of staying in character-something these actors had great difficulty doing because of Simon's material and the combination of hilarious characterizations. Dinner table scenes have their own built-in concerns, such as finding enough time to chew and swallow, arranging the actors so they can be seen by the audience, and using stage food that will not cause the actors to choke. In this play, the actors had to consume a meal of liver which Eugene hated. The audience was sitting close enough to observe the food, so I had to choose something that would look realistic, yet would be easy to swallow and not take a long time to chew. I decided to use soft meat patties covered with gravy. There was also mashed potatoes, and the script called for ketchup, mustard, and pickles. So the dinner table was rather packed. Of course they complained mercilessly about the "soft" meat patties which our prop supervisor, Sheila O'Leary, would tend to overcook. And Sheila, being very conscientious, would cook them in the afternoon to be sure that they would be ready for the evening's rehearsal, so the patties were not only hard, but cold as well. This, however, only added to the general comedy of the situation. I gave the actors a great deal of freedom as we all molded the scene together, and the result was one of the funniest sequences I can remember. It was amazing that the cast could stay in character with a howling audience so close to them. The feeling of joy associated with this scene infused the rest of the play as well.

When I teach comedy in class, I stress the importance of what is called the "comic spirit" which could best be defined as having fun with the material. Without this element of play, the scene or the production runs the risk of becoming too laborious and weighted down with mechanics. *Brighton Beach*, however, could serve as a model for a piece with comic spirit. There was such a freshness and sense of adventure as the actors played, all within the confines of a structured rehearsal, and invented business that was original, distinctive, and outright funny. Even the dramatic scenes were approached with a lively, fresh perspective, and we spent a great deal of time noting the way the comedy and the pathos seemed to evolve from each other.

Brighton Beach raised the spirits of our Theater community. It was a happy time, and the ambiance of the play filtered into our personal lives as we carried this good feeling with us. I have often thought that I would like to direct this play again, and perhaps I will. On the other hand, I know I will always see the animated faces and feel the distinctive rhythms of the Hamden production. I would probably break out in spontaneous, uncontrolled laughter just as we always did, revisiting that place and time in 1987. Such was the power and enjoyment of a very special experience.

I directed *The Shadow Box* by Michael Cristofer the following fall.. It was quite a challenge as it dealt with the lives of three terminal cancer patients and their respective loved ones. I began my pre-production work approximately three months before casting, and in that time I gained an even greater appreciation of the script. It is beautifully written. I seem to be drawn to plays in which the language can be realistic, yet lyrical. While I could feel the intensity of emotion in the text, I also was moved by Cristofer's word choices, phraseology, imagery, and the way the lines spoken by the individual characters overlap each other. This last device often connected three separate conversations taking place in three different areas of the stage into one poetic and rhythmical conversation with a shared theme or emotion. It is no wonder that Cristofer won a Pulitzer Prize for this play.

One of my concerns in directing the play was really a matter of interpretation. I did not want the audience nor the company to think that this play was one solely about death. Rather, I wanted to stress the courage and dignity of the patients, and especially their respective families, as they faced the end of life. In a way, I feel that the play is a celebration of life rather than an examination of how people die. Another difficulty might be in helping the youthful cast empathize with the characters' sense of impending death. How does a director get his company to see the uplifting nature of a play about terminal cancer patients? Of course, the theme is *beneath* the words, and I was anxious for the cast to begin studying, researching, and delving into the text.

I was blessed, once again, with an incredible cast. The eight-member ensemble was very intelligent and talented and was able to handle the emotion and the poetic language. Rehearsals were progressing quite well, and the students' respect for the script was obvious. They knew they could trust the writing, much like actors can when playing a classic. However, I felt that the actors needed a further glimpse into the lives of cancer patients. This decision was not because of problems we were having. In fact, it was just the opposite. Things were going splendidly in rehearsals. Lines were memorized quickly, the cast was flexible, it enjoyed experimenting with subtext and blocking, and it quickly became a close-knit ensemble. I felt, as a director and teacher, however, that I needed to bring them closer to the script and I knew that they could handle what I had in mind.

I arranged a visit to Connecticut Hospice in Branford. For most of the students this was a first encounter with an environment exclusively devoted to terminal patients. I remember the car ride to Hospice as being animated and full of talk and laughter. The ride from Hospice to school, however, was quite the opposite. In our pre-rehearsal, impromptu discussion that evening, the most eloquent thoughts and words came from those students. During that time of sharing they came so much closer to the play's central theme-an appreciation of life and, in fact, realizing a responsibility to it; a responsibility to explore potentials and to make the most of them. I spoke very little and listened in awe at this sensitive, mature discussion among the cast and crew. I knew at this time that no matter what the ultimate quality of the production would be, the students had learned a most valuable lesson, and this, in itself, validated my selection of the play.

From that night on, I was witness to some wonderful moments during rehearsals. The fine efforts on the stage were complemented by so much sharing of feelings off the stage as well. A rich subtext was evolving for the company. The performances of the play were emotional, and I think that many people in the audience identified with the plot. And the acting was exceptional. These eight actors never seemed to be reciting lines they had memorized. Rather, the line delivery was truthful and filled with meaning. Every nuance of voice and gesture was precise and radiated from deep within each actor's soul. As I write this I remember specific moments that were so beautifully acted and I would love to mention them, but the truth is that all eight actors performed unlike I had ever seen them before. In a simple, understated way, they made observations and assimilations so honest, and their dialogue seemed like this was the first time it had ever been spoken. The actors were totally vulnerable, making the emotional moments powerful and heart-wrenching.

An interesting related story is that another high school decided to do a production of this play a few years later but was censored by that town's school board. It seems that they objected to the gay relationship between two of the characters, and for this reason could not understand the value of the play for young people. The director of that production was justifiably outraged at the censorship and went to the newspapers around the State with his story. Several reporters called me asking about the Hamden community's reception of the play, and I responded that it was extremely positive. The experience reinforced my belief in Hamden as an open-minded place, one free of bigotry, and one that valued the education of its children. The reporters' questions also made me appreciate the professionalism and maturity of the Hamden company even more. Censorship never entered our minds as we prepared this play because we believed it was a story that had to be told. I find that when you believe in a project so strongly, the commitment of the company is staunch enough to override the groundless opinions and accusations of any foes. I also found it interesting that two communities—the other one being rather affluent compared to ours—could look at a play from such very different points of view. I so enjoy learning through my observations.

The students wanted to enter the Drama Festival that year, but, as was the case for *Look Homeward, Angel* some years before, I was having difficulty obtaining the royalties. I decided to try to contact the playwright, and I wrote to him in care of the publishing company. About a week or so later I received a late afternoon phone call at work from Michael Cristofer. I never expected the playwright himself to phone me, thinking that agents or publishing companies do that sort of thing. At first I thought it was a prank being played upon me by a friend, a director at a nearby school who was prone to do such things. I remember playing along on the phone and throwing a few sarcastic quips into the conversation. When I finally realized that this was, in fact, THE Michael Cristofer, I was terribly embarrassed and very apologetic! Fortunately, he had a sense of humor and understood the situation. He gladly granted us the rights to do the play at the Drama Festival and wrote a letter to that effect. He also wrote a note to the company wishing everyone good luck at the Festival. He really is an understanding person and I could tell that he was excited that young people were studying and performing his work.

The Shadow Box won the State's Outstanding Production Award that year, as well as an award for Theatrical Excellence. For the first time, every actor was given an award, including three outstanding acting awards for Trisha Fast as Maggie, Lisbeth Shepherd as Agnes, and Felicia Sloin as Beverly-awards richly deserved due to the extraordinary performances they gave. Their power on stage and their ability to play a host of emotions, from hostility and anger to pensiveness and vulnerability, contributed to some of the best work I've ever seen on stage. All-Connecticut Cast Awards were won by Jennifer Barnhart as Felicity, Todd Billingsley as Mark, Dan Miller as Brian, and Joseph Zaccaro as Joe. And Joel Rebhun won an Honorable Mention in Acting Award for his portrayal of Steve, Maggie and Joe's teenage son. The judges were effusive in their praise of the students' work. One wrote me a letter after the festival saying, "The power of that production and the intensity of those performances rise up before me again, and I am in it's grip. I can't shake it! I have to write to you. With that whole weekend of eighteen plays before me, one play leaps up to be remembered and experienced even at this distance of time. The intelligence of those actors-their concern for quality and honesty... I am staggered to see them offstage and to realize that they are, after all, teenagers with all the problems and distractions we all had at that time of our lives, and yet they have so completely dedicated themselves so that all who have seen them will remember them the rest of their lives." Another judge wrote, "I can't believe high school kids can do this. This is professional quality throughout." Another nice note came from a member of the Darien High School community, the host site for the Festival. Katherine Gilliam wrote, "I don't believe I have ever felt so moved by a dramatic production and feel very fortunate to have been able to see it. Thank you...for making such a brilliant production come alive."

Due to the nature of the play, I entered it in the Moss Hart Memorial Award competition sponsored by the New England Theatre Conference. I don't do this often because it's a tremendous amount of work and there just never is any time for it. The Moss Hart Award honors plays that "present affirmative views of human courage and dignity, which have strong literary and artistic merit, and which, in their productions, exemplify fresh, imaginative, creative treatment within the intent of the playwright." Entries for this award included high schools, colleges and universities, community theaters, and professional theaters. I realized that the competition was stiff, but I felt that *The Shadow Box* was an excellent example of a play about dignity and courage, and entering it would send a strong message to the company that I had confidence in their work on the stage and their sense of humanity in their personal lives. In September, 1988 I received a letter from Mary Cavanagh of the Moss Hart Memorial Award Committee informing us that we had won this wonderful honor, and that the award would be given to Hamden High School by Kitty Carlisle Hart, Moss Hart's widow and a celebrity in her own right, at the fall convention of the New England Theatre Conference. Needless to say, everyone was very excited, and congratulations came from near and far. I was very happy for our students who were now receiving accolades for their hard and sophisticated work.

Of course, the true merit of any play comes through the personal triumphs and realizations that the students experience. One member of the company, Andrew Sloin, wrote to me that the play made him think of the last time he saw his grandfather before the latter's death; and he thought also of his mother and a close bout with death that she experienced. And yet Andrew writes, "I made no effort to wipe my tears away because these weren't tears of sadness; they were tears of joy. It was an incredible feeling to know that tomorrow night my mother would be in the audience as healthy as ever." This simple expression of Andy's appreciation of Life speaks volumes for *The Shadow Box* experience. Another wonderful memory was the gift that the company gave me on the final night of performance. They had made a contribution to Connecticut Hospice, and this meant a great deal to me. It illustrates their appreciation of the Hospice workers and shows respect for the valor of the patients. Furthermore, one student, an accomplished singer, offered a concert for the Hospice patients.

And yet one final bright spot of this play was working on it with my daughter, Jennifer, who served as one of my assistants. I always choose plays that I feel are important for young people; plays that speak to them about life values. I think I was especially sensitive to this issue during Jen's high school years. And as much as Jen and I were always close and able to talk about anything, this play was a kind of personal shared experience between a father and a daughter as well as a teacher and student. It provided a way of teaching her something that is very important by letting her experience the lesson rather than just talking about it. In addition to that, I just love working on plays with Jennifer. She has wonderful insight and I value her opinions greatly.

The Shadow Box was one of those productions that could not have garnered any more praise or awards, and as such, it added to Hamden's reputation for high quality theater work. But as I look back on this experience, I see the positive effect it had on those students as being much more important. It enriched their lives and enabled them to see, at least to some extent, the wondrous possibilities ahead. For that reason alone it was worth every glorious moment we spent on it.

The Admirable Crichton, the delightful comedy by James M. Barrie, was my selection for the spring of 1989. *Peter Pan* may be the only play more popular in the Barrie canon. This play tells the story of an English butler, Crichton, who believes strongly in knowing one's place in society and maintaining it. He is the head of a large group of servants in the household of Lord Loam in turn of the century England. The characters are wonderfully penned by Barrie, with the aristocrats who inhabit or visit the Loam household drawn as sophisticated, yet helpless to the point of laughter. When Loam, his family-comprised of three beautiful but spoiled daughters-and friends are shipwrecked on an island, Crichton becomes the new leader due to his qualities of leadership, his character, and his survival strategies.

This reversal of roles illustrates Barrie's theme of equality, as he mocks the strict class structure of England at the time. Breaking down these barriers enables Lady Mary, one of Loam's daughters, to fall in love with Crichton as well as learn survival techniques from him. She becomes quite an impressive, self-sufficient young woman-much the opposite of her initial appearance in the play. Here again Barrie illustrates how societal limitations can limit human potential as well.

Interestingly, when the group is rescued and returned to England, Crichton once again becomes his former self, and in the poignant ending of the play, we realize that he and Mary will not be together as they had planned. She says, "You are the best man among us," to which he responds, "On an island, my lady, perhaps; but in England, no." Mary then says, "Then there's something wrong with England." Barrie was criticized for the ending of the play, critics feeling that he diluted his theme by having the party return to England and assume their former roles. However, I feel quite the opposite may be true, for preventing Mary and Crichton to become a couple only further illustrates the unfairness of class divisions.

No one could criticize Barrie's stage directions, however, for they are simply charming. I heard once that his stage directions were often published as an entity unto themselves due to their immense popularity. Whereas stage directions in contemporary theater are rather minimal, Barrie's seem to go on forever and are filled with a delicious wit and sarcasm.

The large company, some sixty-two students, had a grand time with this play. One of the play's highlights occurs in Act I when Lord Loam calls for the servants, as he traditionally does each year, and orders his family wait on them. He does this in the name of equality and being fair, but, needless to say, his family detests this tradition, as do the servants as well. Each group is satisfied and accustomed to their "place." The servants' parade into the drawing room was wonderfully comical, entering one or two at a time, each actor creating some business that revealed both character and discomfort. The audience howled with laughter, enjoying the most wonderful combination of facial expressions, body movements, and costumes. While Ort's costumes for the upper classes were exquisite and proper, fitting the characters both in personality and size so perfectly, those of the servants evoked character through being too large or too small, too loose or too tight. These actors complemented the humor of the costumes with the way they wore them and carried themselves in them. I can remember Ort's painstaking detail on the costumes-the effort he went through to find the perfect maids' caps, the starched dresses of the higher ranking maids, the detail on the gowns of the upper class women. This is actually the way he approached every play. He concerned himself not only with the color palette of a production, but the fall and drape of the material, the type of character who wears the costume, etc. He then made sure that students were aware of this information. He also encouraged questions about costumes for he believed strongly in this aspect of theater education. This production seems to stand out in this area simply because it had some twenty characters on stage at the same time, throwing even more focus on the costumes than usual.

What I remember most about *Crichton* was the laughter. Rehearsals were so much fun, mostly due to the sense of humor of the cast and crew. It was a large group, so you can imagine how contagious the laughter was once it began, and it took very little to start it. I changed the role of Lord Loam to Lady Loam and was so fortunate to be able to cast Jennifer Barnhart in it. Jen previously played Felicity in *The Shadow Box*, obviously a much different role than this one. Jennifer was tall and physically imposing on stage. She also has a beautifully resonant voice as well and impeccable diction. However, under this bright, womanly exterior is a vivacious girl who loves to laugh. The following year Jennifer was to play Regina in *The Little Foxes*, and create one of the most memorable characters in Hamden Theater history.

Lisbeth Shepherd, a senior that year and the recipient of several acting awards at the State Drama Festival, had played Phoebe in *As You Like It*, Nora is *Brighton Beach Memoirs*, and Agnes In *The Shadow Box*. She now played daughter, Lady Mary Lasenby, with finesse and elegance. Lisbeth was a beautiful young woman with fine facial features and an ability to wear period costumes in a grand yet natural manner. She looked stunning and sophisticated in the gowns she wore in the Loam house contrasted with the rough-hewn clothing including animal skins she donned for the shipwrecked, jungle scene. Due to her superb acting ability, Lisbeth was able to create a marvelous character change and growth during this play. She earned another major award for her work in it. Working with Lisbeth was always a great experience. Not only was she one of the best actors I have worked with, but she was also smart, insightful, and sensitive. She was able to see so much in the text that eventually appears in her performance.

Blaise Wozniak played Crichton. Blaise was a senior at Hamden and new to theater. The would-be directors that scrutinize every audition questioned my casting him since he was inexperienced and this was a major role, but I had a good feeling about him. And this wasn't, after all, the first time I had cast a beginner in a major role. Remember how Charles Shanley excelled as Henry in *The Lion in Winter*, and Jonathan

Davis gave a superior, award-winning performance in *Much Ado About Nothing*. There were many more examples through the years as well. Blaise was a hard working and somewhat reserved person. He was intelligent and usually low-keyed, but I could easily see that there was a lot more to Blaise than what was visible as there is with every human being. He did splendidly in the role, again demonstrating an ability to play the change in the character so convincingly-from the Loam household servant to the island leader, and then back to the butler again in Act IV. In his portrayal of the Island Crichton, or "The Master" as he was called, Blaise showed a very different side of himself. His usually reserved manner melted and a whole new personality emerged; a kind of swaggering, softly-commanding, sensual, and energetic man. I remember the scene with Lady Mary on the island when they hear the horn of a rescue boat, and they know that this unexpected paradise as well as their growing love would now come to an end. Both Blaise and Lisbeth played the scene with a tenderness and vulnerability that could only make one weep.

My daughter, Jennifer, played Tweeney, one of the lowest ranking maids in the Loam household. Jen's portrayal of Tweeny was excellent-and I say that from an objective point of view. It's quite an experience to watch one's child assume a character from a play. I think you initially spend time trying to determine which traits are that person's- those you've seen mature since infancy-and which are specifically created for the character. Finally, the greatest satisfaction is sitting back and watching your child perform as the character in the context of the play. Jen managed to convert her diminutive stature into a powerhouse of a character who, along with Crichton, takes control on the island. It was fun to see the usually shy maid of the Loam household act like a drill sergeant, at one point even chasing Lady Mary with a broom. Jen also fit right in with this particular cast of laughers. At one rehearsal she was exiting the stage briskly and Jennifer Barnhart was simultaneously entering. Somehow they didn't see each other and crashed into each other, sprawling on the stage floor, laughing hysterically. Soon the entire company joined in the laughter, going on for what seemed like hours.

The text also called for Tweeny to pluck the feathers off a bird when she was on the island. For this we borrowed a prop bird from the Yale Drama School prop collection. My friendship with Hunter Spence, the properties master at the Drama School, offered me access to a wide array of the most difficult-to-find articles. Hunter's son, Charles, was also a member of Hamden Theater. Charlie was a skilled technician as well as a kind and affable young man. Hunter's appreciation for the Theater Program's effect on his son often came in volunteering help and support. We found the just the right bird for Tweeny to pluck in the Yale collection. It was chicken-like in appearance, and totally realistic. I must admit that at first glance I became a bit nauseous, and I could only imagine Jennifer's initial reaction to the prop she would eventually have to handle with ease. As I suspected, she balked at the business when she first saw this rather disgusting looking bird. I took the tactic of never forcing her to do it. I knew that when the use of final props was mandatory, Jennifer would eventually use the bird. And that is exactly what happened. We never spoke about it, but I remember a rather disdainful, "I'll-get-you-back" look from my sweet daughter's eye as the bird dangled from her hands the first time she held it.

This play also benefited from the talents of Sophia Salguero and Jennifer Moran. They played the two younger daughters, Agatha and Catherine Lasenby respectively. Both of them were to play major roles in the following year's production of *The Little Foxes,* showing more layers of their acting ability. I witnessed a wonderful growth in Jennifer over the years. She became such a confident and successful young woman, completely at ease in her profession. Sophia studied at Carnegie-Mellon University and, at this writing, already has an impressive list of professional credentials including working with directors like George C. Wolf, Julie Taymor, and Liz Swados and appearing in several Broadway productions. During the summer of 1999 I was able to hire her as the choreographer for my production of *Barnum* and her work was incredible. Not only was the product excellent, but Sophia has a way of bringing out the best in students of all different abilities and experiences. The students loved working with her, and I know she played a large role in the success of the summer program.

Crichton did extremely well in the Drama Festival that year. I should note that this was the first, and unfortunately last, year of Regional Festivals in Connecticut, implemented to address the high demand of participation applications. A constant concern in Connecticut had been trying to accommodate the numerous schools that wanted to participate in the Festival but couldn't due to the Festival's time constraints. The Connecticut Association of Schools, the governing body of all Connecticut student activities, does not allow events to occur on Sundays and halted the Connecticut Drama Association's practice of hosting a three-day Festival. The regional festivals seemed to be the logical solution, but after the trial run, participants-especially those who "won" their respective regionals and then moved on to the State Festival-felt the cost was exorbitant and the paperwork and preparations unwieldy. Personally, I felt that we could have worked out those problems, but the Association voted to return to the original format of the State Festival only.

Be that as it may, *The Admirable Crichton* won yet another Outstanding Production Award as well as twenty other honors, including the coveted Ensemble Acting Award. Hamden actors have always felt honored with this accolade, perhaps even moreso than individual acting honors, because it meant that the acting was superior overall; that the company's work was seamless, and that it collaborated artistically and with ease. *Crichton* also distinguished itself at the Festival by being the first play in the fifty-year history of the Festival to complete a major set change during the performance. In this case, the Loam set was struck, and the island hut was erected. This was a complicated change and had to be choreographed with precision and grace. The crew, which received one of the twenty-one awards, did an excellent job.

After the production, my daughter asked me why more high schools didn't do productions of *Crichton* since it was so much fun and so very successful. I explained that this was a four-act play with four different sets, costumes, props, etc. Somehow our company had overlooked the enormous amount of work and the complexity of this production simply because working on it brought us so much pleasure. I believe that is a telling statement about what can be accomplished in an atmosphere where there is fun and a sense of challenge. Certainly there was no limit to human potential here. I'm sure Mr. Barrie would be very proud indeed.

During the *Crichton* rehearsal period, there was a sudden wave of publicity about Hamden Theater. It began with a phone call from the Connecticut Education Association which published a magazine called *CEA Update*. They wanted to do a story on the department which was now used as a model in The Guide to Curriculum Development in the Arts published by the State Board of Education, and which also had a growing reputation on a national scale. The reporter came to school accompanied by a photographer and they spent a good deal of time talking to students and faculty. This visit was followed closely by an interview in the New Haven Advocate for a story very similar to the CEA's. And finally, just a few short weeks later, I was asked to write an article on educational theater in Connecticut for a publication called *Challenge Update* published by the Connecticut State Department of Education.

I wasn't quite sure what to attribute this recognition to. The previous year I had been the recipient of the American Alliance for Theatre and Education's John C. Barner National Theater Teacher of the Year Award at their convention in Portland, Oregon. Without a doubt, this was one of the most exciting experiences of my life. I'm not quite sure how they selected me, but it certainly was a great honor. I thought that this might have attracted some attention to the department, but I was happy that the articles and stories now being published were about the students' accomplishments and the structure of the department itself. Whatever the reason, Hamden was firmly established as a leader in the field of educational theater, a prestigious position but also one which demanded constant work and constant learning.

"Elegant" has to be the word that most aptly describes our 1990 production of Lillian Hellman's *The Little Foxes*. It was a sophisticated production of an intriguing play. Hellman introduces us to the Hubbards, a rapacious, hate-filled family who dominate a small Southern town at the turn of the century. The twists of the plot, usually brought about by blackmail and other underhanded dealings as each family member tries to outwit the others in his/her path to financial power, hold the audience nearly breathless. The play itself has been described as brilliant and masterful, and some critics have accused it of being almost *too* perfect in construction. Whatever opinion is held, however, there is no doubt that the plot is a principal force that captivates the audience. Arisotle's philosophy that a good plot is the soul of all successful drama is well exemplified here. This does not minimize Hellman's deftly drawn characters. Regina Giddens and company are sought-after roles in American Theater. This may be due in part to our fascination with greed and evil and certainly actors love to sink their teeth into such parts, but perhaps it is due moreso to the challenge they present to actors. They force actors to make new discoveries and understandings. It was interesting for the actors to read Hellman's *Another Part of the Forest*, a play about the same characters, written after *Foxes*, but occurring twenty years prior to the latter play's events.

As I've stated many times, I've always felt a play's message is of special importance in educational theater. As Theater has always reflected society, it continues to provoke, stimulate, prod, and excite us into making our lives better and more meaningful. Addie, one of the Giddens' servants, says, "There are people who eat the earth...and there are people who stand around and watch them eat it. Sometimes I think it ain't right to stand and watch them do it." The thematic implications are obvious. I wanted students to know that evil in society must be resisted or we are all guilty of enabling it. I always found Ben Hubbard's lines particularly haunting when, at the end of the play, he states, "This is just the beginning. There are hundreds of Hubbards sitting in rooms like this throughout the country. All their names aren't Hubbard, but they are all Hubbards and they will own this country someday." How chilling those lines are, and what a call to action for people to speak out against corruption.

Jennifer Barnhart played the evil Regina Giddens, and her wealthy and powerful husband, Horace, was played by Joseph Zaccaro. Their daughter, Alexandra, was played by Sophia Salguero, and Horace's sister, the meek Birdie Hubbard, was portrayed by Jennifer Moran. Oscar Hubbard, Birdie's conniving and controlling husband, was played by Andrew Sloin and their son, Leo, was played by Youngho Sohn. Another brother, Benjamin, perhaps more contemptuous than Oscar, was portrayed by Wyeth Friday. Other members of the cast included Winston Joshua as Cal, Typhanie Jackson as Addie, and Kyle McGee as William Marshall. This cast was exceptional, and every member of it won an acting award at the Drama Festival that year. Jennifer gave an electric performance as Regina, definitely one of the best ever on the Hamden stage. Her work had always been impressive up to now, but Regina was a masterful job. The character manipulated and connived, cajoled and flattered to get what she wanted. Certainly an unforgettable moment was when she sat tranquilly on the couch as her husband, Horace, in desperate need of his heart medicine attempted crawled up the stairs to retrieve it. Part way up the stairs, Horace dies. Jennifer, as Regina, chose to remain seated until she was sure Horace could not be saved. I will never forget her most subtle smile and the fierceness in her eyes as she sat so calmly, awaiting her husband's death. They seemed so much more horrifying during the ensuing silence.

Joe and Wyeth gave exceptionally realistic performances as Horace and Ben respectively. Both looked much older than high school students and commanded the stage with a powerful physical presence as well as an ease that made their acting appear simple. The same was true of everyone else in the cast. In so many of our productions through the years, people have mentioned to me that the actors look so "adult," and while much of the credit belongs to carefully designed and executed make-up and costuming, I am most proud of the actors' ability to motivate internal feelings and external actions, and all the while carry themselves with composure and dignity. This cast looked especially adult and elicited numerous questions from the audiences regarding their ages. To me, these kinds of characterizations were absolutely necessary, for this is a play about adults and their machinations. They had to have a certain physical stature and a resonance to their voices to make the production work.

Ort once again designed a magnificent set. Frank Alberino, who would eventually become an invaluable part of the design team and one of my two professional partners, was a student at the time and served as Master Carpenter. Ort also designed exquisite costumes. In selecting material for the women's dresses, he paid special attention to the drape of the fabric, the colors which would best suit the characters, and, of course, he incorporated the detail of the time period.

The play was enormously successful, and as I look at the crew listing I can understand why. There were fifty-two students who comprised the company of *The Little Foxes*, and most of them were or were soon to become central members of the department. I recognize names of people in the crew who would hold major and demanding roles the following years both onstage and off; technicians who would blossom and enjoy the swiftly growing technical challenges our productions began to offer. Now it was as prestigious to be a crew member as it was to be an actor, something that is rare, at least from my observations of other high school programs.

Much of this feeling was due to the enormous, elegant set and the attention to its detail. It was mainly comprised of the large sitting room in the Giddens home, complete with period furniture and grand piano. Up left was the entrance to the dining room, and the audience was able to watch part of a dinner scene through the French doors which separated the two rooms. This added depth and believability to the set. Up right was the main entrance to the house as well as a stairway with a landing between flights leading upstairs. It was nothing less than amazing that this set could travel to the drama festival and be constructed in less than the five-minute time frame allowed for the set up of scenery. Every crew member had specific responsibilities, and, without verbally communicating, they worked like a well-oiled and precisioned machine in putting that wonderful set together before the eyes of a totally silent and stunned audience. The students presented me with a model of the set for a gift. It was as beautifully built as the set itself, even containing miniatures of the photos on the walls. I still don't know how they reduced those large photographs to such a small size. I suppose the point here is that they constructed the model with the same detail with which they labored on the real set. That speaks for itself.

The Little Foxes was extremely successful at the Festival, earning the top award of Outstanding Production as well as winning awards for every actor for the second consecutive year. What I was most proud of, however, was the interview session conducted by a reporter from the newspaper prior to the play's opening. While the reporter asked the students about their awards, she observed, "The modest group...doesn't flaunt the awards, often changing the subject rather than talk about their successes. 'You do it for something other than the awards,' says Andy Sloin who plays Birdie's money-hungry husband, Oscar Hubbard. Then, quoting a line from the play, he adds, tapping his heart, 'If you don't feel it in here, you don't pick the cotton right.'"

I am constantly in awe of the young people with whom I teach and learn. They are so humble, even amidst the accolades that are heaped upon them and the town and school pride that swells when they succeed. While I try to select plays that teach them lessons, I find that I am the beneficiary of the lessons I derive from their work ethic and humility.

Steel Magnolias, our spring production for 1991, was a departure from plays of the previous years in that it was modern rather than period, and it was performed in a three-quarter rather than proscenium style. We hadn't used the three-quarter round style since *The Shadow Box*, three years before, and I felt that the younger students needed to be exposed to it. Since I wanted to draw the audience into the intimacy of the lives of the six female characters, this production style was certainly appropriate.

Steel Magnolias is a play that deals with friendship, as six women in a Louisiana beauty parlor discuss everything from recipes to weddings to theater to love. The common denominator in all of this discussion is the warmth, caring, support, and sense of humor that the characters display in their relationships to each other. Playwright Robert Harling is telling us, I believe, to reconsider our friendships, all too often ignored, lost, or placed to one side as our lives whirl around us. When one character, M'Lynn Eatenton, played by Catherine Jones, loses her adult daughter, Shelby, portrayed by Diane Bers, to complications from diabetes, the power and strength of friendship enables M'Lynn to move on with her life.

From the start, rehearsals were a great deal of fun. In a way they reminded me of *The Admirable Crichton* rehearsals with the constant laughter, and often they would come to a complete standstill as the cast brought these unique characters to life. In addition to characterization opportunities, Harling's plot and his dialogue were wonderful to work with, as they shifted the play's rhythms from comic to dramatic. It is a great feeling to work with a text that is beautifully written and constantly lifts the company's spirits.

This particular cast and crew were laughers and found much to feed their appetites for humor. They were not only amused at elements within the play, but they would laugh convulsively at anything that would go wrong during rehearsals as well-a doorknob coming off in an actor's hand, a mispronunciation, some bit of business gone awry, trying to learn the appropriate Southern dialect without exaggerating it. I must admit that I laughed just as hard as they did.

Jennifer Ortman, new to the Hamden Theater scene, played Ouiser Boudreaux, the sarcastic, cynical neighbor with a heart of gold. Jennifer had a wonderful, wry sense of humor which she exploited for this role, often causing the audience to fall into fits of laughter. She was also able to handle problems onstage quite easily-such as the time she was sitting in a styling chair and realized that during a recent quick-change, she put her shoes on the wrong feet. She quietly and slowly built the shoe swap into her stage business. And one time her wig was slightly askew which she noticed only when she passed a mirror on the set. Again, she built the adjustment of the wig into her current business and emotion. Jennifer could also deliver Ouiser's sarcastic lines so well! At one point, her "rival", Clairee, the former mayor's wife, accuses her of never doing a religious thing in her life, to which Ouiser responds, "That's not true When I was in school, a bunch of my friends and I would dress up like nuns and go barhopping." Jennifer added a unique quality to the play and I consider myself lucky to have found her.

The play was filled with wonderful lines, both humorous and sensitive. When Shelby talks about her favorite color, pink, and how she plans that color for everything at her wedding, from the bridesmaids' gowns to the carpet to the silk bunting, her mother comments, "That sanctuary looks like it's been hosed down with Pepto-Bismol." And when M'Lynn is terribly upset that Shelby, a diabetic, has ignored her doctor's warning and become pregnant, Shelby delivers one of the play's most famous lines, "I would rather have thirty minutes of wonderful than a lifetime of nothing special."

Catherine Jones played M'Lynn with the mature love of a mother. Catherine had done excellent work in the department for several years, but I feel that M'Lynn was her best work. The scene where she tells her friends of her daughter's death was heart-wrenching and brought the audience to tears. At one point she explodes with anger: "It's not supposed to happen this way. I'm supposed to go first. I've always been ready to go first." And just when the audience is crying with her, Harling lightens the moment. M'Lynn continues, "I just want to hit something...and hit it hard," after which Clairee pushes Ouiser towards M'Lynn and says, "Here. Hit this! Go ahead, M'Lynn. Slap her!" It was a bittersweet moment and a much needed release from the intensity of M'Lynn's grief. But such was the impeccable timing of Harling's emotional changes.

Throughout the rehearsal period, I was continually impressed with the warmth and humanity of Harling's writing and with the ability of the cast to deliver the lines with empathy. The writing was funny, dramatic, intimate-and seemingly all at once. At the end of the play, after the remaining friends have survived the tragedy of Shelby's death, M'Lynn says to them in gratitude for their support, "You have no idea how wonderful you are," to which Truvy, the beauty shop owner, retorts, "Of course we do." I then had the women hug each other center stage, swaying gently to the music of the nearby radio. The tune I used was a moody, sensitive song written and sung by a former student, Rachel Green. Rachel had sent me a copy of her album a few years previous, but I never thought I would be able to use one of her songs for a play. While the music evoked the perfect mood for the end of the play, I also felt good that it was provided by another Hamden family member. This emotional ending had quite an impact on the audience, and at the Drama Festival, one judge wrote that the audience wept for a good ten minutes after the final curtain.

One of the concerns in selecting *Steel Magnolias* is, of course, the requirements of the set. The play takes place in a beauty parlor and most of the business is related to that vocation. Hair must be washed and set and cut. There is a need for running water on stage, and hair dryers that must work. The proximity of the audience in the three-quarter style placed further demands on the detail and accuracy of stage business. We were fortunate to be able to call upon a benevolent member of the Hamden community, Vincent Faricelli, who owned beauty shops in Hamden and New Haven. Vin is a wonderful man who donates a great deal to charities and even sponsors rather large annual fund-raisers in support of charitable organizations. It was not difficult, then, to obtain Vin's help in supplying sinks, counters, hair dryers, and just about anything else we needed. He even wanted to sponsor a haircut-athon on the set to raise money for charities.

Of course, now that we had the props we needed someone to set them up and show us how to use them. Once again, Ort was the answer. He not only designed the set, but he guided the technicians to create special effects such as the running water. He also taught Erika Nelson, who played the beautician, Truvy, how to wash and set hair as well as give manicures. It seems that way back in Ort's past, he attended a school for hair design, and now that skill was being put to good use.

This play about the importance of friendship worked because of the strong bonds among the cast and crew. Catherine, Jennifer, Erika, Diane, Christina DeMeola as Clairee, and Callie Fletcher as the initially shy new employee, Annelle, worked so well together. One judge at the Drama Festival wrote, "Wonderful ensemble work, both in pairs and in large groups. The silences, the breathing, the touching, the eye contact, and the laughter all built this cast interaction. I never doubted the intense underlying love (among them)."

The *Steel Magnolias* cast and many crew members still maintain close friendships some ten years later, a testament to the power of Harling's play and the lessons learned by an exceptional group of people.

The 1993 production of Tom Griffin's ***The Boys Next Door*** dealt with the world of the mentally challenged. It seemed only natural that I would choose to direct it since one of the unique features of the Hamden Theater Program is its interdisciplinary work with the Special Education Department. In 1989 we introduced our first course, joined by a second one in the Spring of 1992. While I looked forward to teaching these classes, I had no idea of just how "special" these students would become to me, and how affected I would be by their enthusiasm, their affection, and even their needs. I suppose it was due to the strength of my feelings that I selected this play for production. I wanted to expose my mainstream theater students, as well as our audiences, to a very important segment of our society; one, however, often treated with fear or apprehension, and sometimes not treated at all.

The world of the mentally challenged is unique. It requires patience, understanding, and attention. I quickly learned that each day would bring new challenges, new problems, creative solutions, and new learning opportunities for me. What one receives in return is immeasurable—like the time one boy rose out of his wheelchair to join a group improvisation; or when one student who "couldn't" talk did just that.

Somewhere during these intervening years I discovered that my world would suddenly seem rather bleak without the company of my special friends; without the whimsical humor of one, the high-pitched, infectious giggle of another, the ultra-sensitivity of a third, and even the spontaneous crying fits of yet another. I remember the class lessons including sign language and music, children's stories and even Shakespeare. We visited relatives in heaven and tried hard to solve the problems of daily living-all through drama. Yes, this was a special experience indeed, and directing *The Boys Next Door* seemed to answer a need rather than just a desire.

The play takes place in an apartment shared by four mentally challenged men in a suburban New England city. There is Arnold, played by Jon Panagrossi, a rather high-strung man who likes to be in charge. He, like the other members of the group home, quickly gains our affection through his innocence, and also when we learn that he is susceptible to the wiles and insensitivity of the larger society. Arnold's following monologue opens the play and immediately illustrates his special needs, his peculiarities, his endearing innocence, and the cruelty of some members of the "normal" society:

My name is Arnold Wiggins. I'm basically a nervous person. People call me Arnold because I don't have a nickname. So I pretend that Arnold is my nickname so that when people call me Arnold, I pretend that they are close personal friends who know me by my nickname: Arnold. I live here at the Stonehenge Villa apartment complex in a group apartment with three other guys. Did I mention I'm a nervous person? Well, frankly, I am. Today I went to the market at the end of the street to get some Wheaties. But I couldn't remember whether I wanted one box or more boxes, so I asked the manager how many boxes should I get. "For just you?" he said. "Yes, sir," I said. "Seventeen," he said. "Thank you," I said. But, and this is what I want to emphasize by nervous, I could only find nine boxes. So what could I do? *(Pause)* I got nine boxes of Wheaties. *(He removes various sized boxes of Wheaties from the bags.)* And seven heads of lettuce. *(He removes the lettuce, studies the situation.)* That made sixteen. *(Pulls out a bag of charcoal.)* And one bag of charcoal briquets. That made seventeen. *(He takes out the milk.)* And a quart of milk. You know, for the Wheaties. But the more I thought about it, the more I thought I didn't get enough...what? Was it (A) lettuce? (B) Wheaties? (C) charcoal briquets? This concerned me. So I asked a girl in line what she thought. I forget what she said, but it was pretty thorough. And then I came home. *(Pause)* Do you think I did the right thing?

Arnold's rationalization was very logical to him, and as the play progresses, I believe his thinking becomes all too logical to the audience as well.

Lucien was played by Greg O'Connell. He was more or less relegated to the confines of the apartment and cleaned it often, constantly wondering where dust comes from. One of the most poignant parts of this play is when Lucien must appear before a State Committee which is threatening to cut off the funding which allows him to remain in the group setting. Suddenly Lucien transforms, in a kind of surrealistic manner, into an articulate man-a device used by the playwright to provide the audience with a glimpse into the mind of the mentally handicapped, but one to which the Committee is not privy. "I stand before you, a middle-aged man...whose capacity for rational thought is somewhere between a five-year-old and an oyster. I am retarded. I am damaged. I am sick inside from so many years of confusion..." This moment of the play affected me a great deal, for I often wondered what the world looked like from my special students' eyes. I spent so much time observing and listening to my students in class, trying to see things from their perspective; trying to figure out how they drew conclusions; how they made sense of things.

The third member of the group home was Norman, played by Jon Walker, who today is a professional actor in New York. Jon won an

Outstanding Actor Award for his work as the mentally challenged man who works in a donut shop and is in love with Sheila, another mentally challenged person played by Samantha Ethier. Samantha did a wonderful job with the role of Hero the previous year in *Much Ado*. Sheila has a fascination with Norman's keys, and when she comes to visit him, he presents her with a gift of keys that Arnold had collected from the movie theater where he works. She, in turn, gives Norman flowers she picked at the local Getty Gas Station. This entire scene is endearing, as so many of them are in this play, as we witness the almost childlike courtship between the two mentally challenged adults. When Sheila leaves, Norman is so excited by her visit that he throws a tray of donuts out of the window, proclaiming, "Free donuts! Free donuts."

The last house mate is Barry, played by Joseph Salvi. Joe would become one of Hamden's finest actors, playing Michael in *Dancing at Lughnasa* and Armand in *Camille* over the next two years. Barry wants to be a golf pro to impress the father who abandoned him many years before. When this father, Mr. Klemper, played with great anger and guilt by Christopher Johnson, finally visits, the latter loses his patience and control and hits Barry, sending the fragile young man into tears and ultimately into a catatonic state for which he must be hospitalized. I remember that very dramatic and violent scene shocking the audience each night.

The men are visited daily and cared for by their social worker, Jack Palmer, played with warmth and sensitivity by Jon Walker's twin brother, Matt. Matt played Benedick brilliantly in *Much Ado* the previous year. But Jack wrestles with the frustration of his job; with the fact that very often the mentally challenged do not improve. Throughout the course of the play it is easy to see how sensitive Jack is to the needs of the men, yet it is equally easy to see his steadily growing anxiety. Jack has demons of his own with which he must deal. The following monologue is found near the beginning of the play and provides some insight into Jack's personality as well as his professional and personal turmoil:

Sometimes I eat lunch down here by the railroad tracks. It's very romantic in a sordid kind of way. *(Pause)* I ran into my ex-wife the other day. She's full of ex-whatever venom. She asked me a few polite questions about my job, then she said, "What happens when they don't need you anymore?" "They'll never not need me anymore," I told her. "Me or somebody else." Who made that rule?" she asked. "God," I said. *(Pause)* Three months ago, Lucien was informed by the Social Security Administration that his benefits were being cut off. They said that their information indicated that Lucien was capable of being fully integrated into the community. We appealed. No luck. Our next step is to appear before a State Senate subcommittee. Lucien has been invited as a witness. I try to prepare him, but I don't think it's taking. He says if he knows "The Alphabet Song," it'll be okay. He says he wants to wear a tie with Spiderman on it. Just so they'll know how important this is. *(Pause)* And as a final note, my ex-wife looked terrific. She drives a BMW now and wears lots of bright green. "Who's that funny little man in the back seat of your car?" she asked me. It was Arnold. "That's Arnold," I said. "Why is reading the phone book sideways?" she said. "He's looking for the road map to Russia," I said. "How can you stand it?" she said. And Arnold, still in the back seat of the car, said, "If the phone people don't want to print maps of Russia, fine, but don't turn around and call it the phone book. Don't deceive the public."

Finally Jack tells his charges that he is quitting his job and won't be seeing them any more. He tries to explain that someone will replace him and take good care of them, but to no avail. The men and Sheila panic, and Arnold runs out of the apartment. Jack finds him at the train station waiting for a train to Moscow where Arnold believes life will be better. In one of the most understated yet emotional scenes I can ever remember, the two men express their feelings, and they bring the production to a close with a long and strong embrace.

It was important to me that the actors in this play create realistic characters and not fall into well-meaning but insensitive caricatures. Fortunately Jon Panagrossi worked as a teacher's assistant in the Special Education Drama Class and met with the students on a daily basis. Other members of the cast visited regularly, and while they led lessons, participated in class, and felt genuine concern and affection for the class members, they were also afforded the opportunity of observing mannerisms, vocal patterns, and the behavioral idiosyncrasies that are so prevalent. Many of these observations were built into the physicality of the characters. But the actors did so in a very sensitive and caring way. They were never "scientific" or too analytical. Nor did they merely mimic gestures, but incorporated all details in a respectful way.

I wanted the set design for the play to be basically realistic, yet reflect the skewed way in which the characters viewed the world. Ort decided to incorporate doors that were taller than the adjoining walls, giving a slightly expressionistic emphasis to the set. Since many doors were called for, his idea worked perfectly.

A unique problem was presented in casting twin brothers in a relatively small cast play. We pondered over how to make Jon and Matt look physically different, and solved the problem by having Ort build a stomach pad for Jon. This made sense since Jon's character, Norman, loved food. It also afforded him the opportunity of creating a new and different kind of physicality for the role.

The play also benefited from the acting talents of Ariella Laskin as the neighbor, Mrs. Warren, whose pet gerbil has disappeared. She never learns that in a previous and riotous scene, the men chase and pounce upon it, thinking it was a rat. Ariella was a directing student of mine and had a rare and wonderful talent in that field. She went on to major in Theater at the University of Connecticut and, upon graduation, work at the Long Wharf Theater in New Haven. Other actors who added immeasurably to this play through their performances included Leah Altman, who played Miss Corbin, the movie theater manager; Carra Gamberdella as Sheila's friend,

Clara; Evan Katz as a golfer, Mr. Hedges; and Theresa Rutz who played the older Mrs. Fremus.

The Boys Next Door produced the effect that I sought. The students and the audience were sensitized to a world many of them knew nothing about. They came to view these mentally challenged people as indeed special.

Sometimes you find a play that seems to be perfect for that particular time and place, and also for the specific group of people with whom you happen to be working. It is the ideal convergence of where you seem to be mentally, and where the needs of your students and the community can be found. This is how I felt about *Boys*. It was an incredibly moving experience. I can't explain how enthusiastically we looked forward to rehearsals every day. They were funny and poignant, and touched something within us all at the same time. Once, again, a playwright's use of language had provided a story so beautifully written—simple, yet eloquent. Doing *The Boys Next Door* was truly an educational and moving experience, and I like to think that all who worked on it or saw it were enlightened to some extent.

The performance of the play at the Drama Festival caused a newspaper reviewer to write, "Never had a play in New Haven, New York or anywhere else moved me so deeply, and I still can't figure out how these kids did it." He went on to comment on Hamden's winning the Outstanding Production Award. "Simply put, for the past two decades Hamden High School has set the standard for theatrical excellence in the State of Connecticut, if not the nation. Year after year, the Hamden students leave audiences spellbound in awed disbelief that they are actually watching high-schoolers perform." We brought the play to the New England Drama Festival that year in Westbrook, Maine, where it exposed hundreds of additional students and their families to the message behind the work. I think our students felt good about this play-not only about its success, but that they were doing something good for society.

Very recently I was on vacation in New England. I had occasion to be in a large department store, and while I was looking at some of the merchandise, I felt a hand grab my arm very roughly. Naturally I was momentarily frightened. When I quickly turned to see who was holding me, I came face to face with a rather large man sporting a grin that took up all of his face. There was an innocence and kindness in his eyes. He was obviously mentally challenged, and was being scolded for his behavior by one of the chaperones of the small shopping group. I told her that I was fine, introduced myself to the man, and shook his hand. In that brief moment my mind flashed back to *Boys* and to my class, and I was immediately transported to this world that had meant so much to me. I have no idea why he grabbed my arm. I'm sure it made sense to him at the moment. But I looked upon this experience as a reminder that the world of the mentally handicapped is always present; that the production had ended, but not the need for sensitivity and caring for this special segment of our society.

When I revisit *The Boys Next Door* I realize that it gave me the opportunity of uniting the worlds of two groups of people very important to me-my hard-working and compassionate mainstream theater students, and those members of my Special Education Drama Classes-loving, unassuming, simple, to-the-point, needy. I always counted my blessings when I realized my ability to call them *all* my friends.

Brian Friel's play, **Dancing at Lughnasa** (1994), was an extraordinary experience. As was the case with so many other plays, this was a very close-knit company, especially the cast. There were eight actors, six of whom had rehearsals every day-and a sense of family quickly developed.

I felt that Hamden Theater was now in a very comfortable place as far as our work was concerned. Earlier in this chapter, specifically in regard to *Becket*, I mentioned the pressure that the press and others often placed upon us to perform as well as the previous year's production. People would say, "You're only as good as your last play," and even though these were good natured remarks, it's often difficult not to let one's ego get in the way of the main objective: to teach the students and to bring out the best in each, producing the best possible production.

There was no doubt that *Lughnasa* had incredible obstacles for a young company. It was a complex and extremely difficult play to bring to life, but the department relished this kind of play, allowing the rewards of working with a superior script to far outweigh any fears and trepidations we might have. The long string of successful Hamden plays strengthened the students' commitment and promoted the feeling that they were part of something large and successful and wonderfully warm and nurturing as well.

One of the most difficult aspects of directing this play was teaching the Irish accent. I prepared for quite a while, listening to tapes and studying my accent/dialect books. And whenever I came across a person with a strong Irish accent, which is more frequently than one might imagine, I paid particular attention to the vocal patterns and melody. The cast was very quick to learn the accent and soon incorporated it into their vocal warm-ups and even into their daily interaction. As a matter of fact, the entire Department was speaking with an Irish dialect for quite a while.

I also became aware of a sense of melancholy and remembrance that underscored this beautiful play, as well as many other Irish plays. The play is actually a flashback, a memory told by Michael, now an adult, who grew up on the Mundy farm in northwestern Ireland with his mother and her sisters, and his uncle. Joseph Salvi, the actor who played Michael, was gifted with a voice rich in coloration and timbre, and when he spoke even the opening lines of the play, "When I cast my mind back to that summer of 1936 different kinds of memories offer themselves to me" the tone was set for a captivating evening of theater ahead. His pitch was deep and full, yet the sounds were gentle and soft.

While much of the mood was also created by strains of Irish music that underscored a good deal of the play, the truly fine acting created a reality that was exhilarating and poignant. In addition to Joe mentioned above, the cast consisted of Kate Esposito who played Chris, Michael's mother, Melissa Beverage as Maggie, Marit Knollmueller as Agnes, Adele Jerista as Rose, Leah Altman as Kate, Christopher Degnan as Uncle Jack, and Anthony Rossomando as Gerry, Michael's father. The performances were amazingly believable, even though this was the first time on stage for many of them. They appeared mature, composed, and completely at ease. One audience member wrote a letter to the newspaper in which she stated, "I could not believe I was watching 'amateurs' in action. Seldom have I seen a performance that could surpass the quality of this one...The acting...was so well done that it astounded me when I suddenly came to grips with the realization that these performers were high school students, not Broadway professionals." Comments similar to this one had been made frequently throughout Hamden Theater history coupled with the audience's perception that the actors look much older than their respective ages. As I've said before, I credit the superb planning and talented make-up and costume designers for this, but I also like to think that the actors grow into the adult roles through a thorough understanding of the text and character, and that intense rehearsal and discussion aids them in projecting the appearance of an adult in his/her thirties, forties, and sometimes older.

As we rehearsed, *Lughnasa* became increasingly important to the company, and everyone seemed to identify with various aspects of it. As I think back, this sense of importance has distinguished so many, many plays. Here again play selection, one of my foremost areas of concern, becomes crucial. Students in Hamden believed strongly in the plays' respective messages as well as enjoyed the challenges presented by sophisticated pieces of dramatic literature. This has caused them to care about and for the production; to nurture it and give so much of themselves to it.

Lughnasa had a ghost-like quality to it. Part of this is visible in the longing which haunts the play as the sisters, much like those in Chekhov's *The Three Sisters*, dream of a better life. Such dreams are basic to all of us, and the audience was immediately drawn into the drama of this family. Some might consider *Lughnasa* a sad play, and I think the way to direct such a vehicle is to have the actors play "against" the sadness; to find and appreciate the things that bring the characters their fleeting moments of happiness. Working with young people, of course, minimizes the difficulty of this task somewhat, for they have an enthusiasm and joy for their work to begin with. I feel that the sadness comes when the audience sees and realizes the characters' inability to improve their lives and that, in fact, their lives are getting even worse. Understanding that this is a memory play gives further insight into the plight of the Mundy family, for we know from the outset that despite the throbbing beat of Irish dance music coming from an old radio, and despite the spontaneous clasping of hands and dancing and laughter, the dreams of the family will not be fulfilled.

Ort Pengue's set design and student Jennifer Lerner's exquisite lighting design complemented the play's almost expressionistic nature. Ort's set consisted of rough hewn wood, a multitude of antiques, suspended windows, and see-through walls, all in keeping with the "memory" aspect of the play. Some memories are vivid and detailed and some are vague, and the set personified that idea. Ort also costumed the play in earth colors—browns and tans, and a splash of burgundy.

While the characters were caught up in their memories, I must admit that I was too. I could identify with the character, Michael, growing up in a home with his mother and aunts because I too grew up in the same house with my maiden aunt and grandmother. Aunt Gert, much like Michael's Aunt Kate, figured prominently in the play for memories of her flooded my mind as I directed it. She played a large role in my life, and in those years of boyhood. I remember many a time when I plagued her with questions about my homework and about life in general. I also remember a green oriental cabinet in her living room, and when I asked her about the figures carved into it, she told me a fascinating story about Chinese lovers who, forbidden to marry by their parents, had to escape together to find their happiness. This was an aspect of Aunt Gert that escaped many a casual onlooker-her own vivid imagination. It took me several years to realize that Aunt Gert, the matriarch of the family who was always concerned with our proper attire for school-and would often check the way we were dressed when we had to pass her on the way to the front door-had another whole side to her. While she herself dressed impeccably, carried herself in a sophisticated manner, and could be be overbearingly moralistic and judgmental at the same time, she also loved adventure. She loved to talk to me and I loved to listen! She told me stories, complained about the news, and kept me constantly afraid that the State of Israel would collapse. I also remember her taking my cousin Jeff and me to Radio City Music Hall when we were youngsters to see *Around the World in Eighty Days*, and I think she was just as mesmerized by the excitement of it all as we were.

Leah Altman played Kate, and after we were well into rehearsals I told her about my aunt. Leah and I have always shared a very special relationship, and I have always felt that her "Kate" was a major bonding experience for us. We spoke so often, and yet we also allude to the fact that we can communicate so much without words. Several years after *Lughnasa*, when I was selected as the recipient of the first Mary Hunter Wolf Award given by New Haven's Long Wharf Theater, it was Leah who sent a beautiful and tender message that was read to the attendees; a message that made me weep and realize once again how important Leah is to me. Leah went to Ireland the following July (several of the actors have, in fact, gone to Ireland in the years since we did *Lughnasa*) , and she sent me a postcard with a picture that reminded her of the Mundy home. Her joy was evident as she noted the "musical voices" of the people and the "green fields of Donegal." She wrote me a letter after the play in which one statement illustrates, in her simple yet profound manner, her powers of perception and sensitivity: "Actors are sort of schizophrenic...we work with some inexplicable passion...to create someone who becomes so amazingly real and familiar, but who must disappear after only a few performances." After graduating Hamden High School, Leah attended Harvard where she directed Tony Kushner's *Angels in America*, and is, at the moment of this writing, in Scotland where she is directing a production of Shakespeare's *Titus Andronicus*. Her talents are obvious.

At one point in the play, Kate returns home from the village of Ballybeg with a toy top for her nephew, Michael. While she addresses the child, she takes off her hat and places it on a stone wall next to her. I directed the adult Michael to move behind Kate, pick up her hat, and bring it to his face. And then, with closed eyes, he inhaled the memories of his Aunt Kate as she was in his childhood. I think I never missed my own aunt more than when Michael performed that action.

Another special aspect of *Lughnasa* was the choreography created by Maury Rosenberg for the one dance called for in the text. It started off slowly and even a bit intentionally clumsy, but then built into a fevered pitch, with each character independently, and yet as a group, drawn into the strong Irish rhythms of the music. It had a frantic, excited, haunted quality to it, with the hard pounding of the actors' shoes on the wooden floor, the vocal shouts by the characters throughout, and the abrupt ending of the dance suddenly exposing the weeping and tears of the character/actors. This sudden end and the subsequent absolute silence and stillness on stage created an eerie and very emotional moment.

Plays have what directors call a "spine" or unifying element which runs throughout the production. *Lughnasa*'s spine was an unseen force, much like a ghost, that wove the scenes, the characters, and even the technical aspects of the play together. Michael's final monologue best describes this:

"...it drifts in from somewhere far away-a mirage of sound-a dream music that is both heard and imagined...a sound so alluring and so mesmeric that the afternoon is bewitched, maybe haunted, by it. And what is so strange about that memory is that everybody seems to be floating on those sweet sounds, moving rhythmically, languorously, in complete isolation; responding more to the mood of the music than to its beat. When I remember it, I think of it as dancing. Dancing with eyes half closed because to open them would break the spell. Dancing as if language had surrendered to movement-as if this ritual, this wordless ceremony, was now the way to speak, to whisper private and sacred things, to be in touch with some otherness..."

I think the entire production was touched by that "otherness"-a sense that we were working on something very special indeed; something which made vulnerable the sacred areas of our own lives. When Joe Salvi delivered this final speech at the State Drama Festival, he underwent a very emotional experience. He tried to find the words to describe what happened to him on stage that day. He said that he was totally immersed in the emotion; that he could not hear the soft Irish music that underscored his speech, but instead could hear a gentle wind blowing throughout the stage. He felt transported to a different time and place, and yet very alert and aware of his surroundings. I could tell by his face and his eyes that he had undergone some awesome and all-too-rare experience. Obviously he moved the audience as well, for there was complete silence at the end of the production, save for the quiet weeping throughout the theater.

We once again were able to represent Connecticut at the New England Drama Festival that year. *Lughnasa* was exceptionally-well received. There was always something special about performing at the New England Festival. Perhaps it had to do with meeting students and teachers from throughout the region who were so devoted to the Theater. Perhaps it had to with the pride of representing one's State. After our performance I noticed several officers of the New England Drama Council sitting together in the audience. As we were striking our set and the audience was filing out, the group approached me. I remember that they seemed quite moved. One spoke for the group, commenting that Hamden provides the reason that so many people attend the Festival; that it provides a learning experience for everyone veiled within an intelligent, polished, and totally moving performance. I was humbled by the comments. I never seem to know what to say or how to respond to praise, except to automatically give the credit to the students who so rightfully deserve it. This definitely was the case for this special production.

After the production I received an outpouring of letters from students in the company and even from their parents. Their words were effusive with thanks-thanks for many things (one girl even thanked me for my faith in "underachievers"), but central among them was their appreciation for believing in them. I find this to be so important for young people-for people of all ages, in fact. We all need someone who has faith in us, in our ability to succeed. Unfortunately we don't often get that positive reinforcement. I believe that every person has something truly special that he or she can offer, making that person unique. It is important for teachers to not only make the student aware of it, but to encourage him to use it. This fosters a positive sense of self; it makes a person think better of himself. This one simple thing can change the whole educational and personal world of a human being. I believe that all teachers should appreciate their students and the wonderful qualities they possess. Understanding this makes me so aware of the important role we play and the responsibility we face in helping young people grow.

One would hardly think of *Camille* as the typical high school play, and our production of it in 1995 may have been one of those high school premiers I spoke of earlier. Based on the novel by Alexandre Dumas, the son of the writer who penned *The Three Musketeers, Camille* is a story of intrigue, mystery, and secrecy; one that unravels theatrically before an audience in a gripping and chilling manner. There are at least three versions of this play that I know of, but the one I liked best was that by the English playwright, Pam Gems. Gems has a gift for capturing the story and telling it with suspense and style. Her use of language is often simple, yet poetic and emotional.

When the two lovers first meet, Armand observes that Marguerite is carrying camelias which prompts the following exchange. Note the brevity of the lines, yet the poetic rhythm they create. More importantly, even with this brevity Gems speaks volumes about Marguerite's playfulness, independence, and hope.

Armand: Why camelias?

Marguerite: Why not?

Armand: They have no scent.

Marguerite: Ah, but you see, I'm an optimist.

Later on in the play they realize that they are drawn together despite the fact that they come from different worlds.

Marguerite: Could it be possible? A life together?

Armand: Why not?

Marguerite: A dream...

Armand: No...real.

Marguerite: Oh my love...

Armand: What else is it all for?

Marguerite: My love...

Armand: What else?

I must admit that selecting *Camille* was not an easy decision. It is a mature play and deals with mature subject matter. Many of the characters, indeed the female protagonist herself, is a courtesan. But there were so many positive aspects to this play. Its tragic and time-honored story is nothing less than compelling. It is more than a love story, although it certainly endures as one of literature's most dramatic. Amidst the glamor of 1866 Paris with its grand opera houses and its fondness for finery in clothing and customs, we are drawn into the intimate lives of two people who defy the odds and seek to control their own destiny; who find and come to cherish the real values of a simple and honest life. Armand, the central male character of the story, says, "Our aim must be to find our true work-to live, to support our children...to read, to think...and to be as clear as we can." Perhaps it is human nature to root for the underdog, and perhaps that is exactly why we become so passionately involved in their lives. We want things to work out for Marguerite Gautier and Armand Duval.

Camille is a "large" play. By that I mean that it deals with major passions in the unbridled, unrestricted style of so much of our classical dramatic literature. And yet at the root of these emotions are the sensitivities, subtleties, and vulnerabilities that unite all human beings. They make us, as audience members, empathize with the feelings of the characters, providing a kind of emotional catharsis. Here again we use the theater to continually evaluate and hopefully improve our own place in society.

While most directors in educational theater anxiously await the next group of talented students, we in Hamden have fortunately benefited from a strong training program that has prevented us from depleting the numbers and talents of each year's graduating class. The ranks of talented and mature students continued to swell in 1995, opening up the doors of possibility as far as play choices were concerned. Many in the *Camille* company had been involved with *Dancing at Lughnasa* the year before, and since that play itself was so advanced, I needed to find a vehicle that would be equally as challenging. An added concern was that the department was so large, and with a relatively small cast in *Lughnasa*, I had to find a play that would employ a large group of people.

I used twenty-five people in *Camille*. The Mundy sisters of *Lughnasa* were all back with the exception of Marit Knollmueller who graduated the previous June. There was also Joseph Salvi who, after his remarkable "Michael" was ready for a substantial role to bring his career at Hamden High School to a close. Melissa Beverage played Marguerite beautifully and with great class, and Christopher Degnan played Armand's father, Marquis de Saint-Brieux. Chris had been our resident technical genius for so long, but had become very interested in acting recently. He played a fine "Father Jack" in *Lughnasa*. His progress was excellent, and his height and good looks gave him a commanding appearance on stage. And there were others who excelled as actors in this senior class: Kristy Merola, Jonas Sansone, Adam Chorney, Marissa Gandelman, and David Fischer. There were also underclassmen who excelled in acting classes and were eager to learn from a Mainstage production. They were bright, insightful, and ready for a script with texture and meaning. The technical staff also was experienced and benefited from the talents of Michael Epstein, Mark Villani, Rebecca Wright, Jaime Grande, Marla Knebl, Andrew Rae, and the wonderful lighting design work of Lynn Provost. This was the ideal group with which to discover the depths and beauty of Pam Gems' sophisticated play.

As I studied the text, I decided I wanted a feeling of grandeur. I therefore placed the action in 1866 although the text calls for it to occur in the 1840's. This may seem like a trivial adjustment, but I found that the women's costumes of 1866 were more elegant than even twenty years before. They were large and hooped, necessitating a grandeur of movement. The men were sophisticated in their black tails and frocks.

Upon my first contact with the script, my first abstract impressions brought visions of rich, exquisite tapestries of roses and pinks and burgundies, colors often associated with elegance and wealth. As a director, I was making a mental connection with the grand and sweeping qualities of the play; with its luxury and depth. These feelings eventually found expression in the costume design where fabrics fell dramatically in sweeping lines, in the set and lighting, and even in the way the actors moved in their Parisian finery. Here the graceful lines were important enough to me to have slight trains added to the opulent dresses in order to achieve the splendor of my first impressions. Even during the intimate moments between the play's two main characters, Marguerite Gautier and Armand Duval, the importance of line was reinforced in the drape of the bed curtains, the covering of the dressing table, or the train of Marguerite's nightgown. I felt that these aspects of the production would not only be visually stimulating for the audience, but would produce an emotional effect as well. I knew that much of the direction of this play would entail teaching the style of the period, and instructing the actors how to wear and move appropriately in the costumes, the women in their elegant gowns and the men in smart black tails and white opera gloves. I also worked with the actors' vocal qualities which I hoped would complement the overall image of the play's intensity and fullness.

The company wanted to continue the tradition of participating in the Drama Festival, but when I pursued the royalties for our sixty-minute Festival version, Samuel French Inc., the play publishers, denied my request. You may recall this happening twice before. I know that cuttings of many plays are forbidden for drama festivals, as are performances of selected scenes. After seeing many of these, I really can't blame the publishers or the playwrights they represent. Many of the cuttings are distorted and done with little or no experience in this area. How could I manage to convince the publishing company that I would treat the script with dignity and respect, and that I would honor the intention of the playwright? How could I get them to at least listen to me? I knew that the Long Wharf Theater had done the play a few years previous, so I began my efforts to obtain the royalties by writing to Arvin Brown, the Artistic Director of the Long Wharf Theater. I prayed that he might have heard of Hamden's pursuit of quality in theater education and might be inclined to support our cause. Not long after I received a lovely letter from Janice Muirhead, the Artistic Administrator of Long Wharf. She assured me that Mr. Brown was well aware of Hamden Theater, and she phoned Samuel French in an attempt to procure the royalties for me. I was very touched by her kindness and her efforts. However, a great deal of time had passed, and the publishing company hadn't made a decision.

It was by chance that I mentioned my problem to Anthony Mark Watts, my former theater teacher and director at Southern Connecticut State University. Mark hailed from England, the home of Pam Gems, and thought that he might know Ms. Gems' agent. Within a few days he supplied me with the agent's name. I wrote to him and received a letter in which Ms. Gems gave us the royalties and extended her best wishes for the full production and the Festival. I was excited to find her to be very caring and understanding, and It was comforting to know that a professional playwright was supportive of the efforts of young people.

The play was very successful at the Drama Festival, winning Hamden it's eighth consecutive "Outstanding Production" Award. Also, the company won the "Ensemble" Award as well as one for Theatrical Excellence. Joe and Melissa won their second consecutive Outstanding Actor and Actress Award respectively, and I was so happy for Kate Esposito who also won an Outstanding Actress Award for her role as Marguerite's friend, Sophie de Lyonne. Leah Altman won an "All-Connecticut Cast" Award to add to her already impressive list of awards, and Christopher Degnan was also honored with the "All-Connecticut Cast" Award for is portrayal of Armand's father.

Chris was excellent throughout the entire play, but he was particularly effective in the scene at the country estate where Marguerite and Armand have stolen to escape the pressures on their forbidden relationship. The Marquis reduces Marguerite to tears as he threatens to use his influence to take her young son from her unless she disassociates herself with Armand, thereby saving the Marquis' family honor. Chris' Marquis was a tower of cunning cruelty. He taught us all a great lesson in acting: that an actor can control through composure and subtlety and needn't resort to shouting and histrionics. He, without a doubt, deserved that acting award.

Camille won great accolades from the audience and the community. My initial fears of selecting this play seemed so distant now, although I'm sure this was due to the mature manner in which the company handled the material. I remember the particularly challenging staging of the love scenes between Marguerite and Armand. There is a series of short intimate vignettes which take place in Marguerite's bedroom. I tried to emphasize the humanity of the text as two people not only make love, but become good friends and find that they can indeed overcome the severe class restrictions of Parisian society. As the scenes were connected by blackouts, I worked incessantly to time those with the actions of the actors, so that the most intimate moments were left to the audience's imagination. This had an exciting and even titillating effect on the audience, and the blackouts were filled with a palpable silence.

The beginning of this sequence contains no words, but only the movement of Marguerite to Armand. They remain facing each other, she lets her hair down, and he effortlessly removes her night jacket. I remember finding absolutely perfect music to delicately and sensuously underscore this moment, and I envisioned Marguerite's night jacket floating to the floor in the rhythm of the music. Little did I know how difficult it would be to attain that effect. Ort built the long, flowing penoir, out of a sheer, lightweight material called voile, and had to wash it numerous times to make it even lighter. Actually, I think he boiled it, giving rise to his oft repeated saying, "Boil the voile." After many washings and alterations, we attained our sought-after effect. I am reminded of that task many times by Ort-who still scowls at the thought of it-but the effect of the penoir sailing weightlessly to the ground at that intimate moment, when both actors were bathed in a soft amber light, was worth every bit of hard work. The audience barely breathed.

I must say that the audience was mesmerized as well by Marguerite's first entrance in the play. She entered the lobby of the Grand Opera, and we wanted her to immediately capture the attention of the audience. For this purpose, Ort designed the most beautiful dress, and we traveled to many fabric stores to find the right material with which to build it. We finally found a shimmering off-white and gold fabric in a shop in Bridgeport. The dress was exquisite, and an audible gasp could be heard from the audience as Marguerite entered.

This attention to detail has always been a trademark of Hamden Theater, both on the stage and off. I feel this separates the "good" theater programs from the truly fine, artistic ones. Programs need to produce plays that help young people grow by working harder; by going the extra distance in their attempt to achieve the very best results. My acting teacher, the late Constance Welch, used to say, "You have to stand on your toes to see far," and I try to instill this same quest for the highest standards in my students.

I received many letters from audience members after *Camille*. One such letter came from a man who had his own production company in New York in which he said, "The level of commitment, truth and integrity that your students brought to this production made every moment, action, word, silence, breath so utterly 'real,' I found I had no choice but submit to the world you so eloquently created." And yet another wrote, "As I watched *Camille* I know I was completely unaware of my own body! Did I even breathe? My soul was fed by its beauty and grace. I can only add that I felt awe...Every gesture, every move.... Thank you for the gift you gave us with this play."

The production also garnered a letter from Connecticut Governor John Rowland. He commended Hamden High School for its seventeenth Outstanding Production Award at the State Festival and its eighth in a row. He also wrote, "Hamden High School's Mainstage Ensemble, under your expert directorship, presents outstanding theatrical productions to residents of Hamden and other communities in Connecticut. Your talents and efforts make your community proud and make your State proud as well." Needless to say, the students and the school were excited to receive the Governor's letter. It's not that often that the highest ranking official in the State recognizes a school's theater group. I feel they were deserving of the honor for they worked so very hard and brought pleasure to so many. They are part of a long tradition of wonderful people, both before and after them, who I like to think have made a difference in the lives of those who witness their efforts.

As 1996 approached I was feeling a restlessness, a longing to add a new and fresh perspective to what had become very familiar and comfortable for me. While appreciating all that had gone before, I felt overwhelmed by the recognition of just how vast this theater umbrella is, and the excitement of bringing something new and different to the stage filled me with an anxiety that was at once disquieting and compelling. Even as life's mysteries continued to unfold, I was swept up in a renewed passion and vigor to capture them and to give them a tangible expression before an audience. I began to feel a strong need to take more risks, to expand, to grow in my attempts to bring the best to my students and to the community, and also to respond to this tidal wave of energy within me. A new voice was growing inside, and I felt good about that.

Antigone is a classic story, but I wanted to give it a fresh and contemporary feel. I took this same approach to *A Midsummer Night's Dream* in 1999, and, of course, the very selection of Eric Overmyer's *On the Verge, or the Geography of Yearning* as my first play in our new theater complex in 1998 signaled the inclusion of more modern, experimental, and even avante-garde works into an already rich body of theatrical productions.

Antigone was an excellent vehicle with which to explore a new path, for Sophocles wrote it in Fifth Century B.C. Athens, a time and place where a great deal of change was occurring. It was an age of enlightenment, one with many playwrights and philosophers. Now the old world was dying out and the new one was yet to be born. Sophocles, like others of his day, struggled with major issues of the civilized world, and his ideas provided excellent material for discussion among my students and ultimately for performance.

Briefly, the plot illustrates the clash between Antigone's sense of morality and Creon's sense of political necessity. She refuses to follow her Uncle Creon's order not to bury her brother, Polynices, a rebel who led the Argive army in an attempt to conquer Thebes. Polynices' corpse lying on the battlefield is a symbol of both Thebes' victory and Polynices' humiliation. Antigone is arrested when she attempts to bury her brother, but

Creon, for various reasons, offers to excuse and spare Antigone's life if she will promise not to attempt it again. She, however, refuses to obey Creon's order, resulting in her death and the suicide of Haemon, Creon's son and Antigone's lover.

While the story of *Antigone* is timeless and well-known, the major question that arises concerning this play is, "Who is right, Antigone or Creon?" This question ultimately enters into the interpretation, directing, and acting of the piece as well. The actions of Creon, the character often considered the antagonist, are actually justifiable when we consider the fact that Polynices was a traitor. Prior to the events of this play, an agreement was made that Antigone's brothers, Polynices and Eteocles, would take turns ruling Thebes, and when Eteocles would not honor it, Polynices led the Argive army to plunder the city. The Argives were cruel and known for killing men and selling women and children. One can only imagine the chaos in Thebes if Polynices were successful.

Another important point to consider is the Greek concept of "the City." It was extremely important to them as a source of unity and sustenance, a much more intense relationship than ours today, and Creon's decision to let Polynices' body rot was a purposeful demonstration that traitors to the City would not be tolerated.

Who, then, is the audience to support in this battle between morality and the law? And who is the tragic hero of the play? Antigone is, by all standards, an incredible person. She has a fierce sense of independence and is more than willing to take action. She is willing to fight against the power of the State, feeling that she is correct as far as morality is concerned. On a higher plane, Antigone is willing to go to the limits for humanity. She, very much like John Proctor in *The Crucible*, has those rare qualities which permit her and others like her to show the rest of us what is possible in the name of civilization. These people illustrate the breadth of human potential. Antigone has the strength of her convictions and is willing to die for her beliefs.

The problem is that Polynices was a traitor, and therein lies the conflict. It is not surprising that judges and lawyers may very well feel that Creon is the tragic hero, one former judge believing that there is no such thing as the "natural" law Antigone vehemently defends; that, in fact, all laws are man-made and must be upheld in a civilized society.

Jean Anouilh wrote his version of *Antigone* during the Nazi occupation of Paris in 1943, a time of censorship. The new government permitted no new plays to be performed, but did allow productions of traditional plays and/or translations of the classics. Anouilh therefore decided to translate Sophocles' play, posing a theme that would encourage the French to resist the Nazi tyranny. In his play he asked his countrymen to closely examine the "happiness" promised by the new Nazi government; one that could only be enjoyed if the government were not questioned.

There is no doubt that Anouilh's *Antigone* was one of my favorite plays and one I had wanted to direct for quite a while. However, I had some doubts as to the "theatricality" of the play based on some productions of it I had seen in the past. *Antigone* is a play of ideas, and it can be a very "talky" play if great care is not taken to introduce a strong visual component. I remember that a friend in another school district had directed it many years before and entered it in that year's drama festival where it placed last. She was distraught, especially since she had devoted herself to the play, and asked me why I thought it placed so poorly. That question had bothered me for years. I felt that the acting was fine, as were the technical components.

My thoughts about this situation led me to a new definition for "conflict," or perhaps an amended one. Long defined as the opposition of forces, I began to think that the definition needed to include *the possibility of one side to control the other*. Much of play is filled with the arguments of Antigone versus those of Creon, and neither one seems vulnerable to the other. My late acting teacher, Constance Welch, often spoke of the "chink in the armor," or the vulnerable spot of a character where he or she was open to the control or influence of others. Could this have been the problem with my friend's production? I felt elated at this discovery. There *must* be something, some way that each of the major characters can sway the other to his/her way of thinking. This vulnerability would then heighten the suspense for the audience as well as add a certain *humanity* to the characters that was not there in that long ago drama festival production. We immediately set out to find this vulnerability in our current production. It became very important to us, and I feel that it added great truth to the characterizations and to the production as a whole.

While remaining truthful to the playwright and his theme will always be utmost in any production I direct, I wanted the outward appearance of this play to be very contemporary. I decided upon a kind of look reminiscent of the Balkans, an unsettled area of the world that seems to be a perpetual battle zone. I felt that this would be ideal for a play dealing with universal questions that stem from war. Creon's soldiers were menacing, dressed in rag-tag army fatigues, bandanas, t-shirts, and wielding monstrous guns. Antigone's first appearance, as the Chorus spoke the opening lines of the play, saw her in a long army coat, nearly to the ground, standing three-quarter back in a shaft of light. Creon was in a specially designed uniform of gray with medals meticulously pinned to his chest.

The set included a large raked platform center stage where much of the action was played. Its rough surface, comprised of a host of materials ranging from stiff wire netting to corrugated aluminum was made to look like twisted sheets of metal, stone, and bronze- the aftermath of the carnage which had destroyed the city. The rake itself provided a flavor of the classic theater, yet its surface and the cold, stark black scaffolding which surrounded it created an eery and forbidden sense of a Twentieth Century war-torn environment. At points in the play soldiers hoisted upon the scaffolding blood-red banners with large, portraits of Creon's face illustrated in a slightly modern style. In addition, the use of a light stage smoke or mist often filled the stage, giving the feeling of a constant battle in some part of the city.

I divided the Chorus' part into roles for three actors, two men and one woman. Their costumes included black collarless shirts, black pants, and black-on-black textured vests. The color obviously personified that of tragedy, but the style of the clothing lent a modern feel. I also cast actors with strong vocal qualities in these roles. I was fortunate to have Patrick Degnan (a brother of Christopher Degnan, the actor whose own vocal qualities enhanced *Camille*) and Adele Jerista in two of the roles. Both were accomplished actors and would play the lead roles in *Summer and Smoke*, our final production in the then-current Hamden High School Theater the following year. The third actor was George Ford who had appeared in *Camille*, had a strong and unique voice of his own, and worked well with Patrick and Adele. The three of them were the anchors of this production due in part to the ever and omnipresent aspect of the role itself, and also because they were always focused, consistent, and part of the action.

There are many things that made *Antigone* an exceptional and memorable production. This was a cast that worked well together, and it won that coveted and hard-to-attain "Ensemble Award" at the Drama Festival that year. Kate Esposito, by now one of Hamden's finest actors as proven by her work in *Dancing at Lughnasa, Camille,* and numerous stunning scenes in acting classes, was truly brilliant as Antigone. While Kate is smaller physically, she makes up for it with a strong, resonant, and melodic voice and a physical self-confidence that forces the audience to pay attention to her. Her face is expressive, and her eyes become the avenue of her subtext and emotion. There were so many parts of her performance that were riveting, including her major confrontation scene with Creon (Joshua Rubin), and her touching dictation of a letter to her lover, Haemon, while she is in jail. Kate's acting has depth, and she is able to create well-rounded, truthful characters.

Joshua Rubin's performance as Creon was extremely effective. Josh and his family moved to this part of the country from the Midwest, specifically selecting Hamden because of its Theater Program. Josh had done theater work in his previous schools, but he told me that the scope of the Hamden program and its discipline forced him to relearn and rediscover much of the work he had done so far. It was wonderful to witness Josh's growth as Creon. He is an intellect and as such enjoyed the many discussions about the political and social ramifications of the play. Well before I cast him, I remember Josh sitting in many classes initiating discussions by asking insightful questions or making astute observations. He often went out on a limb to defend his point of view, even when it was unpopular. His strength and steadfast convictions were useful qualities for the Creon he was soon to create. He also looked the part, sporting a neatly trimmed beard and wearing the sleek modern suit built especially for him. However, what I was most proud of was Josh's perseverance. He worked hard on this role, and it grew steadily until his performance was superb.

Ingrid Nelson played Antigone's sister, Ismene, and Daniel Mendel played Haemon, Antigone's lover and Creon's son. Both Ingrid and Dan provided the "softness" and tenderness to balance the passionate Antigone-Creon confrontations. Ingrid was so believable in her role, imbuing it with a love for her sister that seemed to burst from her heart. She won an award for her performance, and eventually went on to Carnegie-Mellon University in Pittsburgh where she majored in acting. Dan's Haemon was a real step forward for him in his acting training. He was able to play the sensitive love he felt for Antigone while still showing intense anger at Creon for the latter's decision to have Antigone killed. Dan took his acting so seriously from the moment he entered Hamden High School. He once told me that his daily three-hour rehearsals were the happiest times of his school days.

The play also benefited from Jessica Manzi's portrayal of Antigone's Nurse. She was affectionate, sensitive, and real, and added a warmth that was needed in the play. Daniel Kolodny played Jonas, the "first soldier" and also showed remarkable progress in his acting development. Another serious acting student, Dan would go on to Syracuse University.

While we were rehearsing the play, a terrible event occurred. The mother of one of our actors, Kristy Merola, was becoming increasingly ill. She was now in the final stages of her battle with cancer, and we didn't know if Kristy, who played a soldier and delivered a splendid speech near the play's end telling of the deaths of Antigone and Haemon, would be able to perform. As it turned out, Kristy acted in the Festival version of the play, but was not able to perform in the full version which followed the former by approximately a month. Michael Mattie understudied the role and performed it with great clarity and emotion while the smoke of battle swirled at his feet. That speech, as performed by both Kristy and Michael, was a high point of this production. The illness and death of Mrs. Merola was very real and very tragic. And while we did our best to support Kristy, there was no doubt that the enormity of what had happened affected our production as well. It gave the students a closer, more tangible look at life and death and made that aspect of the play more poignant and realistic.

This began a new phase in Kristy's life. Being left alone at such a young age-Kristy's father had died some years before-was difficult at best. I've always admired Kristy's courage in those days, continuing her education and focusing on the future despite the tragedy that had just befallen her. But Kristy always was an exceptional human being; one that I admired and respected and loved very much. I felt very close to her and probably would have been paralyzed with the sadness of those times-in fact, we all would have been-if it weren't for Kristy's courage and composure. It is always a source of the deepest fulfillment and respect for life to learn from one's students. Kristy was a wonderful teacher.

The following summer Kristy joined the Foote Summer Theater program. This was actually quite beneficial for her as it kept her busy doing her favorite thing, acting, while she continued to cope with her mother's death. I had chosen to direct *The Secret Garden*, a favorite of mine, with its unique combination of childlike fantasy and adventure, and the dark secrets looming around the characters dwelling in Archibald Craven's Yorkshire estate. Set Designer, Frank Alberino, and I had been talking prior to the play about the themes and concepts of the play, and we both came across one line which seemed to provide a central image for the "look" of the production. Mary Lennox, the eleven year old orphan who returns from India to live with her uncle Archibald, says, "It is the most forgotten place I've ever seen. With loose gray branches looped all around the tress like ropes or snakes, and dead roots and leaves all tangled up on the ground. So still and cold." Frank and I determined this to be the "spine" of the play, and we incorporated it not only in the set design (Frank created walls that could become transparent with black scrim, within which were rotting branches as if they were actually growing into and suffocating the large mansion), but in the attitudes of many of the characters in the play as well.

However, I personally believe the story is one of rejuvenation, for it is filled with hope and magic as well as a haunted estate filled with ghosts, longings for the past, and a certain sense of despair. It might be easy to surrender to the negative forces that swirl around our lives, but our balance and ultimately our victory come through finding the courage and optimism best described in the play as "wick;" that secret stream of life inside things that appear to be dead and decaying. The character, Dickon, says, "...the strongest roses will fair thrive on bein' neglected if the soil is rich enough. They'll run wild, and spread and spread til they're a wonder."

I feel that *The Secret Garden* celebrates the resiliency of our remarkable human spirit. For this reason, I was very pleased that Kristy was a member of the ensemble. I cast her as Lily, Mary's deceased aunt who returns to comfort both her morose husband, Archibald, and reunite him with Colin, the son he has neglected. The play was poignant and terribly moving, and the audience was swept away by Kristy's superb acting and haunting singing. For those of us who knew of the events in Kristy's life, her singing of "Come to My Garden"-a song meant to comfort her young son, Colin,-and her duet with Archibald, "How Could I Know," for very much the same reason, were spine-tingling experiences. Kristy sang and acted them from her heart, my directing and blocking providing only a shell which she filled with her own longing and spirit. She performed with such fragile, sensitive beauty that those moments were almost epiphany-like. There was not a dry eye in the audience. Perhaps Kristy's exploration of this role, the deceased mother and wife, also helped her come to terms, at least in part, with the passing of her own mother. While our Theater can teach and inform and entertain and enlighten, it can have ironic healing powers as well. One night during the play's intermission, an audience member, the mother of one of the cast members, came up to me and slipped me a note telling me that she was sure I cast Kristy in this role for that very reason. If that were true, some might consider it a terrible risk, but knowing Kristy as I do, I knew she would find comfort in this part and also in this play about rebirth.

Another element of *Antigone* that I found most positive was having Michael Lerner return to Hamden High School. As a student here he had performed so superbly in such plays as *The Elephant Man, Ah, Wilderness!* and *Richard III* and undoubtedly reached a peak with his extraordinary performance in *Children of a Lesser God*. Michael was now a professional actor residing in New York and had experience in stage combat among other theater skills. I told Michael that I wanted a very visual opening to this play and suggested that he choreograph the battle between the armies of Polynices and Eteocles described by the Chorus. Michael worked beautifully and artistically with the students, creating a slow-motion battle infused with gruesome but realistic wartime combat, and also with surprises -such as pulling the hat off a soldier and discovering that the soldier was a woman-that were intriguing, thrilling, and horrifying. Michael's discipline and quest for perfection added immeasurably to the production. It was also wonderful to work with him again, as it always is when Hamden Theater graduates come home to work with their younger "siblings."

Another bright spot of the *Antigone* experience was a program I arranged where area high schools could come to Hamden to view the one-hour Festival version of the play, followed by discussion groups lead by teachers from the various schools. Our new principal, Richard Nabel, participated as a discussion leader and told me how much he enjoyed himself. It felt good to have his support for the project, and over the following years Dick proved to be a true advocate of the Theater program. Our students felt ecstatic as hundreds of their colleagues from the greater New Haven area participated in the program and discussed the play and the performance. The day was filled with excellent discourse, all of which added validity to the importance of the play's theme. There is nothing quite like witnessing the coming together of students from many schools as they share ideas and enjoy the excitement of learning. It was the first time that I had ventured in such a direction and was lucky to have Beverly Canell, our Director of Foreign Languages and a supporter of Hamden Theater for many years, who was instrumental in designing and organizing the day. Bev had been a chaperone for many Drama Festival excursions. She was always exceptionally friendly and organized, and I think she provided a sense of order and calm that the students found very comforting.

The *Antigone* experience was one filled with a great deal of learning. It was an emotional time, one in which we all felt strongly united as we faced the death of a classmate's parent, the thrill of yet another successful Drama Festival which brought Hamden it's ninth consecutive Outstanding Production Award and its eighteenth in twenty years of participation, and a trip to the New England Drama Festival. I also felt that the meaning of this play was especially important. Near the end of the play the Chorus says, "Now and again other Antigones have arisen. Their cause is always the same-a passionate belief that moral law exists and a passionate regard for the sanctity of human dignity." These words are very important to me as a teacher and as a human being. I like to believe in the arrival of new Antigones; people who will stir us up and make us the active, thinking people we should be. Then we will be able to truly value human life and those universal principles which defy all kinds of barriers-race, religion, gender, sexual orientation, ethnic and socioeconomic differences-and bring us together as one living, breathing people.

The two plays that followed *Antigone* were milestones in their own way. Our 1997 production, Tennessee Williams' *Summer and Smoke*, would be the last ever on the "old" Hamden High School stage. The school was undergoing a forty million dollar renovation, part of which was a new theater complex. In 1998 we would present Eric Overmyer's *On the Verge, or the Geography of Yearning*, a new and exciting kind of play which graced the new Hamden Theater. As we faced the new millennium, a whole new Hamden Theater would enable us to stretch even further.

Chapter Three

Endings and Beginnings

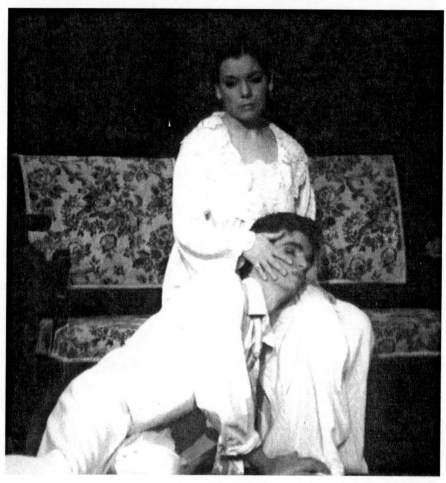
Summer and Smoke, 1997

"When I was seventeen and eighteen my life was so emotionally wrought and stilted that I didn't think I could experience anything more emotionally; that at eighteen life could hold no more surprises for me. Then something happened in rehearsal that made me realize that the emotional traumas I was experiencing were minimal compared to those of the characters I was playing. That freed me to experience my life. Now I like being twenty-three. I like acting my age. I like the process of growing up because it is the process that will some day determine the product."

Joseph

"More than anything I'm blessed to have my cherished little family—a husband more grounded, patient, and devoted than his whimsical wife probably deserves, a daughter who came into this world like a revelation, and a wee baby in my belly who I know little about as yet except that he or she has a kick like a Mexican chillipepper. These are the important things. These are the things which I cherish...And in my thirty years of preparation for these joys, I count my years under your watchful eye as having been particularly instrumental. I will always be grateful for what you taught me as an actress. But little did I know back then that you were laying the groundwork for an ongoing education in how to love profoundly, how to be the wife and mother I wanted to be. I was always arrogant enough to think being a 'great actress' or a 'great academic' would be well within my star. You began to teach me some of the things I needed to know to be a great wife, mother, confidante, and companion, and for that I am truly indebted, because back in those tumultuous years, those were the talents which I secretly held in doubt."

Sarah

The renovation of Hamden High School began during the 1996-97 school year. It seemed strange that this bulwark of Dixwell Avenue was being radically changed. For so many years it sat undaunted by the heavy traffic, blaring horns, and sirens of emergency vehicles fleeting past its front facade, serving as a kind of strong yet gentle, highly respected neighbor. It was a reminder also of Hamden's past, having been built amidst the apple orchards of a rural New Haven suburb; an educational mecca far out in the country that could only be reached by a trolley ride from the bustling city.

There was no doubt that the school was in dire need of repair and updating, but it had been such a centerpiece in Hamden history and played such a large role in the community for so long that it seemed as if every group in town wanted to preserve some part of it. Eventually the front facade, the cupola which sat proudly atop the building, and the main lobby-this last containing beautiful hand-painted murals of Hamden's early days including local resident Eli Whitney's cotton gin-were declared national historic landmarks. The school suddenly became the home of hundreds of construction workers and their machinery, and all kinds of strange industrial sounds bombarded our senses on a daily basis. I often wondered how we would get through this difficult time and still achieve the high academic standards we continually pursued. We had no choice but to incorporate the renovation into our daily existence—and I don't mean that to sound negative. There were many positive aspects of the work as well. Often on-site renovation personnel would visit classes as lecturers; they would present practical problems for math and science classes to solve; they integrated themselves into the school population by attending school functions; and their very presence and magnitude of their goal taught us great lessons in flexibility. Construction workers, electricians, plumbers, and the entire supporting cast became a regular sight, and soon they blended into the ranks without a second thought as we all went our individual ways.

The spring of that year would bring with it the final production in the school's theater-one that had been used for some sixty-seven years. When it first opened, the school's theater was nothing less than a shining jewel. It had a large balcony, sat over a thousand, and was decorated with hand-carved filigree, pillars running along the outer walls, and had a massive stage with a full fly system. It was, without a doubt, one of, if not the most striking and technologically efficient theaters in the State at the time.

It was difficult to choose a play that would end this phase in the development of Hamden Theater. The play would have to be a beautifully written dramatic piece, offering great opportunity for many students. My mind and heart turned to Tennessee Williams' *Summer and Smoke*. Whenever I taught this play in my Literature of the Theater class it generated a great deal of emotion and discussion and was clearly a favorite of the students. They often asked me if we could present it. It had long been a favorite of mine as well, with its poignant moments and excellent characterizations, its sense of intrigue, and the silent, submerged emotions experienced by the characters. It is a fragile and haunting love story between two people from opposite worlds. Miss Alma is a minister's daughter; she is known to be rather stand-offish and proper. Her neighbor, John Buchanan, is the son of a doctor and a wild character who enjoys women and drinking. And yet, as vastly different as their respective worlds may be, these two characters are drawn to each other. Tennessee Williams was a poet well before his mother, Edwina Dakin Williams, suggested that her pale and somewhat sickly son venture forth into the world of playwriting. That suggestion began one of the most prolific playwriting careers in American literature, and we, as the beneficiaries of his poetic genius, have inherited a canon of plays in which this most autobiographical of American playwrights bares his soul through language which is at once elaborate and metaphorical, musical and symbolic. I am always excited when I witness students' enthusiasm with language.

To begin my studies, I read a new book by Lyle Leverich, *Tom, the Unknown Tennessee Williams* which one of my students purchased for me and even had Mr. Leverich autograph. The book was voluminous, but I enjoyed it so much, learning about the playwright's early life, his relationships to his family members, and his struggles as a novice writer. It certainly helped me understand the subtext of *Summer and Smoke*.

When I announced the play, the general feeling among the students was one of great excitement. Students who hadn't read it in the Literature class were swept up in the enthusiasm of those who had, and they quickly found a copy to read. The training program, which had been in place for many years by now, enabled me to find a superb cast.

Adele Jerista captured the role of Miss Alma, a role closely patterned on the life of Williams' mother. I cast Patrick Degnan as John Buchanan, Alma's next door neighbor and life-long love interest. Pat had done much of his work in the technical end of theater, helping to design sets and often serving as Master Carpenter. I admired his desire to act, and he set out to do this in much the same way he performed his technical responsibilities-with order and logic and a calmness that enabled him to handle those "large" moments on stage. It was interesting to me that this desire to act after working almost exclusively in technical theater was something Patrick's older brother, Christopher, experienced as well. Such was the case also for Lynnette Provost, a wonderfully talented lighting designer, who auditioned for and was cast as Alma's senile mother, Mrs. Winemiller.

Fortunately, secondary school provides the opportunity for students to experience the various components of educational theater. Such a situation rarely exists in higher education and, obviously, is not available on the professional level. It is sometimes thought, however, that actors with a strong technical background may approach a role too methodically, much the same way that they deal with executing blueprints or determining the angles of lighting instruments. It is feared that this will prevent them from feeling the emotion of the part. Pat and Lynnette, however, did such a fine job, "jumping the synapse", as I call it, between technique and truly finding the emotion of the scene.

Adele was simply beautiful as Alma. She created a character with such vulnerability and captured the hearts of the entire audience. It is always so fulfilling to witness the development of an actor. I remember directing Adele as "Chava" in a summer musical production of *Fiddler on the Roof*. While this was her first play and she was very young, I could even then see her enormous potential. She went on to give some stunning performances in Hamden Theater, but her Alma was truly the pinnacle of her high school work. When she was announced as the winner of the State's Outstanding Actress at the spring drama festival in 1997, the entire theater rose to their feet instantly to give her a greatly-deserved standing ovation.

Another student in the cast was Jessica Vasquez. Jessica was a splendid actor with a beautiful voice and a gift for making the words her own. She played "Nellie Ewell," the young woman who is a vocal student of Miss Alma's and who eventually marries John. Her work in class was excellent and I always looked forward to her performance assignments. One summer she was cast in an outdoor Shakespearean production with much older actors. The director was greatly impressed with her, and, despite her youth, gave her a major role. Through all of her successes, there was something amazingly humble about Jessica. She was also honestly grateful for anything—whether it was a good scene to study and perform in class, a role of any size in a mainstage production, or just a kind word. I admired her so much. Well before I met Jessica, Professor Leslie Hotson, the famous Shakespeare scholar, gave me a copy of a book he had written titled *The First Night of Twelfth Night* in which he had written a beautiful and moving inscription. I felt it was only fitting that Jessica have this book to honor her love of Shakespeare, and also as a gift for all the joy she had brought to so many audiences.

I remember the rehearsals for *Summer and Smoke* very well, many of which took place in a classroom while the technicians built the set. Adele and Pat worked incredibly hard. They found the perfect Southern dialect which added a musicality to their voices and enhanced Williams' words. I recall being thrilled as I listened to Adele speaking some of the playwright's most beautiful lines, such as the following paragraph in which Miss Alma attempts to define what life should be:

"everything reaches up,....everything seems to be straining out of the reach of stone-or human fingers...The immense stained windows, the great arched doors that are five or six times the height of the tallest man-the vaulted ceiling and all the delicate spires-all reaching up to something beyond attainment! To me-well, that is the secret, the principle back of existence, the everlasting struggle and aspiration for more than our human limits have placed in our reach..."

Another memorable scene they performed together was at the play's end when they try to find some logical explanation for their inability to come together despite their attraction to each other.

Alma:...I haven't come here on any but equal terms. You said, let's talk truthfully. Well, let's do! Unsparingly, truthfully, even shamelessly, then! It's no longer a secret that I love you. It never was. I loved you as long ago as the time I asked you to read the stone angel's name with your fingers. Yes, I remember the long afternoons of our childhood, when I had to stay indoors to practice my music-and hear your playmates calling you...How it went through me, just to hear your name called!...Yes, it had begun that early, this affliction of love, and has never let go of me since, but kept on growing. I've lived next door to you all the days of my life, a weak and divided person who stood in adoring awe of your singleness, of your strength....Why didn't it happen between us? Why did I fail? Why did you come almost close enough-and no closer?

John responds:

> You couldn't name it and I couldn't recognize it. I thought it was just a Puritanical ice that glittered like flame. but now I believe it WAS flame, mistaken for ice. I still don't understand it, but I know it was there, just as I know that your eyes and your voice are the two most beautiful things I've ever known-and also the warmest, although they don't seem to be set in your body at all...

Alma: ...The tables have turned, yes, the tables have turned with a vengeance! You've come around to my old way of thinking and I to yours like two people exchanging a call on each other at the same time, and each one finding the other one gone out, the door locked against him and no one to answer the bell!

As one might be able to tell from the passages above, rehearsals were spent trying to marry the lyricism and the emotion of Williams' words and characters. The actors worked hard to understand the characters' yearning for human love. They also recognized the potential of the language to lift them above the "worldly"- almost to another plane of existence; to some mythic realm.

Summer and Smoke marked the beginning of my professional partnership with Frank Alberino who would go on to design many sets for me at Hamden and also at the Foote Summer Theater. Frank was a student who had gone through the Hamden Theater program and eventually earned his degree in set and costume design from Purchase College. Frank now joined Ort Pengue, our technical director, and became, in my opinion, the best technical team possible. In addition to their technical talents, they were both excellent teachers-knowledgeable, patient, flexible, friendly, and disciplined. They provided opportunities for students to succeed, and that is so important.

Frank's design was magnificent. Williams calls for an expressionistic set, and Frank honored this desire. He used large transparent flats upstage, many of which were on casters so they could move easily. The flats were dyed with paintings of clouds as found in the work of the artist Maxfield Parrish, and some had slowly moving images projected on them. There were also rolling set pieces for both the Winemiller Rectory and the Buchanan house, all designed and built in forced perspective to give the illusion of depth. In the center of the stage was the angel of the fountain which the characters must visit frequently, and which seems to take on a life of its own. The angel and fountain were also on casters so that they could move smoothly, often upstage of the transparent flats where a subdued lighting special kept the angel constantly illuminated as the playwright desired. At the base of the statue is carved "Eternity" and while this was relevant to the meaning of the play, the word and the angel took on a significance for us as well since this was the last play in the old Hamden High School Theater. When Alma made her final cross on stage during the last performance of the play, she touched the angel's wings, looked at the word "Eternity" and exited. It was quite an emotional moment for everyone in the theater, the company and the audience alike, as they realized that the end of an era was upon us. That theater was indeed rich in history.

Spring vacation approached, and renovations forced us out of the theater. This was a trying time for us since the spring drama festival was just ahead, and we were faced with the necessity of finding another large rehearsal space. The cafeteria would have been an ideal spot, but it had been recently demolished. Finally we made arrangements to use the gymnasium.

I suddenly realized that in all of my years of teaching at Hamden High School I rarely, if ever, visited this part of the school and its long, winding, cavernous hallways leading to a myriad of practice rooms and smaller gyms. Hamden High School was large and the physical education area was a good distance away from the theater. It was a challenging task, then, deciding what scenery to bring, making dressing areas for costume changes, and working in that huge and foreign space. Then there was the actual move itself, which could only have been done with the help of the full company of some fifty students. Fortunately, many gym teachers were friends of mine and they were really gracious in helping to make us feel at home and helping out in any way they could. The custodians also, some of my best friends in the school system, were always there to help. I was thankful, however, when we packed our belongings and moved back home after our last festival rehearsal.

Summer and Smoke was extremely successful in both its full run and at the drama festival. The audiences were greatly moved by it, and at the drama festival it continued Hamden's string of Outstanding Productions, this being the tenth successive winner.

After the final performance of the play, we hosted a reception for our Hamden Theater graduates, and many of them returned to say goodbye to a place that was very important to them. There was a great amount of laughter, but also a melancholy feeling as well. This was, after all, more than a theater: It was "home"—the place where countless students found their personal successes; where they overcame obstacles; where they learned to trust and be responsible; where they discovered a sense of "self"-and in doing all of this, they became better human beings. During all of this growth and exploration and experimentation, that "grand lady" had witnessed a great deal—from Shakespeare to Shaw to O'Neill—and had become a storehouse for a mass of energy that could never be measured. She would truly be missed. Martin Harries of *Becket* and *Richard III* among others, was one of the very last graduates to leave that night. I observed him as he moved around the stage and looked out into the house. I could tell that this theater meant a lot to him—even after all these years. As I watched Martin I saw once again how deeply moving and important the Hamden Theater experience had been for so many students.

The following Monday our company performed its traditional post-production "strike"- taking the set apart and cleaning up. This strike was different, however, in that nearly everything was being discarded. There was no room for storage of flats or other large pieces, for the theater would soon become the school's new media center and library. Although we had to pack and account for every single item we had accumulated over the years, I recall a quietness throughout the strike. There was a pervading sense of the end of something; of loss. When all of the work was done, many students lingered on the stage in groups, in pairs, and singly, and several of them were weeping. Parents who came to pick up their children stood by respectfully, even reverently, allowing the students to make this last communion with a very special place.

I stood center stage when everyone had gone and looked out into the semi-darkened theater. I could feel in that eery, yet comforting silence, the palpable energy of so many students over so many years. Ghosts of past productions seemed to lurk behind the curtains and come so close to finally making themselves visible. And if I closed my eyes and listened, I could hear the faint dialogue of plays past, the voices and laughter of students no longer here, the applause of audiences as well as audiences wrought up in emotional stillness. All of this was combined into a cacophony of strangely familiar and beautiful music. Even though I looked forward to a brand new facility on the other side of the school building, the "grand lady" would always be in my heart.

The new theater complex was beautiful. It was 1997-98 and our former theater was now replaced with a 620 seat proscenium theater, a black box/theater rehearsal hall, a full scene shop, dressing rooms with showers, a glass-brick ticket booth, a large lobby, and it was all situated in an area of its own. Plush dark blue seats and carpeting adorned the new theater, which also had a mezzanine containing a control booth housing state-of-the-art lighting and sound systems. A catwalk ran across the theater ceiling providing a multitude of lighting positions and limiting the need for time-consuming and continuous scaffold building, moving, and striking that characterized our productions of the past. The entire complex was sleek and modern. And there was so much space. Finally there was ample room for numerous scenes to be rehearsed and meetings of all kinds to occur simultaneously. Of course it all took a great deal of getting used to. My many first-year concerns ranged from simply identifying the proper keys for so many new locks to deciding where to seat the classes in the black box. Nevertheless, excitement was in the air as that school year began, and our students looked forward to getting a production on the stage.

Planning for and designing any renovated or new structure takes so much time, and budget restraints continually modify the original ideas. While there certainly were modifications in the theater complex, it managed to avoid major alterations and compromises, something I interpreted as a validation of the students' efforts and successes over the years. I looked upon the town's strong support for this facility as a show of gratitude to the students who had created one of the finest Theater programs in the country.

It was much easier than I had anticipated to select my first play for the new theater facility. I initially felt some pressure because I knew the play would attract a lot of attention, but I had confidence in the students and the staff, knowing that whatever I chose, it would be done professionally and with overwhelming enthusiasm. I was looking for something new and different; something that would be boldly refreshing, a bit risky, have both comedy and drama, and say something to the audience. I also wanted to tax the new facility to its fullest and take advantage of the new technical opportunities. The play I selected was Eric Overmyer's *On the Verge, or the Geography of Yearning*, an unusual and contemporary piece, but one which fit my specifications perfectly.

It is difficult to describe this play. I called it a mixture of Indiana Jones, *Around the World in 80 Days, 1984,* and *Brave New World.* It is a fantastical exploration of words and history, filled with simply wonderful moments of mirth and drama. The play follows the adventures of three Victorian lady explorers as they trek through darkest Africa, the Himalayas, and Terra Incognita. It sweeps us away on a safari through time as well, for unbeknownst to the ladies who begin their journey in 1888, they end up in 1952 in a place called "Nicky's Peligrosa Paradise Bar and Grill," a Havana-style nightclub. Along their path they meet a host of eccentric characters such as Alphonse, a cannibal who has taken on the physical appearance of his latest "meal", a World War I German air man who was piloting a dirigible; the Gorge Troll, a rapping guardian of a bridge over which the ladies must cross; Mr. Coffee, a haunting figure from both the past and the future; a yeti; Madame Nhu, a fortune teller; Grover, the husband of one of the ladies who appears to her in a life-like dream; Gus, a teenage gas station attendant, and, of course, Nicky Paradise, the owner of the bar and grill who eventually marries one of the travelers.

On the Verge appealed greatly to my love of language and words, as well as my ever-present sense of adventure and exploration. On another level, I felt that I had found a play that would take us onward. As the play's plot and theme anticipate the future, I was certain that it would encourage us to build upon the successes of the past and encourage us to forge a new and exciting direction for Hamden Theater.

It would be difficult to find a play that concentrates more on words-their evolution and their very sounds. The ladies are avid learners, and as they travel through time, they love the new words and concepts that roll off their tongues: "Air-mail," "blue sky ventures," "so long," "Red Chinese," and a host of others. Part of the play's fun is more closely scrutinizing the everyday words we have come to take for granted.

Then there is the word play that permeates the play, as when Alexandra discovers the word "dirigible."

> Alex: What a succulent word! Dirigible, dirigible, dirigible. Dirigible.
> Mary: Alex!
> Alex: Up your old dirigible. Give us your huddled dirigibles, yearning to breathe free. Have a dirigible on me, big fella. One mint dirigible to go...
> Ineligible dirigible. Illegible dirigible. Incorrigible dirigible. Gerbil in a dirigible! I'll wager it's one of those words which has no true rhyme in English. Of course, it's not an English word, is it?

Fanny writes to her husband about their current surroundings using colorful language that seems to jump off the page:

"Dear Grover...Terra Incognita exhilarates. intoxicates. There is an hallucinatory spiciness to the air. We are in the grip of a communal fever dream..."

And, of course, the rapping Gorge Troll continues the play's fun with language:

"What have we here but travelers three
Comin' cross the bridge to rap with me.
In Xanadu said Ka-u-ba-la Khan
Hey there sweet things what's goin' on?"

Mary's entry in her journal is an example of the numerous passages filled with imagery and alliteration:

"At dawn and dusk, the essence of the jungle increases a hundredfold. The air becomes heavy with perfume. It throbs with unseen presence. A savage tapestry of squawks, cries, and caws presses upon one with an almost palpable pressure. A cacophonous echolalia-snarling, sinister menace-as though the sound of the jungle itself could tear one limb from limb."

Noah Workman, one of my assistants and the production dramaturg, brought his lap top computer to rehearsals, providing us with a luxury we had not experienced before. He was able to instantly research, locate, and even find pronunciations for references in the text. Questions about Baluchistan, Madagascar, Robert Lowell, the Grand Tetons, the Irriwaddy River Delta, and the Masai were answered immediately. It wasn't unusual to find groups of students huddled about Noah, asking him all sorts of play-related questions. This use of technology was fascinating and seemed to reinforce the advancement of our recent move to a vital and contemporary facility. I had heard and used the words, "Theater of the Twenty-first Century" so often. Suddenly it seemed as if I were thrust into it—working in it, living in it, and loving every moment of it.

One of my favorite parts of *On the Verge* was when the three ladies encounter objects from the future in a wonderful scene near the beginning of Act II. They refer to it as "fallout from the future" and "a rain forest of fossils from the future." These include a hula hoop, a silver laser video, a side-view mirror from an automobile, and a copy of the National Review. Designer Frank Alberino created five massive spherical objects from which hung a variety of "futuristic" objects, among them Velveta, a frisby, a can opener, brass knuckles, and a large inflatable banana. The scene was accompanied by mist rolling along the raked stage floor and music, all of which gave the scene a dream-like, esoteric feeling

Frank's design for the play was astonishing, complementing the play's theme of traveling through time and space. He created a large raked platform covered with a black, high gloss sheen. The top of the platform contained grooved vertical and horizontal lines, resembling those of latitude and longitude, in perspective. Upstage of this was a circular cut out in which hung silhouettes of the continents. The entire upstage area from right to left was made up of semi-transparent flats which reinforced the motif of lines of latitude and longitude found on the platform top, so that a map of the world was subtly and appropriately present throughout the play.

As with all of Frank's sets, it was filled with wonderful surprises: well disguised trap doors, a canopy of mosquito netting that appeared to erect itself, and Nicky's Bar and Grill complete with palm tree and coconuts. At one point in the play, snow fell. Alexandra, one of the lady travelers, described it as "snow from the moon." At another moment, stars glistened in the night sky. This play was a visual feast, and the set and the effects won awards at the drama festival that year. Ort was once again the technical director and taught the numerous students construction skills. And while he taught, gales of laughter could be heard once again. The new environment and all of its magical possibilities buoyed all of our spirits, and we never wanted to leave it.

The three actors who played the explorers, Kristi Villani, Patricia Santomasso, and Marta Montgomery, were splendid. Words cannot describe their devotion to the play. They put in long, long hours of rehearsal and created excellent characters. The four of us worked very closely together, as we tried just about anything and everything in bringing the text to life. The three women also became very close, and even seemed to be able to read each other's minds. All three won major acting awards for their performances, as did David Moran for Alphonse, Ben Hecht as Nicky, David Salguero as Mr. Coffee, and Jason Conge as the Gorge Troll. As a matter of fact, *On the Verge* set a new drama festival record, winning eighteen awards between the State and New England Drama Festivals. It also won the "Outstanding Production" Award, marking the eleventh consecutive year and the twentieth in twenty-two years of Festival participation. This feat brought recognition from the Governor of Connecticut, the Mayor of Hamden, and the Board of Education.

One director at the New England Drama Festival wrote to me, "When I bring my students to Festival-especially when we get to come to New Englands-I hope there will be a production that allows me to show my students what high school theater is capable of at its absolute best. You did that for me, for us! All the pieces, all the moments! A rich, full, beautiful show!"

Another satisfying memory of the play was the presence in the audience of the professional actress, Jayne Atkinson, and her husband, Michel R. Gill. They were appearing as Ruth and Charles Condomine in the Long Wharf Theater production of *Blithe Spirit* at the time and were invited to see *On the Verge* by a friend of theirs who was also a Hamden Theater parent. Jayne had played "Mary" in the Yale Repertory Theater production some years before. Both she and Michel were extremely taken by the performance and remained afterward to meet the students and to talk to me. I was flattered to hear their positive comments and see how deeply they felt about the production.

On the Verge was a great way to begin life in a new theater. I look back to the unrest that I was beginning to feel in 1996—a need to explore more of our Theater and to experiment with new kinds of plays, to take more risks, to make new, fresh, and bold choices. *On the Verge* was a realization of that need, and I remember feeling very good about that. For the first time in several years some of that creative disturbance inside of me could subside until the next hunger came along. This play also served as a plateau from which I could see how far I had come and how far I had still to go.

After rehearsals, when everyone was gone, I often would look out into the house from the stage, and I would be filled with strange but exciting emotions. While I thought about where I was physically—in a space I could never have anticipated and all that could be accomplished there—I could feel the presence of the past equally as strong. I yearn for those people and plays of a prior time. Where are they? They are too important to be gone and to be unknown by all but me. Their fresh faces, their eagerness, their performances flash before my eyes. And then, just as quickly and vividly, I think all of the current students and their pride in their new home. There are connections between the past and the present, even if they are in my mind alone. They are strong and distinct and unmistakable. And these combined forces look to the future together, connecting us again and this time to the final words of *On the Verge*.

> "Billions of new worlds, waiting to be discovered. Explored and illuminated...I stand on the precipice. The air is rare. Bracing. Before me stretch dark distances.... What next? I have no idea. Many mysteries to come. I am on the verge. I have such a yearning for the future! It is boundless!..."

Chapter Four

The Shakespeare Plays

Much Ado About Nothing, 1992

"Being part of the theater has been one of the few moments when I have felt real pride. This pride is not only satisfaction that I have done something and done it well, but also that I can be sure that the world is not always "a tale told by an idiot, full of sound and fury, signifying nothing."

Martin

"The theater has taught me how to make decisions, accept challenges, and most of all, open myself to the world and everything in it."

Laurie

I've always loved Shakespeare. Acting in his plays was a great source of joy for me in college. Even in high school, well before I was seriously involved in theater, I never seemed to share the fear my classmates associated with his work; a fear that became increasingly more obvious to me during my teaching career. The word "Shakespeare" is likely to evoke all sorts of negative reactions from students in the general school population, just as it is likely to be a cause for celebration among high school theater students. This latter group acknowledges Shakespeare as the pinnacle of theatrical production. From my earliest days of teaching there were always Theater students who pleaded to do a Shakespeare, disregarding my cautions that it was something to work up to; that it required study and some amount of training. After a few years, however, the fruits of the established acting training program in Hamden made these plays much more feasible.

Whenever I prepared to direct a Shakespeare play I found myself immersed in a certain mood or feeling that seemed to excite me and provide a springboard from which to begin my work. Directors have their own specific and personal ways of getting into an appropriate frame of mind when becoming familiar with a script. With my

Shakespeare productions I would often find myself alone, walking through the courtyards at neighboring Yale University, the architecture of which is permeated with history and emotion. Many of these courtyards are large with expansive green lawns, and many are small and quite hidden away with old, weathered flagstone patios. I preferred the latter to the former. They seemed to harbor many stories within their confines. These courtyards, time-defying nooks, and almost secretive crannies often have elaborate carvings in the stone or in the door frames, or one would have to enter them through unique iron gates. Each appeared to me as a tiny world unto itself, and as I moved from one to another, I enjoyed a feeling of history and even mystery. I felt like any of Shakespeare's characters could walk out from behind a solid old oak door and join me in that courtyard at any moment.

I would also enjoy driving to Witlock's Book Barn in Bethany, Connecticut. There, in a country setting, are two buildings harboring thousands of old books, nearly all of which are out of print. Here I would find many books on specific facets of Shakespeare's work- the flowers mentioned in his plays, or his women, or perhaps a book dealing solely with his clowns. I felt energized from the scholarship that went into the writing, and was often thrilled to be privy to some bit of information that I had imagined must have remained hidden for many years. As I turned the yellowed pages and absorbed the musty odors of leather bound volumes, these books took on lives of their own. They were like aging professors desperately attempting to find an open mind and listening ear before it was too late. Accompanying drawings and bins filled with torn or discarded frontispieces on fragile paper contained elaborate, decorative, and detailed representations of Shakespeare's characters.

Yet another journey into Shakespeare's world was visiting the grounds of the American Shakespeare Theater in Stratford, Connecticut. This is where I saw my first Shakespeare play many years ago as a seventh grade student, and this is where the playwright's magic brought me under its spell. This theater is probably my favorite in the world. It came upon hard times and closed some years ago despite the desperate attempts that were made to keep it open. However, even the locked theater with its faded gray exterior and flagless spires, even the overgrown shrubs that dotted the grounds, and even the adjacent, old vine-covered theater museum with its faded poster of Katherine Hepburn in *The Merchant of Venice* —none of these could dampen my strong personal sentiments for this glorious place. I lived in Stratford for a while, and would often find myself drawn to the solace of the theater's sprawling grounds resting along the banks of the Housatonic River. And as quiet as it was I could still feel the energy that embodies that place. I remember once sitting in front of that theater and blocking a good portion of a play I was working on. I feel inspired there.

Recently I was invited to tour the inside of the theater by Louis Burke, the gentleman who has put his heart and soul into reviving it. I walked throughout as much of it as I could. I revisited the large lobby, once adorned by many exquisite busts of Shakespeare; I walked through the aisles of the auditorium, looking over the sea of now empty seats and turned to admire once again the rich, teak walls; I stepped onto the stage, in the wings of which were still old props, flats, and pieces of scenery; and I ventured into the balcony and the stairwells, and the upper foyer—all of which are still lined with large photographs of productions that occurred there. I was bewitched all over again.

All of this-the research, the pursuit, and the feeling of being part of something grand and historic-eventually would impact the play I was to direct in some way. These things I speak of are personal adventures and very important to both my teaching and directing. I draw from these experiences an energy and subtext that fills the work with depth and meaning. It connects this play, whether it is being taught or directed, to the others, and provides a foundation upon which to explore and discover the work at hand.

Tackling a Shakespeare always filled me with a real excitement. I knew that I could trust the text, that it was always relevant, that the stories were wonderful and universal and struck a chord in all humanity for hundreds of years, and that any concerns or questions I might have would be answered by the playwright's subtle signposts and guidance within the text itself.

As far as my own acting experience is concerned, I remember being in a "mod" version of *the Taming of the Shrew* in college, this being the director's personal twist on the production. Well, it was the '60's, after all, and theater throughout the country was reflecting the rapidly changing social climate. Certainly my college was no exception. "Traditional" seemed out, and directors were looking for something new to say, or perhaps something new to say about something old. I would eventually come to have concerns about this controversial area of dealing with the classics when I started teaching and directing full time, but for now I was totally caught up in the life of the play, portraying Tranio, the servant to Lucentio. I remember the day that we anxiously awaited the arrival of our costumes. A few company members on the costume crew went into New York with little money, but a lot of "interpretation" and brought back a selection of mod clothes that was totally outrageous. We actors were then given our garb, and I recall being taken aback by the gold corduroy bell bottoms, the burgundy shirt with gold polka dots, a vest, and hat. The style of everyone's costume was similar. Even the lead female character, Kate, was married in a mini-skirt, a fashion radically new at the time, to the melody of "Winchester Cathedral" in the background. Each day of rehearsal brought new surprises including the gender changes of some characters and the inclusion of a fashion show on a specially built runway lit from beneath by flashing colored lights. I must admit that once I let go of some of my stodgy preconceptions of how Shakespeare should be done, I had a great deal of fun with that play. And while I didn't realize it at the time, I learned a great lesson, and that was how flexible the playwright's works were; that they were indeed open to interpretation and a variety of styles. This would be of great value in my teaching career.

My next Shakespeare, *A Midsummer Night's Dream*, proved to be another memorable experience, although the production was much more traditional in nature. Constance Welch, the acting teacher and director who was to become my life-long mentor, directed the play and I was given the role of "Peter Quince." Miss Welch was approaching seventy at the time, yet she defied age and any other limitations as she taught, directed, guided, and nurtured us into bringing that play alive.

I recall a similar experience when I took a greatly anticipated voice workshop many years later with the famous theater voice and speech teacher, Evangeline Machline. A person of considerable age at the time, as soon as she started the workshop she transformed before my eyes into an energetic, vital woman who taught with inspiration and moved with ease. I was captivated by her and understood immediately why she was considered one of the finest voice teachers of her day. After the workshop I wanted to thank her and I also had some questions, so I remained in the room until everyone left and I had an opportunity to speak with her. I volunteered to carry her heavy tape recorder back to her hotel room, an offer she gladly accepted, and we started on our way. We enjoyed a warm conversation as we traveled through the hotel corridors, but I also became aware of her rapid change back to an elderly person who moved rather slowly and with a good amount of difficulty. Yet another lesson came my way at that time; that of the ability of passion for one's work to erase a great many physical and mental limitations.

An interesting story about *Midsummer* was that it was supposed to have opened the new Lyman Center for Performing Arts on the college campus. Dr. Kendall, the chair of the Theater Department, felt strongly about initiating the new theater with a festive Shakespearean play (he did the same when he opened the new black box theater in Lyman Center, one which would eventually be named for him, with a production of *Romeo and Juliet*.), and even postponed the production twice, responding to delays in the construction schedule. It was finally decided that the play would go on in May, but in the TV Studio, rather than the new theater. Dr. Kendall's program note reflected his disappointment and, I believe, anger, that the construction deadlines were not met.

While the familiarity of the TV Studio was, as always, comforting, most of the company was rather dismayed that ours wouldn't be the first play to experience the brand new facility. I kept it to myself, then, that I felt rather good about performing in the Studio, and may have even preferred it. It was "home" after all, and a place that meant a great deal to me. I also felt that the final production in a special place was just as important as the first in a new space. I often wondered what that meant or said about me. I would revisit those feelings many years later when Hamden High School replaced its theater of 60-plus years with a modern, new facility.

The production was a great deal of fun. It boasted a large cast, and Miss Welch even brought in an alumnus, Martin Piccirillo, to play "Bottom." This was not uncommon as she used older, more experienced and professional actors for other plays as well. I wasn't sure why she did this except that I suspected she had an agreement with Dr. Kendall about using her former students when no one at Southern was able to play specific roles. After a while, however, I came to the conclusion that the real reason was that Miss Welch wanted us to learn from them. She was very concerned about teaching us as much as possible, and this was a method of introducing us to the work ethics of people in the profession. I remember being very excited about working with these actors, and even being in awe of them. I observed their rehearsal techniques, their experimentation, and tried to absorb as much knowledge from them as possible.

When I acted in Miss Welch's production of *Anna Sophie Hedvig* by the Danish playwright, Kjeld Abel, she brought in Richard Forsyth, an older and highly polished actor, to play a character with whom mine was in conflict. At one point in the play I was supposed to physically attack the man and knock him down to the ground. I had a great deal of trouble with this moment and constantly avoided or procrastinated the real action. I spoke to Miss Welch privately about my discomfort. Physical violence was something with which I could not identify, and then there was my fear that I might, in some way, injure him. She was receptive and understood my dilemma, professing her trust that I would be able to handle the situation before long.

Soon after this conversation, I started noticing Mr. Forsyth toying with his ring in our scenes together. At first I thought it was an interesting gesture, but soon I became focused on the way he would constantly twirl his ring as he glared at me on the stage. I have a vivid mental picture of him resting his arm on the fireplace mantel, using his thumb to move his ring around and around, all the while challenging me with a subtle, wry, and condescending smile. It was as if he were daring me to attack him. The ring and the gesture began to irritate me. I remember feeling somehow akin to the persecuted narrator in Poe's *The Tell-Tale Heart*, a thought which, as I reflect upon it now, amuses me. I worked myself up into such a state that I finally did attack the man, and I did, in fact, knock him down. Of course, I immediately stopped the entire rehearsal by apologizing profusely, much to the dismay of the company and, I'm sure, the director. I often wondered whether Miss Welch spoke to Mr. Forsyth after that conversation I had with her, and together they planned the gesture, hoping to get a response from me. At any rate, something clicked, and the professionalism of Miss Welch's guest actor taught me yet another lesson I could use in my future work.

My college experience with *Midsummer* was so much fun that it may have been the reason that I selected it to be the first Shakespearean production at Hamden High School in November, 1975. As I previously mentioned, students craved Shakespeare prior to this, but the early days were a time for growing and developing, and I didn't think we were ready for Shakespeare yet. Maybe even I felt some trepidation about tackling it. Our production of Maxwell Anderson's *Elizabeth the Queen* was as close as we had come to a Shakespeare, and that was merely in terms of the time period. But I was impressed with the actors' facility in handling Anderson's poetic language and the ease with which they adapted to the style and movement of the period. The performances were strong in that play, particularly those of Maggie Adair as Elizabeth and James Gold as Essex, and I think the production gave me the confidence to do

Midsummer. Many of those cast members even appeared in our first Shakespearean production.

In all of my years of teaching, nothing seems to excite the public more than a Shakespearean production. In fact, people who never go to plays are suddenly enthusiastic about Shakespeare, and so it was for our *Midsummer*. Any intimidation or fear I had about the project quickly disappeared once I began working with the cast. They were incredible. They came to own the language, and there's nothing like a group of young, enthusiastic students to see the humor and, indeed, the pathos in the situations of the this play. Diane Willis (Hermia), Gail Grate (Titania), Ron Munson (Oberon), Edith Meeks (Helena), Theron Albis (Demetrius), Malcolm Smith (Lysander), and Josh Stein (Bottom) were only some of the excellent members of the company. They demonstrated discipline and dedication, and the long rehearsal hours seemed to fleet by. Some of those rehearsals were taped for a possible documentary (it was to come out years later in 1986 and primarily focused on our production of *Amadeus*; the *Midsummer* footage was never used unfortunately) I remember the director, Bill Burns, being very surprised at the ability of the actors to precisely repeat scenes and parts of scenes over and over again. This was Bill's first experience observing high school theater students at work, and his admiration caused him to become involved in Hamden Theater for several years.

This was the group of students I took to see *Twelfth Night* at the American Shakespeare Theater in Stratford, Connecticut. I felt that this would be a good experience for them, giving them the opportunity to witness some really fine Shakespeare and also inspiring them as we worked on our own production. The performance was a matinee and was billed as a student event. The day was beautiful, and hundreds of students from all over the State and beyond were picnicking on the extensive lawn, a popular thing to do at this theater. However, as curtain time approached, I realized that the doors to the lobby were not open. Something seemed wrong. Soon my suspicions were verified when a spokesperson for the Theater informed us that the theater and the surrounding neighborhood had lost their electricity. The company, however, had decided to perform the play outside until the electricity was restored. I remember a very large tree in the middle of the lawn, around which was a circular bench hugging the trunk. This, then, would become the "set." The audience huddled close together, and the actors improvised their blocking, using the tree and the bench and nothing else.

That performance was marvelous, and perhaps one of the finest theater experiences we could have had. The company performed with great spirit and a freshness that is essential to all fine acting. An immediate rapport was built between the actors and the student audience, the latter group loving the spontaneity and exuberance of the performance. Playing outside in the fresh air gave the play a sense of immediacy and freedom. This was, after all, how Shakespeare's plays were presented back in the days of the Globe Theater. What better learning experience for our students.

At intermission we were informed that the electricity to the theater was restored and we would be moving indoors. There was obviously a stark difference between the two acts as far as the technical elements were concerned, and there was no doubt that the set for the production was exquisite. The second half of the play was polished and sophisticated as we would expect of any professional production. However, on the bus ride home many students expressed a preference for the outdoor Act I performance. This experience provided a great lesson for us, especially since we were to perform our own production shortly. We learned that the essential part of any performance is the actors' relationship to the text, to each other, and to the audience; that no matter how glorious the technical components may be, the focus of live performance is on the actor and his sense of truth and believability.

The response to our production of *Midsummer* was extremely positive. A Yale professor wrote me a note thanking me for "breaking ground" with this production and advocated one Shakespeare every year. Reviews in the local newspapers were wonderful, and one reporter, the late P. Scott Hollander, wrote:

> "...there's no need to bone up on your Shakespeare before you go-even someone who's never been introduced to the Bard will have no trouble following this play. This is Shakespeare as it should be; not an intellectual exercise for literary historians, but a theatrical treat with the emphasis on the play, where it belongs."

Howard Stein, then the Associate Dean of the Yale Drama School, wrote:

> "I think the most impressive thing of all in your production ... is the quality of the ambition of the production which never calls attention to itself. You manage to make Shakespeare completely accessible to a group of performers as well as to an audience and that is a very impressive accomplishment."

Howard was to become a dear friend and mentor over the following three decades. I asked him, in 1994, to write the Afterword for my book, *Lessons for the Stage*, and while I labored feverishly on the writing of that book, it is Howard's beautiful words, so simple yet eloquent, which elevate its quality. Howard also set up a visit for my students to a final dress rehearsal of the Yale Repertory Theater's production of *Midsummer* . I remember him telling me to watch the woman playing Helena, for her acting was brilliant, largely due to her vulnerability on the stage. The woman was Meryl Streep, and I was thankful that we had the opportunity to observe her work before she met with her much deserved fame.

Finally, Lee Brockman, a woman with no Hamden ties other than a connection to education (her husband was the Superintendent of Schools in Guilford, Connecticut at the time) and an appreciation for theater wrote:

"...And to think you did it with high school students! But I forgot their young age while watching the show. And I have to keep reminding myself of their comparative inexperience even now, while I remember their superb expressions, their smooth and sure movement, their very professional performance-each and every one of them....I offer you my most heartfelt congratulations, Julian, for what I saw last night. I've already used a lot of words here, but words just won't express my awe. I'm overwhelmed."

Lee was a wonderful supporter of Hamden Theater in those days. She often brought guests to the plays, and she followed each production with a beautiful and heartfelt letter of congratulations. I was sad when she and her family moved away a few years later, for I came to lean upon her honest appraisals as pillars of support and guideposts for future projects as I worked on building the theater program in Hamden. Lee offered an objectivity that I needed, rather than the lavish praise from parents who, although sincere, were so happy to see their children involved that I felt they might imagine a play to be of a much higher quality than it actually was. I jokingly came to name that the "Music Man" syndrome, based on the scene in that musical where parents watch their young children in uniforms much too big for them and playing instruments totally out of tune, but the parents imagine their children to be marching gallantly, each one in perfect step with the others, wearing pristine, well-fitting uniforms and playing their instruments exquisitely.

It is interesting that several members of the *Midsummer* company pursued careers in theater. Gail Grate is a talented actress who has appeared in major regional theaters, in movies and television; Theron Albis is a playwright (I recently was excited to see a full-page ad in a theater magazine for Terry's new play, *An American Passenger*); Edith Meeks has taught acting at the HB Studio in New York; and Malcolm Smith is an accomplished film writer in California.

I was so happy with the success of *Midsummer* at the time. It bolstered my confidence, for I now knew that it was indeed possible to do a top quality Shakespearean production in high school. More importantly, the students were proud of and excelled in their work, and this was important as it represented a step closer to developing a well-trained department where play choices would become unlimited. *Midsummer* opened the doors to a whole new course of study in acting classes as well as lead to the production of more Shakespeare plays in the years to come. But I wasn't finished with *A Midsummer Night's Dream*, although I was unaware of this fact at the time. I was to revisit this play in a special way later on in my career.

In 1980 I directed *Othello* as our second Shakespearean production and first Shakespearean tragedy. This play had always held a great fascination for me. I knew that if it were done well, *Othello* would totally capture the audience with its tale of jealousy, greed, and intrigue. Of greater importance, I was excited about the tremendous experience it would provide for the students.

One of the chief attributes of this play is its dramatic language. Imagine guiding actors to find truthful ways of saying

> A fair woman! A sweet woman! ...
> Aye let her rot, and perish, and
> be damned tonight,
> for she shall not live. No, my
> heart is turned to stone.
> I strike it and it hurts my hand...
> I will chop her into messes.

I was fortunate to have an African-American actor, Tom Edwards, who was one of the best acting students I would encounter in my career. Tom was a handsome and physically impressive man with a voice that could only be described as thick velvet, and yet, as "large" as he might seem onstage, he was a modest and unassuming person with a great sense of humor off stage. For his "Othello", Tom eventually won one of two "Outstanding Actor" awards given at the 1980 Connecticut Drama Association Festival that year. I also remember that Tom had wonderful, large hands, and his gestures with them seemed to be motivated from some secret place within. The other acting award went to another Hamden actor, Andrew Hirshfield who played an unscrupulously cunning, yet alarmingly attractive Iago. Andy and Tom worked so beautifully together and charged the stage with passion and scheming

Tom's abilities continued to develop, and the following year he played Jack Jefferson in Howard Sackler's *The Great White Hope*, for which he not only won another Outstanding Actor Award, but the prestigious "Brother John Memorial Award" given by the New England Drama Council to the single best high school actor in all of New England.

Desdemona was played by Miriam Schmir, a student who will always be dear to me. Miriam was bright and creative, and brought a maturity to Desdemona. She played the character with calmness and composure, carrying herself almost regally and making her appear as a woman rather than a girl. This restraint made her highly emotional scenes near the play's end that much more effective. Miriam was also a beautiful woman, both inside and out, and she brought a sincerity to her character that was enchanting. I recall how she looked at Othello with such love and honesty in their early scenes together. Much of the play's success was due to the audience's involvement in the Desdemona-Othello relationship; the believability with which Miriam and Tom played their love at the play's start, and the calculated destruction of that relationship by the clever and devious Iago.

It was easy to tell that Miriam would have a wonderful future. She graduated from Harvard some years later and eventually became a top writer for television. Miriam visited me a few years ago, and even after all of her success and the time that has passed, she remains sincere and warm.

Othello was, thankfully, extremely well received. The expert acting of Melanie Zyck as Emilia, Michael Prezioso as Roderigo, Brian Drutman as Brabantio, Larry Iannotti as Cassio, Ken Festa as Montano, Andrea Ahrens as Bianca, and Douglas Amore as the Duke of Venice, as well as the other members of the large cast, helped to bring Hamden it's third consecutive "Best Play in Connecticut" Award and it's fifth in the previous seven years. Newspaper reporters were writing of a "Hamden theater dynasty" and these words were also used in several State Education journals.

Things were going well for us as I looked at the array of talented students in the program and their seemingly limitless potential. It was exciting to witness the younger students learning and developing and being inspired by the accomplishments of the upperclassmen. But I was also sensitive to the competitive aspect of the drama festivals. We were, after all, in the arts and not an athletic team. I didn't want students and the community to think that winning was more important than learning. On the other hand, these were the days when the arts in the schools were considered frills, and any kind of positive feedback for an arts program helped to strengthen it. The fame of Hamden Theater did some pretty wonderful things for it over the years. For one, the support from the town and the Board of Education was incredible. Of course, I hoped that this support derived itself from the quality of the program and not a "winning team," but I was willing to accept the support in any manner in which it came. By the time I retired, Hamden had won twenty Best Play Awards, including two stretches of eight and eleven consecutive winners, bringing the town and its Theater national attention and recognition.

By virtue of its success at the Connecticut Drama Association Festival, we were invited to represent the State at the New England Drama Festival which was held in Skowhegan, Maine that year. This experience, as humorous as it is now to look back upon, was one of the most trying times I can remember. I should have realized we were in for a long weekend when I learned that our bus driver's name was Odysseus. We were at the intersection of two major highways when he was advised by a chaperone to take the northern route rather than the northeastern route. I mistakenly assumed he and the bus company had planned out the trip before we boarded the bus, an assumption I never made again. Several hours later, we realized we were heading in the wrong direction, and the only road that could bring us back to the correct highway was a country road that took us through many small towns. Thus began the voyage that culminated in a twelve-hour trip to Maine. By the time we arrived all forty-plus of us were irritable, hungry, and some were ill, and while the performance of *Othello* itself did wonderfully at the Festival, the entire weekend was marked by one terrible experience after another.

The only motel that could accommodate us was thirty miles away from the Festival site, making commuting, especially late at night, a long and grueling routine. The hotel ran out of hot water at one point—the morning, of course, when it was most needed—and we all had to take cold showers in the already chilly environs of this northern section of New England. Of greater concern, one night on our return trip to the motel, a student seriously, albeit mistakenly, thought she was having a heart attack and we had to rush her from the motel to the nearest clinic, several miles away. The only immediate transportation we had was a pick-up truck owned by a neighbor. She sat next to the driver while I rode in the open back for what seemed like hours. The heart attack turned out to be an anxiety attack, thank goodness.

We also had two students who broke toes during an impromptu soccer game, and one actor in a leading role who forgot his costume in Hamden, and we had to find someone willing to take the long drive from Hamden to bring it to us. Yet another student was locked out of her motel room late at night and we couldn't awaken her roommate by any means, whether it was letting the telephone ring continuously or banging on the door or window. This, naturally, caused us to become alarmed that something had happened to the sleeping girl, a fear that disappeared quite a while later when she finally opened the door. Yes, the entire trip was plagued with problems from start to finish, and while it has been the cause for great humor at our theater reunions, I still remember the nightmare of it all.

Othello brings back another memory—and a most horrific one at that. Amidst all of the accolades heaped upon this production, a bizarre and tragic murder rocked our theater family and our school system. Denise Lowney, an art teacher who played a major part in designing and painting scenery for the play, was killed. Denise and I would hold crew sessions on Saturdays, and many students would attend. The atmosphere was relaxed and very productive as everyone worked in groups to build and/or paint pieces of the set. Crew sessions could be very noisy with the constant hum of drills and saws and the banging hammers. There was an ample supply of coffee, tea, juice, bagels, and donuts, and the laughter and fun disguised the extraordinary amount of work that was being completed.

On one Saturday I had to attend a meeting of the State Drama Association, and Denise felt comfortable supervising the work alone. Even though many students might be there, they were so well disciplined, mature, and polite that I didn't think twice about Denise's ability to handle the group. Her last words to me were not to worry and that I could rest assured that everything would be accomplished to my satisfaction.

Denise was divorced and the mother of a teenage girl, yet they looked more like sisters than mother and daughter. Denise was youthful and could easily illuminate a room with her presence. This was a person full of vivacity and fun and a love of life. She was an excellent educator as well and students flocked to her classes. We were good friends outside of school, saw each other socially, and worked on some educational committees together. One of these was planning a new high school that was designed for students who found it difficult to function in large settings. Several of us worked long and hard on this plan, and eventually the school did open, but much of the credit belonged to Denise's innovative ideas and determination to help these students who often slip through the cracks in a large, impersonal educational setting.

On Sunday evening of that weekend, the principal of the school, Carmen Vegliante, phoned me at home and told me that Denise had been murdered late Saturday night. He wasn't certain of the details, but knew that the local news would be covering the story. I was in shock as I watched the news and learned that she had been strangled in her home by a man, supposedly a friend of hers; a man who, I would soon discover, was considered to be a relatively gentle person. The story just didn't make any sense to me. Another gory part of the story was that the man was found running naked down a road in the middle of the night with blood all over his body, a description that has conjured a thousand vivid pictures for me, each one terrible and haunting. But so many details of the story just didn't make sense to me. I heard that drugs were involved in some way, as was alcohol. To tell the truth, I was numb from the stories, the theories, and the daily unfolding of more and more hypothetical details. All I could manage to think about was that my friend was no longer alive. The sudden death of someone close has a resounding effect. Having lost people in this manner and over a long period of time, I don't know which one is "easier" for those who survive them.

A bizarre series of events then unfolded. I was visited very late at night by a another man who loved and wanted to marry Denise. Unlike the man found running down the road, I knew this person and had been in the company of him and Denise on several social occasions. But the happiness of our former encounters was turned to despair and disbelief on this night. I can remember his rather large and strapping frame sitting in my rocking chair. He was crying, telling me that he was going away and I probably wouldn't see or hear from him again. He told me that a lot of terrible things would be disclosed about the murder, but that I should not believe any of it. I had to believe in Denise and the good person I knew her to be. He didn't have to tell me that. He left as quickly as he arrived and, true to his word, I never saw or heard from him again.

After these many years, my only knowledge of the event is that at least two men wanted to marry Denise, but she was reluctant despite pressure from them. Many horrific scenarios have played themselves out in my mind concerning that tragic night, but even after all of these years there is no definite knowledge of the facts. Recently I looked through some old photos, and I found a small picture of Denise sitting in a convertible, her hair flying in the breeze and her infectious smile and laughing eyes dominating the picture. This is how I wish to remember her always. Her loss still causes me great sadness.

The murder occurred weeks before *Othello* opened, and Tom and Miriam and I had yet to face the tumultuous scene in the play where Othello strangles Desdemona. How frighteningly ironic that we would have to immerse ourselves in a scene so similar, at least superficially, with the real life occurrence that shattered our composure so recently. I spoke to the cast and crew about the scene prior to the rehearsal and excused any one who felt uncomfortable. I then went about the rehearsal as I would for any scene. I wanted nothing save the subject matter to interrupt the structure and security of rehearsal that we all depended upon so frequently. I blocked the scene and then we picked it apart moment by moment, motivating and justifying as we brought the text to life. In a peculiar way, the rehearsal almost seemed like therapy for us. It helped to soothe our pain while simultaneously and incongruously providing us with a glimpse of extreme human volatility and ferocity. When Tom mentioned his inability to hate anyone enough to strangle him/her, our company talked about the dark side of human nature and what it would take to get any one of us so angry that we might unleash our fury on someone else. We tried to explore where that darkness resides; what removes the code of civilized behavior and causes an outburst of physical violence. Inexplicably, *Othello* helped all of us cope with Denise's untimely death, and for this reason, the play took on an importance none of us could possibly have imagined only a few weeks earlier.

Save this terrible incident, after we finished our work on Othello I realized what an incredible theatrical experience that play provided for us. I recall one particular student in the cast coming to talk to me at the start of rehearsals about his intimidation with the text and that he lacked confidence in himself for this production. He belonged to that category I spoke of earlier—the general high school student who was frightened of the very word, "Shakespeare." As opening night approached, he spoke to me privately once again. This time, however, he shared his newfound excitement and enthusiasm. He told me that his work on the play brought it alive for him as never before. He came to be intrigued by the story, relish the language which had previously frightened him, and he honestly looked forward to reading more of Shakespeare's plays.

This has happened several times with the various Shakespeare plays we've presented. Most recently, in 1999, a freshman questioned my choice of *Midsummer*, saying that he could never understand a word in any Shakespeare play. He worked on the crew for *Midsummer*, and I would often find him watching rehearsals, being thoroughly engrossed in the content of the scene. After the performances he told me how much he enjoyed the play and how much his original views on the playwright's work had changed. Obviously, we teachers like to hear stories like this one.

Sadly, I know of many directors who shy away from Shakespeare just as so many students do. One in particular, a very capable and talented director and teacher, confided to me that she was very uncomfortable about directing a Shakespeare, and felt guilty about her fear as well. She was well aware of the numerous benefits of the work, yet couldn't bring herself to commit to it. I wanted to encourage her as well as the others to try it and almost made it a personal crusade to persuade them to do so. I talked to them and planned with them, and even subsequently wrote an article that appeared in the *Secondary School Theatre Journal* in the winter of 1981 entitled, "Shakespeare on the High School Stage." In the article I outlined a course of study and preparation and talked a bit about the approach to Shakespeare I take in my own acting classes. Since then I'm happy to say that several of my colleagues have indeed directed a Shakespeare, and they have done excellent jobs, giving such literary and theatrical gifts to their students as well as bolstering their own self confidence.

The weeks of rehearsing *Othello* were so positive and productive. In addition to the exhilaration of rehearsing this great play, I observed so many students engaged in discussions about human behavior, about language, about comparisons to other plays and literary forms; I listened to them spontaneously quoting the play when it applied to daily situations in school; I watched as they individually pursued further knowledge in such areas as music and combat and dancing. This play certainly was a highlight of my career.

In December of 1982 we embarked upon our next Shakespearean venture, *Richard III*. This was to be our first history play, and as such completed one production of each of Shakespeare's major types of theatrical work—comedy, tragedy, and history. Martin Harries played the famous villain. I recall his menacing smile as he directly addressed the audience, saying,

> "And thus I clothe my naked villainy
> With odd old ends stol'n forth of holy writ
> And seem a saint when most I play the devil."

This passage is particularly ironic in that Martin played the saint-like Thomas Becket the previous year in *Becket, or the Honor of God*. Thomas Becket and Richard are polar opposites, one being the epitome of goodness and the other being sheer evil; one is driven by his conscience and the other by ambition and power. I admired Martin for finding elements within himself with which to believably play both roles, but he was that kind of actor. He worked constantly, adding to his storehouse of inner resources and then tapping them to breathe life into these extraordinary historical figures.

One of Martin's greatest assets as an actor was his restraint. He rarely felt the need to shout to make a point or to assert his authority. Rather he held back, he undercut his lines with a calmness which, when complemented by his piercing eyes and expressive mouth, created a man of enormous power. His Richard was lethal and calculating. I remember a judge at the drama festival that year who confided in me that she knew she was in for a treat the moment Martin first appeared on stage. As the ensemble parted and exited soon after the opening curtain, the solitary, black-garbed figure of Richard stood facing upstage. Martin waited a beat, turned slowly to the audience, looked at them, and broke out into a coy smile. This simple series of actions, before he even began to speak, revealed an actor who was in complete control. The audience was excited already.

I cast Martin as Richard during the spring of the previous school year. I wanted to work with him over the summer, exploring the text and discovering the character—at least on paper. I remember he and I sitting by the pool in my condominium in Stratford, Connecticut, with our scripts in our hands and volumes of research material at our sides, spending endless hours discussing, reading, researching and interpreting.

Later that summer Martin went on vacation to England. He sent me a postcard on which was a photo of Edwin Austin Abbey's oil painting, "The Duke of Gloucester and the Lady Anne" in which Richard wore a long, royal robe of deep red. I thought I would surprise Martin by having our costume designers/builders create that robe. It was a way of showing my appreciation to Martin for his summer of study, and while he undoubtedly looked splendid in that costume, it represented a great deal more; it was a special bond between us.

When the acting rehearsals began in the fall, there was great excitement about the production. I hired Bill Burns, the director of the educational theater video mentioned previously, to be the fight choreographer for the play. This is one of Bill's strong suits, and during the play's climactic war scene, he had twenty-one men wielding broad swords in an impressive and greatly-detailed battle. Bill also staged the drowning death of Clarence, played by Alexander Kenney, in the prison near the play's beginning. Again, it was very realistic. Usually reported as offstage action, I chose to have the murder played in front of the audience, believing that it would enhance Richard's villainy. Also, since this was one of Richard's first machinations, I felt it would increase the audience's interest and tension as the play progressed. The more I think about my practices as a director, the more I realize that my appreciation for language has never dampened my belief that plays must have visual action in them. American audiences in particular like to see things happening.

Clarence struggled as his head was forced down into a barrel of water. To add believability to the action, Bill had Clarence momentarily fend off his attackers, suddenly pulling his submerged head from the barrel and sending a long stream of water careening off the side wall of the prison. Once again, it was a highly charged moment on the stage and added even more horror to Richard's deeds.

This cast and crew was, once again, a talented one. Many of them had been students of mine at Whalen Junior High School, so by the time this play came along, some of them had five or six years of acting training. Laurie Pitts played Lady Anne with expertise. The scene where she first appeared, following Edward's casket, was particularly thrilling and difficult. Richard tells us as Lady Anne approaches that he has killed her husband, and will now court her, for he could secure one step to the throne by marrying her. He informs us that he has selected this very moment to propose marriage to her and that she will accept.

Working on that scene took a long time, for Richard's objective seemed not only unrealistic, but, in fact, preposterous. Martin, Laurie, and I discussed and experimented until we found believable motivations. We also needed to find Anne's vulnerability, for this would be the key to Richard's success. I remember the rehearsal when we felt that the scene finally worked. We were thrilled to have found a way to play it that was believable. The audience's loud approval on each performance evening was a testament to Shakespeare's genius, his grasp of the human condition, and also to two wonderful actors who used the seeming impossibility of that scene's premise to challenge them into making it succeed. Martin won his second consecutive "Outstanding Actor" award at the drama festival in the spring of 1983, and Laurie was named to the prestigious "All Connecticut Cast."

In my planning for the drama festival that year, I remember wanting to show more of Richard's driving ambition at the very start of the piece. I felt that many high school students might not know the plot of the play, and I needed to impart this information right away. Also, festival pieces are shorter than full length productions and a great deal of information must be conveyed in an abbreviated amount of time. For this purpose I went to *Henry VI, Part III* and took some lines which I added near the end of Richard's opening soliloquy.

> "Why, I can smile and murder whiles I smile
> And wet my cheeks with artificial tears,
> And frame my face to all occasions.
> I'll drown more sailors than the mermaid shall;
> I'll slay more gazers than the basilisk;
> Deceive more slyly than Ulysses could,
> I can add colors to the chameleon
> And set the murderous Machiavel to school.
> Can I do this and cannot get a crown?
> Tut, were it farther off, I'll pluck it down."

These lines further clarified Richard's intent at the play's opening as well as added depth and texture to his character.

Martin went on to Columbia University and at the time of this writing teaches at Princeton University. Interestingly, he taught history through Shakespeare's plays for a while—a course of his own devising and a fascinating one at that. But Martin was always a unique human being. Even in his earliest days at the junior high school when he played a sailor standing on a large wooden barrel in Neil Simon's The *Good Doctor*, this young man had a talent and a joy for learning that was unmistakable.

The cast also included Kirsten Shepherd as Margaret, the widow of King Henry VI. Kirsten studied theater throughout both junior and senior high schools and was truly a core member of the department through those years. It is a great gift for a teacher to witness the development of students over the course of six years. What a thrill it has been to watch them develop their interests and their skills as they mature, recognizing and appreciating the broad range of possibilities that lay ahead, and hopefully retaining, through it all, their childhood joy and vigor. Kirsten currently teaches courses in theater at North Carolina State University and wrote a book entitled *Ibsen and Early Modernist Theater, 1890—1900*. She was a smart, fun-loving, sensitive young woman from the moment I met her, and she participated in numerous productions. Her brother, Gordon, was involved to some extent in Hamden Theater, but her younger sister, Lisbeth, played a major role in the development of our department a few years later.

One of the advantages of *Richard III* for educational theater is the play's inclusion of a good number of strong female roles, something that is not often found in Shakespeare's works. In addition to Kirsten and Laurie, the cast included Sarah Sherman as Elizabeth, queen to King Edward IV, and Lisa Prezioso as the Duchess of York.

Also in the cast were Paud Roche and Brendan Ledig who would soon play lead roles in Bernard Pomerance's *The Elephant Man,* and Michael Lerner and Patricia McVerry would stun audiences in one of the department's most successful productions, *Children of a Lesser God,* in 1984. Another member of the ensemble, Jane Baird, was to go on to appear in *Aspects of Love* on Broadway some years later.

Once again the press was extremely good to us. Local newspapers praised *Richard III*, especially when it won Hamden it's sixth consecutive "Outstanding Production in Connecticut" Award. One paper wrote "In many sectors of our society, tradition is time honored, sacred. Although the art form has lent itself to some innovation, American theater has held tradition in high regard through the years. Nowhere has this been exemplified in a grander sense than among the young people and adults associated with the Hamden High School Mainstage Ensemble. For them, tradition has meant an attention to detail and singleness of purpose unparalleled in Connecticut scholastic theater in recent years."

A Midsummer Night's Dream (1975)

Othello (1980)

As You Like It (1986)

Much Ado About Nothing (1992)

Richard III (1982)

It was about this time that the Royal Shakespeare Company was visiting New York City with two major productions. One of these featured the famous English actress, Margaret Tyzack whose sister I knew from my association with the Foote School in New Haven where she was employed. Ms. Tyzack and I were introduced via the mail, and this began a series of communications which I found very satisfying and enjoyable. She not only wrote to me, but she sent me several signed photos, asking me which I preferred for specific publicity shots. Not long before she arrived in New York to play the Countess of Rousillon in *All's Well That Ends Well*, I received Ms. Tyzack's personal make-up plot for the role, causing me to be more excited about seeing the play and finally meeting her.

The day of the performance had finally arrived. My friend, Ort Pengue, and I hadn't seen a live performance by the Royal Shakespeare Company, so we were excited about this production. *All's Well* isn't done too frequently, so we were certain the experience would be a memorable one. We had even been given ideal seats, approximately five rows back in the direct center of the theater.

As the lights began to dim at the start of the play, approximately four latecomers took the seats directly in front of us, and it took me no time at all to figure out that one of them was Katherine Hepburn. This unexpected surprise was distracting as I wanted to focus on the play and Ms. Tyzack, but I found myself returning to gaze at the back of Katherine Hepburn's head. When intermission arrived, nearly the entire theater realized that the actress was among us, but few people dared to disturb her. Suddenly Ort struck up a conversation with her, informing her that he was her newspaper delivery boy in Stratford when she appeared there to perform at the Shakespeare Theater. He reminded her how he and his friends would follow her on their bicycles as she went for her daily ride. Miss Hepburn was more than cordial to Ort, and really seemed to appreciate the conversation. I, on the other hand, was anxious to say something, but much too nervous to interrupt. And then, what could I say to her? The second act began, and I spent the next half of the play fortifying myself to find the courage to speak to Katherine Hepburn. After all, I was an acting teacher and I convinced myself that I owed it to my students to at least say hello.

As the lights came up at the end of the production, I realized that Miss Hepburn was not in her seat. In fact, she had already moved swiftly towards the side door where her limousine was stationed. I dashed through the aisles, looking ridiculous I'm sure, pursuing her and calling just softly enough not to make a scene, "Miss Hepburn! Oh, Miss Hepburn!" Finally, as she was about to enter her limousine, she turned sharply towards me, saying, "Yes?" I remember standing so close to her when she wheeled about to face me, her eyes looking directly into mine. Suddenly every movie and play she ever acted in seemed to flash before my eyes. Now that I had Katherine Hepburn's undivided attention, I had no idea what to say. My tongue became dry and thick and I stuttered a meek, "Thank you....", at which point she looked at me rather skeptically and replied, "You're welcome." And then the limousine whisked her away. Feeling rather foolish, I noted Ort in the distance leaning against the theater, smiling wryly, and shaking his head. It seemed that my prediction of a memorable day would come true after all, although it wasn't exactly what I had in mind.

In November of 1984, I had a wonderful experience at the American Shakespeare Theater. At the time I was a member of a committee called "Teachers for Shakespeare" sponsored by the theater, and we were invited to a book signing by author Errol Hill, professor of drama and oratory at Dartmouth College. His book, *Shakespeare in Sable: A History of Black Shakespearean Actors,* covered the participation of black actors in Shakespearean productions from the 1820's to the 1980's, and was sparked by his reaction to the shocking dearth of material about such involvement.

The day was a gloomy one, and a cold, persistent drizzle and accompanying gray skies made me reluctant to drive to the theater. When I arrived, however, I was treated to one of the most important and inspiring experiences I can remember. On the stage before me were seated some of the greatest African American actors of our times: James Earl Jones, Jane White, Moses Gunn, Earle Hyman, Harold Scott, and Gloria Foster. Lloyd Richards, then the dean of the Yale School of Drama, acted as the master of ceremonies, and after some formal introductions, we were treated to readings of Shakespeare by these luminaries of the stage. Earl Hyman, the first actor to ever appear on the stage of the Stratford Shakespeare Theater, read from *The Tempest;* James Earl Jones read from both *Othello* and *The Merchant of Venice;* Gloria Foster then read from *Antony and Cleopatra* , followed by Jane White from *The Taming of the Shrew;* Harold Scott read from *Julius Caesar* and Moses Gunn finished with a reading from *Hamlet*. Each performance was electrifying. I was captivated by their smooth, polished voices and impeccable diction as well as their consummate ability to create a character so instantly. As so often happens to me when I find myself in extraordinary situations like this one, I had that feeling that I was the only one in the room. I blotted everything else out and my focus was totally on the actors. I was caught up in every nuance of sound and resulting image, and I knew, once again, that I was "home" in that beautiful world of Shakespeare I love so much.

I believe that events happen to people, just as this one did to me, quite spontaneously and seemingly by accident, and yet their effect can be felt for years and years. It is almost as if a person is drawn to a place through some power of Fate. This one day at the American Shakespeare Theater was remarkable and will be etched in my memory forever.

It is ironic that I would write about our next Shakespeare venture, *As You Like It* on the very day in 1999 that I received a letter from Sarah Haller Wastell, the student who played the role of "Rosalind" in 1986. Prior to today I hadn't heard from her in many years. Sarah now lives in Swaziland after having resided in a small Basque fishing village on the French/Spanish border for a while. She is a cultural anthropologist, married to a Basque gentleman and is raising her family in Swaziland temporarily. She writes of telling her daughter about her first audition for me and her first role as "Gretl" in *The Sound of Music*, through to the "thrill of playing Rosalind" in her senior year in high school.

Sarah was a marvelous actress and went on to study for a while at a theater conservatory, a place she eventually left. She writes of this experience: "I remember saying that my time preparing myself to become a 'professional' actress had sullied the only pure and beautiful thing I had known in my life, that every day spent learning technique and training my voice saw the erosion of the humanity and magic that had always been the theater's true preserve for me, and that I simply couldn't afford to sacrifice those memories." Interestingly, I never knew why Sarah left the conservatory and didn't think it was my business to ask. Her letter brings closure to that experience and I'm glad she shared that with me.

But Sarah wants to act again someday. She writes, "It won't be the Broadway or the West End I idealized in my youth; it will be a small community theater in whichever corner of the world I find myself when my restlessness has finally exhausted itself, and it will be a theater comprising that quiet grandeur and epic beauty we can invariably find in the lives of all of those around us when we open our eyes to it. It will be a theater just like yours."

As You Like It was the first Shakespearean play I had ever seen. I remember traveling by bus to Stratford, Connecticut from my hometown of Mt. Vernon, New York. I was in the seventh grade. My teacher's name was Miss Tuckwell, and she fascinated me as she would stand before my class, reading poetry and sonnets. I can still see her and hear her voice. She felt it was important for us to see a Shakespeare play and arranged for us to travel so far away to the Shakespeare Theater.

I was fortunate to have other such inspirational English teachers-Mrs. Engel in the sixth grade who encouraged me to write, as did Mrs. Colton and Miss Cahalan in high school. And the wonderful Adelaide Amore, a college instructor, who allowed a freshman into her advanced, upper-classmen-only creative writing class and taught me how to liberate myself through the use of the written word. Those teachers I had early on, way back in Christopher Columbus Elementary School and Charles E. Nichols Junior High School were important figures as it turns out. As young as I was, their love of literature always transported me to some magical world of wonderful stories, beautiful language, and great intrigue.

One educator who had a profound effect on me, although I could never have realized it at that time, was Miss McGivney, our elementary school librarian. One might think it difficult to remember a person who I met so early in my life, but I remember her precisely— the warmth of her smile, the softness of her voice, the sometimes devilish twinkle in her eye, and her fascinating readings. On cold winter days the library radiators hissed with their comforting, noisy steam-heat warmth and smell, and Miss McGivney would stand before us and read Longfellow, and suddenly I could feel the excitement that would come to me over and over again in years thereafter. As I look back, I was very lucky to have such teachers at such an early age, and I'm sure they played a large part in my choice of teaching as a profession and my passion for literature and theater.

I was totally overwhelmed by the beauty of *As You Like It* and I remember my parents telling me how much we should appreciate Miss Tuckwell's efforts to take us to see it. To this day I can remember the deep blue lighting of the forest, the melodious voices of the actors, and the rich costuming. Once again, as I was so prone in those days, I was swept away and taken to some private place of enchantment that I never even thought about sharing with any of my classmates. It was an experience I would always find pivotal in my young life. Directing the play so many years later, then, seemed like a return visit, and I found the experience to be a delight.

I had decided to update *As You Like It* to the Napoleonic Era. The glamorous appearance of the court contradicted the dictatorship of the time, and the unreasonable assertion of power provided a believable backdrop for the dismissal of Celia and her subsequent flight into the woods. Also the flow and softness of the court costumes would provide a visual contrast to the rustic look of the characters in the woods.

Updating, or modernizing, Shakespeare's plays has always been a source of great controversy. Actually this was the case moreso in the 60's and 70's than it is today. When I first began directing, it was a subject I needed to give serious consideration. I always knew that respecting the integrity of the text was of primary importance, and I felt that any updating was permissible as long as the interpretation was still true to the playwright and his theme. Since those themes are timeless, they needn't be pigeon-holed into a strict Elizabethan setting. I recall the Stratford, Connecticut Shakespeare Theater being severely chastised for updating some of its productions in the mid 1970's which seemed to be done as a method of sensationalizing rather than illuminating, one of those being the infamous *Henry V* performed in hockey uniforms.

Our production of *As You Like It*, however, paid utmost attention to the theme and the story, and the language was strictly adhered to. Helen Gardner, the Shakespearean scholar, referred to this play as "the most refined and exquisite of the comedies. It is Shakespeare's most Mozartian comedy." She proposes that the play is composed of two movements, "the first showing the Court with its jealousies and conflicts, and the second illustrating the simplicity of pastoral life." The play progresses from disorder to order, thereby illustrating the necessity for order in life.

This Mozartian reference inspired me to think of using music in the production, and I hired a friend of mine who is an accomplished composer, Susan Hulsman-Bingham, to write some original pieces. I also included operatic pieces at the beginning and near the end of the play and asked two professional opera singers whom I had directed for the CET Opera Company the year before to perform them. This, I felt, would expose my students, at least somewhat, to the world of opera, and also show them how music could easily complement the Shakespearean text.

Susan, Judith Caldwell, and Kyle Pruitt blended into the student company beautifully. I would often see them interacting with groups of students, teaching them about musical composition and opera, demonstrating selections, or just engaging in friendly conversation. I also asked Lorraine Drazba, an English and Shakespeare teacher at Hamden High School, to take a role in the production, which she did most graciously. It was inspiring to witness the students and the adults working on this major project together and the latter group sincerely asking the students for their opinions about line delivery or interpretation and even about the effectiveness of their performances. There was an atmosphere of strong mutual trust and responsibility. There certainly was no condescension on the parts of the adults, for these students were disciplined and approached their work honestly and with determination. So often while directing a play I think about the ways in which students learn. Obviously this is a continuous topic of discussion in educational circles. Then I pull myself out of the rehearsal process long enough to observe the miraculous growth and achievement of these students, and my belief and confidence in educational theater are bolstered once again. It is a discipline that offers such a tremendous range of opportunities. It accommodates all kinds of learners and challenges them to do their best.

I wanted to open the play in a bold and exciting way. Shakespeare helped out here since he places the exciting opening wrestling match between Orlando and Charles near the beginning of the play. I decided to place the action in a palace courtyard amidst a spring celebration. This then allowed me to include the operatic piece and a dramatic fencing match among several actors staged by Bill Burns as additional features of the festivities. The opera, fencing, and wrestling sequences were performed to Susan's most beautiful original score. Before the first word of the text was spoken, then, the audience was treated to visual and auditory feast.

Len Van de Graaff was the student who played the melancholy Jacques whose task it was to deliver the famous "All the world's a stage" speech. As with all famous speeches, it can be somewhat intimidating to act since it has been done by actors through the ages as well as memorized by thousands of students in English classes. But Len did an excellent job with it, giving it a feeling of freshness and truth as he illustrated the various stages in the life of man. The lovely Anne McBride played Celia. Ann was one of those rare students who seemed to have been born with the gift of playing Shakespeare. Her hair cascading in soft strawberry blond curls, Ann's Celia was absolutely delightful. It was thrilling to hear her speak the lines with such clarity and understanding and to bring the beauty of the language alive. David Schwartz played Touchstone, another famous role which could be intimidating to a young actor. David created a character who was wisely humorous, just as the playwright had intended.

I was extremely pleased with the acting in this production. The cast made the lines totally accessible, a factor which I feel is so important in classical theater. Ort Pengue Jr.'s set was superb as well, with its stucco facade for the court scenes and his creation of the forest of Arden through the use of sweeping pieces of dyed tobacco cloth. I admire Ort's instincts when it comes to sensing the mood of a play and his ability to evoke it in such a masterful way.

During the course of our rehearsals, a very special event occurred. I was reading the local newspaper when numerous italicized Shakespearean quotations caught my eye. As I read the article, I discovered that it celebrated the Christmas Day anniversary of Professor Leslie Hotson, a world-renowned Shakespeare scholar, and his wife, Mary. Both were elderly at the time, some 92 years old, and were retired in a small country house in Northford, Connecticut. I had studied Professor Hotson's work in college and was very impressed with it. I felt it was important to write a letter to him, telling him how I was influenced by and grateful for his life-long research on a topic I love so much. I was surprised when he responded to my letter and included an invitation to his home.

I brought Len Van de Graaff, who played Jaques, with me to visit the Hotsons on that wintry day, and I can vividly recall the hours the four of us spent together. I remember being startled by the number of books which filled the floor to ceiling bookcases, obstructing any view of painted or wallpapered walls. A fire blazed in the fireplace, to which the Professor tended slowly and carefully, and the room smelled of burning wood and spiced cider. A silent snow was falling in a picturesque way outside the windows, giving a kind of surreal quality to this once-in-a-lifetime experience.

The afternoon visit was filled with the most wonderful moments, like Professor Hotson showing us his most beautiful rock collection and the gifts sent to him from all over the world by generations of students. At one point, Mary placed a stone in my hand and closed my fingers around it. She then told me that it was walked upon by Jesus himself, and I had no doubt that she was telling the truth. They also showed us a goblet carved during Shakespeare's days from a tree near his home, and a life-like drawing of the playwright—with blond hair. But what I remember most were the penetrating eyes of the Professor and Mary, so totally focused on me. Both of them were so happy that I was directing *As You Like It* at the time, and they were delighted that young people were being given the opportunity to bring Shakespeare's work to life. During the course of the conversation, an enthralling one which spanned the works of Mary Hotson's cousin, George Elliott, to the time they had to quickly bury their treasured books in Europe to hide them from the approaching Nazi army-they also asked me for my interpretation of one of the sonnets. I was momentarily taken aback, and I remember feeling very uncomfortable and insecure. What could I possible say that this learned man and his learned wife would not have heard before? Yet both he and Mary listened so intently to me—as if this interpretation were never before voiced.

And so I learned a great lesson from the Hotsons—the importance of listening. I remember reading a eulogy to my late acting teacher, Constance Welch. Rod Bladel, a former student of Miss Welch's and the head of the Theater Library at Lincoln Center, recalled observing her listening to a young child as intently as one would listen to Aristotle. The value of respecting others' opinions, points of view, and philosophies is one that is applicable not only to the theater, but to life as well. In a thankyou card that the Hotsons sent me sometime after the visit, they remarked, taking me quite by surprise, how they enjoyed my listening to them. The card also contained a simply written but profoundly moving sentence, "You have the humble mind of a searcher for truth." This statement and the treasured memory that accompanies it flatters me greatly, but I feel that it should describe *all* people in the arts, or perhaps I should just say, "all people."

As we prepared to leave that day, Mary Hotson, with great difficulty, walked us to the door. She was more than partially lame at the time and I could tell that she was having trouble showing us out, yet there was no question that she would be the perfect hostess. On a table in her small foyer was a print by Giotto with Halley's comment fleeting across the sky. The year of our visit also happened to be a year that the comet was visible, and I remember Mrs. Hotson taking my hand firmly, looking deep into my eyes, and saying, "Isn't life exciting!" I could tell that she was trying to impart yet one more lesson, giving me a hint of something she had learned in her ninety-two years—one of life's secrets—to be aware of the "connections" that unify people throughout time.

I never saw the Hotsons again, although we corresponded several times through the mail. They sent my daughter, Jennifer, some beautiful handwritten and decorated Elizabethan Christmas songs, a material reminder that the visit wasn't just a dream! The memory of that day, nearly ten years ago, is still fresh in my mind. These elderly people, humble and warm, seemed to defy the well-deserved scholarly acclaim heaped upon them. Their academic and pedagogical honors gave way to the simplicity, honesty, and wisdom that filled that room. To this day I think that the experience was somehow planned for me. Whatever the reason for our crossing paths, I know that I am a better person today for having met them.

Professor Hotson gave me a copy of his book, *The First Night of Twelfth Night* and inscribed it for me. I was very touched by the gift indeed. Years later I had a student, Jessica Vasquez, who was one of the best Shakespearean actors with whom I was privileged to work. I was so impressed by not only her talent, but her disciplined work ethic combined with her sincerity and kindness, that I gave her the copy of Professor Hotson's book, and wrote in it under the Professor's inscription. I told her that she might want to pass this treasure down someday to someone very important in her life.

Years later, during the summer of 1999, I had occasion to visit Louis Burke, the Artistic Director of the new Stratford, Connecticut Shakespeare Festival. Louis was telling me about his research of *Twelfth Night* and how he derived such pleasure from a difficult-to-find book- one which turned out to be the very book Professor Hotson had given me. As a matter of fact, the only copy he could find was in Germany. When I told him that I had been given a copy by Professor Hotson himself, Louis was amazed, perhaps moreso that I had given it away. But there was no question in my mind that Jessica deserved it as a way of saying thankyou to her for all she had done for our class, our program, and for me. The encouragement and support she will derive from it will make it far more valuable than its rarity or its monetary value.

Another fascinating incident that was related to *As You Like It* was my receiving a letter written by a woman in the audience. She was a single mother of a very young child, and she had just moved to Hamden. She knew no one in town at the time, and certainly wasn't related to anyone in the company. However, she was a Shakespeare aficionado and decided to bring her young daughter to see the play. Her letter told of the child's fascination, and how the young girl was thoroughly engrossed in the play. This letter was only the first of many I was to receive from her over the course of several years. She brought her daughter to every production, but, quite interestingly, never introduced themselves to me. It got to the point where I would actually peruse the audience before curtain time, looking for two people who might fit my imagined descriptions.

The years passed, and one evening, following a performance of my summer theater at the Little Theater on Lincoln Street in New Haven, a young woman walked towards me. The lobby was rather crowded, but I remember her approach, her blond hair and such wide, expressive eyes. Somehow I knew immediately that this was the child, now a young adult, who had seen all of the productions. She smiled at me and I at her. We didn't speak for what seemed to be a long while, and then she said quite simply, "I love you...and thank you for doing the most wonderful plays." Her sincerity was so remarkable. She held me riveted by her sense of wonder and excitement-as if I were someone truly special when, in fact, it was she who was so. I thanked her, tears forming in my eyes as if I had found a long lost relative. I kissed her cheek, and I recall how tightly she hugged me. Then an older woman approached, radiating that same enthusiasm and warmth. It's only natural to imagine what people look and sound like after receiving their letters for so long, yet somehow, with them now standing next to me, that didn't matter at all. The mother told me that they were moving away from Hamden and that they would, most of all, miss the plays. They thanked me and disappeared through the front doors of the theater. I stood there for quite a while trying to make some sense of what had just happened. I was somewhat aware of the audience members milling about, but I could only faintly hear their talking. I was in some "other" place, having met two people with whom I felt a strong bond. And suddenly, as joyous as I was to finally meet them, I was likewise as sad, for I knew I would not see them again.

We cross paths with special people in life, and no matter how much we want to hold onto them and never let them go, this is not always the way it was meant to be. Perhaps the meeting is meant to be swift at best, and yet, during that brief but precious time, what miracles occur.

In 1987 I chaperoned a trip to England arranged by high school teacher and future administrator, Janet Garagliano. Janet had been instrumental in setting up an exchange program with the Kirby-Kendall School in northern England. The English students had visited Hamden, and now it was our turn to visit them. While past exchanges between the two schools had involved other departments, its current thrust centered around Theater. I led a joint workshop with their theater teacher, and our students attended classes with their English hosts.

One of my personal highlights of the trip to England was visiting Stratford as well as seeing a production by the Royal Shakespeare Company, one I greatly anticipated. I was thrilled to finally see the Royal Shakespeare Company in their home theater. Approximately eleven minutes into this modernized version of the play, very realistic sound effects of approaching helicopters were heard. Ropes were then dropped from the stage ceiling, and a flurry of soldiers slid down them to the floor. It was a dazzling visual and auditory effect, until I noticed one soldier who stopped half way down his rope. Obviously, something was wrong, and it soon became apparent that the hardware which facilitated the slide had become locked on the rope. Soon after, all of the soldiers as well as the remainder of the cast on the stage looked up at the helpless actor who was now dangling midway down the proscenium arch. After a silence during which the futility of the situation must have become obvious to them, they all began to laugh. And then the audience began to laugh. The stage manager walked out onto the stage, complete with head set, apologized to the audience, and said that the company would begin the play once again. With that, the group exited the stage, and the crew came out to reset the props and scenery. I must have been sitting with my mouth and eyes wide open in shock, for I soon realized that my entire group of students was staring at me. The play began once again, and when the formerly stranded actor completed his journey down the rope he received a loud round of applause from the audience. He received it once again during his curtain call at the play's conclusion, having endeared himself to us through that catastrophe.

Our group talked about the problem after the play and my students were shocked that even the Royal Shakespeare Company was not immune to the problems that face us in the live theater. In an odd way I suppose it made us all feel that we are not alone, but part of a giant theater family which shares the same dreams as well as the same nightmares. At any rate, the occurrence strengthened our resolve to double and even triple check every item prior to the start of any play. I realized once again that we are constantly learning lessons.

Much Ado About Nothing was our next Shakespeare, presented in May of 1992. Like the Shakespeares before it, the anticipation of this production created quite a stir in the department, and theater students began to read and discuss the play long before auditions were announced. Once again, I wanted to do something different with the play and searched the text for clues. I remember feeling the romantic playfulness of the script as I reread it, and I felt the production needed a setting that would complement that idea. I kept thinking of those black and white, rainy Saturday afternoon movies I watched as a youngster and the exotic locations that would easily carry me away on the magic carpet ride of my imagination. Shakespeare places the action in Messina, but once again the prescribed location does not have to be adhered to literally. Messina can be any romantic place inhabited by well-to-do and relatively important people. There is also a great deal of eavesdropping going on in the play, so I wanted the environment to offer some marvelous hiding places for the characters. And lastly, *Much Ado* is about love; about feelings and truth and honesty—which makes the title a bit ironic—for while pretense and make-believe abound in the play, it is actually concerned with reality and truth.

Beatrice and Benedick, the two major characters in the play, are highly independent souls who swear resistance to marriage as evidenced in the following passages:

Ben: That a woman conceived me I thank her; that she brought me up, I likewise give her most humble thanks; but...I will live a bachelor.

Bea: I would rather hear my dog bark at a crow than a man swear he loves me.

Yet, through the plot against Hero, Beatrice's cousin, both protagonists share a sympathy that brings them closer together, and when they finally realize their attraction, they speak quite differently, with directness and honesty:

Ben: I do love nothing in the world so well as you; is not that strange?

Bea: As strange as the thing I know not: it were as possible to say I love nothing so well as you.

My studies and research finally led me to place the action of our production in English-occupied India circa 1914. This would answer the need for army troops stationed on foreign soil. Leonato, who plays host to the visiting army officers, would be an English ambassador/dignitary residing in a lush estate where the central action would occur. I felt that this would offer much possibility for costume and set designs, and provide an intriguing visual backdrop for the play. It is also a romantic time and place, with the mysterious charm of a foreign land and the always-seductive element of adventure.

Ort Pengue's set design was exquisite and included a raked playing surface, stone walls, a wrought iron gate, and lush tropical plants. The costumes were elegant as well, with Leonato, played by Ben Billingsley, in a white suit, and Beatrice, played by Diane Bers, entering in Act I with jodphers, riding boots, a safari hat and carrying a riding whip. This helped to immediately establish Beatrice's tenacious exterior. Diane was a remarkable Beatrice. She played Shelby in the previous year's production of *Steel Magnolias* and, while she was excellent in that role as well, this famous Shakespearean heroine offered rich opportunities for character development and exploration of language unlike Diane had experienced before, and in both of which Diane excelled.

Matt Walker played Benedick. He was an exceptional actor who had an ability to delve deeply into a character's psyche. He could reveal so much through his eyes, and his impeccable diction never drew attention to itself. One of Matt's strongest assets was his sensitivity, and he built this trait into his characterizations so that they were believable and empathic as well. His work with Shakespeare was extraordinary; there was such joy in his performances. Matt would go on to play Jack, a social worker, in Tom Griffin's touching play, *The Boys Next Door*, the following year.

One day Matt came to ask me if I would be interested in starting a Directing Class. He was very interested in this field himself and knew of others that were enthusiastic about it as well. I agreed to teach the class, and that was the beginning of one of the most satisfying courses I taught during my career. The Independent Study Program at the High School sponsored it, so there was more flexibility in class size and meeting hours. That first class had six students, and we met at my home. During our first meeting, we sat in front of the fireplace and talked about directing—what it entailed, what qualities a director had to have, what we hoped to achieve, and so many other things—and I rarely experienced the educational "high" I received that evening. A person knows when something just *feels* right, and that evening's two-hour discussion was nothing less than invigorating.

Over the years, the class fluctuated in size from six to fifteen, but no matter what the size or composition of the group, they all had in common an eagerness to learn and I was grateful for it. The course was rigorous and demanded a great deal of time, but with very few exceptions those students relished the challenge. While each student was required to direct a scene from a play, they often directed one-act plays in a year-end one-act-play festival. As the years went by, the level of production became more sophisticated. I was impressed with the sets, the use of music and sound effects, and the challenge of the selected material. I truly feel that the Directing Class raised the level of proficiency in the entire Department. Directing students became leaders and were often asked for advice and guidance. Students were teaching students, and another component of the learning process was in place. How I loved teaching those classes. I often think of Matt and thank him again and again for being the catalyst for that course.

There were others in the cast of *Much Ado* would have a major effect on Hamden Theater within the next few years as well: Leah Altman, Samantha Ethier, Greg O'Connell, Jon Panagrossi, Christopher Johnson, Anthony Rossomando, and Matt Walker's twin brother, Jon. Taryn Chorney and Carra Gamberdella won awards at the Drama Festival and neither of them spoke a word. They played Indian servants, and drew the attention of the Festival judges by their restraint, dignity, and total composure. Taryn went on to study theater at Adelphi University, and just this past year served as my student teacher. She now teaches in a Connecticut high school.

The *Much Ado* cast also included a young man whom I was advised, rather vehemently, not to cast. He was rather irresponsible for two earlier plays that year, and even dropped out of one. Yet I was impressed with his audition, and moreso with his genuine enthusiasm. I wanted to offer him this opportunity to succeed; he needed it. I phoned him and we had a very honest conversation about the fact that I was about to entrust him with a major role, and that I, and every other member of the large company, needed to rely on him. He told me that he would live up to my faith in him, and he did just that. He never missed nor came late for a rehearsal, but on a higher level, his natural intelligence and curiosity were aroused by his immersion in the Shakespearean text and he loved to ask questions, make observations, see relationships. He went on to win a major award at the State Drama Festival that year, but, more importantly, won the respect and admiration of his colleagues and teachers.

It is interesting that this young man, so easily dismissed by some of my colleagues, could be so successful. I feel that one of the most important things about teaching is to believe in young people; to show them that you trust them. This certainly worked in the case of this young man. To this day he phones me from the west coast to tell me of things going on in life.

Simply put, his story and what he accomplished in those days moves me. I am very proud of him.

The week prior to the play's performance, the New Haven Register Arts and Leisure section of the Sunday newspaper ran a full page article on the play entitled, "That Stage in a Student's Life." This was rather unusual because the Arts and Leisure section rarely, if ever, dealt with educational theater. Rather, it covered our local professional theaters such as the Long Wharf, Shubert, and Yale Rep. The article also included a large color picture of the play in rehearsal. It was exciting to see our work so prominently displayed and discussed in such a notable, vital manner, and it once again verified the professionalism with which we hoped to approach any production. The article obviously attracted a great deal of attention and may have been partially responsible for the magnificent attendance the production enjoyed. It also made our students proud as they realized the wonderful support and respect afforded them by the entire greater New Haven artistic community.

Much Ado won the "Outstanding Play" Award at the Drama Festival in 1992, making it Hamden's fourteenth winner in seventeen years of Festival participation.

After the final performance of *Much Ado* many Hamden Theater graduates held a reunion in the school's cafeteria. It was quite an undertaking and also quite a surprise. The planning committee had received permission to get into the school early in the day and they decorated the space with photographs, posters, and programs of past plays. Following several beautiful speeches in which graduates reminisced and spoke of the importance of Hamden Theater in their lives, I was asked to speak. I vividly remember standing at the podium and looking into a sea of faces—students from so many years, from so many plays and classes, now standing together. I scanned the gathering and a million stories, experiences, and memories raced through my brain. I couldn't speak at first. I could only think about the richness before me. What a vast and limitless amount of energy. Our "family" was together again, the older members mingling with the current *Much Ado* cast and crew. I was incredibly moved.

At the end of my brief talk, a large basket was brought out of the crowd and placed before me, and then everyone formed a long line and put a hand-written letter into the basket. I couldn't believe that they were giving me thankyou letters when it was I who was the beneficiary of their presence in my life. These letters were from the prophets— people who are brightening the world with their goodness.

I can't put my feelings about that night into words. It was at once emotional and spiritual, joyous and fulfilling. Shakespeare best describes it when he wrote, "For thy sweet love remem'bred such wealth brings, That then I scorn to change my state with kings."

My final Shakespearean production was to come in 1999. It would also be my final play at Hamden High School. I think I always knew that my last play would be a Shakespeare piece. I did not know, however, when I selected *A Midsummer Night's Dream* in the spring of 1998 that the following year would also be my final one of teaching. It made the play, the directing, and, most of all, the students that much more special.

Chapter Five

A Fitting Conclusion

A Midsummer Night's Dream, 1999

"Although I did not choose a career on the stage, I know that so much of my job involves what you taught me. I am now a vocal music teacher in New York City. Every day brings back thoughts of things that I learned from my high school theater classes and productions. I often think of those days and remember that it is not my job to make better students; it is my job to make better people."

Samantha

"I find that I use something you taught me every day. It may be something as simple as a physical exercise to loosen up a tense muscle, or it may be something as important as imagining myself in another person's shoes before striking out. You taught me a way to believe in myself, to recognize and praise my achievements as an individual while reaching out to the universal in others. These lessons represent the kind of teaching which prepares students to formulate their own philosophies of life and their own strategies for exploring the world. From Hamden Theater one learns to think and to lend passion to one's thinking. Applying these lessons to any profession or situation is quite simple and something which both unifies Hamden students and makes them unique."

Michael

"I always seem to choke up when I'm around you and can never seem to get away from a pervading sense of formality in my interactions with you. You simply command more respect from me than perhaps any other individual I have ever encountered. I don't believe I could ever express what an impact my experiences with you and the theater have had on me. I strive to impress you, to make you proud, and without even realizing why. I would find myself every day attempting to do something to earn your pat on the shoulder or off-handed

smile, or a coy wink, and I would feel as though I had achieved a great feat upon getting it. I question why the opinion of one man matters so much to me when I had never cared for nor desired the opinion of anyone at all. My conclusion can only be that it is the total and unmatched respect I feel for you. You care for a kid who tries, albeit badly, to catch up to his peers, and give him the motivation, the desire, and the new-found confidence to work harder in every aspect of his life."

Mike

I didn't know when I selected **A Midsummer Night's Dream** for my spring production in 1999 that it would be my last at Hamden High School. The idea of a "last" production still feels peculiar. I suppose that is because the plays over the years represented more than merely rehearsing and performing. It was a way of life-an extension of the school day that was at once welcome, exciting, and really quite the norm. As a matter of fact, it could also be described as a "necessity," for it fulfilled a need that students and I have shared for many years. This was something we did together and now, more than ever, owned together. This further complicated the idea of retirement, making it a difficult decision. Nevertheless, I made that choice in the winter of 1999, a few months before the play went to performance. At first it was difficult to stop myself from thinking, "These will be my last auditions," and "These will be my last blocking rehearsals." The complexity of play production necessitates logic and order, making it all too easy to strike elements off a long, invisible list one by one. I realized, however, that this would put a damper on the rehearsal process, and so I stopped myself almost immediately. Instead, I became engrossed in the process, and I must say I enjoyed every minute of it. How could it be otherwise when there was a constant air of festivity about? This was our first Shakespeare in the new theater, and the play sparkled with a fresh and contemporary approach. Now we had a seemingly larger-than-ever department filled with productive and truly happy students, all of whom were busily working on their respective areas of this huge endeavor.

In many ways, *Midsummer* was a fitting conclusion for my work at Hamden High School and this stage of my career. It had always been a play close to my heart, having performed in it, seen it several times, but more importantly, having directed it as the opening production in the newly renovated Hamden High Theater in 1975. And so, twenty-four years later, it seemed to serve as the other "book end" of my life at this school.

As the production approached there was an increasing sense of anticipation and a groundswell of excitement. All of the performances of the play were sold out in advance, and when production week finally arrived everyone was waiting with baited breath for opening night. What had become very apparent to me was that all of this excitement was over Shakespeare, and what an educational accomplishment that was. It's one thing for high academic achievers to relish the thought of performing a Shakespeare play, but there were many in the company who had academic difficulties Yet here they were, about to bring to life a particular literary genre considered extremely difficult. I often wondered how educators could tap into this enthusiasm. If Shakespeare in particular and the Theater in general could raise the abilities of so many students, how could it be used in other subject areas as well?

During performances I watched some of the play from the balcony/mezzanine area. Beneath me was a sea of people, and I couldn't help but think about how far the program had come in thirty years. I was surprised at how many members of the '75 company of *Midsummer* came to see the '99 production, and I think I spent as much time watching them as I did watching the play. I couldn't help but wonder what they were thinking about. Were they re-living those moments, those rehearsals long ago that were so important to us? Indeed, those moments seemed to be the lifeblood of our high school days. I remember speaking to them before and after the play, and while we exchanged pleasantries something else was definitely going on. I could feel an intensity as our eyes locked and we reconnected after so many years. We were instantly filled with a longing for those early days, that daily contact, that thrill of working so closely together. I realized how much I missed them, but now so many were here along with my current students, and we were all doing what we did best–making Theater together. This elevated the already unforgettable performance evenings to the realm of the extraordinary.

The 1999 production tested the technical limits of our new theater. Frank, Ort, Brian Fagan (who came on board as Assistant to the Designer and relieved Frank of some of the time commitment at the high school due to increased hours at his Long Wharf job), and I met for many long hours discussing the theme, the spine, and the central images of the play. Ours was to be a modernized production of *Midsummer*, and I placed the play in 1936. The color palette was comprised of blues and purples and lavenders. Frank's set included a circular thrust–the first thrust of any kind used in the new facility–that projected into the audience some twelve feet. It had a trap door in it for magical appearances and disappearances of Puck, and also contained long reeds of grass that could grow during various moments in the play due to an elaborate system of ropes and pulleys under the thrust. The upstage area included several wide and sweeping circular stairs that ran the width of the stage to a higher level, and upstage of this level was a series of arched flats, on which were projected clouds, the moon, and various images to create different moods. It was an elegant set, with long, sheer curtains gracefully and dramatically draped for the court scenes, and the forest scenes were splendidly created through the use of tree and leaf gobos projected on the upstage flats and on the floor as well.

Ort's costumes were equally as splendid. I feel he truly outdid himself with this play. Theseus had a military look throughout, but his uniforms ran from red in the opening scene to the stunning white of the final post-nuptial scene in the court. The lovers also wore white in this scene, either wedding gowns or dinner jackets, and all of this was set amidst billowing pale lavender transparent drapes that swagged across the stage. During the forest scenes, the lovers actually had two costumes each, one of which was distressed and reflected their travails as they hobbled and trudged through the thick underbrush. The mechanicals were expertly garbed with time-appropriate hats, vests, aprons, knickers, over-sized pants, and any thing else that made them look humorous. *Midsummer* is done frequently as Shakespeare's plays go, but Ort's design for the forest characters was original and worked perfectly. It defied time and place. The fairies were especially splendid visually, their leotards and head pieces made of stretch velvets in a variety of foresty colors to facilitate movement. Titania and Oberon were regal, and yet still maintained an inhuman quality, and Puck's costume was covered in netting and feathers and designed to enable him to leap, squat, do cartwheels, and anything else required of him.

Working on *Midsummer* was an ideal experience. Actually, the last several years of play production had attained a level of proficiency that excluded almost all of the problems that most directors face in mounting a play. I credit my team with this. Frank, Ort, and Brian are more than theater artists. They are teachers who truly care about young people. While they are compassionate and kind, they are also very organized. Thomas McVety has designed posters and programs for my shows for many, many years and really should be considered a part of that team as well. A student of mine several years ago, Tom was in the 1975 production of *Midsummer*, playing the role of Francis Flute/Thisby. I have always felt that Tom's designs were crucial to the play, for they represented the "PR" work; they were the materials that drew people to the theater and introduced them to the play before its opening curtain. Tom carefully designed according to the play's interpretation, color selections, and theme. I would be hard pressed to pick out my favorite McVety work; each one is outstanding. I was enamored of his designs for *The Elephant Man, Richard III, Ah, Wilderness!, On the Verge..., Summer and Smoke,* and so many, many others—including summer productions of *Big River, Sunday in the Park With George,* and *Barnum.* The team had gotten to the point of nearly reading each other's minds, and while the approach to each new project remained the same, each play challenged us with new ways to overcome obstacles and new ways to express our artistic vision. I know how lucky I was to work with this group. Their work was informed by their artistry and knowledge, but most of all by their genuine love and concern for the students in our care.

Our production meetings for *Midsummer* resembled board meetings of a large corporation. Around several tables pushed together were nineteen of us. In addition to Ort, Frank, and Brian were students Patrick Rousseau and Jon Pleckaitis serving as Master Carpenters, Rebecca Lewis and Aaron Jack, the lighting designers, Rob Britney and Andrew Sargent, the Master Electricians, Marisa Perrotti and Andrew Drozd, the Assistant Master Carpenters, Carolyn Shea and Tiffany Jantzer, the Props Supervisors, Nette Compton, Daina Platais, and Cathie Turner, the Scenic Artists, Amber Castle, the Sound Engineer, and Kevin Carney and Kate Degnan, the Shop Managers. I have always believed in giving students important responsibilities, thereby offering them an ownership of the project. If *Midsummer* was successful, it was because it was important to all of these people. At production meetings, they took copious notes. Time schedules were created with everyone's comfort in mind and then adhered to rigorously in order to meet deadlines. Problems were discussed and solved as a group. The play was like a giant well-oiled machine, and nothing short of a total disaster could have stopped its progress.

While the crew of some forty additional students, all divided into specific production areas, worked nightly at their tasks, I rehearsed with the actors in the Black Box. Here again, the work was exciting, laced with laughter, and yet a serious examination of the text ranging from word definitions and pronunciations to literary references and exploration of subtext. The four lovers-Patricia Santomasso as Helena, Marta Montgomery as Hermia, Michael Ceccorulli as Lysander, and Brooks Kohlhepp as Demetrius-complemented each other so well. Michael and Brooks had done a limited amount of acting prior to this play. Brooks, a senior, had spent much of his time in the technical field, concentrating mostly on lighting. He had, however, taken an acting class and did very well in it. Michael is probably one of the hardest workers I've ever come across. He learned his lines quickly, was never late for one rehearsal, and was always prepared. He allowed himself to be totally vulnerable and open to ideas and experimentation. Michael is the personification of humility and graciousness, and much of the joy of working on this play centered around him.

During the summer following *Midsummer*, Michael told me of a recent experience he had while working at a coffee shop. One night, quite late, he was returning from taking out the trash when a young and rather violent bike-rider accused him of hitting the side of his bike with the trash. Although Michael denied this in his usual mature, gentle manner, the bike-rider continued to harass him. The occurrence finally ended due to the interference of a third party, and Michael was advised by his father to quit the job immediately; that it wasn't worth the anxiety, especially since Michael had already given two-week's notice to his employer a few days before. I agreed with his father. I know many people who have impulsively left such temporary jobs without even offering a two-week's notice. But Michael wouldn't quit, for he felt that he needed to honor his agreement. Also, he felt that his absence would impose a burden on his co-workers because they would have to cover his shifts, and he didn't want to do that to them. I thought about my advice and how it paled in comparison to Michael's integrity, honor, and sense of responsibility. Without a doubt, Michael is quite an unusual person; a model for all of us. And from this experience, seemingly unrelated to theater, I learned, more importantly, about life-about honor and commitment, two things I always talk about, but obviously needed to witness first-hand. I am continually taught by my students.

I remember working on Act III, scene ii with the four actors playing the lovers, one of the most memorable scenes in the play, where Hermia feels betrayed by her close friend, Helena. She thinks that Lysander, with whom she is in love, has been seduced by Helena's charms. Neither of the women know that the men are under the spell of Puck's magic. The talents of the four actors were taxed to the maximum in sustaining this long, but fast-paced comedic adventure. It was filled with the humor of the plot, the language, and a great deal of physical acrobatics. At one point Hermia threw herself into the air and landed in the men's arms as she attempted to strike at Helena. Marta created a character that was feisty and bold, while Tricia's Helena was insecure, even in the face of her supposed beauty. She checked her make-up in her hand-held compact even during this battle scene to make sure she looked good, a bit of business that worked so well since her clothes were tattered at this point and her hat was askew on her head. The two men, in their off-white pants and ripped shirts with suspenders half up and half hanging, wrangled with each other verbally and physically. The scene was so highly charged with energy, and a sheer delight to watch.

In directing comedy I always tell students about the elusive comic spirit which may be best defined as "having fun." The technical aspects of the acting-the voice, the physicality, and the comedy techniques we study in acting class-need to become second nature, and the actors really have to enjoy themselves as they perform. Tricia, Marta, Michael, and Brooks did just that, and their enjoyment was nothing less than infectious. Sometimes the director in me takes a back seat to the viewer part of me, and I become entranced with a piece of work even though I know every nuance of it as well as what to expect. Such was the case with this particular scene. The actors kept it so fresh and seemingly spontaneous that I found myself wondering what would happen next.

In the latter part of this scene, Lysander and Demetrius seek a place to fight, and Puck leads them through the forest by disguising his voice. Puck's aim is to get them so tired that they will fall asleep and he can remedy the confusing situation by administering another magic potion into their eyes. Once again, I wanted to do something a bit unique with this beat of the scene. One popular method of confusing the men to the point of exhaustion is to fill the stage with smoke so that Lysander and Demetrius can't see each other as they run about. Instead, I took a risk and had Puck, in view of the audience, cast spells on the men which instantly stunned them, causing them to do whatever Puck commanded through arm and hand gestures. He controlled them much like one would marionettes. At one point the two men even danced melodramatically about the stage to the accompaniment of tango music, complete with a long stemmed rose in Lysander's mouth, until they were so tired that they dropped to the ground at the completion of the dance. I wasn't sure if this idea would work and paid close attention to the response of any onlookers at rehearsals. Fortunately the audience seemed to love this segment and they applauded wildly during performances.

It is obviously important to allow student actors the opportunity to be spontaneously creative, and while I "skeleton" block scenes ahead of time, I am more than willing to change blocking if it will make an actor more comfortable, or if an actor has a sudden inspiration. I want actors to know that I trust them and will listen to them. This is imperative in creating an atmosphere where actors understand that they are not the pawns of the director, but, in fact, valued collaborators who are encouraged to be creative and original. I know of directors who run the gamut from "traffic cop" directors to those who actually perform the part and tell the actor to mimic him/her. Nothing educational is going on in either of these situations. Obviously, directors should have strong feelings about a play's theme and spine and what it should say to the public before the rehearsal process begins. Scenes can even be pre-blocked to insure balance and picturization. But I also believe that a director who is truly fine, who is confident and really understands the play, should be more than willing to change his preconceived ideas as long as he maintains certain parameters which will not violate the play's intent. Adding the human element to rehearsal, the actors, brings on a whole new phase of the work, and certainly they should feel free to contribute ideas as well.

This was most certainly the case with the mechanicals in *Midsummer*. Once these actors understood that they could make suggestions, they never stopped. While it's often easy to fall into group playing without establishing an individual identity, each mechanical did extensive work in creating his character. Of course, Shakespeare provides a great deal of material about them, but the actors found more to differentiate themselves than relying too much on their occupational distinctions. Visually alone this group, with its combinations of plaids and bowlers and vests and aprons with tools, and oversized and undersized garments presented a funny sight. Their character creations were brilliant, although I'm not sure the actors realized just how brilliant they were. They worked so well as an ensemble,

Noah Workman, last season's dramaturg for *On the Verge...*, played the famous role of Bottom. Noah is an articulate and intelligent man and really was indispensable to me during this, his senior year. He was a teaching assistant for the Special Education Drama classes and daily demonstrated not only superior organizational skills and teaching abilities, but great sensitivity in dealing with the needs of each child.

Bottom is one of those famous roles much like Touchstone and Jaques in *As You Like It*. While they are audience favorites and are expected to project a certain personality, actors need to bring something new to these roles to prevent them from becoming cliche. Noah retained the colorful, boastful enthusiasm associated with Bottom, yet managed to work his own sensitivity into the role as well. His transformation into the ass was splendid, and the audience loved him.

David Steeves' Francis Flute/Thisby was hysterical. His death scene in the Pyramus-Thisby play-within-a-play brought down the house as he stabbed himself with Pyramus' sword and screamed in feigned pain. Ort designed a costume for him that included a blond wig with curls, a large farthingale, and, of course, some outrageous make-up. The other actors were costumed equally as comical for this scene: Pyramus donning a Roman soldier's helmet, the visor of which fell over his face from time to time; Jason Conge as the director, Peter Quince, wearing a French beret, scarf, and carrying a megaphone to call out directions; Hunter Smith, Jr. as Tom Snout/Wall sandwiched between two sheets of muslin upon which were glued large stones; Percy Turner and Brian Huff, alternating performances as Robin Starveling/Moonshine wearing costumes too small and too large for each respectively, wearing a bush of thorns as a head piece, carrying a lantern that was rigged to extinguish itself on cue, and pulling a toy dog on a leash; and Alex Berrios as Snug/Lion wearing a lion's mane that surrounded his face and trailing a long tail behind him. From the places where I watched the play on performance evenings-the balcony/mezzanine or the back of the theater-it was truly heart-warming to witness the entire audience laughing hard and long during the Pyramus and Thisby scene, and interrupting it often with applause.

I need also to discuss three extremely important actors in this play. David Moran played both Theseus and Oberon, Kristi Villani played Titania, and Jason Reyes played Puck for this production. All three had been in *On the Verge* the previous year, and all three had grown tremendously as far as their performance talents were concerned. David was particularly adept at directing, and his work in the Independent Study Directing class greatly manifested itself in his acting development as well. I have long felt that a good director has to have some acting background also just to know what it's like to work under the lights and to create a character. The director is, then, more sensitive to the work of the actor and can guide him along better. David's two year study of directing benefited his stage work, and I noticed a rapid maturation and sophistication in his classwork as well. His observations in class and his critiques of his colleagues' acting work were splendid. He had a great eye for detail, and he was quick to offer alternative approaches to achieving a goal. David was very insightful. He was a tall and good looking man who truly commanded the stage.

I first met David many years ago when his sister, the lovely Jennifer Moran, was a student of mine. She had acted in Barrie's *The Admirable Crichton* and Lillian Hellman's *The Little Foxes*. I still remember meeting David who was just a child at the time. He looked up at me with such large eyes and a great smile, and he told me that he would one day love to act. He recounted his own version of that meeting when he was interviewed for a newspaper article publicizing *Midsummer*, and it was fascinating for me to hear his perspective of that meeting. Little did I know at the time that David would become such a major figure in my professional life.

Kristi's Titania was beautiful and sensuous in a glittering, two-layered costume designed specifically for her. Her natural abilities, her striking voice, vocal control, and stage presence created a character who was able to equal David's Oberon in power.

I divided the other fairies into Titania's followers and Oberon's band. The former moved gracefully, and I was fortunate to have the talent of senior Heather House to not only perform as one of them, but also to choreograph a ballet into Act II, scene ii where Titania calls for a roundel and a fairy song. Heather was a talented ballet dancer, and her work was excellent. Her ballet added to the desired overall visual magic of the play.

Oberon's followers, on the other hand, reflected a very contemporary "goth" look, although they were definitely inhuman creatures. They wore dark make-up on their lips and eyes, spiked hair, and leather vests and pants. I wanted them to appear sinister and threatening to reflect Oberon's anger and vengeance against Titania. I wove all of the fairies in and out of the action. They slithered on the floor, leapt great distances, did cartwheels and some tumblesaults, crept between characters' legs, and performed other movements that illustrated their near animalistic qualities.

Jason Reyes may have come the longest way in his acting. His Puck was spectacular, and I heard some professional theater people in the audience comment that it was the best Puck they had ever seen. I am usually leery of such comments when made about high school students. It reminds me of an experience a good friend of mine had some years ago when he was teaching in a college in the midwest. He was a prestigious figure in the educational and professional theater world, and had been persuaded to attend a local high school musical. After the play, the mother of the female lead found him and was effusive in her praise for her own daughter. She asked my friend if he didn't think that her daughter was just as good as anyone on Broadway at the time, to which he responded quite simply,

"No." She was taken aback, and he tried to explain that this particular locality had little if any contact with the professional quality of Broadway; that there was no standard of excellence to which to compare local work. The mother was offended, needless to say, but the comment was accurate. I'm somewhat amused when I hear comments comparing high school performances to professional performances. It proves once again how unaware most people are when it comes to understanding the many years of rigorous training it takes to be an actor.

I will say, however, that Jason's Puck was a work of art and deserving of the high praise he received. He had worked incredibly hard during his four years of high school, particularly this year. The scenes I gave him in acting class stretched him and challenged him, and I could see his progress grow steadily. Jason did wonderful work with the Shakespeare unit in class, and demonstrated an excellent facility with the language. He created that wonderfully playful and mischievous character we have come to expect, but he proved he could also be a very dramatic actor In Act III, scene ii he delivered a chilling series of images in his speech, "My fairy lord, this must be done in haste," where he describes ghosts wandering, damned spirits, foreboding churchyards, and "black-brow'd night." His final speech, "If we shadows have offended..." was beautifully acted. At the end of this speech, he was left alone on the stage in a spotlight, and a shower of golden sparkling confetti glided down, almost in slow motion from above. Jason looked up into it, reached out gently to touch it, smiled at the audience, and exited upstage. This, accompanied by a very gentle strain of music, ended the play and, I feel rather fittingly, my career at Hamden High School as well. It was a very gentle ending, yet a highly emotional moment, the beauty of which caused some audible gasps in the audience.

As one might imagine, closing night brought many emotions with it. Actually, the entire day was emotional. That Saturday I allowed myself to surrender to a host of "lasts" -the last time I would dress for a Hamden High School production of mine, the last drive to school for a play, the last warm-up session, and so forth. During our pre-play warm-up exercises, I found myself trying to be as "normal" as possible, but there was an obvious and filled silence that surrounded me. I noticed students looking at me and I could feel the warmth that radiated from them. And I thought about the fact that most people probably never know what this is all about; this "theater thing" and this incredible, indescribable exchange of affection between a teacher and so many young people. There are just simply no words to describe the ecstasy of such feeling.

I remember wanting our company meeting before the play that night to go on forever. I didn't want to let go of these students. I thanked them for their work on this play and for their dedication to our department and program. For many years the students asked me to read bits and pieces of plays to them during this time, and I always enjoyed doing that. In the past I had read from *The Elephant Man* by Bernard Pomerance, *The Three Sisters* by Chekhov, *A Life in the Theater* by David Mamet, a good deal of Shakespeare, his plays and his sonnets, from Athol Fugard and Tom Griffin and Tennessee Williams and Eugene O'Neill and so many others. I wanted my students to appreciate the language of these great playwrights, the way they captured emotions, and more importantly, their ideas and philosophies, all of which I knew would have a beneficial effect on those impressionable, sensitive, intelligent, people seated before me.

Company meetings were intimate times, even when the company numbered fifty or sixty. I felt I needed to show my gratitude to them for their commitment to the play, so I always wrote a letter to each person. While it's true that this project was time-consuming, it never was a "task." Rather, it was filled with great joy and love. Each person had accomplished a great deal; had so much of which to be proud, and I wanted them to know how important that was for the overall production and, moreso, for their own personal growth. One student read two poems he had written about being accepted by a "family" of people after struggling with loneliness for a long time, and the seniors read to the underclassmen, another Hamden tradition, and also presented them with awards for their contributions to the department. It was a wonderful way of "passing the torch," so to speak, and encouraging the younger students to accept the responsibilities that go with being the new leaders.

At the end of the meeting, the company surprised me with letters they had written to me. I was overwhelmed. This had happened on two other occasions, *The Fantasticks* and during the reunion after *Much Ado About Nothing*. Their honesty and their undisguised emotion filled me with an entire range of feelings, from gratitude to elation to sadness. The letters were filled with the most wonderful sentiment, and if only a third of what they profess I had done for them was true, I know that my work in Hamden had accomplished something. Validation for one's work is, unfortunately, not common in our society, so I never take my students' appreciation for granted. But I think their thoughts and letters have less to do with my teaching and directing than they do with the realization of their own self-discovery; of finding that very special and beautiful and unique quality within themselves. That discovery of self-worth is a powerful and treasured moment, and students for so many years have been able to find it through their work in the Theater.

One of the performances of *Midsummer* was attended by my good friend, Ann Altman. Ann brought a guest with her, a friend with whom she had studied at Cambridge University in England. Wendy Greenhill was the head of the Education Department for the prestigious Royal Shakespeare Company, and was in New Haven as the RSC had been invited to perform at the International Festival of Arts and Ideas. I must admit I was a bit nervous knowing that Ms. Greenhill was in the audience, but upon meeting her, I found her most kind and gracious. She and Ann were interviewed by the local newspaper, for their reunion after so many years was indeed more than merely a human interest story. It almost seemed as if Fate, with a bit of help from Shakespeare, had planned the meeting. Ms. Greenhill said wonderful things about *Midsummer* which were quoted in the newspaper. "I thought the overall standard was extraordinary," she began. "I thought the clarity and vitality with which they handled the language was superb...They inhabited the language.

They made it their own. That meant they had a wonderful rapport with the audience; the audience loved it." Certainly, Ms. Greenhill's comments were greatly appreciated, and once again proved an affirmation of our students' hard work.

Another newspaper article appeared just prior to the performance of *Midsummer* , and this was one that completely took me by surprise. The headline on the front page of the New Haven Register read, " 'Mr. Theater' Takes Last Bow," and was subtitled, "Hamden High Drama Director Retiring." It included a large color photo of the play in rehearsal and a smaller insert photo of me. It was an overwhelming experience to see this article so emphatically displayed, and I remember feeling a bit embarrassed as well. An unexpected result of the article was the outpouring of letters and cards of good wishes from members of the community. Most sentimental to me, however, were those from so many students, many of whom I hadn't spoken to in several years. What I learned from those letters was that the bond of Hamden Theater was very strong over the years, even when long distances made conversing or visiting difficult.

Of much greater importance than my retirement, I felt that the placement of the article, as well as an editorial within, was a tribute to Hamden Theater and all it had attained over the past thirty years. What had started out with little, if any, financial backing but with a great deal of passion, had grown into a program of noteworthy accomplishments. Likewise, as much "fame" as it had won through its compilation of awards and honors, the true value of the program is what it had done for the thousands of students who participated in it.

As I reminisce I find that thirty years have passed rather quickly, and while so much has happened in that time, it doesn't seem that long ago that we staged *Our Town* at Michael Whalen Junior High School. How could I possibly describe or quantify the amount of learning that has occurred on our stage and in our classrooms since then? There were times, after the regular school day, that I looked around me and saw numerous groups of students rehearsing scenes for acting classes, or discussing a particular play we read in our Literature of the Theater class. Directing students were coaching their actors, and designers and technicians were huddled together discussing sets and lights, selecting colors and responding to challenges. Laughter filtered in from the back hallways where students were making props, and on the mainstage sound technicians were checking volume levels. Our entire theater complex was buzzing with the electricity of learning. At these times I could only beam with pride at the accomplishments of our students, and at their voracious appetite to learn more and more.

So many Hamden Theater students have gone into professional theater, television, and the movies. Just recently one alumnus wrote a play that opened Off Broadway, another was cited in a national theater magazine as "someone to watch," and yet a third had his picture and an article featured in another national magazine. All of this occurred within two days! We have spawned actors and directors and writers and designers and technicians and theater teachers. And as exciting as all of this was, there was something that was even more important to me. I always want our students to use the skills they learned here-and that's not just skills of production, but "life" skills such as trust, responsibility, sensitivity-in any and every walk of life they chose. Some of Hamden's best success stories include the student who learned sign language for a play and then became a teacher of deaf children; the social worker who claims she can better empathize with her clients due to her theater training; the nurse who treats her patients with more sensitivity because she learned to see things from different people's points of view; and the many who went on to teach special needs children after they experienced the Special Education Drama Classes.

On a more personal note, my grandson is well over two years old now. I never knew how my life would change when Kyle Jeffrey came into this world. This beautiful boy, like his mother before him, has brought me immeasurable joy. As I look into my grandson's eyes and I recognize the intensity of his curiosity, his assimilation of this strange world with its new sensations and limitless stimulation, I wonder what I can say to him; how can I guide him? How can he learn from my many mistakes so that his life is free from burden and pain. I wish I knew the answer.

    I do know, however, that the great questions of life have been explored by our great playwrights, and, for me, the "answers" can be found in the vast body of work they have given to us. The very stage I worked on for years came to life with that work, and my classroom was nothing less than vibrant when we discussed the weighty ideas expressed in dramatic literature. We were forced to recognize universal themes and deal with questions of great significance; we learned that we must see things from a host of perspectives, and understand that civilization can only prosper when we honor it and treat it with dignity. Chris Keller, in Arthur Miller's *All My Sons*, says, "There is a universe of people out there, and you are responsible to it." This statement has always been particularly moving for me, for I have always believed that the very nature of the Theater is to sensitize people to look beyond our individual lives and specific needs and to think of and work for the good of all people.

    While our Theater constantly finds new voices, I often wonder about the loss of our great playwrights. I used to think that such brilliant people, such geniuses, should never die. It seemed so unjust. But then I realized that the playwrights' ideas are never far away; that they continue to live on and stir us. The souls, the messages of these writers vibrate in and intoxicate the air around us. They are found in the lyricism of Tennessee Williams and Eugene O'Neill, in the insight of Anton Chekhov and Henrik Ibsen; in the passions of Strindberg and Miller and Inge and Hellman and O'Detts-and so many, many others. It extends beyond the writing itself and taps into the rhythms of the universe; it is felt in the seasons' change and the rhythm of the sea. And it is felt in the absence of sounds as well. For perhaps it is during those poignant stillnesses on the stage that we find the meaning; that we make the "connection" between the ideas and emotions of these writers, these plays, and our own lives.

The joy of performance and the sorrow of seeing students walk out of my classroom for the last time, as opposite as those emotions are, had been regular features in my professional life. These students make their mark in a spectacular fashion, and then Life calls them away, as it should, to use the skills we teach them as they pursue their own dreams. And yet, with their exit, while I felt such heart-pounding pride in their personal growth and achievements, I felt also heart-pounding sadness at their departure. However, as with those playwrights mentioned above, their spirits always remained, adding more ghosts to a theater already rich with a glorious tradition.

I don't think it has ever been easy for Hamden Theater students. The plays of one generation have always been compared to the great ones of the those who have preceded them. Yet I remember every group of students enjoying being a part of the tradition, moreso than trying to prove they are as good, if not better than those who have gone before. Their achievements have been mind-boggling. To me, they all walk among greatness. All of these accolades-the all time-record of twenty "Outstanding Productions in Connecticut", winning over 260 acting, technical and design awards, two Moss Hart Awards for the best play in New England extolling human dignity, praise from the Rockefeller Foundation in New York, serving as the model for the State's Theater curriculum, winning the recognition of journalists, theater professionals, corporations, and individuals-all of these outward marks of distinction are rightfully eclipsed, at least to me, by the personal achievement of thousands of students who have pursued a challenge, taken a risk, and overcome obstacles. In short, they have grown. These are people of character and heart, and I like to think of them as adding their individual and collective talents as human beings to a world greatly in need of them.

Many years ago I had lunch with several Hamden Theater graduates. We were in a rather noisy restaurant. There was Louise Rozett, Diane Bers, Sophia Salguero, Tom McVety, Phil DelVecchio, and Michael, Jeffrey, and Jennifer Lerner. The experience was both happy and sad for me. I suppose I have always been struck by the power of contrasts. The long table around which we sat bubbled over with the talk of Theater. Michael had been out of school for some time by now and was working in New London with a group of actors that traveled to school systems, educating and acquainting young people with Theater. In the summers, this group performed Shakespeare and O'Neill, New London being an O'Neill stronghold. They presented the seldom-performed plays like *The Emperor Jones* complete with drumbeat, and *The Iceman Cometh*. Somehow looking into Michael's eyes that day revealed his passion and knowledge about the Theater, and it was easy for me to see that Michael "knows."

Louise was then a graduate student at the Goodman Theater in Chicago, and Diane was an undergraduate at the Tisch School of Performing Arts in New York City. Each of them had the enthusiasm that exploration of the Theater brings. And Sophia was living in New York after having graduated from one of the top acting programs in the country at Carnegie-Mellon University. I remember that she had a look of trepidation about her; the look of a person now challenged with making a living from what she had learned behind the safe walls of academia. She was taking ballroom dancing at the time while working with an improvisational theater group that explored the social issues of discrimination and racism with inner-city school children. Sophia has always been radiant, and I'm glad to say that the trepidation has been replaced by a great deal of professional success. Phil was a graduate directing student in Illinois, and I was so proud of him for getting full scholarships to study. Jeff worked in Washington D.C. with an environmental agency, while his younger sister, Jennifer, attended a state university, happy to be taking two theater courses the next semester. Tom had long since graduated college and was a successful graphic artist in a big corporation, although he always found time to design program covers, posters, and programs for my productions.

The group sat and laughed, exchanging stories and experiences for three hours. And I realized, all over again, that each of these people was, and still is, so important to me. Each may change pursuits, each will grow, and being with them fills me with such indescribable happiness. The words exchanged are warm and the smiles full of love, but the unspoken word is more potent still. We experience common roots and the invisible threads of a fabric that bind us all together and supports us, each in a different place with a different goal, yet drinking in the sustenance that we so avidly and generously give to each other. What greater gift can ever be given than the love and sharing among friends?

I remember that for a while the raucous background sounds of the restaurant faded away, and even the voices of my companions. And in my silent thoughts I flashed back to their "early" years when they lay bare their hopes and dreams with the fresh enthusiasm of youth. And while they had grown older and become more beautiful than ever, they still clung to those hopes and pursued those dreams, now with a maturity that makes me burst with pride. This is a "family" of true wealth.

I drove home alone that day looking at the bleak, gray winter sky and the barren trees. There is a sense of permanence in Nature and a beauty and a loneliness as well. It seems all the more imposing as it contrasts with the fleeting moments shared with friends. There is so much I want to say; there is so much I feel. I wish we could have stayed together forever, a feeling I have had over and over again throughout the years with each and every group of students, yet I know that is impossible. Only the sky is forever, and the trees, barren and beautiful, and the rivers, and the silent falling snow, and the knowledge that spring will come and summer soon after. But for that moment my heart and my mind embraced the recent memory of those three hours together, and I would see my students' laughing eyes for a long, long time.

When I retired people did a great deal of talking about "legacy," and what mine would be. I smiled, for I feel the same about that word as I do about "memoirs": These things are attributed to people of wisdom and age, and I hardly fit the first, although I'm gently growing into the second. But if I were to seriously think about a legacy I would like to leave, it would be the simple thought that anything is possible. This has been consistently proven over the years by students of all ages, backgrounds, and ability levels. Their passion for learning and for the Theater, together with the feeling of "family" that has existed throughout the years, with each generation respecting the work of its predecessors, has helped them accomplish the most unbelievable goals.

It saddens me to think that I am not sitting in the Black Box at Hamden High School, preparing for rehearsal, overhearing students rehearsing a scene for an acting class, or listening to the exuberance in the voice of a student designer explaining his or her plans for an upcoming production. I do know, however, that the experiences I've had with these students over the years have shaped me and played more than a significant role in my personal growth. My students have taught me and I will always be grateful to them. They are truly people of uncommon grace, and I am humbled by their beauty.

Chapter Six

The Special People

The Boys Next Door, 1993

"I came away from the performance not only in awe of the character's accomplishments in the face of his tremendous disadvantages, but reminded that those of us with so many advantages should not be satisfied with less than our best."
                                                                Terry

"I have found the strength within myself to face what is different and what I do not know, and it is in this way that I have learned the most."
                                                                Noah

These memoirs wouldn't be complete without mention of my special education drama classes, for they have provided some of the most satisfying, fulfilling, and emotional memories of my career. It would be impossible to identify what I did as a teacher without including my work in this area. In retrospect, it surprises me that I would even become so heavily involved in drama for people with special needs as I never anticipated it nor was I trained for this. I was soon to find out, however, that very few people were trained in this area nationally, and no one in the immediate or surrounding geographical location could offer any expertise. I was to venture into this alone.

In my college days I would never have imagined myself possessing the patience or the ability to handle the multiple and vast array of needs these young people have. Now that I can look back upon this phase of my career, I know that patience and individual attention are necessary for teachers in all disciplines. As a matter of fact, I would have to rate those qualities very high on the list of teacher qualifications. Students need to know that there is someone to listen to them and that each of them is viewed as an individual with unique qualities. Becoming aware of this made teaching the Special Education Drama classes much easier.

In my early years of teaching at Michael J. Whalen Junior High School I always had special education students mixed into my drama classes. I admired their perseverance and their enthusiasm for the class, but I felt that they somehow felt a bit distant from the rest of the group. This bothered me because, even then, I knew I felt something for them. They touched some part of me and my response was to take great pains in helping them succeed and feel good about themselves, often at the expense of the rest of the students. I give a lot of credit to my regular education students. They were certainly understanding, but no matter how sensitive they were, I could sense a frustration from both segments of the class, and actually within myself as well. I imagined that a self-contained special education class would enable us to explore many different areas and move at a pace that was comfortable for everyone.

After I transferred to Hamden High School I approached the Board of Education and the Special Education Department, requesting a Special Education Drama Class, and they were most kind in granting my request. I was actually surprised at how little politicking I had to do, especially since this was really new.

Quickly discovering the lack of material on the topic and the lack of trained professionals in this field as well, I was thrilled to find two workshop offerings, one in Portland, Oregon at a convention of the American Alliance for Theatre and Education and another at the New England Theatre Conference Convention in Providence, Rhode Island. Both were extremely helpful in providing materials and also talking to people who had been teaching drama to special needs children for some time, albeit most of those students were much younger than the ones I was to teach. I also spent a lot of time delving into student records in my attempts to learn the backgrounds and needs of the students who were to sit in my room the following year.

Curriculum writing wasn't new to me at all, and I felt very comfortable designing the course. I suppose this is only natural for theater teachers since there are so few courses in theater in secondary school, and certainly fewer established, sequential courses and curricula. This made designing the content of the course easier, and the workshops and numerous discussions I had with Hamden's special education staff enabled me to determine behavioral objectives. I remember designing that first course so meticulously around each student's specific needs. Even so, there was endless modification to do, not only with weekly or long-term plans, but within each class meeting itself. I also kept a daily journal which was a great help in expressing my excitement over student accomplishments and also very often venting my frustrations. At the beginning of the year there seemed to be many more of the latter than the former. Years later I would entrust this personal record to some newer teachers in this field, and it helped ease their isolation and it also validated many of the feelings, questions, and concerns they had which, in fact, were very much like mine.

The particular segment of the special education population that would be enrolled in that first class was labeled, "Behaviorally and Emotionally Disturbed," a label I didn't, and still don't, like. Actually, I don't like any labels. I just have a problem defining people by using phrases that I find limiting. While I can understand a need to describe the special needs that people have, somehow a title such as this defies individuality and the unique qualities that each human being possesses.

Over the years the course changed a great deal. While I used a good amount of the original content, there was considerable change in terms of pace, direction, and related areas of study, all necessitated to meet the widely different needs of the students. It's interesting that I could honestly say that no two "Behaviorally and Emotionally Disturbed" drama classes were alike, another observation that defies this label.

Another element that determined the pace of the class, and often its daily content as well, was the entire pre-class attitude. So often students would come into class angry, frustrated, lonely, and experiencing every other emotion possible from events that happened at home or in school prior to drama class. This was one area that was very different from the regular education classes where, if this happened at all, is was to a much lesser extent. I recall several explosions during that first special education class. Once a boy even picked up a desk and threw it across the stage in a fit of rage. There was no way to predict what would happen. I tried to control this by having the classes end on a note of anticipation for what would happen the next day. For example, we might be in the middle of an improvisation, and we would have to act out the conclusion the following day. We also did a lot of improvising around teenage concerns and problems, dealing with which this particular class was very adept. They enjoyed these and would often forget their own problems, or perhaps sublimate them into the current acting project.

Despite the ups and downs, the emotional exhaustion, and the daily problems, this course went very well. I gave students time to orally evaluate it in June, and I was surprised at the positive comments they made. Of greater importance, I could see progress, and that is often difficult to determine.

Every year since that first class in 1988, my drama class was very different from the previous ones, but as difficult and trying as the classes were, they were also so rewarding. Years later I still maintain contact with many of these students, and it feels good to witness many of them overcoming problems and living productive lives—especially when they were treated with suspicion and sometimes fear in their school days.

I was then asked if I would like to teach the TMR class-Trainably Mentally Retarded. I disliked this label even more than the previous one. I think I objected to the word, "retarded." I have just never like that word, and I could never look into the faces of the students in that course over these many years and think of them as such.

Engrossed in my work with special education, I chose to direct Tom Griffin's play, *The Boys Next Door* in 1993. This play is about people with special needs. I felt that one of the reasons there were so few drama classes in this area, or, in fact, so little information about special needs people at all, was that the general community was unaware of the large and growing special education population, and if they were aware it was usually in the form of cliche images of the worst kind. I wanted to enlighten as much of the community to this subject as possible. I had directed Bernard Pomerance's *The Elephant Man* for the same reason some years before. This play was based on the real life story of Joseph Merrick who suffered from a rare disease that deformed his skin and bones. He became a circus attraction, an oddity for people to mock and even fear, and yet within this ravaged body was a soul of extreme beauty. Merrick was a poet and a philosopher, and once people took the time to listen to him, they could see the richness of the person trapped inside. I felt this was an important play to do. I wanted my students to learn the lesson that Merrick's story teaches.

The Boys Next Door also shows how poorly many people in society treat theTMR population. While I was always sensitive to name-calling in school, I became moreso now, especially to the use of the word "retard" so flagrantly and nonchalantly used by one person to laughingly embarrass another. I suppose this is no different than the other epithets so commonly heard, but working with this class and with this play seemed to amplify these words as they reverberated in my brain. I kept thinking, if the people who use them could only spend some time in my class, or if they would come to see the play. Perhaps then they would understand that special education students had lives and dreams of their own.

One was a gymnast, and one was a swimmer. One wanted to be a ballet dancer, and how many of them loved animals! One girl who was confined to a wheelchair and could barely speak always wore the most beautiful clothes, and her hair was always set impeccably, and when I would tell her how attractive she looked, she would look down and blush. She was one of the sweetest people I had ever met. One boy walked very slowly. One might consider it a shuffle rather than a walk. When he was particularly emotional he also wet himself and so we learned to recognize the signs and be prepared. On the other hand, if we played music in class, this very same boy became a leader and could dance and move as well as anyone in that entire school. It was as if a hidden, secret self would emerge. Another boy went through an emotional crisis when he learned that he would soon be moving away from his family into a group home, and his anxiety would manifest itself in his vomiting every day in class. It was almost like clockwork, and I remember having a lined waste paper basket and rubber gloves hidden, but ready to use on a moment's notice. However, this boy loved to sing, and he was so kind and attentive to others—especially when they were depressed. He would walk over to them and put his arm around them, consoling them in an honest and loving way. Another student was extremely verbal and would often surprise me with his vocabulary which was advanced for any high school student, let alone a TMR pupil. Once he asked me if vegetarianism meant that a person was "non-carnivorous."

Each problem, then, was balanced with some wonderful and totally endearing personality trait; the kind that made you want to do all you could for each person. Teaching the TMR class was bliss. These students were modest and kind and they appreciated every single thing that was done for them. So often as I stood in front of the class I could actually feel myself overflowing with love for them.

They, in turn, loved their drama class and were flexible and willing to try anything. We would travel on imaginary trips to anywhere in the world, and they would tell me what they saw and describe it for me. We would participate in all kinds of pantomime activities -swimming in forest lakes, dining at restaurants, going on amusement park rides. We would also sing and dance often. We would mold clay and paint pictures and then bring them to life. There were just no limits to the class experiences we had. I don't know if the course improved their motor skills or their problem-solving skills or their verbal or observational skills for that matter—but I do know that for forty-five minutes a day we all enjoyed each other's company and laughed and even had some serious conversations as well.

Often our trips were not confined to this world. I had a student for several years whose name was Robin. One day Robin was weeping in class, and when I asked her what the problem was, she said that her Grandpa Jack had died. I was disturbed by the news until an adult classroom aide who traveled with the group told me that Grandpa Jack had died several years ago. Robin replayed this death over and over. Once Robin even brought in a tape recording of Grandpa Jack made at one of her early birthday parties. Obviously, she was very attached to her grandfather.

Also in this class was a young boy who had been badly injured in an accident when he was fairly young. He was now confined to a wheel chair and his hands were replaced by prostheses. Vinny was very quiet. As a matter of fact, he barely spoke and never participated in class activities. He often sat by himself, and It was a struggle to even convince him to move his wheelchair to the rest of the group.

One day Robin was crying about Grandpa Jack, and I decided that we would take a class trip to Heaven, let Grandpa Jack tell Robin that he was pretty content and that she could stop feeling sad. So we all set off on our imaginary elevator to Heaven where Robin got to talk to Grandpa Jack. I played the role and managed to convince her that everything was fine. Robin soon stopped weeping and began to smile. We completed our visit and traveled back down to earth via an invisible elevator.

We took a few more trips above whenever Robin felt sad, and each time Grandpa Jack soothed her feelings. One day as we traveled back down to earth, the drama teacher in me thought that we could use a problem-solving lesson, and I told the group, with fear on my face, that the elevator got stuck. I thought we would then discuss our options and decide upon a course of action. However, Robin became hysterical and no amount of reasoning with her could calm her down. I even told her that the elevator wasn't really there and that this was just make-believe, but Robin continued to wail. And then, out of the corner of the room we heard a voice shout, "Captain Hook to the rescue!" It was Vinny's voice, loud and booming—which startled us since we rarely even heard him speak. He maneuvered his wheelchair to us quickly, used his prostheses to pry the imaginary elevator doors apart, and the class was saved! Robin hugged and kissed Vinny, and everyone else did too. I am still overwhelmed as I think back to that experience. It was one of several miracles I witnessed as I taught that class. From that day on Vinny participated in many class activities, and once again I felt the truly awesome power of drama.

A second story from that class deals with Gerald, yet another boy who was confined to a wheelchair. Gerald, however, had an additional handicap: he couldn't speak, and I spent a year trying to guess what he was attempting to communicate to me. Gerald was very animated and often brought in pictures to share with the class—mostly of wrestlers, his favorite being Hulk Hogan. Just as a blind person seems to develop an acute sense of hearing, Gerald's inability to speak generated expressive eyes, and often he would try to communicate through them. Frequently I knew he was bursting to share something with me, and his animated eyes would widen as he stared directly into mine. I felt completely helpless at these times as I picked at straws trying to guess what he wanted.

One thing that was clear was that Gerald loved drama class. He would watch the class' improvisations, and often we would hear his deep guffaw. If I said something funny in class he would sarcastically roll his eyes and shake his head, as if he were the teacher and I were the student. One day the class was performing an improvisation in the area below the stage in what is commonly called the orchestra pit. The stage was about four feet high. As the class was engaged in the acting scene, Gerald suddenly stood up. I knew he could stand although this happened very infrequently. He pushed himself to his feet and awkwardly labored his way to the edge of the stage, holding himself up by placing his hands on it. And then Gerald "acted," making rough, harsh sounds to communicate. I will always have this picture in my mind—Gerald, such a tall boy, holding himself up, his knees bent severely yet still towering over the class, and acting! That was quite a day for us. A major breakthrough had occurred.

Gerald returned to class the next year with a computer attached to his wheelchair. Now he spelled words to me that appeared on a small screen. I was shocked as I learned that this young man could not only spell, but he was capable of rather sophisticated ideas as well. A whole treasure chest of thoughts and feelings was opened as Gerald was liberated by that machine. It's difficult to describe my feelings even now as I write this. For so long I struggled to communicate the simplest ideas to Gerald, and suddenly I was privy to the treasures of Gerald's mind. How frustrated he must have been before he received that computer.

These are only a few of the stories of this class. While each day had the potential to be filled with laughter or sadness, there was no end to the surprises, nor was there an end to the poignancy. In their simple, but honest ways, these students affected me, touched me, changed me, and I know I will benefit from our shared times for the rest of my life. And how much I learned from all of them—lessons in courage and determination and gratitude. If there is anything right about the label, "special education," it is that these students are truly special human beings.

Chapter Seven

Other Stages

Amadeus, 1986

"I'm not famous or even eloquent as many of the Hamden Theater alumni are, but my life has changed for the better by my association with you and with our Theater program. I would be remiss as a former student and a friend if I didn't tell you that. I have scores of happy stories and reminiscences to tell. Risa and I keep in close touch with many of our theater friends. In fact, our son, Jake, is buddies with Chris Donovan's son, Ryan. Who would have thought! There must be hundreds like us, but we were only a small part of a distinguished and remarkable family."

Gary

Guest-directing was something for which I never thought I had time. The Hamden program required constant shaping and attention as it rapidly grew. There were new courses and classes to teach, plays to read and direct, and a department that strove to be comprehensive while it met the needs of each individual. Advances in technology were also making great strides, and I wanted to incorporate them into our department, affording our students the latest information possible. Most of all, the students needed attention. There were so many of them, and as the numbers grew all of the time, so did their desire to learn about every conceivable aspect of theater. I found myself constantly studying in order to teach them, reading new textbooks and magazines, going to libraries and museums, attending as much theater as possible, researching topics and creating new lessons. And finally, like any one of us, students needed to have someone to talk to about things that very often had nothing whatsoever to do with education. I felt I needed to be there for them in this area as well.

Accepting an invitation from Dr. Vincent Finizio, the department head at Central Connecticut State University in New Britain, to direct *The Prime of Miss Jean Brodie* was something quite new for me. Central's invitation was attractive, and even though the commute to New Britain was approximately an hour each way, I felt an urge to work on this project. My decision to direct the play began one of the most positive experiences I have ever had. Up to then, directing a play meant supervising every aspect of it myself. I was always thankful for talented students who enjoyed design and carpentry, but even then I needed to create drawings and sets of directions, order lumber, supervise costumes, and handle just about every other production component. Suddenly I only had to direct. Vincent Gagliardi, the department's scenic designer, met with me and asked about my concept and needs, and and then went off to work on it. He returned some weeks later, but before rehearsals began, with a model which helped me greatly. Obviously, I wasn't used to this, and it was like heaven to me. Since then, my design partner, Frank Alberino, does the same for every production we work on, and I find it to be one of the most beneficial aids to my work. Lani Johnson, the costume designer and the current department head at Central, presented sketches which were the basis for the costumes. They, like the set, worked perfectly. For once I could direct unencumbered by a multitude of technical responsibilities, and I loved it. It was one of the most liberating feelings I can remember.

It was 1982 and I wasn't sure what I would encounter when I met the students for the first time. I had been so used to my Hamden students, all of whom were involved in a training program and knew what their responsibilities were as well as what was expected of them. They knew they had to work hard and be disciplined to be successful. I wondered what these older college students would be like. When I finally met them my anxiety immediately disappeared, for they were all so kind and friendly. I could easily see how much they wanted to learn, and it took very little time for us to build a strong rapport. Any initial fears that they wouldn't learn lines quickly or wouldn't be flexible and willing enough to explore the characters were quickly dispelled. This was a superior group of people. We would often have long conversations both before and after rehearsals, and I was impressed by their honesty and self-effacing natures.

I was so fortunate to have a large pool of students at auditions, and it was actually difficult to cast the play because there were so many good people from which to choose. Rose Lamoureux played Jean Brodie, and Cynthia Gagne played Miss McKay, Brodie's nemesis and head of the exclusive Marcia Blaine School; Brodie's girls were a strong ensemble and were played by Vicki Rogers, Melissa Jean Feder, Carol Nyborg, and Susan Pauloz. William Nielson played the handsome artist, Teddy Lloyd, the lover with whose feelings Brodie toys and tries to pass on to one of her students, and Patrick Ringrose played Gordon Lowther, Jean's bumbling and humorous suitor. Jennifer Boudreau gave an excellent performance as Sister Helena, and Wayne Horgan complemented her with his own performance as Mr. Perry. The rest of the cast included Gloria Carl, Ken Decker, Sue Evers, Laurel Kastens, Gina Lombardo, and Sandra Wilson.

We worked long and hard on *Brodie*, and I could feel a definite excitement in the air. What I also remember is that rehearsals didn't seem like work because we enjoyed them so much. And at the end of rehearsal each evening, different students would walk me to my car and ask me a multitude of questions about the play and about theater in general. I always enjoyed those walks because I could strongly sense the hunger these young people had for as much knowledge as they could absorb. When the play ended, I realized how emotionally attached I had become to them and to Central. It was an extraordinary experience.

My next guest directing experience, this time at Southern Connecticut State University in 1984, was equally as rewarding. Of course, I always considered Southern my home, having graduated from there in 1969 and having done my advanced degree work there as well. Returning to my roots, then, was a thrill for me. Once again the play had already been selected, and in a way, even that was a relief. I had directed *Brodie* prior to directing it at Central, but William Inge's Pulitzer Prize-winning *Picnic* was new on the directing front to me. I didn't know then that I would fall in love with this play. A few years later I included it in the syllabus of my

Literature of the Theater class at Hamden High School where it quickly became a favorite of my students.

Thom Peterson, Southern's designer, created a masterful set. When we had our first production meeting and he asked me about my needs, I said that I wanted a very realistic feel to this production; that the characters were ordinary human beings like all of us, which made their respective stories and the play's message even more poignant. The dreams and longings of the characters are essentially ours as well, and we cannot help but be moved by them. The play's intimacy would be felt by presenting it in the Kendall Drama Lab and in a three-quarter round production. Another method of attaining the realism of rural Kansas was to use a good amount of dirt in the play's unit setting, that of a backyard which joins the two adjacent homes. I wanted the dirt to kick up as the actors walked; I wanted an earthy feel, one in which the characters were not only familiar with the environment, but seemed as if they were actually rooted in it. The intimacy and realism would combine to allow the audience to feel like it was looking into the lives and souls of the characters. Interestingly, theater scholars and critics have remarked that Inge allows his audiences to examine the characters in his plays as if looking through an ex-ray machine, permitting the viewers to look under the seemingly content and placid surface of their lives.

Thom's finished product was strikingly effective. Not only did the set have a wonderfully realistic feel to it, but Thom had given me many levels and areas with which to create interesting pictures and blocking. A good friend of mine, Frank O'Connor, saw the play and commented on the believable atmosphere and convincing ethos. Frank has strong mid-western ties and visits that part of the country often. He wondered how I was able to create that setting without ever being in Kansas. I thought about that for quite a while. Obviously, much of the credit for the physical set belonged to the designer. As far as the behavior patterns of the characters were concerned, I just had strong gut feelings about them—about the way they walked and spoke and related to each other, their mannerisms, and the effect of the environment on them.

It may sound strange, and even a bit silly, but a lot of the Kansas I wanted to create comes from The *Wizard of Oz*. As I've told my students countless times, inner resources—the information which informs our subtext for acting, directing, designing, and writing—comes from any number of places; from trips, books, movies, museums, foods—anything that we've experienced in life. That movie from my childhood made a strong impression on me as it did on so many others, and I have carried it with me all these years. As much as I appreciated the fanciful story and the colorful land of Oz, I remember, even as a young boy, looking beyond the glitz of the movie and instead being very affected by its black and white section; the Kansas segment. There was something very visceral about the dirt road, the Kansas fields, the house and farm which were very much like those in this play. I'm sure there were many other sources which helped to create the atmosphere as well, including some that were subconscious, but a good deal of the feeling and tone of our production's Kansas came from that movie.

Once again the students were like sponges, trying to absorb every bit of knowledge they could. The cast was strong. Gregg Donnell, a former Hamden student, played the pivotal role of Hal Carter, the drifter. He created the swagger and bravado so necessary for the character's physical appearance, yet allowed himself to be completely vulnerable as well. His performance was commanding. His love interest, Madge Owens, was played by Glena Rogers, a very fine actress who looked the part of the beautiful Midwestern daughter, but also had the range to play the longing and sensitivity that Madge felt. Millie Owens, Madge's younger sister, was played by Julie Morrin who captured Millie's youth and also her tomboyish quality. Their mother, Flo, was very well executed by the Gladys Epstein, an older student at Southern with a considerable amount of theatrical experience. Most of Gladys' work had been in musical and community theater, and this was definitely the most challenging role she ever played. I was moved by her comments to me after the final performance, stating that she learned more about acting from this production than from anything she had ever been in before. Sheila Walsh and Raymond Rourke gave outstanding performances as Rosemary Sidney, the spinster schoolteacher, and her fiance, Howard Bevans. They were nothing less than compelling in Act Three, Scene One in which Rosemary literally begs Howard to marry her. The audience felt such sympathy for her in this extremely difficult scene. Handsome Dean Zaino played the wealthy jock-like Alan Seymour perfectly, and Evelyn Ambriscoe did the same as the Owens' neighbor, Helen Potts. The cast was completed with Eric Foster as Bomber, Donna Lessing as Christine Schoenwalder, and Susan Sayles as Irma Kronkite. Stage Manager Kevin Miller and Production Stage Manager, Richard Smith were an excellent team, and the technical work of Hope Flanigan, Chris Balay, Don Curioso, Paul Marottolo, Dave Starkey, Beth Thompson, Sue Griffiths, Todd Eastland, and Mark Carafano among many others was stellar.

I felt it was important to get to know each and every one of the technicians, to thank them, and to show them that I would never take their work for granted. I did not want to be the kind of director who spent his time only with the actors, so I often came to the theater during the day or remained for a while after evening rehearsals to spend some time with the technical staff. I found that they were not only talented, but, as I suspected, simply wonderful people as well. *Picnic* had to be a success because it was cared for by so many exemplary students of the theater. Needless to say, my stay at Southern couldn't have been more satisfying.

My next directing experience at Southern, however, was unfortunately not quite as positive. In 1985 I was asked to direct a production of Thornton Wilder's *The Matchmaker*, upon which the musical *Hello, Dolly!* was based. The highlight of this experience was working with the cast. They were incredibly friendly and hard-working. Veronica Brenckle played Dolly and Eric Foster, "Bomber" in *Picnic*, played Horace Vandergelder. Both of them gave very strong performances. Andrew Makay as Cornelius and Bob Kenefick as Barnaby were a perfect comedy team, portraying the two young and inexperienced men from Yonkers who journey to New York City in search of adventure. Kim Blakeplayed Mrs. Molloy and her assistant, Minnie Fay was played by Lynn Ann Wood, both of whom were enthusiastic and eager from the very first day of rehearsal. But, then again, the entire cast was eager and their enjoyment of rehearsals was evident in the genuine happiness that surrounded this production. The remainder of the cast included April Castagna, Michael Cook, Sally Kaczynski, Jim McKenna, David Nelson, Carol Platts, Matt Proulx, Deborah Reiff, Edmund Rogers, and Jeff Sabo.

A Thousand Clowns (1990)

Big River (1997)

Brigadoon (1991)

Picnic (1984)

The Matchmaker was to be presented on Lyman's main stage which was adjacent to the Drama Lab where *Picnic* was presented. The largeness of the space, however—some sixteen hundred seats—and the totally different feel of the play made *Picnic* seem a million light years away.

My main problem with *The Matchmaker* was its short rehearsal period. I found it extremely difficult to direct this play in the allotted time of five weeks which included a few days of auditions and the performances. In retrospect, I don't even know why I accepted the job in the first place. I had discussions with the faculty about what I considered a real weakness in the philosophy of doing several plays with short rehearsal periods versus doing fewer plays with longer rehearsal periods. The latter case afforded time in which to experiment, develop, and learn. Southern was not a conservatory program where students spend all of their time in the theater or taking theater-related courses. Students at Southern had the pressures we associate with state schools across the country: a high percentage of the students are commuters who live at home and have responsibilities there; there are traveling concerns and homework concerns and very often students have jobs off campus. These were not impediments to education, but rather realities which I felt needed to be considered. I felt bad for the company of this production because we were working at such a rapid pace. This had to minimize their opportunities of experimenting and making choices, much of what rehearsals are all about. Our production schedule, on paper, was fast-paced, and I had all I could do to create a sense of calm and patience at rehearsals. Once again, it is a matter of opinion and practice, but I believe that actors need to be nurtured and given the time to develop characters. Judging by the touching letters I received from the cast, they seemed to feel that they did, in fact, experience this. If they truly believed this, I felt *really* bad for them, for they probably never experienced a comfortable, relaxed rehearsal period where there was room for all of those wonderful things that are supposed to happen during this time. What was most fulfilling for me is that the actors wrote of how much they learned and grew during the process, and that is the most important thing of all. I wonder, however, how much more could have been accomplished with additional time. Fortunately I had Hope Flanigan as my production stage manager and she was assisted by David Starkey. Both of them had worked with me on *Picnic*, and I respected their talents tremendously. They were organized, trustworthy, always professional, and had a way of troubleshooting problems before they occurred.

One day I arrived at the theater rather early. I sat alone and was engrossed is my work, preparing for the upcoming rehearsal. Soon I saw the side door of the theater open and in walked Joseph Walker, a guest faculty member and director in the Theater Department. I hadn't met Mr. Walker yet, but knew of him as the Tony Award-winning playwright of *The River Niger*. He came over to me and we had a pleasant conversation. He talked of the students' excitement about *The Matchmaker*, something I couldn't witness during the school day since I wasn't teaching at Southern. But then he brought up the subject of my concern about the short rehearsal period. Obviously the faculty had shared my thoughts with him which didn't bother me at all. Mr. Walker totally disagreed with me, stating that he felt actors under pressure and near exhaustion find a new burst of energy which is invigorating, creative, and fresh. I told him that I certainly respected his feelings, but I disagreed with them—at least in educational theater. While there is pressure in any production, I find that creating even more through extremely long and grueling rehearsal hours and constant demands can often become debilitating for actors. My entire philosophy of directing has been helping actors find their potential through revealing their strengths. I simply cannot ride an actor until he is exhausted and feels helpless.

Other problems arose. I was unhappy with the designer's work. He wanted the women to wear corsets, but they were drawn so tight to fit the costumes that some of the cast actually had difficulty breathing, and I had to insist that the those costumes be altered. And then the funny, but sad moment of Dolly Levi's big entrance in our first dress rehearsal arrived. As she attempted to enter the room, her hat hit both sides of the door frame. It was too big for the amount of space in the door opening and she couldn't enter the room. Everyone laughed, including me, but I was upset about the situation, especially since the costume and set designer was one and the same person.

The set, although described to me in theory prior to the rehearsal period as having a cartoon strip feel, looked nothing like I had envisioned. The decorative scenery was flat, black and white, and unappealing. The designer was quite angry and blamed the look on the scenic artists, and the few nights before the play opened he spent repainting everything himself.

Overall, I felt that the technical aspect of this play left a lot to be desired, and my feelings were torn at the end of this production. On the one hand, I was so proud of the actors and enjoyed watching them basking in their well-earned praise. On the other, I felt the department let these students down with a rushed schedule that hindered both the direction and the technical components. I was determined never to work under these conditions again.

In the late spring of 1990 I received a phone call from Mary Mazzacane, one of the two artistic directors of the CET Opera Company. Mary invited me to direct Donizetti's opera, *L'Elisir D'Amore* the following fall. I was excited, although apprehensive, at the idea of directing an opera.

I had previously directed a one-act opera based on the short story, *The Gift of the Magi*. The piece was composed by Susan Hulsman-Bingham and the lyrics came directly from O'Henry's popular story. Susan was an extremely talented composer who lived in New Haven. Her unique compositions were showcased at Lincoln Center in New York, and I felt very privileged when she asked me to direct her newest work. *The Gift of the Magi* had long been a favorite story of mine. When I was a young boy, my father would tell me the story repeatedly, asking me what I thought the message was. Interestingly, he never interpreted it for me, but felt it was important for me to discover this lesson about true love on my own. Often during *Magi* rehearsals I could hear my father's voice in the words of the story. This made me even more committed to the project.

The story's two characters were sung by Judith Caldwell and Kyle Pruett, both of whom brought Susan's mini-opera alive with their superb singing and acting talents. We rehearsed in Susan's living room as we didn't have access to the church where the opera was to be presented until a day or two before the performance. But I had been in such situations before, and Judy and Kyle were flexible enough to quickly adapt to the situation. The opera was presented at New Haven's Trinity Church on the Green, home of the famous Trinity Boys' Choir. The setting—a beautiful church with a constructed stage and theatrical lighting—was particularly emotional for me. I remember feeling very comfortable and warm as I watched the performance from the balcony, completely enraptured by the voices which, for some reason, seemed more exquisite that night than ever before. I was very glad that I accepted Susan's initial offer.

The friendships made from this production were very important to me. The experience was so positive that I knew I had to expose my students at Hamden High School to the world of opera and to the talents of my three new friends. Soon after *Magi*, then, I asked Susan to compose music for my 1986 Hamden production of *As You Like It* and also asked Judy and Kyle to sing at the beginning and end of the play, appearing as Hyman, the god of marriage. Even though they appeared briefly, they added an air of professionalism and class to the play. They also spent a great deal of time with the students, affording them a wonderful opportunity to witness opera singers in action, from warm-ups to performance. This, in a way, validated the students parallel preparation, as they too spent considerable time warming up and performing in a focused yet relaxed manner.

L'Elisir D'Amore was a much more complicated task than *Magi*, however, and I needed to think this through and be certain of my decision. This was new territory for me, although I must admit to being very excited about bold new challenges. But there were other concerns now, rather major ones when I thought about it. First of all, I shamefully never learned to read music which seemed to be the major impediment to directing a successful opera. Then I learned that the opera was to be sung in Italian, a language I don't speak or understand other than a few words and phrases. Somehow, however, I felt the scales were balanced by my brazenness and overriding enthusiasm to dive headfirst into a new medium that was fresh and exciting— one I had always admired and now desperately wanted to try. Mary was the musical director and assured me that she and I would work closely together, which allayed much of my initial trepidation. I also recalled the joy I received from the *Magi* experience. When I look back on this venture, I realize how much I must have wanted to direct it in order to tackle such huge hurdles, but I took relatively little time in deciding to accept the invitation. I quickly began my studies of the opera and its composer, Donizetti. I met with Mary and she gave me the text and a recording. I think I memorized every note of the piece.

Soon after I met the late Carmel Harris, the other artistic director, and immediately realized that I was in for a wonderful time. Mary and Carmel were so accommodating, gracious, and inclusive. I knew something about CET (formerly called the Connecticut Experimental Theater), for it had an excellent reputation as a leading opera company in Connecticut and New England. It was founded by Maestro Francesco Riggio and his wife, Hilda, many years before, and since their passing their very loyal followers were committed to keeping the organization alive and prosperous. I knew the Maestro's daughters, Francesca Riggio Scarpa and Marian Riggio Drobish—both talented performers and teachers—very well, which also made working for the CET seem like a homecoming of sorts.

During the following weeks, I don't think I ever parted with my *L'Elisir* prompt book, even bringing it with me to a doctor's appointment because I knew I would have some time to work on it in the waiting room. I skeleton-blocked the entire opera and listened to the score repeatedly. Mary invited me to the singing rehearsals and to meet the cast well before the staging rehearsals were to begin, and I attended them with excitement and anticipation. I looked forward to hearing the music live. In the large basement of one of the actor's homes the cast was seated before Mary and the piano accompanist, and from the moment they began I was entranced. The music was stunning and the voices so melodious. I remember wanting to begin staging the opera immediately.

Mary and Carmel had already cast the show by the time I was hired which made my job a bit easier. The leads were played by Jill Soltero, Roy Mazzacane, Jeremy Pick, Robin Sellati, and Richard Miratti. Roy had been a student of mine when I first started teaching in 1969 and it felt good to be reunited with him. He had become an accomplished opera singer, having studied in New York and Italy, and having performed at Lincoln Center and all around the world. Jill and Robin and I became friends instantly, and I was to direct them several more times in the future.

The rest of the cast was equally as friendly, exuberant and warm as the principals. I needed to be honest with these accomplished singers from the start and admit to them what my shortcomings were regarding this project. But I assured them I would work my hardest for them. This provided them with a sense of ownership and responsibility. Happily, progress was consistent during the rehearsal period, even though the hall was filled with constant laughter. We were able to use the community room in the Hamden Library for rehearsals which, with its spaciousness, carpeted floor, and excellent facilities helped to provide an ideal working atmosphere.

One of my main objectives was making the opera accessible to the audience even though I knew many of them probably wouldn't understand the language. Therefore I subtly built the meaning into the visual aspect, the physicality of the opera—both in body language and also in the pictures I tried to create on the stage. I was gratified that many audience members commented that they were surprised that they could follow the plot so easily.

The highly respected James Sinclair conducted members of the prestigious Orchestra New England for the opera. This was yet another thrilling aspect of the project for me. I was so happy that Jim and I worked together so easily. I remember once questioning the tempo of a particular section of the score, and I can still see his impish smile as he playfully commented, "You can't even read music, Julian!" When I asked him to humor me and just try altering the tempo slightly, he readily agreed and found that it actually enhanced the piece. He looked at me a bit surprised afterwards and I returned his glance with an impish smile of my own.

The performance evenings were totally sold out. Opera fans are so interesting as they readily applaud and shout "Bravo!" during the performance, something I was not used to. When Roy sang the deeply moving "Una Furtiva Lagrima", the entire theater was so quiet that I thought everyone had stopped breathing. It was an incredible moment.

The success of the opera earned the CET an invitation to perform in Waterbury, Connecticut, sponsored by the Seven Angels Theater. It was quite exciting to move the show, slightly re-staging it for a different venue, and making other necessary accommodations. The Seven Angels Theater decided to project subtitles to enable the audience to understand what was being sung, and while this worked very well, I preferred the performances without the subtitles. I felt the audience could be pulled into the opera more when it had its eyes glued to the action on the stage. The evening was exciting as the opera played before yet another full house, most audience members making it a black-tie affair. Once again, *L'Elisir* was tremendously successful.

L'Elisir was another one of those memorable experiences I was beginning to associate with guest directing. I was so glad that I took on this project. After so many years of directing plays and musicals, this experience opened an entirely new world to me, and I knew it was a part of me now. I hoped I would have the opportunity to direct more operas in the future, but, more importantly, continue to meet such genuine, kind, and diligent people. All too often we get closed off from the exceptional human beings who make up our theater community and the community in general.

The following summer took me to Quinnipiac College in Hamden where I directed *A Thousand Clowns* for The Dandelion Players, a community group that used the college for its performances. One of the groups's founding and artistic directors was Ellen Lieberman, a woman who a few years before had enrolled in an adult acting class I was offering. I could tell that Ellen was seriously interested in theater. She had some experience previously, but I felt she lacked confidence in herself. I gave her a monologue from *A Thousand Clowns* to work on because I thought she could play the role of Sandy very well. Like the character, Ellen was attractive, shy, a bit intimidated, but had such wonderful potential inside her. I felt that Ellen might find it easy to identify with the character and find the confidence that success can bring. Ellen performed the monologue beautifully. Something clicked within her, making her work come alive and the play from which the monologue came quite special for us. Ellen took several more courses and then started to audition in the community, being cast in a variety of roles. She kept in close contact with me, informing me of her projects, and as I witnessed role after role, I could easily see that she was gaining more and more confidence, and her work reflected it.

Soon she met Bert Garskoff, a university professor and theater enthusiast, and together they started the Dandelion Players. I was honored to be asked to direct for them, and selected *A Thousand Clowns* as a tribute to all that Ellen had accomplished. I was able to work with several former Hamden students in this production. Sophia Salguero played Sandy with such charm and precision that one would think the role were written for her. She was quite simply a joy to watch. Ed Scharf played Arnold, and this role illustrated what tremendous progress he had made. Suddenly this former high school student was an adult and playing an adult with an awareness, finesse, and ease. Tom McVety played the riotous Albert Amundson in his own inimitable fashion. Tom has the ability to be funny and also reveal such sensitivity as well. The cast also included the talented Gary Littman as Leo Herman who night after night brought the house down with his antics as "Chuckles the Chipmunk." Young Michael Kayne played Nick. Michael would become integrally involved in my Foote Summer

Theater program for several years before eventually attending NYU's Tisch School. And Bruce Connelly, a consummate actor whose friendship went back to college days, played Murray Burns and did an extraordinary job. I think that his preparation, his discipline, and his acting itself actually taught everyone else in the cast as they rehearsed together.

Maury Rosenberg and Michael Lerner were the stage managers for the play. Maury played Nick for me when I directed *Clowns* in 1969 as a senior in college. It was fun to have him with me as we re-explored this play, reminiscing and laughing. Michael was a product of Hamden Theater, having played many roles with expertise. I really believe that Michael's work is one of the reasons that Hamden achieved such stature in the educational theater community. Sheila O'Leary was the properties supervisor. I always enjoyed working with Sheila as she was so committed to every task. She was a perfectionist. Our small running crew was comprised of two people, my daughter, Jennifer and Anne Marie Conway.

In many ways this production was a "family affair." It was a totally different experience from that of the opera just a few months before, but each was singularly rewarding. I felt I was growing so much and so quickly as I continued to venture away from Hamden High School. Yet I must admit I felt a bit guilty as well. In no way would I jeopardize the education of my Hamden students, and I scrutinized every aspect of my outside involvement to make sure that nothing would interfere with their education. With each project, I found ways to include them, either getting them to play smaller roles or giving them opportunities to work on the technical crews. I wanted them to learn as much as possible, and the offers I was receiving during those years provided them with a wealth of opportunity.

In the early 90's I was to renew my partnership with the CET Opera Theatre, directing a twin-bill of one-act operas in '92, *The Telephone* by Gian Carlo Menotti and *Il Maestro di Musical* by Battista Pergolesi, and also directing *The Song of Norway* in 1993.

In both cases I was reunited with Jill, Robin, and Roy as principal singers as well as so many other people who were good friends by now.

The Telephone was a charming piece to work on. It recounts the story of a man who wants to propose to a woman, but every time he begins, she receives another phone call. She also seems to enjoy the calls and gets very involved with each one. Finally the man has an idea. He leaves the apartment and calls her from a public phone, at long last able to propose. This wonderful ending brings the delightful piece to a happy conclusion.

Il Maestro di Musical (The Music Master) is a short, gay tale of love. A woman, Lauretta, is pursued by two men, her music teacher, Lamberto, and an impresario, Colagianni. After some clever thinking and planning, all three are happy in the end. Lauretta signs a contract with Colagianni that she and her soon-to-be-husband, Lamberto, will give a grand tour where they will perform and Colagianni will collect the money.

These small comic pieces were great fun to work on and, once again, drew very large audiences. Their intimacy was starkly different from the production of *The Song of Norway* which was to follow approximately a year and a half later. The CET, then in its 44th year, wanted to celebrate the 150th anniversary of Edvard Grieg's birth, Grieg being the major character in this opera. This production was large and lavish, featuring approximately fifty cast members ranging in age from fourteen to seventy. The production also featured dancing by members of the New Haven Ballet School, and since the play needed teenagers as villagers, I was able to secure ensemble roles for eight Hamden students. Many more were afforded technical opportunities. Once again I felt good that I could pull my students into the world of opera, and I felt the diversity in ages among the cast and crew members was particularly stimulating.

I was lucky once again to work with my long-time friend and professional partner, Maury Rosenberg, who choreographed the piece. It seemed like Maury and I went from project to project, and nothing could have made me happier. He was so creative and added so much to anything we worked on. His death at such a young age some years later was a great loss for the theater community, and for me personally and professionally. I still expect to be able to phone him and tell him of a new project we can work on together.

My stage manager was Ariella Laskin, another Hamden student, whose organizational skills were excellent. Ariella graduated from the University of Connecticut as a theater major, her real talent being in the field of directing. I was very fortunate to have her on my administrative and artistic team for this production. She kept it from becoming unwieldy, and added immeasurably to the overall artistic impression of the work.

Carmel Harris' death a few years after *The Song of Norway* and the aging of the core members of the CET have unfortunately stalled the work of this productive and talented group. When I read the reviews of their work and study their history, I realize what an impact the CET had and what a loss its termination was for the Greater New Haven community and the State as well. I can only be thankful for my role in their last major productions, for this opportunity was a rare one and it taught me a great deal.

All of my guest directing experiences enhanced, in some way, my appreciation for theater and for the diversity that makes up the theatrical community. I was selective as far as what offers I would accept, and I hopefully made the right choices. I do know, however, that my work at Central and Southern, with the CET and Dandelion helped me to grow as a director and as a human being, to meet and enjoy the company of new people, and to explore even further this large umbrella of the theater world.

It has been said that the world of the theater defies definition. It's landscape is limitless. From the shelves surrounding me playwrights and play titles of every kind and representing every faction of society call out to me, as do books on theory and style, on acting and directing and voice and movement and design and playwrighting. Titles include such words as essential, contradictory, challenge, perspectives, vision, fundamental, modernist, period, believing, power, irreverent, doing, legacy, image, art, representative, brave, violent—these are formidable words and perhaps provide a paintbrush-stroke effect, much like the very beginning work of a director as he begins to see images and formulate ideas about a play he is soon to direct. They are a beginning, but cannot provide that elusive definition for this soul-stirring and overpowering art form.

I think all too often theater people become so ingrained in their own respective areas that they tend to be blinded to the enormous wealth and diversity Theater has to offer. People have become highly selective, choosing to perform in or see only musicals, or only non-musicals; to participate only in children's theater productions, and so forth. Unfortunately, they cheat themselves of the beauty of the overall picture. Appreciation and awareness of the scope of Theater enriches our lives and perpetuates that art form which has nourished us, and which the society of people around us is greatly in need of.

I mention this because guest-directing has enabled me to become somewhat familiar with the luxurious quilt work that is our Theater and meet some of the people who make up that fabric. And yet, this is only a beginning. I have to proceed slowly and logically or I feel I will be overwhelmed by the power of its incredible force. The longer I am involved in this beautiful world or Theater, the more I realize I have yet to learn.

Chapter Eight

Deaths and Inheritance

Dancing at Lughnasa, 1994

"I hope I will never forget what Hamden has taught me about Theater, but I'm sure I will never forget what Hamden has taught me about life."

Julie

"I've learned so much about the Theater and myself, but most of all, I've learned about the importance of friendship and the closeness between people."

Callie

My grandson, Kyle Jeffrey, stared up at me innocently and with large, curious eyes. I was telling him the story of Jack and the Beanstalk. It all started rather innocently, as he had taken a bag of beans from a low cupboard and was wielding it about like a lasso. I took it from him and tried to distract him by launching into the story of Jack, never really expecting this sixteen month old boy to become steadfastly interested in what I had to say. I'm sure it was my tone of voice rather than the story itself, most of which I struggled to remember, that held his attention, but he was certainly captivated and even smiled broadly several times as if he understood every word I spoke, and never did he break the flow of communication between our eyes. It was the first time that I can remember holding his attention for any more than the split second it usually takes him to go from one childhood discovery to another, from the swinging pendulum and ringing chimes of the wall clock to his fascination with a large hibiscus blossom on a nearby plant. Something very wonderful was happening during that discourse. There was a real sharing of a moment; a spontaneous kind of communication between people that happens much too infrequently, and the nice part about it was that I was aware of it all the time and didn't punish myself for not having appreciated it as it occurred—something we all do too often.

That wonderful experience happened on my father's *yortzeit*, or the Jewish calendar anniversary of a person's death. And that evening, while I said the traditional prayer of remembrance and I looked into the eyes of my father in a nearby photograph, I was saddened at the thought that he was not alive to participate in the great joy that is Kyle Jeffrey.

I sometimes think of myself as an intermediary, a bridge between generations of people. I know how happy each would have been to have known the other; a new dimension would have been added to each other's life. I often think that all of my students know each other, failing to realize that the age difference between the oldest and the youngest is rather large at this point. I will see a student and happily relay the good news of a former student until I see a slightly bewildered look in the eyes of the younger, and I suddenly realize that he has no idea about whom I am speaking.

So I become the "story-teller;" imparting facts and anecdotes that I feel are important and that may enrich the lives of those who are willing to listen. Much of this comes from my fascination with the stories my dad would tell me, or my mom, or other of my adult relatives who would fill a wide-eyed youngster's boundless imagination with the most wondrous tales.

I remember a distant, much older cousin—my mother's cousin, actually—coming to a family get-together. I had never met him before, and I don't recall if my family had either. He was visiting from Europe and didn't speak any English. I remember so vividly my family sitting around him, listening to an interpreter as this stranger who had entered our family circle held them spellbound with a very personal story; one he had difficulty in telling even after the passing of time. I remember sitting outside of the group, as fascinated by my family's intense concentration as by what the man was saying. And I also remember the finite movements of his facial muscles and the sadness in his eyes.

He told of the Nazis breaking into his house when he was a boy, and how his parents had hidden him in a closet just prior to their arrival. He watched through a crack in the wooden door as the invaders took his family away, never to be seen again. When he completed his story, my family was very still and silent. As a matter of fact, I remember a long silence, one which somehow frightened me because, for perhaps the first time in my life, I thought that my family was frightened. I wanted to run to my parents and hug them, but I was afraid to move. That moment was so long ago, yet so alive to me still.

Years later I was to meet Professor Leslie Hotson and his wife, Mary, and they related another wartime story; of the time that Mary's cousin, a famous European writer, had to bury her books in a field to protect them from the approaching Nazi army just prior to her escaping the country.

I tell these stories to my students because I feel they provide a sense of history and add dimension and perspective to their limited but expanding experiences. Much of what I seem to tell has to do with the lives of those who have died, for I feel we can learn so much from them. And in a way the stories keep those people alive in our memories.

I wish there were some place and time that the living and the dead could meet. We wouldn't even have to speak, but let our eyes communicate for us. Maybe this would relieve some of the suffering we go through when we lose someone close to us. I so often long to hear a now-distant voice, to hold a hand, or to feel the warmth of an embrace I cherished a hundred times, but one which is possible no longer.

Unfortunately death has not been a stranger to me over my thirty years of teaching. I've always felt this to be unusual since I primarily deal with young people, but that, in itself, makes the pain of losing someone in our family much more acute. As recently as this very morning I received word of the death of a former student who had resided in Florida for the past few years. I can easily remember her as she looked in her junior high school years, and I see once again the vivacity and enthusiasm which enveloped her as she rehearsed or worked on some technical aspect of theater. How can we ever come to terms with the taking of a young life.

When we studied the great playwrights in my Literature of the Theater class, the question would invariably arise as to whether death and emotional pain were necessary components in a life dedicated to art. I was asked if the death of someone close somehow allowed artists to see with a depth that many people have not experienced. It seemed uncanny to me that this question would be asked so frequently, but students had much upon which to base the question. Certainly the lives of the playwrights we studied -O'Neill, Williams, Inge, and so many others—were marked with a great deal of suffering.

I've given considerable thought to my students' questions. I've also thought about death itself ever since I was buffeted by its first major impact on my life, my father's in 1974. Since then the losses have continued, some expected, some ironically hoped for in the midst of terrible suffering, but most of which have been premature and therefore jolting and painful. The faces of so many lost loved ones swirl around in my head. I feel that people who are important to us provide us with a certain fuel for life; they become an energy source, and their loss creates a void where we once found sustenance, comfort, and warmth. It's only natural that we search for ways to fill that void and restore a balance to our life. But a fascinating component of this balancing effort is that the void allows a person to see under the surface of life, exposing us to a secret place; a vast, infinite territory containing feelings we may never have experienced before. So while the loss is obviously painful, in a strange way it can also be illuminating. It puts us in touch with our own mortality and exposes us to something much larger than the life of any one human being, or perhaps even the human race for that matter. I believe that artists hunger to bring this larger picture alive through their work as they wrestle to determine where humankind fits in. While there are many factors that determine the impact of an artist's touch, a glimpse at this unexplored territory may add a certain magnitude, and even a disquiet and urgency that can make a work resound in the hearts and minds of the spectators.

Each time death strikes the young I am at a loss to figure out its meaning. Why would someone with such potential be taken from us? I look for some reason, but my efforts seem to fail me. I only know that the effect of each passing has caused Hamden's Theater Department to grow stronger and more closely bonded over the years, as if that person's spirit has become part of the very foundation of our work.

I was a student teacher in 1969 at Michael J. Whalen Junior High School. Joseph Cristiano served as my cooperating teacher, or as it was called then, my "master teacher," and as I observed him that very first day of my student teaching tenure, I realized how very effective he was. Suddenly I was looking at teaching from a totally different perspective—the doing and not the theorizing—and I didn't know if I could measure up to the job.

My first day of student teaching found me sitting in the row of desks against the side wall. My notebook was opened, my pen in my hand, and I was ready to begin this new chapter in my professional life. I remember the details so clearly—the wood grain in the desks and the slightly antiseptic smell of the classroom. I also remember the sunny sky just outside the window, and I suddenly wanted to run into that brightness and that breeze and postpone, or maybe even halt altogether, this lonely journey into the real world.

At one point, the boy sitting in front of me turned around and smiled at me. He told me I needn't be nervous about this student-teaching "thing" and he was sure I'd do fine. I must have been projecting my apprehension and, to some degree, panic. That contact was my first one-on-one moment with a student, and I remember being somewhat surprised at both his perception and his boldness. I had convinced myself that my smart-looking jacket and tie had disguised my anxiety. I guess I was wrong.

That student was Larry Biller, one whose insight was apparent, although a casual observer would first be charmed by his engaging sense of humor and attracted by his headful of curly hair. I would come to enjoy having Larry in my class a great deal as he was bright and interesting and always had much to contribute to class discussions.

Larry auditioned for *Our Town,* the play I had "inherited" when Barbara Mastroianni, a faculty member at the school and also a Crescent Player friend of mine, decided that her many commitments would interfere with the time needed for rehearsals. I cast the play and gave the role of "George" to Larry. He had a certain innocence that informed the role perfectly. Even today I can see his slender, somewhat lanky frame onstage pounding a baseball into his mit in Act I, and appearing so much more mature later on in the play as he visits the grave of Emily, the childhood sweetheart who eventually becomes his wife and dies in childbirth. Larry's work was simple, yet moving, and most of the audience was surprised to find itself weeping at the latter moment of this, the first play to be performed at that school.

Many years passed and Larry married and became a father of several young girls. One day at work a disgruntled, and obviously deranged, client pulled out a gun and shot Larry and his partner repeatedly. Both of them died instantly. Larry's death sent shock waves through Hamden, a town not used to such gruesome happenings. It was felt even more considering Larry's loving and generous nature. He was always doing for others. A few years later the town built and named a playground after him in honor of his work with the many children to whom he was so devoted. I still have difficulty believing this terrible thing actually occurred, as visions of Larry in ninth grade with his shock of curly brown hair dance playfully in my memory.

Soon I was to have Larry's nephew, Daniel, as my student. As is the case with any particularly important moment, I have retained a mental photograph of our initial meeting. I was returning items to a costume storage area in the middle school, and a young man approached me with an amazingly warm smile and an offer to carry the costumes. I was taken aback by his outgoing, friendly nature that seemed to burst from within. Maybe I even subconsciously recognized a bit of Larry in Dan's exuberance. When

I taught him two years later, Dan was still as energetic as ever, and he still retained that radiant smile.

During the fall of his freshman year at the high school, I took a group of about forty students to a theater convention where we saw a play that dealt almost too realistically with the murder of a family member. Dan was noticeably upset by the play, the first time I had ever seen him in anything but a positive mood. During intermission I asked him to take a walk with me. I remember us walking along leaf-filled sidewalks and the crispness of the autumn afternoon, as I tried to give him the opportunity to talk about his feelings. I asked him if he would rather sit out of Act II, but he felt better having shared his emotions a bit and was appreciative that I took the time to try to comfort him. I think Dan and I bonded on that day. I know I felt especially close to him. He was intelligent and sensitive and not afraid to be vulnerable—certainly a special person.

Today, when I think of *Our Town* I think of Larry Biller. In a way, the understated beauty of each complements the other. I must admit, however, that when I was younger I was never very fond of the play. That production at Whalen did much to endear it to me. Over the years it has grown on me even more, maybe because I've had a glimpse of that boundless territory I spoke of earlier; a place seamlessly and matter-of-factly built in to the narrative of the play. Now *Our Town* seems to be the one play to which I turn when I need to find some personal comfort or to provide a reading for a special occasion. When my daughter was married, I read part of the wedding scene aloud to our guests, and when I was asked to do a reading at the funeral of a close friend's mother, I found the perfect words once again within its text. The dedication of my book, *Lessons for the Stage*, quotes the play when I remember my parents:

"We all know that something is eternal, and it ain't names and it ain't houses and it ain't earth and it ain't even the stars. There's something eternal about every human soul."

The playwright, Thornton Wilder, lived in Hamden for many years and had a way of looking into the human soul. He could express the most profound ideas through the use of the most simple words and phrases. It seems only fitting that Larry Biller played such a crucial role in the production of a play that illumines the human heart.

David Bowles, a student from my early days of teaching, died suddenly of a brain aneurysm while he was still in high school. David had a terrific sense of humor, and his popularity drew large audiences when we first began the theater program. Character roles were his specialty, and he fleshed out remarkable personalities for Fagan in *Oliver!* and Paravacini in *The Mousetrap* among others. I truly loved David. He could brighten anyone's spirits, even in the darkest of times. I was a relatively new teacher when David died, and the idea of one of my students dying was, at once, bewildering and shocking. We try to believe in a pervading fairness in the world; a sense of justice that rules our lives. But I could find none in David's passing. I was shaken by it, for his loss was accompanied by yet another awakening to the stark reality of our existence.

Just after his death, I recall visiting his family, and David's mother, Malissa, and I sat on the couch, far from the rest of those paying their respects, and perused his scrapbook. I didn't know that David saved momentos from each play. There was the beard he wore as Fagan, and old scripts with his blocking notation, and also the opening night letters I had written to him. For some reason it seemed very important to Malissa that we do this. It was almost like a final communion with David. At first I thought of this as odd, and then I thought that it was obviously important to Malissa. As I thought about it years later, however, I wonder if Malissa, who I have come to characterize as a very wise person, wasn't doing it for me. I remember her hands turning the corner of each page, not knowing what the next would bring and what memories would fly off the page and rush into my head.

After David's death, his parents wanted all memorial contributions to go to Hamden Theater. Malissa and Robert Bowles felt that the theater did a great deal for their son and this was their way of showing their gratitude. I admired the Bowles greatly. At the small ceremony during which a check was given in David's name to the department, my memory of them is very clear. They are standing side by side, Melissa's arm tucked under her husband's. Robert was dressed in a dark suit, his face set and composed, both of them surprisingly strong and peaceful, nearly stoic.

My admiration for Malissa only grew stronger when she lost both her husband and her remaining son as well some years later. I often wondered how she got through those three deaths. How is it possible for us to imagine the enormous pain of losing a spouse and two children? But Malissa is an unusual human being; a woman of great faith. She is a living lesson in courage. Sometimes, perhaps all-too-rarely, you cross paths with someone in life and, even in that short period, your life is illumined. Malissa was an inspiration for me. She attended my final production at Hamden High School in the spring of 1999, radiating an inner peace and that same joy for life that was always so characteristic of her. There was not much I could say, and maybe it was better that way. I do know, however, that her presence there that night added a validity to my thirty year career in Hamden.

That same evening I was reunited with David Dippolino, another student from the early 1970's and a close friend of David Bowles. He introduced me to his daughters and then we hugged each other hard. During that embrace twenty-five years vanished instantly and we were transported back in time to the Michael Whalen stage, remembering David Bowles' laugh and even his vain attempts to balance a cane on his nose in every play. David Dippolino and I wept, but they weren't sad tears; they were tears of happiness because we had the opportunity to share a brief time with a rare and gifted human being.

Other students who died over the years include Gary Conte in a boating accident, Jimmy Ardito and Billy Sargolini; JoAnn Coppola and Michele Plant and Charles Shanley; Alan Tiernan and Jim Adair, Carlos Gonzales and Sheila O'Leary.

Carlos had cancer and fought the disease so bravely right up to the end of his life. He came into school one afternoon wearing a bandana to hide the baldness caused by the radiation treatments. Yet I remember him being particularly exuberant that day, smiling and laughing; being in the theater that was undoubtedly a special place to him and where he had spent so much of his time. Carlos was a fighter. He provided yet one more lesson in courage. Isn't it strange that I can remember the touch of his skin as we shook hands. It is so interesting to me that the everyday things we all take for granted can become so significant. The touch of Carlos' hands will always be with me.

Sheila O'Leary died from diabetes-related causes. We kept in close contact even after she graduated from high school as she and I had grown very close over the years. Whenever she was home from college she would come to school to visit, and it wasn't unusual for her to sit at the back of the theater, listening to class after class, sometimes for two or three hours, before we even got to have a conversation. In addition to her battle with diabetes, Sheila also dealt with a sensitivity to light caused by her albinism, for which the only remedy was her wearing dark glasses at all times. But part of the wonder of Sheila O'Leary was her determination to surmount these problems in her quest to become a professional theater technician. She spoke with me only once about the feasibility of this dream. We sat together backstage late one afternoon and talked at great length about the possible obstacles, but Sheila had such a passion for this work. We knew it would not be easy, but I could see that Sheila had made up her mind long before asking my advice. We never spoke of it again, but rather shared her excitement about the projects she worked on over the subsequent years. One would think the obstacles to Sheila's dream were insurmountable, but she didn't think that way at all. This brave young woman was a true example of the indomitable human spirit.

Sheila worked on construction crews and props while she was in high school. A memorable story is that of the time she was the properties supervisor for *Brighton Beach Memoirs*. At one point in the play the character,

Eugene, a rather innocent and naive teenager, has to look at a picture of a naked woman in a magazine and react as if he had never seen one before. The actor was having a bit of difficulty with it, mostly because he was rather innocent himself and I suspect he might have been a bit embarrassed to broadcast the wide-eyed shock of the moment. One night in rehearsal, that moment was about to come and I was thinking about how I could tactfully help the actor play it more believably. All of a sudden, however, as he opened the magazine, his faced turned bright red, and he gasped uncontrollably as he struggled to deliver the line. It was the perfect reaction! I glanced at Sheila who returned a characteristically sly smile, and I immediately knew that she had planted a photo in the magazine that I personally did not want to see! As she passed by me a few moments later she nonchalantly mumbled, "Made your job easier, Schlusberg!" As we laughed about that episode, I realized that one of Sheila's many talents was her ability to get right to the heart of a problem and solve it as quickly as possible. Another obvious trait was a wonderful sense of humor.

I recently came across a card Sheila sent me in 1990. In it her sentiments about theater were so clear as was her passion to make it her life's work. I think I will always be impressed with her inability to accept limitations in her life. Sheila never gave up her dream. Sometimes I still expect to see her walk through a doorway or hear her voice on the phone. The world is a sadder place without Sheila although, in a strange way, my respect for her makes me see things more clearly and with more appreciation.

There is yet another student's death that had a great effect on me. This boy was not a theater student, but one I met when I was in charge of the "Indoor Suspension" room at school. This particular student was frequently in attendance. My understanding of this room's purpose was that it served as a warning for students who were repeatedly tardy or who were guilty of some minor infraction of the school's policies. However, this young man was a real problem, and his behavior often caused me to send him to one of the assistant principals for further disciplining. I never could quite figure out why this young man caused such a ruckus and almost taunted me, daring me as well as the other teachers who supervised the room at different times during the day to send him out.

A few years later I read an article in the local newspaper about a terrible car crash in which the driver drove into a building in the middle of the night. The driver died immediately upon impact. I must admit that, while saddened at the loss of life, I really was not surprised that the driver was the same troublesome student from the indoor suspension room. From my observations, he had an anger-a turbulence within him that would unleash itself in inappropriate language and behavior.

Soon after learning this news, I met the parent of a former student named Christina in a grocery store. She told me that her family and the late young man's family were quite friendly and had been for a long time. She also revealed to me information that both surprised me and made me rethink my estimation of the young man. It seems that he had an interest in Shakespeare, and at family gatherings Christina and he would often go off on their own and read from the plays. Christina even gave him her valued collected works of Shakespeare which he cherished and often would read alone.

I could never begin to describe my shock and despair when I learned this. He never would have admitted his love for Shakespeare or literature because that just wasn't "cool" in his circle of friends. I seriously thought about this boy for weeks and weeks, realizing that somewhere deep under this care-free and seemingly hostile attitude was a young man with great sensitivity and a passion for language and philosophy. As time passed after his death, I found myself deep in thought, often to the point of being in my own world in the presence of friends. They would often try to snap me out of it by asking me what was wrong, but I wasn't ready to share this story with them. I just kept thinking that I might have been able to help him. I wondered if I could have made a difference. If I had only known about the boy's "secret".

Life presents so many surprises. I am constantly reminded not to give too much credence to superficial appearances; that just as I teach actors that a believable character on the stage has many layers, the same is true of any human being in life. We should not be deceived by appearances. We must constantly be aware and sensitive; we must constantly question and look into situations and behavioral patterns from so many perspectives.

Death did not spare my colleagues. I've spoken of my friend, Denise Lowney previously in the Shakespeare Chapter. Her violent death, still shrouded in mystery, seems so antithetical to the happy, spirited person I remember.

Death also claimed the life of my wonderful Maury Rosenberg. How do I even begin to describe Maury? It seems as if I had known him all of my life. Maury choreographed many musicals for me as well as dances found in non-musical scripts. The last project we worked on together was *Dancing at Lughnasa* in May of 1994 for which he choreographed the frenetic, almost demoniacal Irish dance the playwright calls for. That one dance took so much rehearsal time, but the actors loved working with him. As far back as I can remember, all actors loved working with him. Maury had such a friendly way about him and a unique sense of humor as well. He was a good, kind, talented man who gave so much to others.

I first met Maury when I was a student at Southern Connecticut State College. I was given permission to student-direct a production of *A Thousand Clowns* in 1969 and I needed a young boy to play the role of "Nick", the precocious nephew of Murray Burns. Just prior to the auditions Maury walked into the Theater/TV Studio, asked for the director of the play, walked over to me and nonchalantly informed me that he was the Nick I was looking for. I remember looking down at this boy with blond hair and sparkling eyes, and him looking back at me with a seriousness and maturity that belied his young age. He had an innocent, yet direct attitude that immediately won me over. I didn't know him, but there was no doubt in my mind, even after a few seconds, that he had all the right qualities for Nick. As rehearsals progressed, I remember relating to him often as if he were a colleague of mine rather than a preteen. I think this had to do with his serious intent and remarkable work ethic. Even at that early age, Maury added a special quality to the play, and I knew that we would cross paths many times.

Actually, Maury and I did more than cross paths; we became very close friends over the years. He was a talented man, who was not only a choreographer, actor, and dancer, but an exceptional director as well. When he had an idea that he thought would benefit a production, he would go to any lengths to execute it. Two days before we opened *Guys and Dolls* in 1970, which Maury choreographed, he had an inspiration for new outfits for the Hot Box girls. Despite opening night looming just forty-eight hours away, Maury took up shop on the stage all day long and built new costumes as students ran in between classes for fittings. Maury was like that—always filled with surprises. His mind never stopped racing as he always tried to improve what was on the stage, often right up to curtain time. What separated Maury from the rest of us was that he brought his ideas to fruition all of the time.

Maury died of AIDS. He was diagnosed a long time before he died, and I had a hard time believing that he would one day no longer be with us. It just wasn't possible. It would take an enormous force to quiet this man with his inordinate amount of energy and charisma. As foolish as it seems, I really thought that I knew the one person in the entire world who would beat this disease. During the course of his illness, Maury rarely stopped working. He was vital and vibrant, directing plays and musicals, acting and choreographing, and all the while running a balloon and novelty shop in New Haven called "Monkey Business."

One of my last memories of Maury was seeing him in Connecticut Hospice. Maury had traditionally thrown a Groundhog Day's party every year, saying that it was the only holiday he could think of that didn't have festivity surrounding it, making it the perfect day to celebrate. Even while he was in the last days of his life at Hospice, his spirit was uplifting and he had endeared himself to the staff so much that they decided to have the party. I remember decorations and food galore, and so many people celebrating the way Maury would have wanted them to. Maury was noticeably absent for most of the get-together, although the room was alive with laughter and genuine good feeling, all of which came from stories about him. Near the end of the party Maury appeared in his wheelchair. A silence came over us as everyone looked at him in the center of the room. And while so many of us had tears in our eyes, he would not allow us to be sad. He then delivered what could only be described as a late-night talk show monologue that had everyone laughing hysterically. And It was all spontaneous, which only proved how miraculous and indomitable this man's spirit was

As the guests were about to leave, we knew that we would never see Maury again, and so each person took the time to speak with him. When I knelt beside him I could tell he was obviously weak. We looked into each other's eyes for such a long time, and finally he whispered words I will never forget. He thanked me for being the most important influence in his professional life. I was speechless and I remember the tears streaming down my face. This man who had done so much for so many and who was adored by hundreds and hundreds of people—including me—was thanking me. Somehow I think Maury was unable to see the effect he had on us. *He* was the one to be thanked.

Prior to his admittance to Hospice, when Maury realized that the end of his life was coming, he planned his funeral and ceremony. He made all of the decisions, including the selection of his own coffin—to relieve his family and friends of the pain of such tasks. He wrote a piece which his brother read at the memorial service—one laced with funny anecdotes. I remember that service, and I remember looking around the huge hall filled to capacity with the people whose lives Maury touched. The crowd was so large that many people couldn't even get into the building. He also arranged for a video to be shown; one in which he was dressed in a banana costume entertaining the elderly in area senior citizen centers as he often was want to do. He wanted us who survived him to remember him that way—with laughter.

His brother told me that Maury wanted me to be a pallbearer, an honor I will always cherish. And when I helped to lift the coffin, I began one of the longest walks of my life— putting Maury's body to rest. As we huddled together in the cemetery on that cold day, I found solace in the realization that I was very lucky to have Maury in my life. He was a gift to all of us. He taught us to laugh; that life could be very good indeed, despite the hardships we all encounter. My heart will always ache for Maury Rosenberg.

Edith Dyen was a teacher at Michael Whalen who was very supportive in those early days of Hamden Theater. She died in 1974. Edith was a lovely woman who would bring me gifts from the places she traveled, thinking I could use them in the next play. I remember her frequently telling me that I was doing important work, and that I should continue it even when times and situations seemed difficult. Edith attended every play, and always on Thursday nights. It was still early in my career, and I was impressed that this veteran, established teacher would take the time to support our fledgling program and to provide personal encouragement to this novice teacher. But Edith was always there, and always with a smile and special warmth. Edith's passing greatly affected me, and I felt an urgency to remember her in some formal way. After discussing it with the company of our production at the time, we decided to dedicate *Funny Girl* to her, a fitting tribute as that project was filled with such love.

I clearly remember that rainy day in August when we gathered for Edith's memorial service. It was a quiet service, and a sad one. The Whalen staff sat closely together that afternoon, trying to find comfort in each other's presence. We had not encountered the death of a colleague at this point. The eulogy was beautiful, but equally as moving was that with her passing Edith had united us; had drawn us together, so that for those moments we were one. Edith was very important to all of us—a person loved and one who would be missed for a long time afterward. We had lost the joy of talking with Edith, but we never lost the joy of remembering her.

Other losses included Barbara Mastroiani, a college friend and a colleague at Whalen who invited me to direct my first play there; Grace Pasqualoni Scalese, who I will always remember as the young, fun-loving friend who started teaching about the same time I did, and whose life ended much too early due to Multiple Sclerosis; P. Scott Hollander was a friend and theater critic/reviewer whose beautifully-written newspaper articles brought attention to our young theater group in the very late sixties and early seventies. As was the case with all of these people so instrumental in my professional and personal lives, I was saddened and shocked by her death, for it was difficult to think of our world without Pat's brightness; her laugh and her caring nature.

When I first began my career, I thought of work as a place to go to; a place apart from my personal life. But I soon learned that this would be impossible. Just as I carried home the joys related to my job, the deaths of my colleagues followed me as well. I often felt pummeled by it until I was in some kind of daze, often saddened and numb simultaneously. It was then that I knew I needed to try to find some meaning behind the losses, just for self-protection if nothing else. I thought about this for many years until I learned to take something from each of those precious lives and make it a part of me—something that would honor their memory and make my own life more meaningful.

Other deaths have altered my life substantially, and while they are personal in nature, they certainly have affected my professional life as well. My cousin Jeffrey's death, just two days after his forty-eighth birthday, was a terrible loss for me as it was for our whole family. Jeff was always bright and full of energy, and he had a great sense of humor. I can't say I was shocked by his death as he had been sick for quite a long while and we both knew what the end result of that illness would be. Fighting the inevitable, as futile as it is, became the stuff of our Sunday evening phone calls, and he from Manhattan and I from Connecticut would collaborate on ways to fight the imminent shadow looming over and encroaching upon us. And yet we laughed as well, just as we did as kids growing up in New York. We were like brothers, Jeff and I, sharing secrets and learning about this world that titillated us with its overwhelming possibilities. Our parents let us travel to the New York City by ourselves at an early age, and that noisy, beautiful, thrilling, expansive, humming metropolis became a challenge of sorts, and we hungered to experience every aspect of it.

One of our adventures took us to our first Broadway play, *Guys and Dolls*, a production that I believed had to be the most exciting event in the world. To this very day I can remember the romantic smell of that elegant theater, the plush seats and curtains, and the exquisite and seemingly immense hall itself with its intricate carvings and filigree that adorned the proscenium arch, ceiling, and walls. We must have looked a bit out of place, two wide-eyed young boys amidst a sea of well dressed people who appeared so elegant, cultured, and sophisticated. Jeff and I also went to the New York Public Library, determined to find our family's coat of arms. No one ever told us that there was little chance of poor European Jews having one. And on another occasion we decided to walk through every ethnic neighborhood we could, from "Little Italy" to romantic Chinatown to one area that reminded us of the Arabian knights. Another memorable excursion was to Radio City Music Hall, but this time we were taken by our Aunt Gert. There we saw the movie *Around the World in Eighty Days*, and suddenly hot air balloons, India, and even actors David Niven and Shirley MacLain took on special significance in our young lives. Yes, our childhood consisted of shared secrets and shared excitements, and that provided a bond that we would enjoy as we grew older.

We also shared a fascinating experience when we were about twelve years old. The Jewish High Holy Days were approaching, and among the many things we were taught to do and not to do in our nearly-daily Hebrew School classes was to observe the strict rule of not looking at the high priests, or "Kohanim" as they are called, while they chanted a very special prayer on Yom Kippur, the holiest day of the year. Refraining from doing things was not unusual for us. Orthodox Judaism has so many "never questioned" laws, and actually was fundamental in helping me attain a strong sense of discipline. But I questioned so many things as a young boy, and perhaps I still do so today. It wasn't unusual for me to be reprimanded by the rabbi and threatened with the most frightening thing of all: *he would tell my grandmother* who must have appeared like a stern, unforgiving matriarch to him. I'm sure he thought I was in for a great punishment from her, but after a lecture, Grandma would smile, make some of her wonderful old-world sugar cookies, and we'd talk about things we weren't "supposed" to.

Yom Kippur approached and I told both Jeff and my then seven-year old brother, Joey, that I intended to do the unthinkable: I was going to look at the high priests. For many years I listened to the their melodious, almost mystical chanting, and I heard the thud of their knees hitting the floor as they kneeled for the one and only time during the entire year that they were required to so. Next to us my uncles, like all of the other men, were hidden under prayer shawls, and all of the Hebrew School boys were instructed to turn our backs to the altar or cast our eyes down. Our synagogue was huge and opulent, with marble imported from Italy, a large balcony, and the most radiant and enormous stained glass windows along the side walls. They seemed to soar hundreds of feet upward! On the High Holy Days the ark was dressed in white velvet curtains, adorned by Hebrew letters embroidered in shimmering gold. It was quite a sight, and one that could help fill the most unreligious soul with at least a temporary feeling of holiness.

Jeff was standing to my right and Joey to my left when the sacred moment arrived. I could see my uncles Aaron, Lou, and Hy moving rhythmically back and forth, lost in the immediacy of prayer and security of prayer shawls. It was then that I touched both Jeff's and Joey's hands, glanced at each of them, and mouthed the words, "I'm going to look now." My little brother was frightened, perhaps thinking I'd disappear or maybe turn to salt if I lifted my eyes upward. Jeff, however, knew I was determined and gave me his silent approval. And then I looked. What I saw amazed me, for the sunlight was streaming through the amber stained glass windows, casting a bright and vibrant golden beam of light upon the altar. The chanting, while I was conscious that it was indeed happening, could only underscore the serenity and splendor and inspiration of that moment. Jeff and Joey, feeling the increasing pressure of my hands upon theirs, also looked upon the scene, and we three shared one of those fleeting yet memorable experiences. We may have been very young at the time, but we could recognize the rarity and importance of that moment.

I realize that this happened long ago. And I realize that the passing years and the "forbidden" quality of this experience my have added a certain "theatricality" to my memory. But the one thing that has remained with me all these years is the picture of three boys holding hands, awestruck at something they could and yet could not fully comprehend. Personally, I have always felt a part of something larger since then; some "plan," some rhythm that dictates the seasons, that defines beauty, that determines when the tides will ebb and flow. There is some higher power. I know this.

And now my cousin Jeff is gone. But I find comfort believing that he is a part of that plan; and even of that beautiful golden stream of the brightest light that shone upon the altar on that special day so many years ago.

The deaths of my parents, as Jeff's, had an enormous effect on my life. Their respective passings, like pebbles dropped in a pond, ripple endlessly outward, reaching places in my mind and heart I would have hardly imagined possible, and adding new potency to words like "never" and "finality." Many books have been written about coping with the death of a parent, and I'm afraid I have little additional insight to offer except that I think everyone deals with this occurrence in a very different way.

I was very close to my parents and they were very supportive of my dreams. I could best describe them as simple, hard working people. Family came first, and they sacrificed a great deal for their four children. Education was of utmost importance to them, even though my mother did not go to college and my father only completed eighth grade. They felt, however, that we needed to go to school because that was the only way to improve our lives.

Naturally, I have many memories of my parents, but those memories are different from those of my siblings, Stan, Marcia, and Joseph, since we are all approximately five years apart from each other in age. To me, memories of little things stand out—like the Saturday afternoon trips we would take, or watching my parents as they sat on the front stoop on summer nights talking to the neighbors while we children played all kinds of games. A favorite memory of mine is seeing the figure of my father walking across a small field on his way home from work. Running to him and hugging him felt warm and secure. How I envy the young boy who was able to do that, and how lonely it often feels for the older man who can never feel his father's warm embrace again. Dad died first, and several years later we lost Mom.

I remember taking many walks with my mother when I was very young, helping her push a stroller with my baby brother, Joe, bundled up inside. I remember the smell of fresh-baked rolls on the main street of our hometown and begging Mom to let me buy one; and as we shared it we would push the stroller to a park and engage in one of our favorite pastimes—searching for four-leaf clovers. Finding one of these rare beauties, my mother was quick to remind me, was the epitome of good luck. I searched so hard, but could never find one. It became a preoccupation. Sometimes I tried to fool her and shape a three-leaf clover into four, but Mom was too smart for me. The pursuit of the four-leaf clover became a goal of our combined efforts for many years. It also became a secret between us, something we talked about in a whimsical way every so often, as if finding one would be the answer to all of our problems. Perhaps what was more important than finding the clover, however, were the flashbacks to my youth that the hunt provided, and the bond with mom that just grew stronger through the years.

When Mom died I was sure the world could never be right again. I was relieved that her suffering was over, but all the same, the future seemed very cold and hollow. How could I go on without being able to receive the comfort I always found in her eyes? What about the advice she gave me throughout my life that could easily clear my clouded brain? And her touch—would I never feel the warmth and kindness of those hands again?

Near the end of her life I traveled daily to New York to visit her in the hospital. I had just arrived home in Connecticut when I received a phone call from her doctor telling me to return immediately, that mom's time to leave us was here. That lonely final ride to New York was filled with memories and also with the uneasiness of what the next few hours would bring.

Those were the days that families and even the medical profession to some degree weren't as honest with patients as they are today. No one ever told my mother that the form of leukemia she had would eventually take her life. I could only imagine what she must have been thinking as that disease made her life more and more unbearable. I often thought she must have known she was dying, although a day or two before she died she looked up at me from her hospital bed and plaintively asked, "Julie, what's happening to me?" I couldn't find the words or the courage to tell her the truth. That moment of cowardice haunts me. I keep thinking I should have been honest with her so that that she could have prepared herself in some way, or she could have had time to reflect upon her life, or at least found some peace with the knowledge that her suffering would end. Instead I sat down next to her, took her hand into mine, and told her I loved her.

When I arrived at the hospital, my mother had already died. My brother, Stan, met me outside her room and told me the news, and then asked me if I wanted to go in to see her one last time. I couldn't do that. I knew that seeing her at that moment would be the image I would always carry with me, and I didn't want that. Although my thoughts and emotions were in turmoil, that was a clear and definite decision on my part, and I have never regretted it. Somehow I just couldn't see my mother lifeless before me.

The most memorable experience of my life occurred on the afternoon of my mother's funeral. After the service, my friend, Ort, and I were driving out of the cemetery, when we came to a red light at the cemetery's gate. I stopped the car and Ort spontaneously opened the passenger door, leaned outside, and returned with a small green object in his hand. He gave it to me—a four-leaf clover. I was speechless. I felt as if an angel had touched my shoulder, and I almost expected to turn around and see my mother sitting in the back seat. That moment erased the sorrow that made speaking and even thinking clearly impossible tasks. For a moment my life seemed to be lifted in some spiritual way.

This experience seemed like a divine event. I've shared it with a few, select people and usually they react to it in common. First of all, there is a kind of incredulous silence, but there is also a strong desire to believe that a communication took place between two souls. Perhaps believing that it could happen to me would enable it to happen to them.

The four-leaf clover story does not end there, however. Ort's mother, Marie, died a few years later. Her death was sudden. She drowned. I was forty-eight at the time, and I would like to think that I'd be somewhat used to Life's shocks, yet this one took me by surprise once more. I try to outweigh the horror of her death with the thought of her spirit being in some peaceful place. It's difficult for me to think of a person "here" one moment and not the next. All of that energy of being alive-where does it go?

When I think of Marie now I often think of her church—a place very central to her life. I had been in it on many occasions as this was a religious family, and they invited me often to celebrate the many events in their lives. I can smell that church so distinctly—that sweet fragrance so foreign to this Jewish man. I see the priest ceremoniously dissolve the circular wafer in his mouth and drink from a cup which he wipes and wipes—in fact, nearly kneads- with a fresh white napkin. The giant crucifix of Jesus' body is a comfort to all who reverently kneel and pray, yet I feel like the outsider; a stranger to the ritual and even to this cavernous, echoing edifice. Yet I recognize a warmth here; a gravitation of many to the security of this holy place. And this, I like to think, is the departure place for Marie's spirit.

Ort and his father chose a relatively new cemetery for Marie, or maybe it was a new section of an older cemetery. At any rate, there were many burial plots to choose from in this field of endless green peace. In discussing which plot would be best, there was no guidance, and the two of them were not sure how to select it. Do they look for a knoll, a tree, a spot with a beautiful view? And then Ort looked down and his eyes immediately and miraculously rested upon a four-leaf clover. He knew this was the spot.

We live in a highly technical and sophisticated world. At least I like to think so. I try to believe that rational thinking and a sense of order characterize most of our existence, and that events in our society are all part of a huge chain of human actions and reactions. How, then, does one begin to explain the uncanny experience of the four-leaf clover story; a story which does not end with this event either.

When Ort told me about his experience at the cemetery, I could hardly believe it. But to this very day we have both clovers. Since then I have been to Marie's grave, and I think the air is warmer and sweeter there. The poignancy of the four-leaf clover story helps a bit in dealing with the death of Ort's mother and mine as well, and I find comfort in believing that there is some divine intervention involved. Most humans revere God's omnipotence, but how many of us give Him enough credit for His poetry?

Marie had a wonderful and often sarcastic sense of humor, and she would often tell me stories about the family and also about the church. I'll do my best to relate this one, but I'm afraid no one could tell it like Marie.

Father Hogan was a controversial figure, and not a very-well-liked priest in Marie's parish. She had many disagreements with him over the years. Upon his death, his body, garbed in his priestly vestments, lay in the church for the parishioners to pay their final respects. During the service, as the Cardinal was sprinkling holy water upon the Father's body, the cap of the aspergillum, the small, baton-like object which holds the holy water, broke and flew in the direction of the body, whereupon it hit Father Hogan on the head and promptly disappeared into the coffin. Needless to say, the Cardinal, his fellow priests, and the parishioners were appalled, and no one was sure what to do next. Finally several priests decided to ease the embarrassment of the moment. Many hands swiftly searched the folds of Father Hogan's vestments as well as the deeper recesses of the coffin. However, there were too many people searching at the same time, and the church aisle was too narrow for all of them. To everyone's shock, the coffin slipped off its runner base and toppled over, and Father Hogan fell out of the casket. The congregation was horrified, and now two priests and a Cardinal were desperately trying to get the body back into the coffin. Marie said that Father Hogan was a fairly heavy man which made the task very difficult. They finally managed to get him back into the coffin, but his arms and legs stuck out in all directions. The priests and Cardinal did their best to adjust the body so it would look more becoming, but then realized that Father Hogan's crucifix, which just moments before was hanging around his neck, was now gone—probably under him. Marie described the faces of the three men as they exchanged panicked glances. They realized they had to find the crucifix. By now the parishioners were aghast and simply stared, seemingly without breathing, until the crucifix was found. Marie recalled the experience as a memorable one and an all-too-appropriate way for the Father to depart his congregation. I'm not sure how much of this story was fact and how much was exaggerated, but I've retold it exactly as Marie originally related it to me, illustrating her unique sense of humor.

As I mentioned above, there is yet one final chapter of the four-leaf clover story. May 28, 1995 was the day of my daughter's wedding. Naturally, I had been thinking of Jennifer for many days and weeks leading up to it. The ceremony took place in a gazebo by the water, just as Jennifer wanted. My daughter looked beautiful in her wedding gown. I remember the breeze whispering through her hair ever so slightly, and many thoughts went through my head. When and how did my pig-tailed little girl become this beautiful woman? Her life raced past me, from the first time I ever saw her as a newborn in the nurse's arms right through her childhood and adolescence to now. I suppose these questions become almost cliche, and that every parent of a bride or groom thinks these things.

My friend, Bruce Connelly, was on his way to the wedding. He was nearly late and grateful for a last-minute ride offered by a friend. He remembers rushing down a path from the house to the car, when he somehow spied a four-leaf clover on the lawn. He picked it for good luck and, upon his frantic arrival at the wedding where the wedding party was already lined up and the musician about to begin, Bruce gave the clover to Ort. Ort was dumbfounded, thinking about the history of the four-leaf clover story. He ran to Jennifer and placed it in Jennifer's bouquet.

I suppose the three clover episodes may have been coincidence. The rational side of me says that they are. However, I must admit that there is a part of me that wants to believe that all of this was meant to be, and I indulge myself in the belief that this may be the closest we can come to those we have lost; to that place I spoke of earlier where the dead and the living can feel each other's presence.

Death takes people away from us, but I believe it gives us something back as well. Often that something is difficult to find and time needs to pass before our sight is cleared. I like to think that I have inherited things from the people who are no longer a physical part of my life—and that inheritance is much more valuable than money or material belongings. So many of my students and colleagues faced their deaths with courage, and I have learned through their example. I have witnessed, first hand, the qualities of integrity and honesty that have marked the lives of others, and I have observed the bonding of human beings as they come together to comfort each other. These special people have added so much to my life and have taught me to appreciate the uniqueness of the human spirit.

I am a theater teacher and director, and the theater reflects life. I like to think I can guide my students into better work on the stage by offering them the insights I hope I have gained from the lives of my departed friends as well as from those who fill my life each day with their enthusiasm and joy. In this way we do more than create realistic characters. More importantly, we make the connections that compel our audiences to feel the wonder of being alive.

I so firmly believe that a person lives on after his death through the good things he has done in his life. Perhaps he has provided some hope or inspired a dream. This is the greatest gift of all—to help people see how beautiful life can be.

Chapter Nine

Foote Summers

The Secret Garden, 1996

"I remember starting the Foote Summer Theater program in my freshman year of high school and feeling intimidated when I first walked into the theater. I was pretty young compared to the older, more experienced students, but the program provided such a comfortable environment that I immediately knew I wanted to be a part of it. That was four summers ago, and this program has become an important part of me. Over the years I learned a lot about theater, but, more importantly, to always believe in myself and what I do."
Bethany

"Each summer I return thinking that my love for the Theater could not possibly grow stronger, and always I am proven wrong as my eyes are continually opened to new experiences."
Emma

"These past summers have been so wonderful for me. Every morning would be filled with a sense of excitement and anticipation as I traveled to Foote Summer Theater. I loved being there."
Amy

I don't know what the summers would be like without the Foote School Summer Theater. I've been working in this program for twenty years now, and what started out as a small program for young children taking place in a cafeteria-like space on the Foote School campus has developed into a major enterprise—a full-length musical production for high school aged students housed in a renovated performance space in downtown New Haven. Everything about the current program is wonderful, from its location in the arts district where the very air hums with creativity, to the diversity of the students who come from many high schools throughout the State. There have been strong ties among the students for many years, completely eradicating the belief that high schools need to be competitive. Instead their friendships are genuine; they are supportive and loyal to each other throughout the year, and always enthusiastic about welcoming new students into the fold each summer.

I actually began my work for this program in the summer of 1981 as a technical director. I received a phone call at Hamden High School the spring before from Patricia Chernow, whose idea it was to begin the program. Pat was a music teacher at Foote , a private/independent school in New Haven. She was seeking a student who could serve in this capacity, and was surprised that I immediately offered my services. It was a difficult time for me financially, and the idea of a six-week summer theater job sounded very nice.

That phone call started a strong friendship with Pat. I remember meeting her for the first time at her elegant home in New Haven. The house was previously owned by an art enthusiast, and the ceilings were lined with spotlights aimed where paintings used to adorn the walls of long hallways. Interestingly, the former owner's son became a central figure in Hamden's Theater program a few years later.

I could tell that Pat had grandiose plans for the Foote program, and as much as she valued working with nine to twelve year old children and recognized the importance of creative dramatics in their lives, I knew that she had a larger plan in mind. She wanted an older, more mature group, a plan I agreed with since most of my work had been with high school students. We talked also about changing the material from the necessary original pieces and small children's theater plays to something more substantial. Pat was an accomplished musician and played piano for *The Fantasticks* at the Sullivan Street Theater in New York some years before. Although she taught music, I often thought of her as someone who was longing to go back to work in the professional musical theater rather than an academic. But I was new to this program and didn't know how long I would be involved in it, so I tried to be as supportive as I could, often discussing with Pat her plans for the future but not knowing if I would be part of them.

As I approached Foote School and its beautiful, sprawling campus on my first day of work that summer, I sensed that I was entering a new phase of my professional life. I was taken by the intimacy of feeling and the personalized attention to every student that characterized the teachers' attitudes towards their students. I could assess this from the bulletin board displays in the faculty room and the student-written poetry and art projects cluttering the coffee tables and walls of that space, one that, in other schools, is nearly-always relegated to teacher concerns only. I was also privy to conversations of faculty members who would wander in and out during the summer, often with their children and even their dogs, the latter seeming totally at ease and even natural to this setting. I also observed teacher and parent volunteers watering the grounds and planting flowers and shrubs to beautify the campus, something seldom, if ever, done in a public school setting. I was beginning to like the feeling of family I was observing, and the obvious pride this community had in its school. I was soon to meet the Head of School, Frank Perrine and administrators like Bill Friday and Laura Altschul who were welcoming and warm, making me feel at home. As the program proceeded during that summer I met many teachers and I could easily tell that their work and that of the administrators far exceeded the parameters of a given contract. It was easy to tell that they were devoted to this school. Now, after twenty years of association with Foote, I'm happy to say that this same attitude still pervades the campus under the current Head, Jean Lamont.

Working as a technical director in a first-year program with little if any money was not a stressful job, and I enjoyed the challenge of working on a component of theater other than acting and directing. It was a welcome relief not to be in charge of every aspect of a production, although Pat asked me countless questions during those weeks. I know that technicians and designers have their own set of stress-causing problems, hectic schedules, and deadlines to meet, but for that summer the technical demands were minimal at best. As a matter of fact, I felt like more of an art teacher than a technician, working with the students on painting and making props.

Pat told me often that she wished she knew I was available that summer, and that I could have been directing the play rather than painting on large pieces of paper. But it was fine with me. Maybe I needed that summer to get a feeling for the program. The director was a Yale theater student, Tom Whitaker, with whom I struck up a friendship. He was a talented and kind person, and the fact that he was graduating and moving away from New Haven made accepting Pat's proposal to be director the following summer much more palatable. I certainly did not want to compete with him for the job, nor would I have.

Directing nine to twelve year olds in a small cafeteria that next year was a far cry from my job at Hamden, but it really was refreshing and a much-needed break. Quite often during rehearsals I would be distracted by some movement in the large windows of the room and see Hamden High School students approaching, paying a brief visit as they enjoyed a summer walk through town. Often they would bring little gifts with them. One summer Larry Iannotti quite unexpectedly brought me a basket filled with an antique collection of Shakespeare's plays, and Martin Harries showed up one day with two Eugene O'Neill plays, wrapped in a purple ribbon. Larry and Martin, like many others, would frequently happen by, as if Foote School was the natural course on their daily travels, bearing what have become some of my most prized possessions. I must say, however, that I needed to see them. Their visits grounded me, connected me to Hamden, and also gave me a sense of professional identity and purpose. As the years passed, this became more and more the case as I came to understand the fundamental roles the Hamden students would play in my life.

Within a few summers, our students were older and Pat asked me what I thought about renting the Arts Hall at the newly renovated Educational Center for the Arts (ECA) in downtown New Haven. Our current venue was too small for the number of audience members who came to our plays, and the lack of air conditioning made it terribly uncomfortable in the summer heat. That space truly was small and originally had been used as a place for students to eat lunch. It had a low ceiling—or at least a lower one than is necessary for lighting a performance space—a few drapes and lighting instruments, and the fact that it could be used for major productions during the school year was more a testament to the ingenuity, creativity, and flexibility of the drama director, Bob Sandine, than the practicality of such a use.

I welcomed Pat's idea to move due to the necessity for a larger space, and we went downtown to the ECA to get a first-hand look. The building was originally a synagogue, and a grand one at that. It was built in the 1800's and still maintained a formidable appearance on the corner of Audubon and Orange Streets. The small silver letters spelling out "Educational Center for the Arts" seemed dwarfed by the sheer size of the reddish-brown edifice with its spires, stained glass windows, and large stone bricks.

The main sanctuary was gutted to become a theater, although it still retained the large stained glass windows on one wall. Lighting and sound positions were accessible by walking on a flexible grid that was nearly the size of the room itself and ran close to the very high ceiling. I remember walking on it with great trepidation, knowing full well that it was totally safe, and yet experiencing the strangest sensation in the pit of my stomach every time I ventured out onto it. There were other rooms in the building, but we were more or less relegated to this wonderful space. The fact that it was a sanctuary made me feel immediately comfortable, perhaps in some way due to my Jewish background. I am amused as I recall stories of the building being haunted—what theater isn't?—by the ghost of a rabbi, angered that this holy place would now be used for entertainment. It seems that groups renting the theater would discover props missing, scenery slashed, and other disconcerting and unexplainable mishaps. I would sometimes tease the students that they better be respectful or the ghost would get them, and as they laughed off my warnings, their eyes darted in the direction of any slight sound in the darkened corners of the room. I'm glad to say that the ghost must have liked us, for our production of *Brigadoon* went exceptionally well! Maybe this is because we always thought of the theater as a holy place to begin with.

I was glad that our first major endeavor at the ECA was *Brigadoon*, a musical I was to direct some years later for Foote once again. Brad Blake was our choreographer. I remember Brad's extraordinary energy well before that summer when he was a student at Hamden High School. He was an excellent dancer in his own right, but more importantly, the students learned a great deal from him and had a good time doing it. One night during a performance, the actress playing Meg Brockie, Andrea Drobish, stumbled over her lines in one of those incredibly fast patter songs. I had heard of this happening very often with productions of this play and tried to guard against it. Brad and I were standing in a small alcove just outside the control booth well above the audience, and our eyes instantly darted to each other in panic. How, we worried, would she ever be able to remedy the situation? The song hardly provides any time to breathe let alone figure out a solution. Remarkably, Andrea managed to remain calm, invent lyrics, retain the rhythm of the musical number, and even make her lyrics rhyme in that verse. I still don't know how she did that.

Isn't it strange that I would recall that moment with Brad so vividly so many years later—especially when his work was so memorable that I could have retained of a host of other memories. It was one of those moments in the theater that is difficult to describe: on the one hand, the very idea of a live performance implies the possibility of things going wrong in front of an audience, yet the problems themselves create an intense support system—whether we are able to spontaneously help solve them, (which can be the greatest of learning opportunities for young people) or, as in the case of Brad and myself, we can only look on helplessly and pray for the best.

We were to do one more production in the Arts Hall at ECA. The following summer we presented *Grease*. Brad was unable to be our choreographer and we knew we had to replace him as soon as possible. One day Pat phoned to tell me someone was interested in the job, and I drove to her house for the interview. That was the day I met John Paolillo, someone who would figure prominently in Foote Summer Theater and remain with the program for many years. John and I became good friends immediately. He had everything that was needed for the program: he was a talented dancer, he had a terrific sense of humor, and he was someone to whom the students could really talk. He had dreams of going to New York to dance, but felt that he was too short and didn't possess the right "dancer's build." Nevertheless, he was tenacious about that dream, and I'm happy to say that today he is doing just that. John's laughter was infectious, and I remember so many rehearsals coming to a complete standstill because something would strike him funny. The students loved him, and as happy as I was for him when he decided to move to New York, I was saddened that our long-standing working relationship would now end.

I was fortunate to find two other choreographers whose work was excellent and whose personalities sparkled. Nefra Sullivan choreographed *Big River* in the summer of 1997, and Sophia Salguero did the same for *Barnum* in 1999 and *Chess in 2000*. I love to watch talented choreographers, especially those who can bring a lot out of a teenager. Many students, mostly boys, feel awkward about dancing on stage. It takes a patient and giving choreographer to make them feel good about themselves. The mother of one of those insecure boys recently told me that her son, now in college, gained so much self-confidence because he felt, after Nefra and Sophia worked with him over the course of three summers, that he could finally be proud of his dancing. This is such a tribute to those two women and their talent and dedication. Nothing can be more positive in the educational sphere than helping students understand that they have enormous potential.

Soon after *Grease* ended in 1985, Pat moved to the southern part of the State, preventing her from continuing both the program and her teaching job at Foote. It was a sudden move and caught me by surprise. Suddenly the destiny of the program fell into my lap. I felt I needed time to restructure it, to redetermine its goals, and decided to temporarily move it back to the Foote campus.

During our summers away, Foote had constructed a new building with a large multipurpose space. This, then, would be yet another temporary home. There was also a need for a program that would include younger children once more, so I decided that we would focus on that age group while I deliberated about the direction we would take in the future. Judith Caldwell became my new musical partner, and we embarked on a series of smaller plays with music. Judy was the head of the music department at the Educational Center for the Arts, and we had worked together previously. We also employed Susan Hulsman-Bingham to play the piano for several small productions. I'm almost embarrassed to admit that Sue, Judy, and I formed a little production orchestra. They, at least, could legitimately play their instruments. I, on the other hand, played the kazoo and the bongos, often simultaneously, and also rather poorly. I will only say that our orchestra added to the "informality" of the program. Yet, the lack of a high-powered, production-oriented experience did not diminish the quality of the work nor the fervor with which the students approached it. In fact, numerous children from those summers went on to successful theater careers in college and after. I can only say there was a freedom built into the process that enabled these young people to boldly experiment, learn to make choices, and enjoy themselves immensely—just as the adults did.

As much fun as those days were, the program was caught between parents who wanted a process-oriented experience for their children, and those who wanted a product-oriented one. I argued that it was difficult to supply both in such a short amount of time and with young children. I felt that my hand was being forced and knew the time had come to make one more decisive choice. I opted to return to what I knew best—working with high school students and seeking a permanent home, a legitimate theater space somewhere off the campus. Gail Brand, the director of the Foote Summer Program, agreed with me, and I started to search for the ideal spot. Gail was totally supportive and is, to this day, one of the finest administrators with whom I've ever worked.

I was fortunate to find a brand new renovated theater with quite a history. Known formerly as the Lincoln Theater, a small but popular arts-film hall, the building had recently been totally altered to a performing arts space. Interestingly, it was originally founded by Jack Crawford in 1925 specifically for live productions of the Little Theater organization. At the time there was a strong little theater movement, and many groups in the area were relegated to town halls and church basements for their performances. The Little Theater on Lincoln Street thrived for quite a while, but its use as a live-performance space began to disintegrate during the war years. There was also competition from New Haven's Shubert Theater and other professional organizations. When there was talk of the building being razed in the early 1980's, Ken Galdston of the Yale School of Organization and Management worked with Nancy Brown, another New Haven arts advocate, and formed the Committee to Save the Lincoln. With financial backing from the State and from private contributors, the Lincoln was indeed saved and declared a national historic landmark, recognizing its historical and cultural importance in the community.

I had never known the Lincoln as a performance space, but had indeed visited it frequently when it was a movie theater. There was something wonderfully warm and intimate about it. In 1969 I saw the Zefferelli production of *Romeo and Juliet* there, and when I got home after the movie, I realized that I had lost my wallet. I went back to the theater the next day, and the manager allowed me to pick through the large trash bin that was actually located directly behind the movie screen! I remember desperately, but quietly, rummaging through the trash to the movie's score and all of the time knowing that only the movie screen separated me from a full house of people staring in my direction.

It felt good to bring the Foote program to the Lincoln. It was a perfect space located at the end of a short street and situated in the newly created arts district of the city. Artists abounded in the neighborhood, and there was an energy on the street that easily filtered into our theater as well. We finally had a home, and I was certain that the strong tradition of theater that existed there would enhance the efforts of our young people. We were to be the first group to rent the newly renovated Little Theater which made it even more special to us.

ECA owned and operated the building, and its Executive Director, Robert Parker, was extremely gracious to us. Bob was a Southern Connecticut graduate and we knew each other somewhat during those college days. Over the years, our friendship was to grow considerably. He is the best "landlord" you could find—extremely cooperative, attentive, and supportive. Bob also troubleshoots a lot, anticipating problems concerning conflicting times in the Little Theater and solving them far in advance. And it seems as if he solves them to our benefit. He is also a greatly respected leader in the New Haven arts community.

Part of the rental agreement was that I would hire ECA's two technicians, Jamie Burnett and Steve McGuire, both of whom had graduated from Carnegie Mellon University as technical theater majors. We chose to do a production of *The Boyfriend* in the summer of 1990 as a kind of tribute to the early days of Foote Summer Theater when we performed this musical in the old cafeteria/theater on the school's campus. Steve's set was wonderful and seemed so professional compared to what we had done in the past. My experience as technical director that first summer was laughable compared to Steve's expertise. Jamie's lighting was in a class by itself. He had a way of not only creating mood, but punctuating emotional moments as well. The three of us worked together for several years, and each year the technical end of the program became more complex.

Certainly the Little Theater could handle it, for although it was a small space, it was magnificently equipped with the latest advances in the field.

I was always aware of how talented Steve and Jamie were, and I knew that before long they would have to answer their professional callings in other places. I was grateful for my time with them, but I knew it would ultimately end. Jamie left first, and Steve a few years later. We had done some excellent productions together, including *Brigadoon* in 1991, followed by *Fiddler on the Roof, Funny Girl,* and *Pippin.*

Pippin was a departure for us into a musical that was a bit more contemporary. When Steve and I talked about the play, we decided to try something a bit different with it. We placed the action in the Bronx in contemporary times, hoping to make the story a bit more relevant to the age group of our students. I'm not the kind of director who feels he needs to put a distinctive signature on his work by taking a play out of its original time period. Nor do I like to shock people with a radical interpretation of any piece of work. If a production style needs to shock, the play probably isn't that good in the first place. *Pippin* was a hit for a quite a while. Our updating of it had nothing to do with a lack of power or the play's being dated. It was just an artistic voyage; something we thought would be appealing and different, yet strictly adhering to the play's message. Nothing was altered other than the time, and since the time period is modernized through the writing of this musical anyway, we felt it was well worth the risk.

The production was thrilling as it told the story of a boy who was trying to "find himself" amidst the power and pressure of the Bronx. Having grown up on its border, I remember being able to feel the palpable presence of that area of New York and its role in the lives of those who lived there. Working on *Pippin* brought a lot of boyhood memories back; memories of visiting relatives in the Bronx with my parents when I was very young—so young that I remember using crayons and a coloring book as "The Lone Ranger" played on an old television in the background. I also recall taking the overhead train that would eventually become a subway as we got closer to Manhattan—hearing it rattle loudly from both within its cars or when I was standing beneath it, deafening me to anything else for what seemed like hours. I'm always amazed at the personal responses that plays elicit from me.

Our set contained graffiti-marked brick walls, and all of the necessary props for this play-within-a-play were retrieved by the characters from "the neighborhood." For example, the body parts needed for one of the musical numbers were mannequin pieces from a clothing store. Many of the characters wore bandanas on their heads as well as other clothing articles representative of a youth culture—tank tops, muscles shirts, doc martin boots, etc. With this interpretation, and staying true to the intent of the work, this musical took on a visceral, youthful muscularity, resounding with excitement. The audience loved it.

Pippin started a trend of musicals that were not often performed in high schools. We did *Joseph and the Amazing Technicolor Dreamcoat* in 1995, followed by *The Secret Garden, Big River, Sunday in the Park With George, Barnum,* and *Chess* in 2000. I hired Frank Alberino as my designer and technical director, a professional partnership that is simply wonderful. Frank also designed my last three plays at Hamden High School. Not only is he an artist, but he works so well with young people. He teaches as well as designs, and the students have tremendous respect for him. He managed to gather a technical staff each summer that was extremely talented: Mark Villani, Lyn Provost, Pat and Chris Degnan, Michael Epstein, Andrew Rae, Noah Cain, Marisa Perrotti, Pat Rousseau, Rebecca Lewis, Rachel Castiglione, and so many others.

Each of Frank's designs is magnificent, from the eery mansion and surrounding gardens in *The Secret Garden* to bringing George Seurat's painting alive in *Sunday in the Park With George*. Frank's designs are always splendid and can never be compared to each other, but *Sunday* definitely stood out as one of his very best. We hung a large print of the Seurat painting in the lobby on performance evenings, and I witnessed the amazement of so many audience members as they compared it to the stage picture they had seen just moments before. The similarities were striking. Franks' set design and Ort Pengue's costumes were responsible for this achievement.

Frank and I have many meetings during the year to plan for the summer musical, and I am the beneficiary of Franks' meticulous planning, perfect models, and designs that flatter the production and the theater itself. I know that Jack Crawford, the Little Theater's founder, and his associates would be proud to see how this facility is taxed to the maximum during the summer musicals.

I've been very fortunate to work with incredible students in the Foote program. They have honored the texts of these vehicles by investigating them thoroughly and working diligently on characterization or on the technical aspects of the production. This work has resulted in some very moving performances. I have great disdain for "professionals" and even college/university theater educators who are condescending to high school actors. One of my students visited me soon after starting his freshman year at college, visibly upset by the acting teacher's remark, "The first thing you have to do is forget all that stuff you learned in high school!" I find that high school actors often have an immediate connection with the text. Often they are more vulnerable and willing to take risks in discovering their character. Obviously this can and does happen on all levels, but one should never rule out a high school actor's ability just because of his age.

Foote Theater audiences have been treated to solid performances over the last ten or so years. I particularly remember Dan Whitman's Tommy and Diane Bers' Fiona in *Brigadoon,* David Eiduk's remarkably mature Tevye in *Fiddler,* Jennifer Phelan's Fanny in *Funny Girl,* Michael Kayne's Leading Player in *Pippin,* Kristy Merola's Lily in *The Secret Garden* and Kate Esposito stopping that show with her singing of "Hold On", Baron Poitier's Jim in *Big River,* Ted Bailey's George and Kristi Villani's Dot in *Sunday in the Park With George,* and Eric Santagata's spectacular work in *Chess.*

Diane Bers came offstage after a performance of *Brigadoon* with an almost incredulous yet familiar look in her eyes. She told me that something had happened to her while she was performing; something quite spontaneous and wonderful that connected her to Fiona. I am at a loss for the words to describe this transformation—this sudden awareness. It occurs when the mind is clear and focused and the body is calm and open to sensations. Suddenly an internal light becomes brighter, the music we hear becomes sweeter, and there is the profound sensation of being at one with the character. Once this happens to an actor, he longs to rediscover it over and over. I refer to that moment—rather clinically and unromantically, I'm afraid, as "jumping the synapse"—when all of the technique we've been storing up and at which we have been laboring suddenly becomes unconscious, and a very real and honest emotion surfaces. The actor's everyday tensions give way to the tensions of the character, and a communion of sorts, physical, mental, and spiritual, occurs. Fortunately I have seen many actors experience this. I say fortunately because this minor miracle is as wonderful for the teacher/director to experience as it is for the actor, not because it validates our "worth", but because we witness a magnificence, a growth, a sudden understanding in a student.

It hardly seems like twenty years have passed since we began the Foote Summer Theater Program. Once again nostalgia gets the best of me, and my mind flashes back to incredible moments on the stage; moments when the actors and the audience became so bound up in each other, and where there was a free and rapid exchange of energy and excitement. Obviously, as is the case with the Hamden students, the older students are now living all over the country, all over the world, in fact. Many have children of their own. But I see them in my mind's eye as they looked so long ago. Some little thing will spark a memory; will cause me to smile. Some lighting effect or piece of music or specific fragrance will propel me back in time and I will become reacquainted with those miraculous students who breathed life into a program that became very special to all of us. Those students were radiant. They remain so close—just on the other side of my eyelids, in fact. Many of them grew up in the program, enrolling in it for many summers, and adding their distinctive spirit to it. I remember Sarah Moore, Arielle Verinis, Claire DePalma, Eliza Fiorentino, Matt Wolf,

Christina DeMeola, Bess Paupeck, Abbie Paine, Chris Johnson, Catherine Miller, Jonas Sansone, Brian Canell, Ingrid Nelson, Kim Reiss, Kara McGuire, Michelle May, David Steeves, Eliza Sayward, Jessica Gusberg, Bethany Fales, Ted Bailey, Ariana Balayan, Ben Johnson, Amy Hellman, Emma Anderson, Caitlin Doonan, Claudia Ostojic, Jim Clark, Rachel Smirnoff, Alex Forte, Chris Smalley, Molly Nuland,—and, of course, Michael Fasano whose eleven summers of involvement set a record for the most summers dedicated to this program.

There were and continue to be many others, each working so hard during the day, basking in the excitement of performance at night, and then walking away into the warm summer evening. After everyone is gone, I will often walk back into the empty theater. It is eerily silent. Some play programs litter the floor. The natural sounds of the building reign now—the soft creaks emanating from the far corners, the drip of a faucet in the dressing room— whereas just a short time before the building exploded with a joyous noise. There is something simultaneously astonishing, powerful, and comforting about sitting in a dimly lit theater amidst the energy that still lingers here. I can almost hear the sounds of plays before ours, way back to the days of Jack Crawford. Perhaps a theater never sleeps, but after the audiences leave and the actors leave and the crews leave, a peace so silently descends, protecting and nurturing this proud but aging Grand Lady where so many have practiced their art, and through that work have brought joy to so many.

Chapter Ten

Awards

Camille, 1996

"I went to an award ceremony for your uncle yesterday afternoon and I wanted to tell you about it. It was excellent. The award was called the Mary Hunter Wolf Award. It's for excellence in education and was awarded by the Long Wharf Theater. I hadn't a clue as to who Mary Hunter Wolf is since I know so little about theater. But she's an impressive lady and she's had a long and successful career in the theater. Her friends and colleagues included Agnes DeMille, Stanislavsky, and a whole bunch of people whose names even I recognized. She performed and then directed theater all over the country including many Broadway shows. Even now, as a woman well into her 90's and confined to a wheelchair, she is still active in arts committees in New Haven.

The Long Wharf Theater, itself an institution in New Haven, initiated the award this year and Julian was the first recipient. The award ceremony took place in the lower lobby of the theater with speeches given from a landing on the stairs going up to the upper lobby so that everyone could easily see the speakers. The lobby was filled to capacity. An organizer noted to me that they hadn't expected the turnout.

Last year Julian was among a number of people who were recognized by the Arts Council of Greater New Haven for their contributions to the arts. I remember being just a bit nervous for him when he got up to speak, but he was excellent. So this time I just looked forward to hear him speak. There were some good talks before his acceptance speech and there was a tribute to Mary Hunter Wolf who was there, and then the presentation of Julian's award. Julian got up calm, casual, smiling, and his talk eclipsed all of the others. He spoke about educational theater and how Hamden is dedicated to it (they built a new theater complex at Hamden High). And then he presented personal examples showing how all students, from straight A to Special Ed, benefit from the program. It was a superb talk. I noticed that a woman standing near me was almost in tears, and I looked around and saw that other people were also.

I feel a little awkward at these things because Julian and I resemble each other and I notice people looking at me in an odd way. Two people actually thought that I was him. One gentleman shook my hand, introduced himself, and gave me his title. I shook his hand, introduced myself, and gave him my *title as Julian's brother. He was a bit taken aback. It was a good afternoon and evening. Julian is wonderfully talented.*

Dad"
Stan Schlusberg

Hamden High School Theater's astounding record of awards and recognition over a thirty year period is a testament to the ceaseless efforts, dedication, talents, and diversity of an enduring and caring family. I like to think it is also, and more importantly, a tribute to possibility; to energetic, risk-taking young people who see no limits to what they can achieve. The awards represent the material proof of a thirty-year miracle, but they hardly tell the whole story. Actually, I don't know if there is a way of telling the whole story; of adequately describing the sense of tradition, the pride handed down from generation to generation, or the love with which so many people treated the process of learning about theater over the years. It was a glorious time, and I know that I grew as a teacher, a director, and, most of all, a human being as I was touched by the fervency, sincerity, and kindness of those many students.

Hamden Theater participated in the annual statewide Drama Festival sponsored by the Connecticut Drama Association and, over the years, distinguished itself with numerous awards. In twenty-three years of participation, twenty productions won the highest award given, that of "Outstanding High School Production of the Year." There were also over two hundred individual and group awards won for acting, design, and technical components.

I feel that the following comments attest to the accomplishments of these exceptional students. We were certainly honored to receive them.

"The most remarkable thing about the Hamden Theater program, the thing that makes it most unique, is its level of sheer consistency when it comes to providing audiences with excellent theater; and providing superlative theater training for the students attending school there. Hamden

Theater is a program of staggeringly high levels of quality. It brings enrichment and education to the town, the Hamden area, the State, and the whole New England Region."
>	Robert M. McDonald
>	Chair of Graduate Studies in Theater
>	University of Connecticut

"Even one award deserves kudos, but when one group consistently returns year after year with the highest honors, it is evident that something special is going on."
>	Editor, the Hamden Chronicle "

The work of Hamden is work that is actually unusual in this country anywhere."
>	Joanna Rathgeb
>	Saint Michael's College

"Hamden Theater represents some of the very finest high school work I've ever seen."
>	William Grandgeorge
>	Wesleyan University

"You have done it again, Hamden. Your style was impeccable, your script challenging, and your interpretation on target."
>	Brother Ron Santoro
>	Saint John's Preparatory School
>	Danvers, Massachusetts
>	New England Drama Festival
>	Adjudicator

"I learned much and had my life touched."
>	Kelly Morgan
>	New England Drama Festival
>	Adjudicator

The following list notes participation in the New England Drama Festival for several years as well. Many invitations to this event, however, offered to the New England States' winning schools, had to be declined due to the enormous cost of transporting the company and scenery to other states in the region, lodging, food, and a myriad of other expenditures. I was always overwhelmed by the amount of paper work and organization it took whenever we did participate, and the relatively brief amount of time allotted for doing it, so I must admit I wasn't too disappointed when we chose not to. On the other hand, the New England Drama Festival was always a thrilling event and a wonderful opportunity to see the finest high school theater in the region. However, my choice to use fifty or more students on our plays, coupled with the complexity of our productions, unfortunately curtailed our involvement in that event. I felt bad about not providing this opportunity to the students whenever we had the opportunity of participating, but the costs to the school system were staggering and unjustifiable to an extent in times of budget crises.

The list will also note Connecticut's only Regional Drama Festival in 1989. While the statewide venture was rather successful, it was discontinued by the organization due, once again, to the financial burden on schools who would have to hire buses, rent trucks, and pay hotels for each Festival.

In 1984 and 1986 I chose not to enter the Festival. For one of those years we hosted the event, and it is rather difficult to host and participate as well. Also I felt the awards won at the Festival were becoming an evaluative measure of our overall program, and I did not want that to happen. The controversy of "competition" in the art world is age-old, and at the time I thought that those two years away from the competitive aspect would benefit us in the long run.

Since then I have worked hard to lessen the competitive aspect of our participation, and strengthen the Festival aspect. In this regard the Drama Association also wanted to create a more celebratory and sharing environment, and it therefore introduced Special Recognition Awards in 1983 to further recognize and reward participating schools for specific areas of expertise. This provided an avenue to bolster the confidence of many participating schools and their students. Personally, I encouraged our own students to befriend students from other schools and was particularly proud of them when they made long-lasting friendships; when they gave standing ovations to other schools' performances; when they went out of their way to seek out students from other schools and ask questions, make observations, and praise their work. In their own quiet, reserved, and humble manner, I felt that the students from Hamden were always in a class by themselves.

In 1978 and 1988 Hamden's productions of *The Crucible* and *The Shadow Box* respectively captured the coveted Moss Hart Award presented by the New England Theatre Conference for the Outstanding Production in New England extolling human dignity. Entrants for this award included high school, community, college, university, and professional theaters, so winning it was a distinct honor. In 1984 our production of *The Elephant Man* won the secondary school division honor for this award. Unlike the State Drama Festival to which we had to travel, the judges for this award traveled to the entrants' theater which, after preparing the application and all of the related paper work, was a welcome relief. I felt that participation in this event was particularly important since it provided opportunity for the students to explore the text in terms of social mores and what it had to say about living a life of honor, courage, and dignity.

An examination of the list of awards illustrates most distinctively the technical achievement of the Hamden students over the years. While most high schools seem to stress acting over technical work, students at Hamden High School enjoyed the technical challenges of each production, and there was a certain prestige to being a technician. Here again, crew sessions were marked by excitement and enthusiasm, and certainly the artistry and skills of designers Frank Alberino and Ort Pengue only created more risk-taking journeys in recent years. Elaborate, permanent-looking sets were designed and built to travel to the Festivals where they could be constructed and taken down within five minutes as dictated by Festival rules. Over the years sets included running water, collapsible scenery, projections, two story sets, objects that "grew" before the audience's eyes, and numerous other surprises that kept the audience in visual wonder constantly. And yet the technical aspects never overshadowed the acting. Rather, the entire production was tightly-knit and each component complemented the others. I've always felt that the finest productions are those in which no one aspect of the play draws attention to itself.

I was once asked, "What is the secret of Hamden's success? What makes Hamden 'different' from the rest?" I do not know the answers to these questions. I attribute the success to the enthusiasm and dedication of the hundreds of wonderful students who have felt an ownership of this program. Hamden Theater has long been a family where the members looked after and helped each other; where each person—even in a company of fifty or sixty—felt special and also assumed responsibility that he or she was trusted to fulfill. These students loved their work, and perhaps that is the greatest stimulus for success.

Here, then, is the list of productions and the awards each garnered:

1973 *Elizabeth the Queen* by Maxwell Anderson
    Colleen Ledig   All-Connecticut Cast
    James Gold   Honorable Mention in Acting
    Margaret Adair   Honorable Mention in Acting

1974 *The Miracle Worker* by William Gibson
    Outstanding Production in Connecticut 1973—74
    Colleen Ledig   Outstanding High School Performer
                               (special award created for this performance)
    Colleen Ledig   Outstanding Actress
    Donna Urquhart   Outstanding Actress

1975 *The Lion in Winter* by James Goldman
    Colleen Ledig   Outstanding Actress
    Donna Urquhart   Honorable Mention in Acting

1976 *The Prime of Miss Jean Brodie* by Jay Presson Allen, adapted from the novel by Muriel Spark
    Outstanding Production in Connecticut 1975-76
    Gail Grate   Outstanding Actress
    Donna Urquhart   All-Connecticut Cast
    Theron Albis   Honorable Mention in Acting
    Malcolm Smith   Honorable Mention in Acting
    Helena Whalen   Honorable Mention in Acting

1977 *Look Homeward, Angel* by Keti Frings, adapted from the novel by Thomas Wolfe
    Gail Grate   Outstanding Actress
    David Rosenberg   All-Connecticut Cast

1978 *The Crucible* by Arthur Miller
    Outstanding Production in Connecticut 1977-78
    Joshua Stein   Outstanding Actor
    Marcus Stern   Outstanding Actor
    Joanne Piscitello   All-Connecticut Cast
    Michele Durocher   Honorable Mention in Acting
    Joshua Stein   All-New England Cast*
    Joanne Piscitello   All-New England Cast*

*awarded at the New England Drama Festival of 1978, Hamden's first year of participated in this event.

Winner of the Moss Hart Award sponsored by the New England Theatre Conference for the Outstanding Production in New England (high school, community, college, university, professional theater) extolling human dignity.

1979 *Desire Under the Elms* by Eugene O'Neill
   Outstanding Production in Connecticut 1978-79
   David Rosenberg   Outstanding Actor
   Margaret Emley   Outstanding Actress
   Paul Teitelman   All-Connecticut Cast

1980 *Othello* by William Shakespeare
   Outstanding Production in Connecticut 1979-80
   Thomas Edwards   Outstanding Actor
   Andrew Hirshfield   Outstanding Actor
   Miriam Schmir   All-Connecticut Cast
   Thomas Edwards   All-New England Cast*
   Andrew Hirshfield   All-New England Cast*

   *awarded at the New England Drama Festival of 1980

1981 *The Great White Hope* by Howard Sackler
   Outstanding Production in Connecticut 1980-81
   Thomas Edwards   Outstanding Actor
   Jeanne O'Day   Outstanding Actress
   Ken Festa   Outstanding Actor
   Larry Iannotti   Outstanding Actor
   Thomas Edwards   All-New England Cast*
   Thomas Edwards   Brother John Memorial Award for Outstanding Performance in New

England*
    Ken Festa   All-New England Cast*
    Larry Iannotti   All-New England Cast*

   *awarded at the New England Drama Festival of 1981

1982 *Becket, or the Honor of God* by Jean Anouilh
    Outstanding Production in Connecticut 1981-82
        Larry Iannotti   Outstanding Actor
        Martin Harries   Outstanding Actor
        Anne Clark   Honorable Mention in Acting
        Kirsten Shepherd   Honorable Mention in Acting
        Larry Iannotti   All-New England Cast*

   *awarded at the New England Drama Festival of 1982

1983 *Richard III* by William Shakespeare
    Outstanding Production in Connecticut 1982-83
        Martin Harries   Outstanding Actor
        Laurie Pitts   All-Connecticut Cast
    Special Recognition for Total Effect and Challenge of Production

1984 did not participate in the Festival

1985 *Children of a Lesser God* by Mark Medoff
    Outstanding Production in Connecticut 1984-85
        Michael Lerner   Outstanding Actor
        Patricia McVerry   Outstanding Actress
        Leonard Van de Graaff   All-Connecticut Cast
        Michael Lerner   All-New England Cast*
        Patricia McVerry   All-New England Cast*
        Heather Wainwright   All-New England Cast*

Special Recognition Award for Challenge of Production*
Special Recognition Award for Actor Preparation*
Special Recognition Award for Integration of Theatrical Elements*

*awarded at the New England Drama Festival of 1985

1986 did not participate in the Festival

1987 *Amadeus* by Peter Shaffer
    Award for Theatrical Excellence
Todd Billingsley	Outstanding Actor
Jeffrey Lerner	All-Connecticut Cast
Mia O'Day	Honorable Mention in Acting

    Special Recognition Award for Challenge of Production
    Special Recognition Award for Period Movement and Blocking
    Special Recognition Award for Make-up
    Special Recognition Award for Theatrical Elements

1988 *The Shadow Box* by Michael Cristofer
    Outstanding Production in Connecticut 1987-88
    Award for Theatrical Excellence
Trisha Fast	Outstanding Actress
Lisbeth Shepherd	Outstanding Actress
Felicia Sloin	Outstanding Actress
Jennifer Barnhart	All-Connecticut Cast
Todd Billingsley	All-Connecticut Cast
Dan Miller	All-Connecticut Cast
Joseph Zaccaro	All-Connecticut Cast

Joel Rebhun   Honorable Mention in Acting
Special Recognition Award for Voice and Movement

Winner of the Moss Hart Award given by the New England Theatre Conference for the Outstanding Production in New England (high school, community, college, university, professional theater) extolling human dignity.

1989 *The Admirable Crichton* by James M. Barrie
 Outstanding Production in Connecticut 1988-89
 Award for Theatrical Excellence
 Outstanding Regional Production
 Ensemble Award
 Lisbeth Shepherd   Outstanding Actress
           Outstanding Regional Actress*
 Jennifer Barnhart   All-Connecticut Cast
           Outstanding Regional Actress*
 Sophia Salguero   Honorable Mention in Acting
           Outstanding Regional Actress*
 Andrew Wildstein   Outstanding Regional Actor*
 Jennifer Moran   All-Regional Cast*
 Blaise Wozniak   All-Regional Cast*
 Special Recognition Award for Voice
 Special Recognition Award for Design Excellence
 Special Recognition Award for Ensemble Period Acting
 Special Recognition Award for Technical Merit
 Special Recognition Award for Running Crew
 Special Recognition Award for Setting
 Special Recognition Award for Challenge of Production
 J. Bryan Juliano   Outstanding Technical Design Award

*awarded at the Connecticut Regional Drama Festival.

1990 *The Little Foxes* by Lillian Hellman
    Outstanding Production in Connecticut 1989-90
    Award for Theatrical Excellence

Joseph Zaccaro	Outstanding Actor
Jennifer Barnhart	All-Connecticut Cast
Wyeth Friday	All-Connecticut Cast
Sophia Salguero	All-Connecticut Cast
Typhanie Jackson	Honorable Mention in Acting
Winston Joshua	Honorable Mention in Acting
Andrew Sloin	Honorable Mention in Acting
Youngho Sohn	Honorable Mention in Acting

    Special Recognition Award for Set Design
    J. Byran Juliano   Outstanding Technical Design Award

1991 *Steel Magnolias* by Robert Harling
    Outstanding Production in Connecticut 1990-91
    Award for Theatrical Excellence

Catherine Jones	Outstanding Actress
Diane Bers	All-Connecticut Cast
Erika Nelson	All-Connecticut Cast
Jennifer Ortman	All-Connecticut Cast
Christina DeMeola	Honorable Mention in Acting
Callie Fletcher	Honorable Mention in Acting

    Special Recognition Award for Set Design
    Special Recognition Award for Ensemble Acting
    Special Recognition Award for Stage Crew
    Special Recognition Award for Wig Design

1992 *Much Ado About Nothing* by William Shakespeare
    Outstanding Production in Connecticut 1991-92
    Award for Theatrical Excellence

Benjamin Billingsley All-Connecticut Cast
Jonathan Davis All-Connecticut Cast
Matt Walker All-Connecticut Cast
Taryn Chorney Honorable Mention in Acting
Kurt Fusaris Honorable Mention in Acting
Carra Gamberdella Honorable Mention in Acting
Special Recognition Award for Technical Excellence including Set, Costumes, and Props
Diane Bers All-New England Cast*
Matt Walker All-New England Cast*
Special Recognition Award for Effective Use of Voice and Articulation*
Special Recognition Award for Excellence in Execution of Scenic Elements*
*awarded at the New England Drama Festival of 1992

1993 *The Boys Next Door* by Tom Griffin
Outstanding Production in Connecticut 1992-93
Award for Theatrical Excellence
Jonathan Walker Outstanding Actor
Samantha Ethier All-Connecticut Cast
Christopher Johnson All-Connecticut Cast
Greg O'Connell All-Connecticut Cast
Jonathan Panagrossi All-Connecticut Cast
Joseph Salvi All-Connecticut Cast
Matt Walker All-Connecticut Cast
Special Recognition Award for Ensemble Acting
Samantha EthierAll-New England Cast*
Greg O'Connell All-New England Cast*
Jonathan Panagrossi All-New England Cast*
Jonathan Walker All-New England Cast*

*awarded at the New England Drama Festival of 1993

1994 *Dancing at Lughnasa* by Brian Friel
    Outstanding Production in Connecticut 1993-94
    Award for Theatrical Excellence
    Ensemble Acting Award
    Melissa Beverage   Outstanding Actress
    Joseph Salvi   Outstanding Actor
    Leah Altman   All-Connecticut Cast
    Kate Esposito   All-Connecticut Cast
    Marit Knollmueller   All-Connecticut Cast
    Adele Jerista   Honorable Mention in Acting
    Special Recognition Award for Set Design
    Special Recognition Award for Lighting
    Special Recognition Award for Technical Crew
    Leah Altman   All-New England Cast*
    Melissa Beverage   All-New England Cast*
    Kate Esposito   All-New England Cast*
    Joseph Salvi   All-New England Cast*

*awarded at the New England Drama Festival of 1994

1995 *Camille* a version by Pam Gems
    Outstanding Production in Connecticut 1994-95
    Award for Theatrical Excellence
    Ensemble Acting Award
    Joseph Salvi   Outstanding Actor
    Melissa Beverage   Outstanding Actress
    Kate Esposito   Outstanding Actress
    Leah Altman   All-Connecticut Cast
    Christopher Degnan   All-Connecticut Cast
    Special Recognition Award for Set Design

Special Recognition Award for Stage Movement
Special Recognition Award for Make-up and Hair Design

1996 *Antigone* by Jean Anouilh
    Outstanding Production in Connecticut 1995-96
    Award for Theatrical Excellence
    Outstanding Ensemble Acting Award
    Ingrid Nelson   Outstanding Actress
    Kate Esposito   All-Connecticut Cast
    Joshua Rubin   All-Connecticut Cast
    Special Recognition Award for Ensemble Acting
    Special Recognition Award for Set Design

1997 *Summer and Smoke* by Tennessee Williams
    Outstanding Production in Connecticut 1996-97
    Award for Theatrical Excellence
    Adele Jerista   Outstanding Actress
    Patrick Degnan   All-Connecticut Cast
    Jessica Vasquez   All-Connecticut Cast
    Daniel Kolodny   Honorable Mention in Acting
    Kristi Villani   Honorable Mention in Acting
    Special Recognition Award for Technical Design and
        Overall Technical Effect

1998 *On the Verge, or the Geography of Yearning* by Eric Overmyer
    Outstanding Production in Connecticut 1997-98
    Stage Manager's Award for "the most professional and courteous crew"
    Jason Conge   All-Connecticut Cast
    Benjamin Hecht   All-Connecticut Cast
    Marta Montgomery   All-Connecticut Cast
    David Moran   All-Connecticut Cast

David Salguero	All-Connecticut Cast
Patricia Santomasso	All-Connecticut Cast
Kristi Villani	All-Connecticut Cast

Special Recognition Award for Ensemble Acting
Special Recognition Award for Lighting
Special Recognition Award for Set Design
Special Recognition Award for Set Building
Special Recognition Award for Costumes
Special Recognition Award for Properties
Special Recognition Award for Dramaturgy
Special Recognition Award for Set Crew

Benjamin Hecht	All-New England Cast*
Marta Montgomery	All-New England Cast*
Patricia Santomasso	All-New England Cast*
Kristi Villani	All-New England Cast*

Properties Supervisor Award for Rebecca Lewis*
Sound Engineer Award for Benjamin Bausher*
Stage Magic/Special Effects Award for Lisa Oblena, Andrew Drozd, Cathie Turner, Nette Compton, Brian Huff

*awarded at the New England Drama Festival of 1998

I was sitting on the stage at the awards ceremony of the Connecticut Drama Association's Spring Festival 2000, anticipating delivering my acceptance speech for the organization's Lifetime Achievement Award. I had retired a year before, and now looked out into the sea of young faces in the theater with a sudden longing to teach again. I envied my colleagues the opportunity of learning and sharing with such remarkable and talented students. In just one year away from the classroom I could feel a certain void in my heart.

After my acceptance speech, I was ready to step down from the podium when the President of the organization, Rona Rothhouse, asked me to remain on the stage. I was bewildered by her request, but obediently and warily stepped back as she began to address the audience. It seems that everyone in the theater was aware of a new award to be instituted that year, one that had been advertised for several months but which was kept from my knowledge: the Julian Schlusberg Commitment to Excellence in Educational Theater Award which would honor the work of a particularly hard working student in the State. Needless to say, I was dumbfounded and humbled by this honor. Meeting the winner and her family was heart-warming, and as I drove home that night I realized how fortunate I have been in my career, and how graciously I have been treated by various local, state, and national organizations for my work in educational theater. The awards they've bestowed on me touch me greatly, but I always think they must have made some giant mistake. I know that people like their efforts to be rewarded, but to tell the truth, I have always felt a bit uncomfortable about this.

To the general population, those of us who work in the Theater should be outgoing and gregarious people. I guess I don't quite fit that category. Personally, I have felt that my rewards have been working with exceptional students; a highly diverse group from all academic levels, ethnic and socio-economic backgrounds; a group that is unselfish and works hard. Our rewards have been felt in the classroom and on the stage as we study about this wonderful theater and how to use it to learn about ourselves and bring joy to others. I would much prefer seeing my students awarded for their work. They give so much of themselves.

I am very grateful for the following awards. They have validated a career laden with rigorous lesson planning, with new theories and instinctively-created lessons, and with production choices that might be considered too risky by some, and have, in fact, caused controversy in other communities. I can only thank our town for its open-mindedness and unwavering support in providing the best possible theater education. Truthfully, I feel a bit guilty for receiving an award for things that are integral to the work of any theater teacher and director—the long hours of planning and organizing, making charts and graphs and attending many meetings, listening to and advising students and colleagues, those long, long nights and lost weekends, sacrificed vacations, bargaining, trading, shopping, and a host of other time-consuming, but greatly rewarding activities; rewarding because, in the end, they benefit the students. But all of it is necessary to build and maintain a solid theater program. I am truly thankful for all of the following:

The John C. Barner National Theater Teacher of the Year, given by the American Alliance for Theater and Education

The Long Wharf Theater's first annual Mary Hunter Wolf Award for "Excellence in the art and teaching of Theater"

The Arts Council of Great New Haven's "Award for Excellence and Mastery in Educational Theater."

The Hamden Teacher of the Year

The Alumni Citation Award from Southern Connecticut State University for "Outstanding Achievement in the Performing Arts"

Prominent Alumni List for Southern Connecticut State University

Governor John Rowland and the State of Connecticut Official Citation for directing 20 winners of the "Outstanding High School Production in Connecticut Award" at the annual Connecticut Drama Association Festival

Hamden Notable Award, given by the Friends of the Hamden Library, for distinguished service to the community

Namesake of the Connecticut Drama Association's

"Julian Schlusberg Award for Commitment to Excellence in Educational Theater"—awarded to a student from a Connecticut High School

Connecticut Drama Association's Lifetime Achievement Award

Connecticut Drama Association's Distinguished Service Award

Hamden Board of Education's Golden Apple Award for service "beyond the classroom"

Four Hamden Legislative Council Awards for "brilliant guidance and leadership"

Author of *Lessons for the Stage,* nominated for the Barnard-Hewitt Award

Directed *Amadeus,* the focal point of *Places, Please* , a nationally distributed documentary on educational theater

Directed or supervised students to winning 223 acting, design, technical, and dramaturgy awards

All of these awards have their special distinctions, and each is so greatly appreciated. Receiving the Long Wharf Theatre's first "Mary Hunter Wolf Award for Excellence in the Art and Teaching of Theater" was especially wonderful because it was given in the name of a most distinguished person of the Theater. Mary Hunter Wolf made a major impact on both professional and educational theater. She collaborated with Tennessee Williams, Horton Foote, Agnes DeMille, Sinclair Lewis, Katherine Dunham, D.H. Lawrence, and Willa Cather, to name a few. She also co-directed the first African-American musical on Broadway, and was the assistant director for Jerome Robbins' famous production of *Peter Pan*. There are numerous other credits to her name, but what impresses me so much about Mary is that she changed her focus from professional theater to educational theater midway through her life. Riding acrest a remarkable career in the professional theater, she suddenly decided that her calling was to help young people. She then proceeded to make strides in this area that rivaled those in her former field. Her accomplishments are substantial and range from work with the American Shakespeare Theater in Stratford, Connecticut, to establishing arts organizations and an art magnet school that has been nationally recognized.

More moving to me than receiving the award, however, was presenting it the following years. Mary sat in a wheelchair before me in the lobby of the Theater, and, while I spoke of her great work to the many people attending the event, I took great joy in looking into those ninety-five year old eyes and noticing the smile on her lips. Someone once said, "Oh, to travel the caverns of Mary Hunter Wolf's mind! What treasures there must be!" I have often thought about this and the rich history through which she has lived and helped create.

My brother, Stan, came to the ceremony at the Long Wharf Theater in 1997. I was very touched that he made the journey from upstate New York, but his letter to his adult children recounting the event affected me even more. It reflects a man who is humble, intelligent, and kind. I have looked up to Stan all of my life, and when I am in his presence I realize over and over again that the one "award" I would cherish most of all would be to be like him.

The 1996 Arts Council of Greater New Haven's Award for Excellence and Mastery in Educational Theater was yet another memorable event. Ronald Ebrecht, the Arts Awards Committee Chairman, had very kind words at the ceremony; words I appreciated because they recognized my belief that *all* students can benefit from a solid theater program:

"Your exceptional career in the development of a comprehensive program of education in all aspects of the theatrical arts is a model for artists and teachers throughout the country. Your belief that the theater arts are accessible to all students has imparted a deep understanding of dramatic literature, developed and nurtured great talent, and provided a sense of self worth and accomplishment to students of a wide range of abilities and skills. Your work of the highest artistic excellence is essential to the future of the American Theater."

All too often, our work is very lonely. I have heard this repeatedly from my colleagues, and I have certainly felt it myself. Organizations such as the AATE, the New England Drama Council, the New England Theatre Conference, the Connecticut Drama Association, the drama guilds of each of the New England States and, of course, the time-honored National Thespian Society provide student and collegial ties that are at once supportive and necessary. I am glad that similar organizations exist all over the country and that nearly every State has an educational theater organization of its own. These groups provide a foundation we all need—a feeling of constituency, of fellowship and belonging, and simultaneously reflect the growing importance of this most magnificent thing called educational theater in the curricula of our schools.

About the Author

Julian S. Schlusberg is the author of *Lessons for the Stage, An Approach to Acting*. His honors include ones from the American Alliance for Theater and Education, the Connecticut Drama Association, New Haven's Long Wharf Theatre, the Arts Council of Greater New Haven, Southern Connecticut State University, and Connecticut Governor John Rowland and the Connecticut General Assembly.